THE DEFINITIVE
DIANA

An Intimate Look at The Princess of Wales
from A to Z

SALLY MOORE

W9-AYZ-122

CB

CONTEMPORARY
BOOKS

CHICAGO

Library of Congress Cataloging-in-Publication Data

Moore, Sally.
    The definitive Diana : an intimate look at the Princess of Wales
from A to Z / Sally Moore.
       p.   cm.
    Includes bibliographical references.
    ISBN 0-8092-3948-5 (cloth)
        0-8092-3844-6 (paper)
     1. Diana, Princess of Wales, 1961-   .   2. Great Britain—
Princes and princesses—Biography.   I. Title.
DA591.A45M66   1991
941.085′092—dc20
[B]   91-29980
                                             CIP

The color photographs in this book are reproduced by permission of the
following organizations.
    Press Association: page 1 top and page 7 bottom. Rex Features:
page 1 bottom left. Photographers International: page 1 bottom right;
page 4 top left, top right, and bottom right; all on page 5; page 6 top left
and top right; and page 8 top left and top right. Camera Press London:
pages 2–3 and page 4 bottom left. Nunn Syndication: page 6 middle and
bottom, page 7 top left, and page 8 middle and bottom. Alton Towers:
page 7 top right.

Cover photograph © Chancellor/Alpha Globe

Copyright © 1991 by Sally Moore
All rights reserved
Published by Contemporary Books, Inc.
180 North Michigan Avenue, Chicago, Illinois 60601
Manufactured in the United States of America
International Standard Book Number: 0-8092-3948-5 (cloth)
                                       0-8092-3844-6 (paper)

To Zena, Leslie, and Claret
with love

Contents

Preface   *ix*
Preface to First Edition   *xi*
A to Z
   America   *1*
   Arab Gulf States   *14*
   Armed Forces   *15*
   Arts & Handicrafts   *16*
   Astrology   *18*
   Australia   *20*
   Austria   *33*
   Autographs   *34*
   Barnardo's   *36*
   Baths & Bathrooms   *48*
   Beauty Secrets   *51*
   Beds & Bedrooms   *58*
   Belgium   *60*
   Birthright   *61*
   Blind   *64*
   Books   *65*
   British Lung Foundation   *67*
   Cameroon   *69*
   Canada   *72*
   Child Accident Prevention Trust   *74*
   Children   *76*
   Collections   *80*
   Cooking   *84*
   Courtship   *86*

Dancing   92
Deaf   101
Drugs   104
Education   106
Family   110
Famous Relatives   119
Fashion   120
Favorite Things   128
Fiji   132
Food & Drink   133
France   138
Friends   140
Germany   151
The Guinness Trust   152
Gulf War   153
Hawaii   160
Health   160
Help the Aged   165
HIV   166
Holidays   168
Honeymoon   170
Hong Kong   171
Hospitals   173
Hungary   177
Indonesia   180
International Spinal Research Trust   183
Italy   185
Japan   192
Jewelry   197
Jobs   199
Key Dates   201
Kuwait & the United Arab Emirates   204
Leprosy   208

Letters   208
London Symphony Chorus   210
The Malcolm Sargent Cancer Fund for Children   212
Marriage   213
Monaco   242
Money   242
Motoring   248
Museums & Exhibitions   254
Music   255
Names   260
The National Meningitis Trust   263
National Rubella Council   265
New Zealand   266
Nigeria   269
Norway   273
Orchestras   275
Orders, Decorations & Honors   277
Parkinson's Disease Society   279
Pets   280
Portugal   281
Pre-school Playgroups Association   282
Presidencies & Patronages   285
Press   290
Public Engagements   295
Quotes   305
Radio   313
Red Cross   315
RELATE   315
Residences   325
Restaurants   329
Royal Protection Squad   330
Shopping   336
Spain   338

Speeches   *341*
Sport   *342*
Staff   *351*
Television   *362*
Thailand   *368*
Turning Point   *368*
Uniforms   *373*
Videos   *375*
Wales   *377*
Wedding   *379*
X-Rated   *386*
Young England Kindergarten   *392*
Zoo   393
Bibliography   394

Preface

Just as this edition was going to press, some of Diana's closest friends and relatives made world headlines with their shocking disclosures about the Princess's "loveless marriage" (from which it was suggested she might soon escape) and her health.

Already reeling from the recent separation of the Duke and Duchess of York—followed by Princess Anne's long-expected divorce—the British monarchy now finds itself embroiled in its most sensational crisis since Edward VIII abdicated to marry Wallis Simpson in 1936.

As I now write, the Palace and people await the next act in the astonishing public drama that began following the publication of Andrew Morton's sad biography, *Diana, Her True Story.*

Will the Princess quit the Royal Family? Will she become reconciled with Prince Charles? Will they separate and divorce? Or will the Palace officials make the royal couple soldier on publicly despite the private unhappiness?

Any continuation of the charade would seem farcical. If the allegations are true, the deception has gone on long enough.

But whatever decision is made, and whatever dirt is dished out during the current mudslinging, nothing can detract from Diana's public work and achievements over the past eleven years.

She has carved a unique role for herself as a force for good in the world, and in the process she has deservedly earned the admiration, affection, and esteem of people everywhere.

The Definitive Diana remains the most detailed and insightful record of a career that made history and won hearts for the Princess worldwide.

Sally Moore
London
July 1992

Preface to First Edition

As an ardent royalist, I believe that Diana is the best thing to have happened for the modern-day British monarchy. Alongside Prince Charles, she is also the most likely person to ensure its future survival. Over the past ten years Diana has brought youth, color, warmth, and vitality to the institution and a genuine sense, through her, that the monarchy today is really in touch with and in tune with the people it serves. However, marrying into the Royal Family and everything which that entails has not been easy for the Princess. As she has since admitted, when she walked down the aisle at St. Paul's Cathedral as a twenty-year-old bride in 1981, watched by seven hundred million television viewers around the world, she didn't really know what she was letting herself in for. But she has confronted her fears, survived the pressures, developed, and matured. She has emerged as such a perfect choice—as the Queen herself said—and so utterly irreplaceable that it is impossible now to imagine public life without her. She once asked, "What's so special about me?" I hope this book, covering her life from birth to the end of her remarkable first decade as the Princess of Wales, will make that clear to any who still have doubts. However, she knows she is not perfect, and this book is not uncritical of her or Prince Charles. That they have had problems individually and as a couple is beyond doubt. Nevertheless, Britons can feel blessed, and very lucky, to have two such fine and worthwhile people as their probable future King and Queen.

One of the most enduring problems they have to cope with are inaccurate stories about them which appear in the newspapers, particularly in regard to the state of their marriage. Most of the British Press are not junk journalists, but all face difficulties getting accurate facts.

Early in 1983, when wild stories had been circulating, I was asked to try and get at the truth about Diana. In pursuit of this, I rang the shrewd and urbane Michael Shea, then the Queen's Press Secretary. Between us we arranged a meeting at Buckingham Palace with my then bosses, the Editor and London Editor of a Fleet Street newspaper. Historically, relations between the Palace and the Press in general had been fraught for many years, with mistrust on both sides. Royal reporting is a notoriously difficult field for any responsible journalist: rumors abound, you can't check facts personally with the Royal Family, their close friends seldom talk, and too often in the past it seemed staff at the Palace Press Office either didn't know the facts themselves or wouldn't reveal them. They were very ready to complain about inaccuracies in the newspapers but less ready to supply the information which would have prevented them. It was a no-win situation all-around. Faced with the latest barrage about Diana, the meeting was held to try and find a new formula which would be mutually beneficial.

The agreement reached at the Palace was that we would have a closer relationship, based on trust. In practical terms it meant, as I recall, that staff in the Palace Press Office would be more open and give us straight answers, even if it meant they sometimes had to talk off the record, and that we on our side would check facts with them so that stories published would be accurate. The first tangible result, which I wrote with Andrew Morton, then my colleague and now a royal author, was a major piece on Diana and Charles (see MARRIAGE) which revealed fresh facts and demolished several myths in the process. (*Time* magazine followed it up on February 28, 1983, with a cover story featuring Diana, titled "Royalty vs. the Press.") This promising beginning unfortunately did not lead to a permanent solution. When Michael Shea and I compared notes long after, we both felt there had been hiccups in the opposite camp, though not from the principals. But it was a sincere attempt to improve a difficult problem, and it seemed like a good idea at the time. Michael Shea, much missed, left the Palace in June 1987, two years before I began research on this book.

When I outlined the project to the Palace, I pointed out that this guidebook to the Princess—assembling more detail about different aspects of her life, work, and interests than had ever before been published in a single volume—would not only be of interest to her many admirers but might also help reduce the number of inquiries about her from around the world to the hard-pressed staff in the Press Office. It was essential, however, that I should obtain accurate information, preferably directly from the Palace. I therefore asked at the outset to be allowed access to staff in the Princess of Wales's private office, to her personal staff, and, if possible, to the Princess herself. This was refused on the grounds that all the relevant people would be too busy. Instead I was told I could get help from the Press Office, and I was directed to Dickie Arbiter, Assistant Press Secretary to the Queen, who acts as Press Officer for the Prince and Princess of Wales.

I visited him at the Palace and made several basic initial requests, all of which, since they were simple and I've been on good terms with the Palace for at least twenty years, I expected to be met easily and without problems. However, when I asked what Diana's titles are, to check whether she had taken on all of Charles's titles or only some, he didn't appear to know and said I would have to look them up in a reference book. When I asked for copies of the past itineraries of Diana's overseas tours, which are routinely supplied to the Press, he said that I was "asking the impossible" because there were too many of them and they were stored downstairs. If, as I believe, the Princess's advisers are keen to emphasize her serious working role, this response seemed incomprehensible. I offered to look through the relevant files myself, to save him time. He refused. He did agree to send me copies of Diana's speeches and of official Palace announcements concerning her, plus a copy of the list of the organizations of which she is Patron or President. However, they took six months to arrive, after a reminder, and the former were incomplete and the list was inaccurate. Further inquiries through the Press Office produced a second list, which was stated by the Princess of Wales's private office to be their own working list and absolutely accurate. It wasn't. Months later, at my request, I was sent an additional updated list from the Press Office which was still not entirely correct, though they clearly had problems themselves. A later "checked," computerized Palace list dated November 1990 also contained errors. Naturally I am grateful to the Palace, some of whose officers were very helpful, for what assistance they were able to give. But the situation I have outlined cannot be in Diana's interests, and I find it incredible that the Princess of Wales should not be better served.

One can only guess at the level of personal distress caused to members of the Royal Family by inaccurate stories about them. Most of these could be avoided if the Palace employed sufficient Press Officers to cope with the work load and made sure they were fully briefed and ready and willing to give responsible journalists whatever help is required to make facts known. Naturally the Queen and her officers try to keep Palace costs to a minimum. But it seems to me, with respect, that to run the Press Office on what appears to be a skeleton staff is a false economy and an unwise and shortsighted policy. Until something is done about that, some authors who write regularly on royal matters will go on avoiding the Press Office, seeking their information from contacts elsewhere. And journalists trying to write with complete accuracy about the Royal Family without similar sources will continue to find that it is like trying to keep your shoes dry while dancing in the rain. I would have liked to submit the manuscript of this book to the Princess personally before publication. Since that opportunity was not open to me, I can only say that if, despite my best efforts, she or others named discover any factual errors, I apologize and will naturally correct them for any future edition if I am supplied with the details.

Because the book covers so much ground, I owe a debt of gratitude to all the authors and journalists whose work I waded through during my research. The numerous books I consulted are listed in the bibliography. Two which I found particularly helpful in my research were Penny Junor's *Diana, Princess of Wales*, for Diana's life before marriage, and Judy Wade's *Charles & Diana, Inside a Royal Marriage*. I thank them for their kind permission to reproduce brief extracts. My gratitude also goes to Brian Hoey and Daily Express Newspapers, particularly Brian Hitchen, Editor of the *Daily Star*, for permission to quote from material published in the *Daily Express* and *Daily Star*, and to Tim O'Donovan for supplying figures from his research on the number of public engagements carried out by members of the Royal Family. For other help, I should like to thank Hugo Vickers, Harry Arnold, Judy Wade, Ashley Walton, Donald Zec, Charles Kidd and David Williamson of Debrett, Independent Television News (ITN), the Central Office of Information, John Kelly, and Douglas Matthews, Librarian of the London Library. My thanks are also due to the heads, public relations, or Press Officers or other representatives of numerous organizations, companies, or individuals connected with the Princess who found time in their busy work schedules to supply me with information or comments, often both. These include David French and Zelda West-Meads of RELATE, Roger Singleton and Geraldine Doyle of Barnardo's, Harold King and Nadine Kettaneh of the London City Ballet, Arne Christensen of the Anglo-European College of Chiropractic, Vivienne Parry of Birthright, Bernard Quinn of the British Deaf Association, Debbie Bloomfield for the British Lung Foundation, Emily Rae and Charlotte Lindsey of the British Red Cross, Alison Neurauter of the British Sports Association for the Disabled, Louise Pankhurst of the Child Accident Prevention Trust, Leon Yow of the Commonwealth Society for the Deaf, Lydia Cassidy of the English National Ballet, Pamela Allison of the English Women's Indoor Bowling Association, Margaret Fenn of EUREKA!, Pat Spooner of and Louise Greidinger for the First International Covent Garden Festival, Steve Large of the Freshfield Service, Gloucestershire County Cricket Club, Penny Uprichard of the Hospital for Sick Children, the Guinness Trust, Janet Johnstone of Help the Aged, Jasper Woodcock of the Institute for the Study of Drug Dependence, Valerie Dunk of the International Spinal Research Trust, David Leonard of the London Symphony Chorus, Sylvia Darley of the Malcolm Sargent Cancer Fund for Children, Vivienne Price of the National Children's Orchestra, Helen Buttery of the National Meningitis Trust, Julia Lindley-French and Gordana Jakolevic of the National Rubella Council, Gail McKenzie of the Natural History Museum, Don Lenox of the Parkinson's Disease Society, the Pre-school Playgroups Association, Jonathan Benthall of the Royal Anthropological Institute, Dr. Alistair Beattie of the Royal College of Physicians and Surgeons of Glasgow, the Reverend Bernard Coote of the Royal School for the Blind, the Scottish

Chamber Orchestra, Deborah Newbury of Turning Point, Alan Williams of the Welsh Bowling Association, Alison Norman of the Welsh National Opera, Dr. Naren Patel of the Royal College of Obstetricians and Gynaecologists, Rear Admiral Richard Hill of the Honourable Society of the Middle Temple, Nina Andrious of the Albany community center, staff at the Emanuels, Jane Harris for the Chelsea Design Company, Sharon Bevan of Colourings, Barbara Daly's personal assistant, Samantha Loggie, and Judith Sin for The Body Shop. My apologies for the fact that lack of space prevented me giving more information about some of them. For allowing me to check various details with them, I am grateful to the Royal Hampshire Regiment; the 13th/18th Royal Hussars (Queen Mary's Own); the Worshipful Company of Grocers; the Merchant Taylors' Company; the Ford, Jaguar, and Mercedes-Benz motor companies; and to anyone I've inadvertently left out. My thanks also to my agent, Carole Blake, Robert Smith, Susan Hill, Helen Gummer, and to those who would prefer to remain unnamed. For helping me in various ways to complete the task, my gratitude to Colleen Meehan, Dennis and Peggy Young, Abbey and Shireen, Himat and Ranjan, Joyce, Harry and Sue, Miles, Pat and Jonathan, Sandra and Wayne.

Though time has been short and the road long, I have found this book a pleasure to write and hope you will find it a pleasure to read. To discover in greater detail the wonderful work the Princess does, and to come into contact with so many solid-gold souls in many fields whose magnificent efforts achieve such worthwhile results, is a humbling and very heartwarming experience.

Sally Moore
London
April 1991

AMERICA

Though Diana was the first Englishwoman to marry an heir to the British throne in three hundred years, her great-grandmother, Frances Work, was an American. Fortunately for the modern-day monarchy, however, Frances, known as Fanny, rebelled against her father's wishes and married a Briton. Fanny's mother had been born out of wedlock in India, and her father, Frank, started out as a clerk in Ohio. But he made millions of dollars in finance in Manhattan and, being very patriotic, threatened to disinherit any of his children who did not marry Americans. Frank particularly disapproved of rich Americans marrying titled Europeans. However, like Diana, Fanny had a mind of her own and after crossing the Atlantic, she married James Boothby Burke Roche, who was to become the 3rd Baron Fermoy. It was more than a decade before the marriage broke up and Fanny returned to New York, trailing a set of twins, Maurice and Frank, and a daughter, Cynthia. Her father forgave her, but he made her promise not to marry another European or live in Europe again. To secure their inheritance, even her children had to agree to stay in America and become U.S. citizens within twelve months of his death. However, in 1905, fourteen years after Lord Fermoy divorced her in 1891, she married another European, Aurel Batonyi, a Hungarian racehorse trainer employed by her father, with whom she is said to have run off. That marriage soon ended, followed by a second divorce in 1909, and her father again forgave her. After Frank died in 1911, lawyers managed to get his will overturned because he'd been "unduly prejudiced against foreigners," and the family inherited his £12 million fortune. Lord Fermoy died in 1920, and Maurice, then in his mid-thirties, inherited the title, becoming the 4th Baron Fermoy. Back in Britain, he settled at Dersingham in Norfolk, where he became a Tory MP and the Mayor of King's

Wherever she travels, Diana appears relaxed and confident.

Lynn. In 1931 he married concert pianist Ruth Gill. King George V offered the couple a home at Park House on the royal Sandringham estate in Norfolk, where Diana's mother, Frances, and later Diana herself were born. In 1956, after Maurice died, Ruth, Lady Fermoy, became an Extra Woman of the Bedchamber to her friend the Queen Mother. When Fanny died, she left money in trust for her great-grandchildren once they reached the age of eighteen. Diana used part of her inheritance to buy the three-bedroomed bachelor-girl flat at Coleherne Court, estimated to have cost £60,000, on a corner of the Old Brompton Road in London, where she was living when she became engaged to Prince Charles. See FAMILY and RESIDENCES.

Diana still has cousins in America, including Mrs. Sheila Platt, the wife of a diplomat in Washington, and Cynthia's son-in-law, Walter Maynard, a New York financier. Cynthia's husband (she *did* stay in the United States and marry an American) was the rich but tragic Arthur Scott Burden, who suffered brain damage playing polo when he was thrown by his pony (Prince Charles, please take note) and died in 1922 after being kept, insane, in an asylum. Cynthia remarried and had two children, Guy Cary and Cynthia Russel, who are cousins of Diana's mother. Walter Maynard married Arthur's daughter, Eileen, and Diana is a second cousin to their three children, Walter, Sheila, and John. The Princess is also distantly related to three former Presidents of the United States: George Washington, Calvin Coolidge, and Franklin D. Roosevelt. See FAMOUS RELATIVES. A book called *American Ancestors and Cousins of the Princess of Wales*, by Gary Boyd Roberts and W. A. Reitwiesner, was published by the Genealogical Publishing Company of Baltimore in 1984.

Diana's first visit was eagerly awaited in America, where Myrna Blythe, Editor of the *Ladies' Home Journal*, declared in 1983, "Every once in a while, there is a public personality who captures the imagination of not only her own country but of the world. There was Jackie Kennedy in the sixties who had this same appeal. It would be fabulous if Diana came. Americans admire her looks, her style and her charm. She is definitely our leading lady—like Jackie." America's First Lady, Nancy Reagan, who had attended the royal wedding in 1981 (which was watched on TV by nearly forty million U.S. households) was pressing too. But it was November 1985 before the Princess made her first trip to the United States, when she accompanied Prince Charles on a five-day visit to Washington, D.C., and Palm Beach. The American view of her as another Jackie O was reemphasized then by a columnist who commented, "Her keen interest in fashion has done for the dowdy House of Windsor what Jacqueline Onassis did for the Kennedy White House—blown away the cobwebs." The build-up to the visit was so intense that "Di-mania" was renamed "Dimentia." The *Washington Post*, whose Editor in Chief, Ben Bradlee (see FAMOUS RELATIVES), became internationally known as a result of his newspaper's exposure of the Watergate scandal and

All the President's Men, the Robert Redford movie of the book which followed, offered advice to its readers in case they encountered the royal couple. Remarks Americans were advised *not* to make to Diana included "Do you all still see Koo Stark much?" and "Do you ever use that bowl the Reagans gave you?" Americans were similarly advised *not* to tell Charles "I can't stand my father either" or "I use a ouija board too." See TELEVISION.

After flying in from their two-week tour of Australia via Honolulu (see AUSTRALIA and HAWAII), Charles and Diana were greeted by President Ronald Reagan and Nancy at the White House, though because they were not on a state visit, they did not stay there. However, that evening the Reagans laid on a fabulous White House banquet for the royal couple. Visiting the Washington Home for Incurables beforehand, Diana confessed to an old lady that she and Charles were suffering from jet lag and had not slept for two days, so she was afraid he might nod off at it. (He didn't, but he did forget the toast.) Competition among status-seeking socialites and celebrities to be invited to the banquet had been fierce, but there were several notable exceptions. Robert Redford, whom the Princess had specially asked to be invited, had to cry off because of filming on his movie, *Legal Eagles*, in New York. But he spoke to Charles on the telephone, sent him two £70 bottles of his favorite champagne plus three dozen red roses for Diana, and invited them, with William and Harry, for some cowboy riding on his ranch in the future. Diana Ross, a favorite of both the Prince and Princess who they had hoped would sing at the do, was so tied up with her new movie and her plans to wed Arne Naess that she allegedly forgot to reply. And Madonna, who was also said to be on the original guest list, reportedly refused to assure the First Lady that her dress would be suitably dignified, and she later caused shock waves by portraying the Princess as a brandy swiller in a TV sketch.

Among those who were present at the dinner dance, where Diana wore a dazzling pearl choker with a vast sapphire clasp and an elegant midnight blue off-the-shoulder velvet gown which she had spotted on a rack at Victor Edelstein's, were several of her other favorite stars. These included Mikhail Baryshnikov (see AUTOGRAPHS), Tom Selleck of "Magnum, P.I.," Neil Diamond,

President and Mrs. Reagan welcome the Prince and Princess of Wales to the United States. (Globe Photos)

Clint Eastwood, and John Travolta, all of whom, except Baryshnikov who was out of commission, danced with her. The highlight came after Nancy Reagan confided to John Travolta, star of *Saturday Night Fever* and *Grease*, "The Princess is hoping you will ask her to dance." Travolta, who had found himself cold-shouldered by Hollywood after a string of more recent film flops and had become a near-recluse, could hardly believe his luck. The fact that Diana, whom he described as "charming, adorable and down to earth," wanted to dance with him "made me feel I was somebody again," he said later. Other dancers cleared the floor as they disco-danced to his hit single "You're the One That I Want." "It was really sensational—very wild, very swinging, very sparkling," said a royal aide. The disco-dance with the Princess at the White House brought Travolta worldwide publicity, and once again film offers began to come in. Celebrating renewed fame in 1990 with his smash-hit movie *Look Who's Talking*, Travolta was quoted as saying, "Princess Di did me one of the greatest favors of my life. I owe her. She's a really warm, nice person." Of her dancing, he said, "She's good, she's got style and good rhythm. She knew how to follow me and we did quite a few turns and spins. She did real well. I'd give her ten out of ten." Asked later at a Press conference how Diana had enjoyed it, Prince Charles declared, as she grinned broadly, "She would be an idiot if she didn't enjoy dancing with John Travolta." The American Ambassador to Britain, Charles Price, commented, "The Princess gave [John] a real run for his money. She was every bit as good as him. It was real Hollywood tinsel town stuff. What an evening!" See DANCING.

The menu for the banquet included lobster mousseline and crab, chicken capsicum, brown rice, and peach sorbet in champagne sauce. The entertainers were Neil Diamond, who had forfeited thousands of dollars to be there after having to cancel a vital recording session with eighty-five musicians booked for the same date; American opera star Leontyne Price, who sang an aria from *Madame Butterfly*, Gershwin's "Summertime" from *Porgy and Bess*, and a spiritual; and Nancy Reagan, who serenaded the guests with a verse of "I Concentrate on You" because Charles declared it was one of his favorite songs. President Reagan helped make the evening memorable with a gaffe at the top table when he referred to Diana as "Princess David."

The following day, the royal couple officially opened the spectacular "Treasure Houses of Britain" exhibition, of which they were Patrons, at the National Gallery, where they saw more than seven hundred works of art on loan from two hundred British stately homes, covering five hundred years of art collecting and private patronage. That evening the royal couple had dinner at the British Embassy, where the guests of honor were Vice President George Bush and his wife Barbara.

On the third day they were in Virginia, where they had a private lunch at the mansion of billionaire philanthropist and art connoisseur Paul Mellon, whose family founded the National Gallery. At one of the J. C. Penney department stores, which were staging a $50 million "Best of Britain" promotion of British products, Diana asked, "Don't you have double-breasted suits?"

and, pointing to Charles, who wears them, added, "Don't you think they are much more flattering?" People in the crowd outside included cops taking snapshots of the royal couple and a California graphic designer there to promote his mural of the Princess made from ten thousand jelly beans. (Diplomatic jars of jelly beans, President Reagan's favorite sweets, had been provided for the royal bedsides at the British Ambassador's residence by the Ambassador's wife.) With Nancy Reagan, Diana visited an adolescent drug rehabilitation center in Springfield (see DRUGS) before rejoining Prince Charles to lay a wreath, marking Veterans' Day, at Arlington National Cemetery, where she wore a stunning blue outfit by Bruce Oldfield, possibly his most successful design for her. The dinner and reception at the National Gallery which followed were restricted, it was reported, to VIPs and benefactors who had donated at least half a million dollars to the Gallery. That evening the Mayor of Washington, Mr. Marion Barry, discussed the problem of poor inner-city blacks with the Prince and said, "Have you seen downtown Washington?" Charles allegedly replied, "No, they won't let me come downtown. I wanted to do it."

The next day Charles and Diana said farewell to Washington and left for Palm Beach, Florida, home of America's millionaire lotus-eaters. There Prince Charles played in a polo match at the Palm Beach Polo and Country Club, scoring the winning goal before a crowd of twelve thousand while police helicopters headed off a light aircraft trailing a banner which read, "Charles and Diana please help to free Ireland." At a previous polo game in Palm Beach in 1980, the Prince had been overcome by heat exhaustion and, thinking he was dying, had asked his aide, Oliver Everett, for help. See STAFF. Bill and Jane Ylvisaker, who own the club, provided a luxury £360,000 house there, on Wellington Estate, for the Prince and Princess to use on their visits. That evening the royal couple attended a banquet and ball at Breakers Hotel hosted by Charles's friend, Occidental Petroleum Corporation chief Dr. Armand Hammer, who died in 1990 at age ninety-two. The gala raised an estimated $3 to $4 million for the United World Colleges, which seek to promote world understanding through education, and of which Charles is International President. With the thirty-two couples in the Magnolia Room who had paid $50,000 (£35,000) a pair for the privilege of meeting and being photographed with the Prince and Princess before dinner (the other couples had $10,000 tickets) was newly wed "Dynasty" star Joan Collins, who had just married her fourth husband, Peter Holm, in Las Vegas. Diana had met Joan the previous March at a charity evening in London given by Bruce Oldfield in aid of Barnardo's, where the soap opera star had reportedly told her, "We will get you a part in 'Dynasty' when you come to Los Angeles." See TELEVISION. True or not, Diana, wearing a raspberry pink velvet gown with a low-cut back, congratulated the couple on their wedding. "She was perfectly sweet to me. The conversation was warm and friendly," said the splendid, unsinkable Joanie who, dressed in a *Gone with the Wind* gown and dripping with diamonds, later danced at the ball with Prince Charles. Diana danced with Gregory Peck. Other guests included Bob Hope and Cary Grant. Chairman of the ball was Baghdad-born former belly dancer Mrs. Pat Kluge, aged thirty-six, a British national and wife of Paul Kluge, an American billionaire twice her age. But Mrs. Kluge resigned after it was revealed that the skin-flick magazine *Knave* had published full-frontal nude pictures of her and sex advice under her maiden name, Patricia Rose, in the seventies, when she was married to the owner, Russell Gay. On the big night the Kluges, whose marriage has since ended, were "traveling abroad."

The royal couple flew back on an RAF jet to celebrate Prince Charles's thirty-seventh birthday with their two sons at home. In Britain, Prince William, then aged three, appeared with a black eye, explaining, "I tripped over a brick." And there were brickbats too. So much of the visit had been connected with riches. Washington political scholar Joseph Kraft of the Brookings Institution had written before their arrival to promote the "Treasure Houses" exhibition, "We borrow prestige from an aristocracy we can buy. Britain . . . sells its prestige to the highest bidders." And back in Britain, controversial American-born royal commentator Harold Brooks-Baker of *Burke's Peerage* reportedly claimed that the couple's "rent-a-royal" routine in the States had threatened to cheapen the monarchy, adding, "To require the Prince of Wales to visit Palm Beach is like asking the Pope to visit Sodom and Gomorrah."

In February 1989, Diana visited New York for three days on her first major overseas trip without her husband, becoming the Uptown Girl in the Big Apple. Her advisers seemed to have learned a lesson from the previous trip, and this time she concentrated as much on the grit as the glitter. One New York tabloid heralded her as "The Most Publicized Woman on Earth," "Bigger than Gorby, Better than Bush." On network TV morning shows, pundits questioned the state of the royal marriage, which had undergone strains since the previous visit (see MARRIAGE), and asked, "Are they really mad at each other?" For the benefit of eager fans, they also inquired, "Do you think there'll be any chance of Princess Di actually pressing the flesh?" (She certainly did!) But some prearrival comments were surprisingly anti, citizens being urged in print not to succumb to "Di-mania." "We once revolted against the British and should be ashamed of any pro-monarchist yearnings," wrote one political columnist. *New York Post* writer Pete Hamill, a seventies date of Jackie Onassis and Shirley MacLaine, penned a Di-lashing article calling the Princess "the most famous welfare mother in the world—a permanent recipient of the British dole," which she isn't. See MONEY. He added that although she "seems to be a decent person," she "doesn't work, has no known talents, and derives her celebrity entirely from the man she married," which shows how ill informed *he* was!

Amid all this, Diana arrived on the Concorde and went straight to a fashion reception held by a British knitwear company in a skyscraper in Manhattan, where she was deafened by the cheers of thousands of New Yorkers and almost blinded by photographers' flashlights, joking, "Someone will have to lead the way. I can't see for all these flashbulbs." Upstairs on the fiftieth floor, one of the first New Yorkers to meet her at the reception rhapsodized, "She's wonderful, elegant, enchanting, amazing!" Diana gazed at the famous Manhattan skyline from the windows and declared, "New York is marvelous, quite dramatic. But I've never seen so many blue and red flashing lights in my life." Those lights beamed from police cars, part of a security network which included a special "Di-squad" of four hundred extra cops wearing gray bulletproof flak jackets and toting machine guns, anxious about Irish threats to disrupt the visit. Cops on motorcycles preceded a twelve-car motorcade when the royal party, the Princess in a bulletproof Cadillac, moved off to the Plaza Athenee Hotel on East 64th Street, where she stayed in the same $2,000-a-night luxury duplex suite used by star guests like Elizabeth Taylor and rock star Prince when they are in town.

Next morning, she was given a 7:00 A.M. dawn serenade outside the hotel by Cockney exile Lennie Metcalfe, who had been hired by Rupert Murdoch's Channel Five TV company to dress up as a pearly king (a leader in a community of pushcart peddlars whose clothes have mother-of-pearl-covered buttons) and play an accordion. Elsewhere, the winner of a Princess Diana look-alike contest doled out helpings of British shepherd's pie. That day, Diana found herself sharing front-page billing in the New York tabloid newspapers with a story about a three-year-old toddler used as a human shield in a drugs-deal shoot-out. There was more grit in the slums of the Lower East Side, where Diana toured the Henry Street settlement center, a halfway house for homeless families, where she chatted to a homeless mother of three and, noticing that a little boy's shoelace was undone, crouched down to tie it up for him. Behind the center, out of sight, groups of winos huddled over bonfires, sipping their booze. Traffic hold-ups caused by the royal visit had already been nicknamed "Di-lock," and when the chill February wind and rain suddenly gave way to an unseasonal warm spell, a radio announcer christened it "Diana weather," which was a contrast because the British royals are usually said to bring rain. (See KUWAIT & THE UNITED ARAB EMIRATES.) At a promotion of British toys at "the ultimate toy shop," F. A. O. Schwarz on Fifth Avenue, the local version of London's Hamleys, where the tales of Thomas the Tank Engine were making their New York debut, the Princess was greeted by sales staff dressed up as Popeye, Olive Oyl, and Paddington Bear. Chronically ill teenager Hope Manley, for whom she made a dream come true, presented her with roses. See LETTERS.

That evening, resplendent in a richly embroidered white-and-gold gown and bolero jacket by Victor Edelstein, Diana attended the first American performance of a production of Verdi's opera *Falstaff* by the Welsh National Opera, of which she is Patron. See

MUSIC. On the sidewalks around the Brooklyn Academy of Music, which had been scraped free of chewing gum in her honor (provoking enraged front-page comments in *Newsday* that city employees had better things to do), the cheers of one thousand admirers drowned out chants of "Princess Di must go" from about sixty to a hundred IRA and Noraid supporters. About eight hundred New Yorkers bought $1,000 tickets to attend the opera and a banquet later at the Wintergarden, where Diana was to have been joined by *Fatal Attraction* star Michael Douglas, one of her favorites. However, like Robert Redford before him during the Washington trip, he cried off because he was busy filming *Black Rain* in California: a second royal snub in a year, since he'd previously canceled an engagement with Fergie, also because of movie commitments. (Diana met Douglas later at the London premiere of *Wall Street*.) *Superman* star Christopher Reeve, who once danced with the Princess to the music of Kid Creole and the Coconuts at a charity event in Britain, was roped in as a new partner for Douglas's wife, Diandra. But when she went down with the flu, neither of them turned up either. Among those who did make it were the upper crust of New York society and other A-list ticket holders including Astors; Rockefellers; billionaire publisher Malcolm Forbes, who'd been at the White House banquet too; and glitzy megarich property developer Donald Trump, prior to his matrimonial and financial problems.

The next day, Diana was greeted by hundreds of rainswept New Yorkers lining the streets of Harlem where she arrived, in a cheerful red woolen suit, to spend over an hour visiting seven dying children in the AIDS ward of the pediatric unit at Harlem Hospital. See HIV. Staff reached tearfully for their hankies as the deeply touched Princess cuddled, talked to, and played with the children. A one-year-old toddler named Monica, wearing a pink frock, curled her fingers around Diana's hand. The Princess asked a little boy, "How heavy are you?" and lifted him up, cradling him in her arms for a hug. As he laid his head on her shoulder, his big brown eyes smiling, she herself seemed overcome and close to tears. "She knew this was going to be harrowing," a Buckingham Palace official said, "but I don't think she has ever been so touched by anything. The youngster in her arms was about the same age as Prince William." Usual life expectancy for the children—a few of the 1,300 youngsters in the United States at that time with AIDS, contracted by most of the mothers through intravenous drug use—was said to be three years. The little boy Diana cuddled had reached the age of seven but was thought to have only one more year to live.

Despite her alleged pro-Irish sympathies, which had provoked an FBI security check, Dr. Margaret Heagarty, the Director, wore a small Union Jack on her hospital outfit for the royal visit and was clearly impressed with the Princess. Describing Diana as "a deeply sensitive and kind young woman," Dr. Heagarty said that she was an inspiration and an example to American leaders. "Our own royalty, whatever that is in . . . a republic," she said, "have not done anything nearly so symbolic as these things you are doing for us today." She told Diana, "You cannot get [AIDS] very easily and your presence here and your work in Britain has calmed many people. People with the disease can be hugged and loved. We need to care for these patients and not be afraid of them." Her colleague Miss Lulu King, educational coordinator on the children's AIDS ward, added, "Thank you for bringing love, youth, and vitality to us here, and God bless you." Standing with tears in her eyes as the visit drew to a close, Dr. Heagarty declared that the Princess had given the hospital "and our community of poor people an enormous uplift" and had shown "great courage." "We have been so moved," she said. "Princess Diana is a mother herself, and she understands." No photographs showing the faces of the ailing children were allowed to be taken during the visit. Previously, when a child had been recognized as an AIDS sufferer from a news photograph in the United States, his family's home was burned to the ground.

In an America paranoid with fear about AIDS, Diana's compassionate and spontaneously affectionate gestures toward the children made a huge impact—as British-born New York publicist Peter Brown pointed out to her later. "Well, I just turned up," Diana replied humbly. "No more, no less." However, the memories stayed to haunt her, as she revealed later on her flight home on the Concorde. See PRESS. A Buckingham Palace spokesman said, "Visiting Harlem Hospital was a very emotional experience for her. She has been working nonstop for two days, and the full impact is only just catching up with her.''

Diana's final engagement was a reception at the residence of British Consul General Gordon Jewkes for supporters of the American Foundation for the Royal Academy of Music, where guests introduced to her included Yoko Ono and rock singer Mick Jones of Foreigner.

The visit to the Big Apple, without Prince Charles at her side, had been stressful, emotional, and exhausting for the Princess, but it had also proved a great success. The brickbats which had heralded Diana's arrival were followed by bouquets once she was seen in action. ''Diana's doing a helluva job for the Empire,'' remarked Malcolm Forbes. Bianca Jagger declared, ''She's stunning. The people of New York are charmed by her.'' And the *New York Daily News* declared, ''Princess Diana broke the heart and soul of the city when she cuddled several AIDS patients at Harlem Hospital and grabbed the outstretched hands of rain-soaked well-wishers.'' A headline which expressed the general feeling when New Yorkers bade her farewell said fondly, ''Bye bye sweet Di.''

In October 1990, Diana returned to Washington, D.C., for a gala fund-raising evening in aid of the Washington Ballet, London City Ballet (of which she is Patron), and Grandma's House, a home in Washington for children with AIDS. The Princess's work for the London City Ballet had virtually kept it going, but it had reached an ''extremely perilous'' situation financially and Diana's mission to Washington was partly, if not mainly, to save the company. See DANCING. However, because of the high price of the tickets—$2,540 a head, or $3,517 for those who wanted to meet the Princess—fewer people than expected attended. The evening raised $826,542, somewhat short of the million dollars hoped for. Washington socialites were reported to have been put out that the event had been organized from London. Despite any embarrassment, Diana made the most of her brief visit. At Grandma's House, when one three-year-old girl nicknamed First Lady asked her, ''Can I ride in your car?,'' the Princess said, ''Of course you can,'' then picked her up and sat her on her lap for a drive in the British Embassy Rolls-Royce. The Reverend Debbie Tate, President of Grandma's House, where First Lady lives, said, ''The

Princess is a wonderful person and she really does care deeply."
Earlier, Diana discussed AIDS babies with Barbara Bush at the
White House, where President George Bush joined them and
praised her efforts to help American charities. He also asked the
Princess about reactions in Britain to the Gulf crisis following
Iraq's invasion of Kuwait that August. See GULF WAR.

ARAB GULF STATES

In November 1986, Charles and Diana made a ten-day tour of the
Arab Gulf States, visiting Oman, moving on to Qatar, and stopping briefly in Bahrain before traveling on to Saudi Arabia. Apart
from the jet lag and fierce desert heat, both of which affect Diana
badly, she had to remember to keep her elbows, chest, and legs
modestly covered to avoid insulting Islam, and included in her
tour wardrobe high-necked, sleeved, calf-length dresses and a
trouser outfit, which allowed her to sit on cushions on a carpet for
a banquet in a Bedouin tent where roast sheep, head and eyes
intact, was served with vegetables and yogurt.

Still there were gaffes. From the royal couple, when they
kissed after a polo match in Oman—a kiss promptly banned from
local television screens in case it inflamed and outraged viewers.
And from Crown Prince Abdullah, brother of King Fahd of Saudi
Arabia, who decamped to the Canary Isles, allegedly on medical
grounds, rather than play host to the visiting VIPs. His reason,
apparently, was the row between Britain and Syria over terrorist
allegations during which diplomatic ties were broken: he sided
with Syria. In Qatar during a desert display, both Charles and
Diana looked put out by what seemed, to British eyes, cruel
treatment being meted out to a camel by its rider. See ZOO. On
the other hand, it must have seemed very odd to the Arabs that
the Princess was the focus of Press attention on the tour, and that
when she went off to one engagement while the Prince went to
another, the media pursued her rather than him. Arabs regard
women as second-class citizens, which may account for one Press
claim later that at times Diana had felt "humiliated" on the tour.

True or not, the trip had its compensations. The Sultan of
Oman presented Diana with fabulous jewels (see JEWELRY) and

Charles with an £80,000 Aston Martin convertible. He also opened his personal guest palace to the Press for the first time so that photographs could be taken of him inside with the royal couple, as they were when Diana curtsied to him at an official banquet. In Qatar, it is taboo for the sexes to mix socially, and it looked as if Diana would have to spend the evening of her husband's thirty-eighth birthday on November 14 apart from him at a women-only dinner. Instead the Amir made her an "honorary man" for the evening so that she could join Charles at his special banquet. And in Saudi Arabia, King Fahd made up for the Crown Prince's snub by acting as personal host to the royal couple, even giving his own banquet for them at his palace, which had not been originally planned. These honors and the warmth of the welcome and friendship shown to them by their generous hosts during the tour made a great impression on Charles and Diana.

One event which got the accompanying Press quite worked up, visualizing headlines about a third royal baby on the way, was the surprise appearance of the royal gynecologist, George Pinker, at the official dinner in Bahrain. See CHILDREN. But hopes of that big story faded when Diana herself asked in surprise, "George, what are you doing here?" It turned out his arrival was pure coincidence: he had flown in to attend a local wedding the next day.

At the end of the tour, the royal couple had a brief one-and-a-half-day second honeymoon sailing through the Red Sea on the royal yacht *Britannia*, as they had after their wedding five years previously. Charles then went off to visit the Parachute Regiment in Cyprus, while Diana flew home, loaded with presents for their two sons. See MARRIAGE and GULF WAR.

ARMED FORCES

The Princess is Colonel-in-Chief of the Royal Hampshire Regiment, which she has visited abroad (see GERMANY) in Londonderry, Northern Ireland, and at its headquarters in Winchester, where for a regimental dinner in February 1990, she wore her own version of mess dress. See UNIFORMS. She is also Colonel-in-Chief of the 13th/18th Royal Hussars (Queen Mary's Own), and spent her sixth wedding anniversary in July 1987 presenting new colors to them at Tidworth Garrison, 250 miles apart from Prince Charles who was on a private visit to his tenant farmers in Cornwall. See MARRIAGE. (In 1989 they spent their eighth wedding anniversary apart when Charles presented new colors to the Royal Regiment of Wales, of which he is Colonel-in-Chief, while she celebrated a friend's wedding in Leicestershire.) Diana is sponsor of HMS Cornwall. See LETTERS. During a visit to the frigate—armed with Exocet, Harpoon, and Sea Wolf missiles—in Plymouth in October 1988, when she presented good-conduct and long-service awards, she also sat at the controls of a 30-mm antiaircraft cannon and fired a blank shot from a 4.5-inch gun. The visit involved clambering up ship's ladders, so Diana cleverly contrived to look ladylike and avoid giving the sailors an eyeful by turning up in a smart pair of culottes. See FASHION and PRESS. The Princess also has links with the Air Force as Honorary Air Commodore of RAF Wittering. The Red Devils parachute team landed at Kensington Palace when Prince William was a toddler, much to his delight. Abroad, Diana is Colonel-in-Chief of the Royal Australian Survey Corps, and of the Princess of Wales's Own Regiment in Canada. See GULF WAR.

ARTS & HANDICRAFTS

Both Diana and Charles enjoy sketching. Diana has made several drawings of her children, some of which are apparently lodged in the royal archives at Windsor for safekeeping. Charles takes time from the busy royal schedule whenever he can to practice the hobby. On the tour of Japan with his wife in May 1986, for example, he sat alone sketching a scene in a palace garden in Kyoto between official engagements. Though he claims he is "not good" at sketching, he has also said, "I get completely absorbed in it . . . it teaches you to be observant and to notice your surroundings in detail and, to me, it provides enormous relaxation." He also paints watercolors of landscapes and seascapes, and he likes to give his paintings as wedding or other gifts to members of the Royal Family. Some of his watercolors were reproduced in his book A Vision of Britain (Doubleday, 1989). Like Prince Andrew's early photographs, many of his pictures have a sense of remoteness, isolation, and loneliness, a feeling of being set apart. Charles usually signs his paintings with the initial C, plus the place and the year when the picture was painted. He keeps his paints in an old canvas fishing bag, which always accompanies him to Balmoral and, on occasion, on trips abroad. He has made at least four painting expeditions to Italy, a country he has "a passion for." In May 1990 he opened his first one-man show of fifty-seven of his watercolors in Urbino, where he said, "These sketches are very much a part of myself and I am sure those who paint will understand how hard it is to part with something into which, when inspired, you have poured your heart and soul." One of the pictures had just appeared at the Bath Contemporary Art Fair, and two more of his works were included in a celebrity exhibition in July 1990 to raise money for a new forest on the London-Essex border. One of his watercolors, of a farm scene in Norfolk, was hung at the Royal Academy of Arts summer exhibition in 1987. The work, entered under a pseudonym (see NAMES) and from the home address of Sir John Riddell, his Private Secretary at the time (see STAFF), was chosen on merit. Though the hobby can be lucrative (Charles sold one of his paintings to a friend for £10,000), it does separate him at times from Diana and the children. However, he finds painting a great relaxation, like sketching.

The couple love paintings and have many hanging in their homes, including a wedding portrait and a painting of the family at Prince William's christening, both by one of Charles's favorite artists, John Ward, who is in his seventies. They have been friends for years, and in 1985 Ward was with the royal couple on their Italian tour (see ITALY) to help the Prince perfect his painting technique. Another friend, artist Bryan Organ (see FRIENDS), did portraits of them both in 1981. The one of Diana, the first official portrait of her as Lady Diana Spencer, was later slashed but repaired. They have several paintings, gifts from the Queen Mother, by Roy Petley, an artist who was brought up in a children's home and exhibits on the street railings at Green Park close to Buckingham Palace, where the first royal to discover his work was the Duchess of Kent. She has bought many of his pictures, and both she and the Queen Mother have commissioned him to paint more, including one of Sandringham House and another of Wood Farm near Sandringham.

Diana studied drawing and painting at Riddlesworth Hall school (see EDUCATION) in addition to basketwork, weaving, and pottery. Though needlework wasn't something she excelled at during her time at West Heath, she enjoys tapestry, and in early 1989 was spotted emerging from the Women's Home Industries shop in Pimlico, London, with a tapestry kit. She is said to have cut Charles's hair with her tapestry scissors before now! Tapestry was also a hobby of her grandfather, the 7th Earl Spencer, and the tapestry backs on some of the chairs at Althorp are his handiwork. By coincidence, the 7th Earl's wife, Lady Cynthia, daughter of the 3rd Duke of Abercorn, had once been romanced by the last Prince of Wales, later Edward VIII and later still the Duke of Windsor, whose own hobby was embroidery. Charles's grandfather, King George VI, the Duke's brother, was an expert in petit point and made a dozen chair covers which the Queen Mother has at Royal Lodge, Windsor.

Diana is an avid photographer and has albums full of photos she has taken of her children and homes. She showed some to top royal cameraman Tim Graham, who reckoned they were "very competently done" with a "nice eye" for composition.

The Princess is President of Wales Craft Council and is particularly involved in the performing arts. See DANCING and MUSIC. She is also keen to encourage business sponsorship of the arts, as she showed in a speech she made in December 1989 when she presented a dozen winners with that year's awards of the Association of Business Sponsorship of the Arts (ABSA).

ASTROLOGY

Diana was born under the home- and family-loving astrological sign of Cancer the crab. Typical virtues of the sign: loyalty, patience, helpfulness, and sympathy toward others. Typical faults: dreaminess, frivolity, and irritability. Crabs can be very sensitive and crabby. Charles was born under sexy Scorpio, sign of the eagle and scorpion—beware the sting! Typical virtues: love of responsibility, physical courage, readiness to work hard, thoroughness, and caution. Typical faults of the sign: secretiveness, suspiciousness, callousness, and jealousy. A Scorpio seeks sensation, fresh experience, new associates. Cancer and Scorpio are both water signs, motivated by emotion and intuition, and the bond they share can be exceptionally strong. A negative view, expressed in Sayers & Viney's *Bad News Zodiac* (Grafton, 1985), is that the union of Cancer and Scorpio could be like mixing Pepsi with paraquat, a lethal cocktail which the fair Cancer could survive only by total submission to the dominating demands of the dark, brooding Scorpio. Which sounds not unlike the plots of the romantic novels Diana so enjoys! However, the more popular and positive astrological view is that these two signs are highly compatible, forming good unions and excellent partnerships in marriage and other relationships. With this pair there should be no problem over who wears the pants, provided the Scorpio is the male. Prince Andrew, whom Diana once had her eye on, is an Aquarian. A Cancer-Aquarius link does not get the astrological thumbs-up long-term. By coincidence, Charles and Diana share the same astrological signs as fashion designers David and Elizabeth Emanuel, who made Diana's fairy-tale wedding dress. Elizabeth once declared, "We balance each other well because I'm dreamy and he's more orderly. We make a great team but we like to do different things, and so give each other plenty of space. Our star signs are supposed to be an excellent match." It was only when they split up on the eve of their fifteenth wedding anniversary in 1990 that she revealed they had "lost the ability to communicate" and had been leading separate lives for years. See RELATE.

In March 1985, when astrologer Carole Golder surveyed the marriage of the "rebel" Diana, whom she claimed has "leanings to overpossessiveness and jealousy," and Charles, who "likes to be boss," she predicted "big changes coming in 1987," saying, "His star chart shows Charles to be a devoted husband and father. But with his Scorpio sex appeal, he wouldn't be averse to admiring glances thrown his way!" It was in 1987 that stories claiming the royal marriage was on the rocks reached a peak. See MARRIAGE. According to *Royal Chinese Horoscopes* (Equation, 1989), Diana

was born in the Year of the Buffalo (1961) and Charles in the Year
of the Rat (1948), a combination which author Barry Fantoni
declares is totally incompatible, adding that "practically all Rat
and Buffalo marriages tend to end in disaster." Various astrologers have hinted in the past that Prince Charles would never be
king but that greatness lay in store for Prince Andrew. At the time
of their wedding, it was predicted that Charles and Diana would
have three children. However, an astrologer who prepared Prince
William's birth chart later predicted that he would have a brother
and *two* sisters (see CHILDREN) and that he would be crowned
king in about the year 2025, by which time he would be aged
about forty-three. One unconfirmed report claims that Diana
consults an astrologer.

AUSTRALIA

Diana's first major trips abroad both before and after her wedding
were to Australia. Her mother and stepfather, Frances and Peter
Shand Kydd, who have since separated, had invited her to go on
a vacation with them to their thousand-acre sheep station near
Yass in New South Wales for the first time. And since they flew to
Australia in 1981 shortly after Prince Charles proposed, the
holiday served several purposes. It gave Diana a break from the
glare of the media spotlight trained on her every activity since her
romance with the Prince first became known. It gave her the
chance to "think over," as Charles had suggested, whether life as
a royal would be too awful a prospect, though in fact she had
accepted his marriage proposal instantly. And it also allowed her
to spend her last days of freedom on vacation in private with the
Shand Kydds before the Palace officially announced the royal
engagement, ending her privacy forever. Astonishingly, although
they flew out together to Sydney on a scheduled Qantas flight,
Diana managed to arrive in Australia undetected. And when her
disappearance from Britain suddenly set Mrs. Shand Kydd's telephone ringing, she told the Press, fibbing, "Diana is not here and
is not coming." Under the circumstances many other mothers
would no doubt have done the same.

Australian journalists descended on the estate; but by de-

While touring Australia, Diana meets with well-wishers at Macedon, Victoria. (Glenn Harvey/Camera Press London)

ploying various adventurous tactics, which he relished, Peter Shand Kydd ensured that for the ten days they spent swimming, surfing, and lazing around at a friend's beach house, they weren't found. The determination to fend off inquirers and keep Diana's whereabouts secret was such that when Charles tried to ring his sweetheart from Britain, even he had difficulty getting through on the telephone. At one number he tried, the person who answered (apparently a member of the staff) told him, "We're not taking any calls." "It's the Prince of Wales speaking," he said. "How do I know it's the Prince of Wales?" asked the voice. "You don't. But I am!" Charles protested. Fortunately, he eventually got through to Diana on another number. But even the privacy of their calls was put in doubt when it was suggested that outsiders might be illegally tapping their around-the-world sweet nothings, though Charles thought that "highly unlikely." See MOTORING. (A claim that their calls *were* tapped and taped during Charles's later pre-nuptial visit to Australia proved false.)

Diana's return to Australia in 1983, two years after the royal wedding, was a very different matter. It was her greatest test to date—her first official overseas tour as the Princess of Wales. She accompanied Charles on what was to prove, in her own words, a "baptism of fire." And baby Prince William went, too, which was a complete break with royal tradition. See MARRIAGE. The Queen, when a baby, had not been taken on tour abroad by her parents, and as an infant, Prince Charles had also had to be left at home. So little Prince William became the youngest member of the Royal Family ever to go on an official foreign tour. Estimates of the items needed to be packed in William's luggage included at least 246 disposable diapers, a potty, a minimum of twenty day-time outfits plus twelve cardigans, stretch sleepers which could also be used as pajamas, bibs, several sunhats, a woolen coat, more than two dozen pairs of socks, two hundred jars of baby food, his favorite toys, and much more. Professor Charles Stroud, pediatrician at King's College Hospital in London, assured report-ers that most babies travel well, suffering less jet lag than adults, and indicated that the twenty-four hour flight would pose few problems for the royal infant. The aircraft had been specially converted to include a private bedroom and sitting room for the royal couple, and William had his own bed in a separate cabin he shared with his nanny, Barbara Barnes, and Olga Powell, her assistant.

The grueling six-week tour of Australia and New Zealand was not only Diana's debut abroad but also one of the most compre-hensive planned since 1953–54. The program involved engage-ments in Australia from March 21 until April 17—moving from the Northern Territory to Canberra, New South Wales, Tasmania, South Australia, and Western Australia to Queensland and Victoria—before traveling around New Zealand until April 30. Palace officials regarded this as the "Big One" and endless preparations were put in hand. It had to be a success—and so did the Princess. London-based reporters used to following her around on her normal public duties at home had few doubts. No royal captured hearts and minds in quite such a natural, open, spontaneous way. No royal enchanted crowds more, responded better to children, or showed so much genuine, and appropriate, emotion. No royal was prettier, and few women anywhere dressed with such style, elegance, and pizzazz. With Diana, no reporter stuck for copy ever needed to fall back on the hackneyed royal description of how "radiant" she was. She was the living, breathing, real thing—a flesh-and-blood People's Princess and a world-beater (on form, of course). Why should the Australians and New Zealanders feel any differently about her?

For Diana, whatever her personal doubts or fears about the arduous and lengthy task ahead, there was her first tour wardrobe to plan. With temperatures likely to be up to 38° C (100° F), the materials for daywear needed to be cool, natural fibers like cotton and silk. The colors had to be bright and vibrant, so that she'd stand out in the inevitable crowds. Red was a top choice: that always gets you noticed. She chose lots of pink as well, from the palest shade to bright fuchsia. Blue, to match her eyes. And sunny bright yellow, a new choice for her. The wardrobe would be a mix of old and new, so that she could intersperse outfits she'd worn in the past with brand-new creations from favorite designers including Catherine Walker, Bruce Oldfield, Bellville Sassoon, and Victor Edelstein. To cover all her engagements, she is said to have organized about eighty outfits. Day dresses and smart suits with hats to match, evening gowns, casual clothes for tour breaks, shoes, handbags, jewelry, and don't forget to pack at least one tiara—an endless array which would make the average family's summer vacation packing seem a cinch. Planning, choosing, and ordering for her wardrobe began the autumn before, and work was still being done up to the last minute. Refuting claims that the Princess was spending money like water, a Palace Press Officer pointed out that she'd had to get lots of cool new clothes anyway because the summer before she'd been in maternity frocks, and she could hardly take those. Only a day before she was due to leave, Diana admitted that she hadn't yet finished putting her wardrobe together and was still mulling over exactly what to take with her. In 1981, when she'd traveled to Australia with just two suitcases, it had no doubt been easy. This time, a royal baggage master would be required to take charge of the tour party's ninety cases and trunks.

Although the first and second heirs to the throne are supposed to avoid traveling on the same flight, the Queen allowed Prince William to go to Australia on the same Royal Australian Airforce Boeing 707 as his parents. The family flew in to Alice Springs on Sunday, March 20, 1983. Little Wills or Wombat, as his parents call him, became the immediate focus of attention as he emerged from the plane with Nanny Barnes and was transferred to the loving arms of his mother for his first Press photo opportunity on foreign soil. A wag in the crowd yelled, "Here's Billy the Kid!" William squinted in the sunshine, while Charles tried to flick away a "ubiquitous Australian fly" which settled fitfully on his son's nose, cheek, and head. The exhausting flight, Charles said, had left them with "tertiary jet lag," but nevertheless the arrival of the royal party was sunny and cheerful and in marked contrast for local people to the drama and tragedy they had suffered in recent days past.

Alice Springs had been enduring torrential rains, during which three people drowned, trees and bridges were swept away, a hundred people were evacuated from their homes, and the central part of Alice was cut off for thirty days. The causeway to the luxurious Federal-Casino Hotel, where Charles and Diana were due to stay, was swept away by floodwaters, so emergency plans were quickly made to put them up at the newly opened, two-story Gap Motor Lodge instead. In the meantime, car dealer Dino Diano stepped in and allowed them to freshen up at his pool and bungalow in the shade of Snob Hill, where they swam, sunbathed, and relaxed for four hours before moving into suites 301 and 303 at the motel. Their own suite (the other was for their clothes) came complete with a TV they could watch from the queen-size bed, a brick-built bar stocked with cans of Australian lager, and a tub for two. See BATHS & BATHROOMS.

While his parents settled in, apart from an hour when they climbed out through a hole in a fence to inspect the flood damage at Alice Springs, William and his nannies were flying off to their haven. Arrangements had been made well in advance for the baby prince, who was then aged nine months, to remain permanently at his own base. On the Australian leg of the forty-five-thousand-mile tour, that meant staying with Nanny Barnes at Woomargama near Albury, at an isolated New South Wales homestead with four thousand acres of land which Charles and Diana had chosen to become their home away from home. Here they would be able to relax in private with their son whenever a break in the packed schedule gave them the chance. The seventy-year-old house at Woomargama, filled with paintings and antique furniture from Europe and China, had six bedrooms, a cozy kitchen, wicker chairs on the vine-covered veranda, and a courtyard and swimming pool, shaded by a silk tree, which could be seen from William's quarters. There were English trees and roses in the garden. And before they made way for the royal guests by moving out to their city home in Toorak, Melbourne, the owners, rich company director Gordon Darling, aged sixty-one, and his wife Margaret, made sure that the pantry was well stocked and that there were fresh flowers in all the rooms. The Darlings already had nursery furniture at Woomargama which their grandchildren used on visits there, plus an English baby carriage, which was brought out of storage and dusted off in case William needed it. And they said he could use the changing room near the swimming pool as a playroom, if he wanted to.

At Woomargama, which in contrast to Alice Springs was suffering the forty-sixth successive month of its worst drought in memory, many of the hundred residents, including Onore "Norrie" Sutton, an ex-truck driver who ran a pub called The Swamp, were thrilled at the lightning response once local authorities discovered that the royals would be staying in their area. They had been at the local council "for years to do something about our town," said Norrie, yet suddenly "everything started happening." Swarms of workmen arrived in vans and trucks to fix the roads, turn on sprinklers, cut the remaining grass, and water trees. While at the nearest airport, thirty-four miles away at Albury, men worked till dawn laying tarmac while a further team waited in vain on twenty-four-hour standby for some rain to fall in order to plant grass seed.

Though no permanent staff were kept at the house at Woomargama, the royal couple took a twenty-strong retinue with them on the tour, including Diana's key team of seven close aides, all of whom she addressed by their first names. These were Oliver Everett, aged thirty-nine, her Private Secretary, whose task each morning was to brief her on the day's events (which would sometimes involve traveling hundreds of miles to fulfill up to eight official engagements per day); Anne Beckwith-Smith, aged thirty, Diana's full-time Lady-in-Waiting; dresser Evelyn Dagley, aged thirty; Press Secretary Victor Chapman, aged fifty; detectives Inspector Graham Smith and Sergeant Allan Peters, both in their late thirties; and of course Nanny Barnes. In addition, at an estimated cost of almost £4,000 each, Diana's hairdressers, Kevin Shanley and Richard Dalton, were flown out in turns to tend her locks so that one of them could still attend their clients in London. See STAFF and BEAUTY SECRETS. Because of the length of the tour, there were back-ups for some of the staff too.

Prince Charles had spent six months at Geelong school in Melbourne in 1966, which according to Prince Philip's Equerry, Squadron Leader David Checketts, had turned him from a shy, seventeen-year-old boy into "a man." The Prince retains a particular affection for the country and its people, finding Australians friendly, forthright, humorous, and kind, despite being ribbed as a schoolboy in Oz ("Down Under" or Australia) about being a "Pommie" (somewhat disparaging term Australians use for English immigrants) this or that. For him the tour was a return to what he regards as "a sort of second home."

But for Diana it was her first time on duty as an official royal ambassador abroad, and she later admitted that the first few days came as a "shock." Apart from having to cope with the jet lag and heat, royal tours are very arduous with enormous distances to cross, thousands of people to see, and umpteen events crammed into the schedule to try and please as many local people as possible. Even for experienced royal travelers, a six-week tour, with short breaks for relaxation, is an exhausting business. Diana must have found it daunting. Later she declared that touring overseas, when she's kept even more busy than she is at home, is not the "holiday" some people might think. However, she not only survived but was the star attraction. Charles commented good-naturedly to part of a crowd in Sydney meeting him rather than her during a royal walkabout, "It's not fair, is it? You'd better ask for your money back!"

Her face, neck, chest, shins, and feet painfully red from overdoing the sunbathing at Mr. Diano's pool in the 27° C (80° F) heat the previous day, Diana chose a high-necked yellow and white dress for one of their first visits, to the Alice Springs School of the Air, which then broadcast lessons to 110 children living in isolated areas of the outback, where she and Charles answered questions posed by youngsters over the radio. That evening, they traveled two hundred miles to climb the lower slopes of Ayers Rock, the world's largest monolith, revered by the Aborigines and the scene of the start of Australia's infamous dingo baby case. Then, like tourists, they went to a good viewing point and waited to see the sunset over the rock. Diana got out her camera, but just as the colors changed between scarlet, purple, and black, she turned away to look at a little lizard handed over by a ranger and missed the big moment. She handed her camera back to her detective with a rueful smile.

Next day, the royal couple crossed the Tropic of Capricorn to visit the old gold-rush town of Tennant Creek and Karaguru school, where the children had spent a month rehearsing a song called "But I Can't Spell Hippopotamus" to perform to the VIPs, Charles commenting that he hoped they now could. "I am not coping with the heat too well," Diana revealed during a walkabout in the 38° C (100° F) heat which followed.

But soon they were off to Woomargama for a reunion with Prince William, whom they had not seen for three days. Diana rang ahead to say they would arrive at 7:00 P.M. and to ask Nanny Barnes to keep William up beyond his usual bedtime so that they could give him a cuddle. "I know it's only been a short parting," said one of the royal staff, "but they can't wait to see him again."

As it happened, they drove up two hours late, having been held up by crowds in Albury, extrajoyful perhaps because after the four-year drought, William's arrival at Woomargama had produced a sudden nonstop deluge. Charles and Diana even had to relax indoors during the break with their son because of the downpour.

Back on duty on March 24 (Diana now had not only jet lag and sunburn but also a slight cold from the rain at Woomargama), they traveled 190 miles to Canberra for the official welcome to Australia by the newly elected Labor Prime Minister Bob Hawke, who was committed to a policy of getting rid of the monarchy and declaring Australia a republic. He refused to bow to the royal couple at Canberra airport, though his wife Hazel did a small curtsy and his eighty-five-year-old father, the Reverend Clem Hawke, said firmly, "I am still one of the Queen's men." Protocol prevented Charles from mentioning the subject, though he spoke of the strong ties between Britain and Australia during a speech to seven thousand people later at the Civic Centre. However, when the Waleses and the Hawkes met later at Government Lodge, the Australian leader's retreat, they seemed like old friends. Of Diana, who had clearly won him over with her charm and sense of humor, Bob Hawke said, "She's a lovely lady."

There was prolonged cheering during a walkabout in Canberra, but the Princess revealed how much she was missing William. When twenty-nine-year-old Aussie housewife Jill Shoebridge told her, "I wish I had a nanny just like yours to look after my son," so that she could get out and do the shopping, Diana replied, unsmiling, "I would swap with you anytime. I wish I did not have to leave William with his nanny. I would rather do what you are doing." She told others in the crowd that William kept waking them up at 2:00 A.M., apparently because he was teething. See CHILDREN. "He's waking in the night and having a good scream," she said. "He just can't settle down to Australian time. But he is very well." She also said with a smile, "He's getting a lot of affection from a lot of people."

That evening, at a dinner given by the Governor General, Sir Ninian Stephen, at Government House, Diana wore an apricot taffeta gown with a V neck, dropped waist, and puffed sleeves.

With it she wore the Spencer diamond tiara which she had worn on her wedding day, plus a diamond necklace and her prized Royal Family Order from the Queen. See ORDERS, DECORATIONS & HONORS. Two of the guests, millionaire art collector Kim Bonython and his wife, had lost everything in the South Australian bushfires: their mansion, a unique jazz record collection, priceless works of art, and even the clothes they had planned to wear at the dinner.

The bushfires had killed forty-six people, destroyed more than two thousand homes, and devastated thousands of acres that February shortly before the start of the royal tour. At their own request, Charles and Diana cut short their stay in Canberra to visit the worst-hit area, around the township of Cockatoo near Melbourne. Many of the seven thousand people who waited to greet them had horrific tales to tell. Of the kindergarten which civilian firefighter David Adams hosed down from the roof while inside a hundred children lay huddled beneath dripping wet towels, placed on them by headmistress Iola Tilley, which dried within three minutes because of the fierce heat. Of the firemen who dropped from exhaustion after getting only seven hours of sleep in nearly four days. Of the houses and forests which had been lost and were now bleak, charred remains. And tragically, of the bodies of relatives, friends, and neighbors which had been found. Diana turned her head away sorrowfully when Mrs. Sheila Griffiths, from Birmingham, England, revealed how her only son, Christopher, aged twenty, had died when they were overtaken by fire which had traveled at eighty miles an hour as they drove to take food to the firefighters. Mrs. Griffiths was too badly burned herself to shake hands with the royal couple, but she was "very touched" by their concern. "They seemed to understand and were so upset themselves," she said. Fire captain William Marsden's widow, Gillian, told how he'd been found dead with four other firefighters under their tender after being trapped by the flames. "Princess Diana asked if I minded talking about it," she said. "I said I didn't and told her that I was glad that at least they didn't suffer because it was quick with the intense heat." Before leaving, Charles and Diana planted a young tree as a symbol of new life.

When Diana met more bushfire victims at Stirling Oval in

the Adelaide Hills, she said to one woman, "I do hope you don't mind the intrusion." Two thousand people turned out to see them on that visit, during which the couple talked to the crews of fourteen fire trucks. One of them commented that Prince Charles seemed to be "one of the boys too" and presented him with a souvenir fireman's helmet inscribed with the message: "From the boys of Cudlee Creek." Diana shook the scarred hand of one Cudlee Creek fireman, eighteen-year-old Phil Williams, who had been trapped by a ninety-foot wall of flames and so badly burned that he'd thought his hands would have to be amputated. "My heart goes out to you," she told him. "I admire your bravery." Her sympathy touched many. District fire chief Mike Kemp, from Millicent where fourteen people died, said, "She is a wonderfully warm person. There was more depth in her care and concern for us than any words can describe." Charles and Diana took many sad memories back with them when they spent that Sunday quietly with William at Woomargama.

In Sydney, Diana was mobbed by wild crowds as they drove in an open-topped maroon Rolls-Royce to the famous Sydney Opera House, where Charles thanked Australians for taking his wife to their hearts. She had been "enveloped," he said, "by warmth and affection," a fact underlined by the ten thousand flag-waving fans who had gathered on the forecourt to greet them. A few protesting antiroyalists had to be protected by the police from the crowds, and their "Go home, Royals" placard was ripped to shreds and flung at their feet by an old lady. The ball that evening at the Wentworth Hotel, where the royal couple danced for an hour—Diana wearing a frilled blue-and-silver gown by Bruce Oldfield—was immediately tagged *the* social event of the year.

The tour continued to Newcastle on the Pacific coast, and on to Maitland and Hobart in Tasmania where, during a speech at the official reception, Prince Charles recalled the good-luck wedding messages he had received during his prewedding trip to Australia in 1981 and declared of his wife, "I was indeed lucky enough to marry her." At this, behind him, Diana grimaced, everyone laughed, and Charles, swiveling around, added with a grin, "It's amazing what ladies do when your back is turned." From Hobart, they drove off at a heady pace, visiting Kempton, Oatlands, Ross,

Campbell Town, and Launceston, where they each planted a tree and saw the Australian Maritime College before returning to Woomargama to spend the Easter break, complete with Easter eggs from admirers for Prince William. That gave them a chance to do their own thing, and after church on Easter Sunday they went to Warwick Park, where polo-mad Charles played his first match in six months while Diana watched from the stands, catching up on the news and exchanging gossip with her former flatmate Ann Bolton, who had emigrated to Australia. See FRIENDS.

Adelaide, Renmark, Port Pirie, and Fremantle came next on the itinerary, followed by Perth, where Charles was given two jars of the Aussies' favorite Vegemite and another kiss from a well-wisher—they both got several kisses from fans during the tour. The departure from Perth was delayed by a cyclonic downpour, and during the sunny welcome when they finally arrived at Bunbury, where a rally of thirteen thousand children greeted them at the Hands Memorial Oval, the breeze blew the notes for Charles's speech aside and made him cuss. See X-RATED. Then it was on to Holbrook and Brisbane, where under a blazing sun the Princess was almost mobbed by dense crowds. The following morning they traveled in a nut-mobile at Palmwood's Macadamia Nut Plant and in a yellow-roofed train which matched Diana's dress at the Sunshine Plantation. At Melbourne, where they met Australia's *Crocodile Dundee* star Paul Hogan, nearly two hundred thousand people turned out to cheer the couple, though 150 IRA sympathizers demonstrated outside a concert they attended there.

They traveled by royal train to visit Ballarat, an old gold-mining town, and at Bendigo they watched a dancing Chinese dragon from a hotel balcony. There was more fun at Sovereign Hill where they rode in a Wild West–style Cobb stagecoach—Prince Charles high up in shotgun position with the driver—and were "threatened with arrest" by a police trooper in 1850s costume as "a wanted couple newly arrived in the Colony." For their final engagement, a dinner dance at the Melbourne Hilton Hotel, Diana stunned everyone, including fashion critics, by turning up in the sexiest gown ever worn in public by a British princess—a slinky white off-one-shoulder number, covered in silver and gold bugle beads, by the designer Hachi, which was making its debut

Princess Diana jokes with an Australian lifeguard team during the bicentennial tour of Australia in 1988. (J. S. Library/Camera Press London)

but which has since become one of her favorite choices for glamorous occasions.

When the couple waved good-bye to Australia exactly a month after their arrival at Alice Springs, they did so knowing that the visit had been a remarkable success and that Diana had found her feet as a princess on duty abroad. By the time they left for the second stage of the trip (see NEW ZEALAND), Diana felt she had "actually been able to achieve something," was "so amazed that I was capable of that," and found touring from then on became "easier."

Diana and Charles returned to Australia in 1985 to mark the 150th anniversary of the state of Victoria, in 1988 to join Australia's bicentennial celebrations, and again in 1989.

The Princess is Colonel-in-Chief of the Royal Australian Survey Corps; President of Barnardo's, Australia; Patron of the Australian Junior Red Cross, the Australian Council on Smoking and Health, and the Malcolm Sargent Cancer Fund for Children, Australia; and Joint Patron of the Royal Children's Hospital Foundation Appeal, Victoria, Australia.

AUSTRIA

The royal couple paid a three-day visit to Vienna from April 14 to 16, 1986, chiefly remembered for the outrageous way sexy Austrian actress Dagmar Koller flirted with Charles at a gala dinner hosted by her husband, the Mayor of Vienna. She teased him with her colorful shawl, Marlene Dietrich style, and then raised it to screen them both while she passed on some private joke, which made Charles laugh. Diana, who is not immune to jealousy, looked distinctly frosty. See MARRIAGE.

They were actually there to wave the flag and help promote British trade. A British Airways Concorde—charter rate £28,000 then for a ninety-minute flight—had made a special detour to Milan, costing thousands of pounds, to pick up Charles who'd been on holiday in Italy, before flying him and Diana to Vienna to help launch "British Week." But BA pointed out that there were "no cut rates, even for royals" and that the sixteen in the royal party, plus the British Week exhibitors, businessmen, and models on board, all had to pay for their flight. The royal couple arrived at the City Hall through cheering crowds in an open horse-drawn carriage, Diana in pink and black. They stayed at the British Embassy residence, being driven around with a leather-jacketed Austrian motorcycle escort. It was a packed and varied visit.

Members of the celebrated Vienna Boys' Choir gave a concert for Diana at the Augarten Palais. The night before, the royal couple narrowly missed meeting controversial Presidential candidate Kurt Waldheim, former Secretary-General of the United Nations, who sat in a box opposite them at an Elgar concert in the Vienna Konzerthaus. But he was not invited to the cocktail party during the intermission.

There was one of the familiar walkabouts. And a fashion show, to earsplitting music by George Michael and Queen, at the Hofburg Palace, where Diana told top model Melissa Stockdale, "I would love to have been on the catwalk with you today." Said Melissa, "All the girls had been talking about what a super figure Diana has got and what a marvelous model she would have made." The Princess commented on the "overwhelming" smell of hairspray, asking the models how they managed to put up with it. Charles has tried to ban her from using it, to help protect the

ozone layer. See BEAUTY SECRETS. She put questions to them
about life on the catwalk, and she asked six-foot-tall model Michele Paradise to explain how she slicked back her hair. "She was
having a lot of fun," said Michele.

Not so, however, at the banquet, at least during Dagmar's
other big moment, when she dropped a lipstick from her bag onto
the floor and she and Charles, she said, bumped heads under the
table looking for it. "Then a waiter's big hand came along and
picked it up. My big chance to get really close to Prince Charles
had gone," she said. Diana's reaction to that went unrecorded.
However, if there was a slight frost in the air as the royal couple
went home on the Concorde (which flew supersonic over the
English Channel for the first time by special permission, with
Charles in the cockpit with the crew), a present sent to them as a
memento from Austria might have helped. It was a love potion
from quarry owner Robert Schindele, who declared, "It has transformed my love life."

AUTOGRAPHS

Unlike stage, screen, and pop stars, members of the British Royal
Family do not, as a rule, sign autographs. Arriving in America for
her visit to Washington, D.C., and Palm Beach in November
1985, Diana refused to sign a copy of Penny Junor's acclaimed
biography of the Princess for fifteen-year-old schoolgirl Ann
Waymire. According to Ann, Diana shook her head and replied,
"No, it's a bore." "I don't know if she meant giving her autograph
was a bore, or if she had found the book about her boring," Ann
said. "I really loved reading it." She cheered up when Di agreed to
show her her engagement ring instead. A rich Texan who asked the
Princess for her autograph at a charity do later in Palm Beach had
the temerity to complain when she refused, and apparently he got
a "tough luck"–style response. At the White House banquet in
Washington, D.C., however, one admirer succeeded where others
failed—Mikhail Baryshnikov. Diana has been a huge fan of the
Russian ballet star for years. When he made his request, instead
of the usual royal refusal, Diana gave him her autograph and

revealed, "I've got yours, you know. It was at Covent Garden years ago. I was one of the girls who were waiting for you for hours and hours after the performance." When the Princess visited New York in 1989, the newspapers warned readers in advance not to ask for autographs. See AMERICA. On a private visit to the Sussex AIDS Centre in Brighton in July 1990, Diana was taken aback when she was confronted by an AIDS patient demanding her autograph. Possibly out of compassion, she complied, but declared, "This is a one-off."

However, church warden Reg Little, aged sixty-three, tossed a successful letter over the wall at Highgrove in July that year asking for the plaster cast from Prince Charles's broken arm, once he'd finished with it. Reg intended to auction it to help raise £46,000 for repairs to the storm-damaged roof of St. Thomas of Canterbury church at Kingswear, Devon. He was quoted as saying, "If it has Diana's signature on it, it will be worth a lot." It didn't. On their trip to Hong Kong in November 1989, Prince Charles broke the royal rule by autographing two first-day covers commemorating the royal visit for a Chinese taxi driver at whose home he was given a cup of tea. But these examples *are* exceptions, so if you don't wish to embarrass the royal couple, don't ask.

BARNARDO'S

Diana's great empathy with children, her commitment to family life, her background as a child from a broken marriage, and her friendship with one of her most brilliant fashion designers, the charming Bruce Oldfield—who was a Dr. Barnardo's boy himself and is now a committed fund-raiser—all make her a natural as President of Britain's largest child care charity. Since the days of Dr. Barnardo more than a century ago, the charity—which used to look after orphans but has since vastly changed and expanded its services—has always had the ruling monarch as Patron. In addition to the Queen, the two other current royal Patrons are the Queen Mother and Princess Margaret, who had been President herself for almost forty years until she suggested that a younger member of the Royal Family might take on the role. Barnardo's invited the Princess of Wales because she was young, highly popular, loved children, and seemed an ideal choice. To their delight, she agreed. She is also Royal President of Barnardo's, Australia, which she has visited on tour, and International President of Barnardo's, New Zealand, which she is likely to visit on her next trip there.

Though the royal Patrons in Britain take an interest in Barnardo's, it is the President who is the "working royal." Diana has given heart and soul to the charity and has been amazingly active on its behalf, attending engagements virtually once a month. Since she became President in November 1984, she has made at least fifty-eight visits to Barnardo's projects, fifteen of them within the space of twelve months in 1987. In November 1985, she attended no less than three Barnardo events in a week; in November 1987, three in four days. In October 1988, when Barnardo's was relaunched and dropped the *Dr.* from its title as part of its new up-to-date image, she helped gain essential publicity for them in the

More than a figurehead, Diana becomes personally involved in all her royal duties. This visit to a North Sea oil rig in 1985 was arranged at her own request. (Ron Bell/Globe Photos)

newspapers and on radio and television by using the occasion to make her first major speech. And in 1989, launching the charity's "If you let me" campaign to help mentally handicapped youngsters get the chance to find homes and jobs in the community, she invited three handicapped young people and the media to her drawing room at Kensington Palace where she signed the campaign charter. Barnardo's Senior Director, Roger Singleton, comes from Yorkshire, where folks aren't easily impressed. But he is.

"We had no idea when we asked her to become President that she would be willing to commit herself to the extent which she has done," he said.

And therefore that's a source of enormous delight to us. She has a manifest love of children and people in general—and such a natural matter-of-factness about her in conversation, so informal. On one visit in February 1990, the wind was so bad

that her helicopter was canceled and she had to get from
Canterbury to Tunbridge Wells, which I gather meant a journey on winding roads with the official cars traveling pretty
fast. And she arrived making some comment about being
mighty glad to be out of them because of being hurled around
in the back. It was the sort of comment any of us would have
made, and it put everyone at their ease. That's one of the
things which strikes people who, until the second that they
meet her, have been a bit obsessed with "What do we call
her?" and all that sort of thing. She's so *human*.

In theory, the Princess could simply arrive, look around,
shake a few hands, smile at the cameras, and go away again,
shaking people and their problems off like a pet coming in from
the rain. She could be cold and aloof, dying to get back to her
children, and still technically be a figurehead "doing her job." But
that is not Diana's style at all. See PRESIDENCIES & PATRONAGES.
Roger Singleton says:

She does very much more than just turn up. It's difficult to
put into words the sheer excitement and deep sense of satisfac-
tion that she brings on her visits to our projects. After the
Princess has gone and the police and the barricades and the
mayoral chains and Lord Lieutenants have all cleared off, if
you then go round and talk with people whom she's met and
talked to, there are two or three things that are sure to come
out. One is how *easy* she is to talk to, to "relate to" in jargon.
Secondly, the speed with which she seems to be able to talk to
people about things which are *really* important to them. I mean
you don't need half an hour's warm-up—she really gets down
to the nitty gritty. Despite television cameras and all the inevitable fuss and commotion and hangers-on that go with a royal
visit, the Princess can have a private personal conversation
with a couple, for example, about what it's meant to them to
have a child with serious Down's syndrome. Now that can be
the third, fourth sentence, having only just met them for the
first time. And those people really feel that what they've said
has been listened to and has been understood. If you watch
parents who have children with serious mental or physical
disabilities, you will see that they always look at how another
adult reacts to their child. And the message they get from

watching the Princess with their children is that she accepts them as people. And they go away from that feeling, "Well, if my kid's good enough for the Princess of Wales, then he, or she, is good enough for anybody." You can't *buy* that—it's a unique sort of quality.

I come from Yorkshire, where we're used to saying things pretty plainly. And I always feel after conversations like this about the Princess that people will go away feeling that I'm just being sycophantic, or that I wouldn't say anything adverse about her anyway in case it cocks up the relationship. But the fact is I truly believe that she has some unique personal qualities. And to be able to put those to good effect in the glare of publicity and still leave people feeling pleased and proud and valued, is, I think, quite a rare ability. We particularly value what the Princess is prepared to say or write for us. Because sometimes our message is about the importance of trying to provide opportunities for young people with mental handicaps, and that coming from the Princess of Wales is far more likely to have impact than a hundred professional speakers at a conference standing up and mouthing it. She's sincere, she has personal integrity, and I think there is something about her which would make it very difficult for her to say something which didn't square with her feelings on any issue.

Barnardo's was founded by Dr. Thomas Barnardo, a Victorian visionary who began his pioneering child care work in 1866 by helping waifs and strays in London's poverty-stricken East End. His work expanded to encompass needy children throughout the country, who were offered a safe refuge in his children's homes, regardless of their race, creed, or sex or whether or not they had disabilities. Of his own seven children, one, a daughter, was mentally handicapped. In addition to his other work, Dr. Barnardo found foster families for illegitimate babies. He even ran a revolutionary scheme, which had to be kept hush-hush in those straitlaced days, whereby a young single mother could have access to her child, provided she paid part of the foster family's fee from her wages and led "an industrious and responsible life after her one lapse." Dr. Barnardo kept records of each child he encountered and its family. He wrote of one little girl that she was "reared in filth and immorality, sent out to beg, cruelly beaten and kicked about with an abandoned mother's example going before her. If not rescued soon she will be a moral pest." For over a century the name Dr. Barnardo's meant orphans and children's homes. Up to the 1960s, the charity ran about 120 large children's homes throughout Britain, including West Mount, the Georgian house just outside Ripon where Bruce Oldfield lived; boarded out hundreds of other children, usually younger ones, with foster families; and assisted families who were able to care for their own children but needed help of some kind to keep going. By the end of the sixties, however, poverty levels in Britain had declined, and the need for the type of work Barnardo's had been doing had diminished. So the charity looked to the new needs of the seventies. "Had we not acted when we did, at the end of the sixties," Roger Singleton said, "we would have been stuck with all these homes with the number of children in them decreasing and no children coming in. The writing was on the wall, so we changed tack." Instead, Barnardo's recognized that there were hundreds of "forgotten" children, many with either mental or multiple mental and physical handicaps, "parked away in vast mental hospitals, and the nurses looking after them—without criticizing the nurses—had an impossible job." The charity made helping handicapped children the major part of its work—setting out to bring them out of the hospitals and give them a proper family, placing them with foster families or in small homes among the community, in many cases reconnecting children who had been abandoned by their parents at birth with their own families. In addition, the charity also developed projects throughout the country. It now has about two dozen, providing a wide range of services to help the "many thousands of quite seriously handicapped children living at home with their parents, but at enormous cost in an emotional, physical, and material sense to the parents and to their brothers and sisters."

Apart from the problem of mental, physical, or emotional handicaps, Barnardo's also helps families in cases of child abuse and where youngsters are in trouble with the law or nearly so. It still deals with foster care and adoptive care, but today's problems include looking to see whether it can do something to help the increasing number of children who will be born HIV positive. It helps young people who've spent much or most of their lives in hospitals or residential homes learn to stand on their own feet, offering not just practical and emotional support but job skills through youth training programs. And it helps families under stress to stay together, providing family centers with playrooms for the children plus counseling for the parents and social events to give them a break. Altogether, at 167 different projects across Britain, the charity works each year with more than eighteen thousand young people, and their families, who have special needs—caring, as it says, "for the person—not just the handicap or problem." The cost works out at about £1 million a week, more than half of which is donated by the public. But a public which still wasn't aware of the fact that the charity was no longer "that old-fashioned organization which looks after orphans." As a result, the sad stigma which still lingered about orphans was sometimes carried over to nonorphan children and families then being helped. So in 1988, Barnardo's dropped the *Dr.* from its name, hoping this would prompt a curious public to ask "Why?" and then listen to the explanation. The charity relaunched itself with a brand-new, modern image to reflect its current work. Diana tried to help get the message across in a foreword to the charity's annual review in 1988, when she wrote from Kensington Palace:

> It is now four years since I became President of Barnardo's and during that time I have undertaken a number of visits throughout the United Kingdom. I am always extremely impressed by the very wide variety of work I see, but I am also aware that many people lacking this first-hand knowledge are totally unaware of the range of work covered by the charity.
>
> Barnardo's believes that every one is capable of reaching their full potential. Today, in partnership with families, Barnardo's tries to find ways to make this come true—whether for children with mental handicaps, youngsters with physical disabilities or young people who have had a difficult start in life.
>
> I realize that it is a time of tremendous activity within Barnardo's and that 1988 marks the beginning of new efforts to make the public more aware of its work. The new look opens up fresh opportunities for everyone to tell people exactly what it is Barnardo's does today.

Diana tried again at the annual general meeting held at the Queen Elizabeth II Conference Centre on October 18, 1988, when, to mark the relaunch, she mastered her nerves and delivered a speech. Considering that it was her first major speech and that the message she was trying to get across had taxed (and some might think defeated) professionals at the communications game, she made a pretty good stab at it. During the speech, which received wide media coverage, she said:

Before accepting the Presidency, I, perhaps like the majority of people, associated Barnardo's with orphans. This, as I have learnt during over fifty visits to projects throughout the United Kingdom, is inaccurate.

During these visits, I have had an opportunity to see the organization at work and to see the needs and problems faced by many people who use Barnardo's services. One aspect which has remained as a constant theme throughout is the enormous importance which Barnardo's attaches to *family* life. I have seen this both in the efforts made to help families remain together and in the work undertaken to provide foster homes or personal residential care for those young people unable to live with their own families.

Recently I visited three projects which in quite separate ways were examples of family life bringing new hope, help, and security to children and young people in very varied circumstances.

In Liverpool, for instance, it was the family of a profoundly handicapped teenager. In this case the demands made on her family were so great that, when young, her parents had no option but to place her in a long-stay hospital. After many years in the hospital she went to live [in a Barnardo's bungalow] at Croxteth Park, where the experience of having personal, committed care, linked with a carefully worked out learning programme, has enabled her to make enormous progress. Now this young woman spends each weekend with her parents and the weekdays with Barnardo's. A fine example of a family "reunited."

I fully realize that for many young people, family life is not always a happy experience. They may have been thrown out of their homes, or circumstances may have forced them to leave. Some are homeless. Others are at risk of drug addiction or prostitution. It is even more of a challenge if such young adults are themselves parents.

In Leeds, I met one young woman with her five-month-old baby, who after several years in care is now being helped by Barnardo's to establish a home with her boyfriend and to provide some real security for her child.

In North London, I visited Beryl and Banji, which is a name I greatly enjoy. Having come to this country from Jamaica in 1962 and successfully brought up their own children, they have now offered a loving home to three teenagers who desperately need a family.

I heard from both sides how the boys had put their foster parents' devotion to the test. But slowly they have grown in self-confidence and trust—a fine reflection on the firmness and commitment of their care.

In this area, Barnardo's have recognized the importance not only of finding long-term foster parents for children whose own families have disintegrated, but also the significance of placing children with families of the same race.

I know that family life is extremely important and, as a mother of two small boys, I think we may have to find a securer way of helping our children—to nurture and prepare them to face life as stable and confident adults. The pressures and demands on all of us are enormous.

I do realize that the view of what constitutes a family is broader today than it was a century ago. Today few children lose parents through early death, but many do experience that loss through divorce, and increasingly more complicated families result from separation and remarriage. A statistic which brings this home is that one in eight children live in single parent families. These children's experience of family life may be different, but I do not believe it need necessarily be any less satisfying or effective.

When the good Doctor started his work at the end of the last century, he was concerned with orphans. Today, over a century later, the organization which carries his name, while still deeply involved in the care of children, is now working with children *and* their families.

I have been asked today to reveal to you all Barnardo's new identity. I believe, and I hope you will agree with me, that it captures many of the elements which are important in family life—commitment, togetherness, and building the way ahead to the future.

With everyone's help, support, and enthusiasm, I know Barnardo's can look *forward* with confidence, and it therefore gives me enormous pleasure to say goodbye to the old and to reveal the new Barnardo's.

Not perhaps as succinct as saying, "Yesterday Barnardo's helped orphans. Today it helps the handicapped and their families—and many more besides." But it was a good start.

The Princess followed this up by spearheading Barnardo's first national campaign, called "If you let me," to help mentally handicapped young people get proper homes and jobs and to encourage everyone else to be "more accepting and less hostile" toward them. She invited three young people to join her in front of the TV cameras at Kensington Palace when she signed the campaign charter. One of them was a girl named Donna, who had been featured in Barnardo's special campaign video as a shining example of what those with a mental handicap can achieve. She had first been presented to the Princess when Diana visited Dr. B's Kitchen in Harrogate, a restaurant and coffee bar open to the public, run by Barnardo's, which trains young people for jobs in the catering industry. Donna, aged twenty-two, trained there, landed a permanent full-time job with Trust House Forte, and became Employee of the Month. At the hotel in Harrogate where Donna works cleaning thousands of pieces of silver, copper, and stainless steel, head chef Peter Rathbone pointed out that she had started off doing 30 percent of the job and before very long was up to 65 to 70 percent, adding that he wished "the rest of the brigade would commit themselves 30 percent plus" in the same time.

Also at Kensington Palace with the Princess were two other mentally handicapped young people, nineteen-year-old Mandy, profoundly handicapped and in a wheelchair, and seventeen-year-old Gerald, a real character who'd been in care since he was born. He wanted somewhere to go and something to do to maximize his potential and determine his own future rather than spend the rest of his life in an adult training center. He swiftly became the star of

the show, handing Diana his pen to sign the charter while they sat
with her on the famous sofa in front of the tapestry (and the TV
cameras) in the Prince and Princess's drawing room. But when he
had difficulty getting it back into his pocket and Diana offered to
help, he moved away from her to assert that he could do it
himself—neatly demonstrating the "If you let me" theme!

After they were all offered orange juice, coffee, and biscuits,
Gerald started to wander around, so Diana took him to see her
study, off the drawing room. And at the point when Roger Singleton began wondering how to suggest politely that perhaps they
should leave, Gerald beat him to the punch by putting his hand on
Diana's arm and declaring, "I've got to go now." Roger Singleton
recalled:

> The reason why he had to go was because we'd come up from
> the local hotel in a minibus and he'd been promised that he
> could sit in the front seat on the way back, and he wanted to
> make sure he got it! The Princess played along with it beauti-
> fully: "Right! Fine," she said. So we all trooped downstairs
> and she came down with us and out into the courtyard at the
> back of Kensington Palace, and we eventually loaded up—it
> got all a bit of a riot there—and away we went. But we'd had a
> grin and a joke about it. I said to her, "Here's me trying to find
> a way of politely saying, 'Is it time we went?' and he goes and
> says that!" And she laughed. She knows about all that—she's
> been a nonroyal.

Diana referred to the visit in her foreword to Barnardo's
annual review 1989, in which she wrote that she had "much
enjoyed" meeting Mandy, Donna, and Gerald and added, "They
were representative of those young adults we are aiming to help by
speaking out. It is important that we all do as much as we can to
help change attitudes toward the thousands of similar young
people and help them live their lives to the full." And in September 1989, she made a speech on the subject at a Barnardo's
conference in Liverpool for parents of handicapped children
which showed she well understood their anxieties. She told the
audience:

> Today's conference is an important part of Barnardo's "If you
> let me" campaign, and I was so pleased earlier this year to sign

the charter which marked the launch of this, Barnardo's first national campaign. Its importance cannot be too strongly stressed.

To you, here today, its relevance is all too clear. But we need to bring home to *everyone* the message that young people with mental handicap *should* have somewhere to live, *should* have something to do, and *should* have the opportunity to enjoy life to the full.

These are the hopes that all of us, as parents, have for our children. As parents, we all share certain fears—for our children's safety, their health, that they will not fit in or be accepted by other children.

But I know that you as parents of children and young people with mental handicap have an additional and very special fear. The tremendous worry as to what will happen to your child when you are no longer here to cope. Who will bother about their likes and dislikes, remember special occasions like birthdays?

The fear is that your child's future may be in a bleak institution, and I realize you know that, given a chance, your son or daughter could have a more secure future.

People with mental handicap are not life-long children. As they grow up they have a right to greater independence, to more choices and to richer experiences. The challenge is to emphasize the message of hope and to obtain the commitment of other people.

Of course, more could be done if more money was available, but there is never enough and it is a sad reflection on our society that people with mental handicap would appear to be the losers when resources are short.

But it costs nothing to think more positively about young people with mental handicap, and so many of the difficulties could be eased by a change in public attitudes.

Perhaps more could be achieved if more ways could be identified to "give them a chance."

To give people with mental handicap a chance to live in a house in an ordinary street; with training, preparation, and encouragement, to give them a chance to hold down a proper job; and to give young people with mental handicap a chance to enjoy life to the full.

To everyone—friends, relations, employers, and authorities: give young people with mental handicap a chance to achieve their full potential. We all need to create a more caring environment for those young people whose needs have been neglected for too long.

In 1987—her busiest year, with fifteen Barnardo's engagements—people at a Barnardo's project at West Wickham were lucky enough to be visited in November by Diana and her two sisters, Sarah and Jane, since all three were on their way to a nostalgic trip down memory lane at their old school, West Heath, where the Princess opened a new sports hall. See EDUCATION. The day before, Diana had had one of her most moving meetings—with tragic fifteen-year-old Claire Bosworth from Heage in Derbyshire, who had been nominated by her school friends for one of the charity's Champion Children Awards. The awards are given to youngsters outside Barnardo's who have excelled in artistic or other skills, bravery in helping others, or triumph over adversity themselves. Claire had struggled through schoolwork and gained seven CSEs (Certificate of Secondary Education—awarded for passing standard examinations), despite having leukemia, losing her sight in one eye, and losing her hair four times during chemotherapy and radiation treatment. In November 1987, she willed herself out of bed, apparently against medical advice, to travel the 130 miles to London, determined to meet the Princess and be presented with her award at the Champion Children lunch at the Dorchester Hotel. Hardly able to walk, she staggered a few steps up onto the platform from her wheelchair to receive her award. Roger Singleton recalled, "The Princess was very moved, and as for a lump in the throat, that was very much the atmosphere in the whole room." When, in a touching gesture, Diana handed her bouquet of yellow roses and orchids to Claire, the teenager burst into tears. A few days later, Claire died in her sleep. She had drained her last reserves to make the trip, her sister, Mrs. Karen Rice, said, adding, "But whatever it took out of her, it was worth it for all the happiness she got from meeting the Princess." Diana was told the sad news after visiting a Barnardo's project for young offenders at Newport in Gwent. She was said to be "deeply upset," and later she wrote to Claire's parents. Mrs. Rosaline Bosworth, Claire's mother, found the letter deeply moving and said, "The fact that the Princess wrote it herself has made it so much more appreciated by us. It is a very private letter and there are a lot of comments which are very personal." Roger Singleton said, "The letter became public knowledge when it somehow leaked into the papers. But the whole poignant story underlines that there is some depth and meaning to the events that the Princess engages in—and what a rare woman she is."

BATHS & BATHROOMS

Prince Charles once said on American television that the Queen's bathrooms at Sandringham were "the best bathrooms in the business" and that the nineteenth century, when Sandringham was built, "produced the best bathrooms that have ever been." His bachelor bathroom at Buckingham Palace was decorated with his favorite newspaper cartoons of himself, which now adorn the walls of downstairs bathrooms at Kensington Palace and Highgrove. See COLLECTIONS.

As a schoolgirl at Riddlesworth Hall, Diana used to enjoy sliding down the back of the bathtub, which she described as being "really naughty." See EDUCATION. The bathroom at her bachelor girl flat at Coleherne Court years later had a bright red cherry wallpaper. When she broke the news of her secret engagement to her three flatmates, one of them, Carolyn Pride, had to listen through the door because she was closeted inside the bathroom at the time. See RESIDENCES and COURTSHIP.

Highgrove, the couple's country house in Gloucestershire, has six bathrooms. Charles's bathtub has mahogany sides. At Kensington Palace, Charles and Diana have separate His and Hers mirrored bathrooms off the master bedroom. Both are marble, and Diana's contains a bidet. The couple decided they should have a second bathroom late in the day when their Kensington Palace apartments were being prepared for them, causing last-minute adjustments for their interior designer, Dudley Poplak.

Charles, who knows all about aromatherapy and wants to

produce scent and aromatherapy oils from flowers grown at High-grove, likes to lace his bathwater with rosemary, which is said to calm the nerves, and lavender, to aid relaxation. Diana likes to use Strawberry Body Shampoo & Shower Gel and Milk Bath, products she buys from the Kensington High Street branch of The Body Shop. See BEAUTY SECRETS. She has always been obsessive about cleanliness, even as a schoolgirl. At Riddlesworth Hall, the rules allowed a bath on alternate nights, and at West Heath three times a week on rotation, which wasn't nearly often enough from her point of view. So at West Heath, Diana took "illegal" baths nightly, after lights out, and washed her hair more often than the regulation once-a-week too. She washed her clothes extraoften as well.

In May 1989, there was an unconfirmed report that the Princess had been spotted by local residents visiting a clinic on Boscombe Road in London's Shepherd's Bush district where Guyanese health guru Lady Veronica Price allegedly gave "electric" baths and hot mud baths to Prime Minister Margaret Thatcher. However, Lady Veronica's millionaire ex-husband Sir Frank Price, a former Lord Mayor of Birmingham, confirmed that his former wife had treated four members of the Royal Family, including Princess Margaret and Princess Michael of Kent, tantalizingly not naming the other two.

Diana once told Capital Radio disc jockey Roger Scott that she always listened to his program, on between four and seven in the evening, while bathing Prince William as a baby. See RADIO. She also revealed that Charles bathed William "all the time," reveling in his new role as a father. He even got into the tub with him. On one occasion, it is said, when Diana was anxious about leaving for an engagement and couldn't find Charles, she eventually tracked him down to the bathroom, where he was splashing around in the bathwater with little Wills. In Australia in 1983, she told children over the Alice Springs School of the Air that William's favorite toy, probably a bathtime one, was a plastic whale which spurted little balls out of its spout. (Charles rode on the back of a real whale at Windsor Great Park in 1976.) At Alice Springs on that same Australian tour, Charles and Diana stayed at a motel where their suite boasted a special barrellike "love tub" for two, which bubbled like a Jacuzzi and was much enjoyed by honeymooners taking a dip together. And on their brief stopover at the Kahala Hilton in Hawaii in 1985, the royal couple are thought to have shared a king-size Jacuzzi complete with foaming scented liquid soap.

The Princess stands no nonsense at bathtime. Even as a child, when she helped with her young brother Charlie, she would tolerate no protests when it was time for him to put his toys away and be bathed. However, she is well aware that boys aren't often very anxious to wash or be washed. In March 1990, visiting refugees at an emergency center who had been flooded out of their homes at Towyn in Wales, she met fourteen-year-old Darren Stansfield and joked, "I bet you are glad there's no school and you don't have to have baths!"

One old flame of Diana's brother, dishing the dirt after their romance ended, claimed that he didn't clean the bath after using it. Another of his ex-girlfriends, Katie Braine, is the inventor of a bathroom device which whistles an alert when the bathwater is being run if there's a danger of the bathtub overflowing.

In 1981, Prudence Glynn, former Fashion Editor of *The Times*, attacked Diana for wearing her famous black strapless dress (see X-RATED), saying it made her look as if she was sitting in "a hip bath."

BEAUTY SECRETS

Diana is a fan of the natural, beauty-without-cruelty skin and hair products from The Body Shop. She uses their Milk Bath and their Strawberry Body Shampoo & Shower Gel, a mild skin cleanser which can also be used as a liquid soap. She likes The Body Shop's Elderflower Water, a skin tonic and freshener, their Elderflower Under Eye Gel to soothe tired eyes and reduce puffiness, and their Rich Night Cream with Vitamin E, which she buys from the branch on Kensington High Street or, if she's at Highgrove, from the branch in Bath. She gets their Chamomile Shampoo and Banana Conditioner and buys some of their men's products, including shampoo, for Charles. To soothe her weary feet after all that royal footslogging, the Princess uses Peppermint Foot Lotion,

A natural beauty, Diana always radiates style and grace. (Terence Donovan/ Camera Press London)

which The Body Shop came up with after footsore competitors in the London Marathon begged for something to help them. She likes to polish her toenails, but, unlike one of his predecessors, there is no suggestion that Prince Charles helps her with this task. (Edward VIII, who allegedly had a foot fetish, was once spotted at Fort Belvedere polishing Wallis Simpson's toenails by a footman who promptly decided to quit.) The Princess now polishes her fingernails, which she finally stopped biting after acupuncture, it is said, helped break her of the habit.

Two American magazines have praised Diana's wonderfully long, shapely legs. In 1988, *W* gave them eight points out of ten, commenting on her "slender calves and slim ankles," and the following year, *People* rated her legs "sexy." But the Princess herself is critical of them and has complained in the past about them being too thin or knobbly. Trying on an outfit once at the Kensington branch of Benetton, she astonished a sales assistant by checking how she looked in a long mirror and remarking that her legs weren't good enough to wear it. See FASHION. She prefers to keep her legs bare and cool in the summer or on visits to hot countries abroad, and she was the first lady in the Royal Family to appear bare-legged at Royal Ascot and at Buckingham Palace garden parties. She has her legs and underarms waxed and wears leg makeup when she is without nylons or a tan.

At 5 feet, 10½ inches, she's about an inch taller than Prince Charles, and at first she seemed embarrassed about her height. She'd wear flat shoes, and early photographs with her fiancé were posed to make her appear shorter. For the engagement pictures taken on the garden steps at Buckingham Palace, Diana stood on a lower step. Posing for photographs for the commemorative stamp, Charles apparently stood on a box. (Humphrey Bogart wore five-inch platform soles for his love scenes in *Casablanca* with the statuesque Ingrid Bergman.) In those days, Diana walked with a sort of stoop, her shoulders rounded, her head held down, peering at the ground. However, as she gained confidence and poise, her attitude and posture changed. Now she walks tall, proud of her modellike stature, and has even apparently said she would like to be taller.

In her teenage days helping at Young England kindergarten, she was rather plump; weighed more than 140 pounds; and had a jolly, round, countrified face (which she doesn't miss) and an ample bosom (which she does—see X-RATED). In the five months before the royal wedding in July 1981 when Diana started shedding her babyfat, she lost nearly fourteen pounds. By the time it was announced that she was pregnant, she had lost almost another fourteen pounds. And after the birth of Prince William in 1982, she became practically emaciated, drawing gasps of concern from crowds. See HEALTH. However, she did eventually recover her weight. Last summer she was said to weigh 133 pounds. Endless words have been written about "Diana's diets," but she has repeatedly said that she has none. "I cannot diet," she declared in 1988. "I am not strong-willed enough." She keeps slim because she prefers light, healthy, nonfattening meals and exercises regularly. See FOOD & DRINK and SPORT. She gets fed up when people go on about what she is, or isn't, eating and told Japanese journalists during her tour of Japan with Charles in May 1986, "I don't know why there are all these stories saying I am too thin. I am eating a lot." She is said to go off her food when she is upset. In December 1988, readers of *Slimming* magazine voted the slender Princess "The Most Stunning Figure in the Public Eye" for the fourth year running. She also got the most votes to win the titles "Best Royal Body," "Most Attractive Royal Face," and "Best-Dressed Royal," and she has won further titles since. For vital statistics, see X-RATED.

To keep her perfect English rose complexion, she has facials at the Wyndham Place, Marylebone, salon of Yorkshire-born beauty therapist Janet Filderman. The Princess uses her products, including Milk of Roses cleanser and Bright and Clean skin freshener, which are also available, with beauty advice, by mail order. She also likes the Clarins products Sensitive Skin Day and Night creams, Alpine Herb Cleanser and Yellow Toner, and she had a Clarins Paris facial while staying at Champneys Health Farm (see HEALTH) in January 1990. She has followed the Erno Laszlo skin care routine from America which involves, among other things, splashing her face with warm water sixty times a day. She has used aromatherapy oils by Daniele Ryman to help her relax, overcome jet lag, and scent her homes; and she has had massages at Aromatherapy Associates in Fulham. See BATHS & BATHROOMS.

Though Diana is regarded as one of the most beautiful women in the world, her individual facial features are not perfect. But she has learned to make the most of herself, and in recent years she has recognized and used the power of her beauty. See MARRIAGE. If there is a flaw, it is her nose. The Princess is alleged to have told friends during a hen party at Kensington Palace, "I'd love to have my nose fixed. It's too big." One plastic surgeon,

Stephen Pincus from Los Angeles, used a video computer to show how her nose could look redesigned if he got busy with his scalpel, removing a bump here and producing a tilt there, and sent photos to the Palace. But despite rumors over the years that Diana has had a nose job—some claim after Prince William was born—she has denied it, saying she likes her nose the way it is. The only alteration that's known is that she had her ears pierced as a schoolgirl.

Diana wore virtually no makeup until she had a flat of her own in London. Which meant that when she suddenly came into the public eye as a teenager and started to wear more, she had very little experience or technique. So it wasn't surprising that she made beginner's errors. Powder blue eyeshadow, presumably meant to enhance her lovely blue eyes, was old hat, unflattering, and lacked subtlety. Pink blusher bang in the middle of her cheeks made her rather chubby face look even more round and accentuated her nervous blushes. But she was given some early professional tips by Felicity Clark, then Beauty Editor at *Vogue*, where her sisters used to work (see FASHION), and she learned some important lessons from Barbara Daly.

Barbara Daly is the world's top makeup artist—the genius *every* woman would like to be made up by. Even Joan Collins, that perennial glamourpuss, goes to Barbara for the Daly magic for special occasions. But Barbara's greatest claim to fame, of course, is that she made up Diana's face for the royal wedding. It wasn't the first time, so she already knew which of her features to accentuate or play down, which areas to shade or highlight, which tones and colors would produce the most perfect result. Despite that, Barbara was so anxious to ensure that she arrived in good time that she turned up at Clarence House with her makeup brushes and kit at 4:00 A.M. on the royal wedding day! Then she had to sit there for hours until Diana was ready for her. Barbara recalls waiting "poised like a mummy," trying not to crease her John Bates wedding outfit—a red floral silk dress, worn with a tiny hat which Barbara had borrowed from her cousin and pinned on the back of her head. With Diana's looks there had never been any doubt that she would make a breathtaking bride, but the romantic dewy-soft look which Barbara gave her certainly enhanced her natural beauty.

From Barbara, Diana learned to ditch the pink-blob-on-the-cheek look and instead to highlight her cheekbones—which revealed themselves gratifyingly once she'd lost her babyfat—with subtle rust and peach blushers which suit her coloring better. She learned to use a concealer to hide any cheek blemishes or dark areas under her eyes, to shade her eyelids in more flattering gold and browns, and to blend her makeup softly with cosmetic brushes to avoid hard edges of color. Though Barbara has made up Diana many times since the wedding, and still does for special occasions, the Princess now generally does her own, taking about twenty minutes in the process. "She is a stunningly beautiful girl and she's got great natural style," Barbara said. "I didn't specifically tell her anything, other than the tips you'd normally give someone while you're making them up. But she's learned to be very expert at applying her makeup, and I think the way she does it is extremely professional and very good. She doesn't seem to wear a lot, and she's got such a wonderful complexion. She's an utterly gorgeous lady. Anyone who looks that good all the time deserves enormous credit." Barbara has so many royal and celebrity private clients that your chance and mine of getting the Barbara Daly look from her in person is extremely remote. However, you *can* do it yourself by following a highly instructive fifty-five-minute video she has made showing women step-by-step how to apply makeup the expert way. It is called *Face to Face with Barbara Daly*, available from The Body Shop.

Diana uses makeup from Barbara's Colourings range, also sold exclusively at The Body Shop, and particularly likes the Colourings concealer and lash comb. She's also said to use Colourings' blue eyeliner and red lipstick with tawny pink lip gloss. She has used cosmetics by Clinique, including Wild Roses blusher and Electric Light Eye Shadow Pencil, and Christian Dior, including their blue mascara.

Does she still make mistakes with her makeup? In my view, yes. For evening she often draws a bright blue line on the inner rim below her eyes, which is not a good idea since, although it does emphasize how blue her eyes are, it makes them seem closed-off and smaller. It is also a dicey beauty tip for others to follow because on fair skins, heavy dark lines drawn on the lower rim or below the eyes can look hard and aging. A barely perceptible trace of liner blended softly at the outer edges beneath the lower lashes would look more subtle and perhaps more effective. Diana's eyelashes are dyed regularly to look darker, but she sometimes overdoes the mascara, leaving cloggy spikes. Two thin, almost dry layers of mascara, after using an eyelash curler, followed by a careful brushing or comb-out with her lash comb, would give a lighter, more feathery and feminine effect. Nothing opens eyes up more than beautifully done lashes. But even minor criticism seems churlish when Diana almost always manages to look gorgeous. She carries a makeup kit around with her, as became clear when an eighteen-month-old girl fished it out of Diana's handbag and took the top off her lip gloss, during a royal visit to a home for sick children in Jaywick, Essex, in September 1989. Typical of the caring Princess, instead of being miffed she showed the toddler how to apply the gloss.

Because Diana's hair is very fine, as a young schoolgirl she wore it in pigtails, then braids when it was longer, to keep it tidy. From the age of sixteen she had her hair styled by Cockney Kevin Shanley, owner of the Head Lines hair and beauty salon in South Kensington. Her sisters, Sarah and Jane, were among his regular clients, and he has also done the hair of their mother, Mrs. Frances Shand Kydd. Shanley did Diana's hair for her first date with Prince Charles, for the royal wedding, and for years afterward, sharing the job during Diana's long first tour of Australasia with his Scottish colleague Richard Dalton, the son of a baker. See AUSTRALIA. (Prince Charles had had his hair cut at Truefitt and Hill for fifteen years until his wife got Kevin to take the scissors to him too. See ARTS & HANDICRAFTS.) Diana's early "Lady Di" hairstyle, which sent girls around the globe rushing to their hairdressers for a similar cut, was created for her by Shanley. It was the first of many fashion trends Diana sparked off, and it made her from the start the most-copied modern-day member of the Royal Family. But her hair tends to flop, so she has her roots permed every couple of months to give it lift and body. Because the natural color is mousy, every two months or so she also has her hair lightened with highlights. The "Di-lights" became a fashion trend too, and in 1983 top London colorist Daniel Galvin reported that highlighting at his salon, where clients included

Twiggy, Joanna Lumley, and Susan Hampshire, had "gone up 100 percent since Princess Diana came on the scene." "Nearly half my customers have highlights in their hair now," he said. Diana's hair got paler and paler, becoming so blond around the time when Prince Harry was born in 1984 that the Press nicknamed her Dynasty Di. The bouffant effect she had then, it is said, was achieved partly by blow-drying her hair upside down.

Several of Diana's hairstyles have drawn criticism. Insisting on having her hair put up for the first time in public for the State Opening of Parliament in November 1984—against the advice of Kevin Shanley, who thought it wouldn't suit her and would spoil her soft, fresh, natural image—was a real mistake. The Press cameramen concentrated on the new hairstyle instead of on the Queen. Which, since that could have been foreseen, made it look as if the Princess was trying to upstage her mother-in-law, even if she wasn't. And as Shanley had predicted, people didn't like the chignon anyway, the Press calling it "Di-abolical" and a "Di-saster." Nevertheless, the Princess had had her way; and after that Richard Dalton, who had put her hair up, became her regular hairdresser. When Shanley revealed some of his royal memories in the *Sunday Mirror* in 1985, Dalton, aged thirty-nine, left Head Lines and went freelance, basing his work schedule around the Princess. The 1940s shoulder-length style he gave Diana wasn't popular. And neither was the short 1950s Teddygirl DA cut he gave her before her tour of the blistering-hot Arab Gulf States in 1986. (Earlier the same year, Diana had been quoted as telling a voluntary hairdresser at a hospice, "I would love to have my hair cut short. But they won't let me because I need to wear it long . . . it goes better with tiaras and hats. The compromise is lots of lacquer." See AUSTRIA. However, in "greening" their homes, the environment-conscious Prince Charles banned the use of aerosols to avoid damage to the ozone layer.) There was further criticism in 1989 when Diana tried having her bangs brushed rather severely back and away from her forehead, which critics declared emphasized the size of her nose.

Her hairdressers have found that they can be on call around the clock: for a blow-dry at Kensington Palace at 7:30 or 8:00 A.M. after her morning swim (see SPORT), sometimes in the evenings and at weekends prior to engagements, and of course on tour abroad. The relationship between a woman and her hairdresser is often close, and in Dalton's case his influence grew to the point where he even advised the Princess on her clothes. But he found himself somewhat awkwardly in the headlines at the beginning of July 1990 after singer Dionne Warwick wrote an apology to the Princess over a gala planned for London this year for an AIDS charity called That's What Friends Are For. Dionne reportedly claimed that Dalton told her he had access to the Princess and could persuade her to support the gala. Dalton countered by saying that Dionne had "no right" to suggest that he could get Diana to attend, and he insisted he would "never embarrass" the Princess. Coincidence or not, within days Diana emerged in public with her hair restyled by a new crimper, Scottish stylist Sam McKnight from the West End salon of Daniel Galvin. Temperatures were about to hit some of the highest in living memory in Britain, and of her new, elfin short cut, Diana declared, "I feel much cooler. My old hairstyle was a bit too hot for this weather." As always, where she led others followed, and hairdressers around the country were immediately besieged by girls wanting to have their locks shorn too. In August 1990 it was announced that Dalton had ceased to be Diana's hairdresser and would be concentrating instead on his salon at Claridge's and his ambitions to expand his business.

Since then, the Princess has also had a wash and blow-dry from stylist Ivor at Prince Charles's new hairdressers, Carey Temple McAdam, at Hay Hill in Mayfair, where other clients are said to include Prince Andrew and Prince Edward. One of the partners, Denise McAdam, who does Charles's hair, also did Fergie's for her wedding. Diana, who sported an even shorter swept-back hairstyle with bangs in March, told one young visitor to Kensington Palace that Prince William likes to gel his hair into a fifties quiff, adding, "He likes the greased look too."

BEDS & BEDROOMS

Diana slept on what she described as a "very uncomfortable" metal bed as a schoolgirl at Riddlesworth Hall. She and her schoolchums used to jump over the beds in their dormitory, including one nicknamed "the Water Jump" because, the Princess explained, the girl who slept in it used to wet the bed. The bed Diana slept in at West Heath school, where she and her friends used to have pillow fights, coincidentally stood directly beneath a portrait of Prince Charles at his investiture as the Prince of Wales. At Kensington Palace, Diana and Charles have a huge seven-foot-six-inch-wide oak four-poster bed, which Charles had had in his bachelor apartment in Buckingham Palace before their marriage. Because of her back trouble (see HEALTH), Diana's side of the mattress has been resprung for firmer support. They keep their favorite soft toys on their bed, including Diana's toy frogs and Charles's rather worn childhood teddy bear. See COLLECTIONS. Like other royals, they prefer sheets to duvets. Their sheets are white. Traditionally, upper-class couples have His and Hers bedrooms, which should temper speculation on the fact that Charles and Diana do not always sleep together. Charles has a single bed in his dressing room at Kensington Palace and a sofa bed in his dressing room at Highgrove. This does not necessarily mean, as some seem to have assumed, that he and Diana no longer do It. See BOOKS. The Prince and Princess made their strong physical attraction for each other obvious from the start. (Indeed, an Italian magazine once claimed that Diana was a "sexual volcano" who studied erotic manuals from Japan!) They were the first royals to kiss openly in public, and Charles often used to pinch Diana's bottom or rest his hand on her rump, regardless of the cameras. If, like other couples married for ten years, they make less of a public display of their affection now, it does not follow that they are any less loving in private. When they sleep apart it may be so that Charles can avoid disturbing Diana when he arrives home late or has to leave very early next morning, because of her bad back or his polo injuries, or indeed because he snores. See MARRIAGE.

The fact that the Princess has disturbed nights—and not simply when the children wake her up for a cuddle or a drink of water—is no secret. Charles has snored for years. During a visit to Erskine Hospital near Glasgow in July 1989, when former soldier Ted Harrison revealed that the racket he'd made snoring had kept his friends awake, Charles confessed, "I get into trouble for snoring myself. . . . I get a good ticking off." As a schoolboy at

Gordonstoun, the Prince made so much noise with his nighttime blasts that boys in his dormitory used to put toothpaste up his nostrils to try and get a quiet night's sleep. Charles referred to this unusual "cure" when he and Diana visited Towyn in March 1990 to cheer up flood refugees camping in an emergency center. See WALES. When he was told that snorers were keeping people awake, Charles asked, "Do you have snoring competitions?" and then suggested two treatments for the snorers: "Stick toothpaste up your nose and eat boiled onions." If Diana has to put up with snores *and* the smell of onions from her spouse, it may explain why she sometimes goes to bed as early as 9:00 P.M. and why earplugs have been spotted at her bedside. See MUSIC. She gets up at about 7:00 A.M. for her morning swim. See SPORT. Charles is often awake earlier listening to the 6:10 A.M. "Farming Today" program on BBC Radio 4. According to author Andrew Morton, the tiny roof garden built by their Kensington Palace neighbors, Prince and Princess Michael of Kent, overlooks the Wales's bedroom.

On royal tours abroad, the couple are usually given separate bedrooms so that they can each have a separate dressing room. This saves time and is more convenient for them and their dressers, given the number of times they have to change clothes for engagements. See PORTUGAL. In Japan, considerate hosts made a point of giving Diana a Western-style bed, knowing how badly she suffers from jet lag, so that she could sleep well and recover from the flight.

In June 1990, it was revealed that Charles and Diana had been left a lifetime's supply of pillows in the will of Lincolnshire farmer Sir Joseph Nickerson.

BELGIUM

Three IRA suspects with a cache of weapons were arrested in Antwerp a few days before the Princess paid a whirlwind seven-hour visit to Brussels in December 1990. However, she was not believed to be a target, despite "DIANA DEATH PLOT" Press headlines. Wearing a thin suit in a snowstorm, she visited a car catalytic convertor plant, a hospital specializing in sudden infant death syndrome, a city center store, and opened new offices for HelpAge International. See HELP THE AGED and ROYAL PROTECTION SQUAD.

BIRTHRIGHT

In 1987, the same year that her gynecologist George Pinker began his three-year term of office as President, the Princess became an Honorary Fellow of the Royal College of Obstetricians and Gynaecologists, an international professional body concerned mainly with the health of women and babies which conducts examinations and maintains standards in obstetrics and gynecology. She was invited to become an Honorary Fellow because of the "enormous support" she has given to Birthright, the charity arm of the College, and because of her "caring concern for children and those afflicted with disease." In July 1989, the Princess opened the College's Silver Jubilee Congress. Several of Diana's friends are involved with Birthright, including Mr. Pinker, now Sir George, who became its President; Lady Romsey, who was a member of the appeals committee; David Frost, a member of the charity's council, who has helped raise massive funds; and Anna Harvey. See FRIENDS and FASHION. Whether any of them lobbied Diana is not known, but one day Birthright received a message out of the blue in "Palace-speak" to the effect that if an approach was made to the Princess, she might well consider it. She did, becoming Patron in 1984.

Birthright began as the Childbirth Research Centre at University College in the mid-sixties, later became known as the National Fund for Childbirth Research, and finally gained its current name in 1975 when the Fund was adopted by the Royal College of Obstetricians and Gynaecologists. Its original brief, to prevent babies being born handicapped (which about thirty-five thousand a year currently are in the United Kingdom) or dying at birth or a few days later (which seventy-five hundred a year currently do), has since expanded. It is no longer simply a mother and baby charity, funding research for the better health of women and their babies, but also does a great deal of work on menopause, women's cancer, gynecological problems, and male infertility.

Princess Diana shares a lighthearted moment with Princess Anne at the Derby. (Bryn Colton/Camera Press London)

"The Princess came on the scene in 1984, and at that time Birthright was a very, very small medical research charity giving away about £100,000 to research," National Organizer Vivienne Parry recalled. "She personally set the Birthright ball rolling, and we are now a charity which is just about to spend £1 million a year on research projects—and that's not to mention all the research centers we now have that work in lots of other areas like infertility and cervical cancer. I'm sure Birthright wouldn't have grown half as fast, or half as well, without the Princess."

Diana was pregnant with Harry when it was announced that she had agreed to become Patron of Birthright. The very same day she officially opened the charity's first research center, at King's College Hospital, which works on high-risk pregnancies and other aspects of fetal medicine. The center had actually been open for some time, and at the ceremony Diana had some heartwarming encounters with women who had already had treatment there.

"There were some absolutely wonderful stories, people whose babies had been saved who would certainly have died, all those sort of things," Vivienne recalled. "For instance, she met a lady who had lost about six or seven babies because of rhesus blood group disease. The lady had gone to King's, and they'd given the baby five transfusions while still in the womb. The baby, a girl, was born early and only had a fifty-fifty chance of making it. But she *did* make it, and that little girl presented a bouquet to the Princess on the day. So it was wonderful." Finding one particular woman to meet the Princess proved a hilarious problem in retrospect. At the time, said Vivienne, Birthright was "looking at a new type of ultrasound which could tell how much blood was getting through to the babies," and before the ceremony Diana had asked to meet some of the women who'd had this treatment. But *eight* women selected in succession for the honor had to be ruled out—because, one after another, they went into labor within days of being told they were to be presented to the Princess of Wales. Diana finally met the ninth, who managed to contain her excitement until afterward.

Vivienne said:

> The Princess has a huge effect as Patron. She's committed, and very good at talking to people as well, and making them feel loved and wanted. The classic thing is that always before an event, people come up and say, "Oh, what shall I say? How shall I address her? What's this? What's that?"—terribly twitched. And then afterwards they all come up and say the same thing. I can guarantee it almost. It's always, "Oh, isn't she *normal*? Isn't she *nice*? I forgot I was talking to the Princess of Wales!" Because she'll chat about going to Sainsbury's and ordinary things that people talk about. Beforehand there is always this image that she and Prince Charles sit at home both wearing crowns, with her in a ball dress, do you know what I mean? There's this idea that people who are part of the Royal Family are not quite normal, that they're terribly grand and must drink out of crystal all the time. But actually they're just the same as anyone else, really, when it comes to home and family and ordinary things in life. I went to a meeting recently about infection in pregnancy, and a virologist got up and said that the incidence of rubella in pregnancy had dropped dra-

matically, and that he felt the Princess of Wales, who has encouraged people to have rubella vaccinations, had played a key part in that dramatic reduction. Because she is so photographed and so followed, she does have the ability to influence in a way which other people don't. I mean, the fact that she held the hand of that man with AIDS is hugely significant, it really is. We're just beginning to do AIDS, but only just, because there still aren't that many cases of AIDS in pregnancy.

See NATIONAL RUBELLA COUNCIL, HIV, and SPORT.

BLIND

In 1982 the Princess became Patron of the Royal School for the Blind (she is also Patron of the Royal New Zealand Foundation for the Blind) in Leatherhead in Surrey, whose title these days is rather a misnomer. It was one of four schools, all for the blind, founded in 1799 by a group of male philanthropists as a result of a trip to Paris, where they learned of facilities offered for the blind there. The schools were set up in Bristol, Liverpool, Edinburgh, and London, the latter starting life in a room in a pub called the Dog and the Duck in Southwark until 1810 when it expanded. During the nineteenth century, the school provided education and training for blind boys and girls aged from twelve to twenty. In 1900, it moved to Leatherhead and, after the Second World War, changed its role, becoming a center for multihandicapped, visually impaired adults. About 130 blind and partially sighted people, aged from twenty to ninety-six, now live there, the majority permanently, though others stay temporarily while they learn skills which will allow them to live independently in the community. "We're helping people who've been told they were helpless," said the Director, the Reverend Bernard Coote. "And it can be a long process. It took one man over a year to learn how to tell the time. Since she has been Patron, the Princess has attended concerts and a world premiere, and has given us proceeds. Most years residents are invited to Buckingham Palace garden parties. And she's visited us twice. On her visits she met everybody possible and was very warm and understanding. Some people can be very patronizing to the blind, but the Princess talks to them as equals. We've had a royal Patron since Queen Victoria, but I think it's a much more *personal* link than in the past." During one visit, the Princess made a brief speech in which she referred to the "extremely valuable work" done at the school.

BOOKS

It has been estimated that more than 112 books have been written about Diana, selling twenty-seven million copies around the world. One of the most surprising, Patrick Montague-Smith's *Royal Family Pop-Up Book*, even allows fans, by pulling the right tab, to make the bridal Princess and her Prince repeat their famous wedding-day kiss on the balcony *ad infinitum*. (Pull a tab on another page and hey presto, William crawls!) Diana herself enjoys reading two-box novels—the kind you read feet up with a box of chocolates at one hand and a box of Kleenex at the other. As a schoolgirl, she read hundreds of romantic novels by Barbara Cartland, who declared in 1987, "She loved my books. She used to smuggle them into her boarding school." See EDUCATION. Miss Cartland, Diana's stepgrandmother (see FAMILY) is the world's most famous romantic novelist and top-selling authoress with global sales of over five hundred million for five hundred titles in twenty-seven languages. Diana's other favorite writers include Colleen McCullough, author of *The Thorn Birds*, and Barbara Taylor Bradford, author of *A Woman of Substance*, *Voice of the Heart*, *Hold the Dream*, and *Act of Will*. See TELEVISION. She also enjoys the work of Daphne du Maurier, Mary Stewart, and Danielle Steele. As Lady Diana, when she was being besieged in her flat at Coleherne Court by the Press, she said, "I'm an avid reader. I'll read almost anything I can get my hands on, from women's magazines to Charles Dickens. Don't make me sound like a bookworm, because I'm not. I read because I enjoy it and I find it relaxing. Especially when I think of the photographers waiting outside to chase me round the block." She likes to tuck blockbusters into her luggage to read when she goes abroad. Before her debut overseas tour of Australasia in 1983, she spent twenty minutes browsing with her detective at W. H. Smith's in Sloane Square, where she was overheard saying, "I just love Jeffrey

Archer's books." However, she came out with three paperbacks by other writers: two romances, *Indecent Obsession* by Colleen McCullough and *Remembrance* by Danielle Steele, and James Herriot's novel *Lair*.

According to a survey carried out by the American-based Pocket Books in 1990, women who enjoy reading slushy romantic novels have the healthiest sex lives. Editor Linda Morrow declared, "They have the best love lives and the most sex. The survey punctured the myth of readers being dowdy middle-aged ladies with no lives of their own. Those who are married report having sex more frequently with their husbands than those who don't read romances. Theories that women devour these books because they are unhappy with their own love lives don't stand up." Indeed Barbara Cartland herself was quoted as saying, "My readers like nothing more than making love very often."

However, in May 1986 Diana revealed that "unfortunately" her husband "disapproves" of the books she reads. "He doesn't like me reading light novels," she said. Charles reads history and philosophy, writers like E. F. Schumacher, author of *Small Is Beautiful*, Franz Kafka, and Alexander Solzhenitzyn. He has written and contributed to several books himself, including a children's book, *The Old Man of Lochnagar*, which he wrote for his young brothers. He also wrote *A Guide to the Chatting Up of Girls* for soldiers in the Royal Regiment of Wales, which has never been published. Diana has written forewords to books, including one for a book on Birthright (of which she is Patron; see BIRTHRIGHT) and another for *For the Sake of the Children*, a history of Barnardo's (of which the Princess is President; see BARNARDO'S) by June Rose, published in October 1987 by Hodder and Stoughton. She has also written forewords from Kensington Palace for annual reports of other charities and organizations with which she is linked. She has yet to pen a book. In November 1984 it was reported that she had been approached, unsuccessfully through an intermediary, by Jacqueline Onassis, working as an editor at the American publishers Doubleday, with an offer to ghostwrite her autobiography.

In February 1989, Tim Brown and Alan Rustage's Penguin novel *Princess*—in which a Princess Diana–like character is kidnapped by Spanish ETA terrorists, members of the Basque Marxist-Leninist separatist movement there, while on a motorbike ride with King Juan Carlos of Spain and then held hostage—was attacked by security men and MPs as "absolute bunkum" because of loopholes which would apparently never be allowed. It was also called "irresponsible" and "dangerous" on the basis that it might tempt fanatics to try to make fiction fact.

BRITISH LUNG FOUNDATION

Our lives depend on our lungs. Yet lung disease—including asthma, bronchitis, emphysema, pneumonia, pleurisy, asbestosis, tuberculosis, and many others—is one of the most common medical conditions. In Britain alone it affects five million people of all ages from newborn babies to pensioners, costs the loss of more than fifty million working days each year, is the biggest single reason why people visit their family doctors, causes suffering and disability to thousands of people daily, and accounts for 20 percent of all deaths. Everyone is potentially at risk. At work many adults suffer lung damage from dust and other pollutants. Lung disease is the most common illness among children and the most frequent reason they have to go to a hospital. Lung cancer kills more men than any other cancer, and its incidence is on the increase with women. Pneumonia can kill, especially during flu epidemics and among AIDS patients. It is the lungs which are mainly attacked by dangerous new diseases such as Legionnaires' disease. Five thousand new cases of TB, which fortunately can be cured, are diagnosed in Britain annually. And one in ten people over the age of sixty suffers from chronic bronchitis and emphysema.

The only hope of finding ways to improve prevention, diagnosis, and treatment of lung diseases lies in research. But until 1985, support for lung research fell way behind funding for other medical charities. So in that year a group of medical specialists set up the British Lung Foundation (BLF), which has since raised over £2 million allocated as grants for selected research projects throughout Britain. Diana became Patron of the charity in 1986, and she has visited hospitals to see research it funds. A visit to St. Bartholomew's Hospital in London on March 8, 1989, was on "National No Smoking Day." The Princess is a vehement antismoker, as are most other members of the Royal Family, including Prince Charles. (Prince Philip and Fergie both felt obliged to give up tobacco when they entered the family "Firm," though Princess Margaret, complete with a long cigarette holder, still puffs away.) In November 1988, Diana attended the BLF charity premiere of *Who Framed Roger Rabbit*, where she met the movie's executive producer Steven Spielberg; she and Charles are Spielberg fans. In June 1989, at the Grosvenor House Antiques Fair charity gala, which was also held in aid of the BLF, she was presented with one of her favorite Halcyon Days enamel boxes (see COLLECTIONS) which had been specially designed to feature the charity's distinctive red balloon logo. One of the most famous off-duty photographs of Diana shows her at Smith's Lawn, Windsor, in 1988 wearing jeans, cowboy boots, a jacket, a baseball cap, and one of the charity's white sweatshirts, also bearing the red balloon logo. In September 1989, she had coffee with show-biz stars at Claridge's to launch a six-month chain of fund-raising coffee mornings nationwide. The BLF says that the Princess "has shown great interest in the problems endured by people who suffer from lung diseases and in the hope that medical research can offer them." In September 1990, Diana visited a BLF stand at London's Barbican Centre while attending a meeting of European respiratory physicians, of which she was Patron, held jointly between the Societas Europaea Pneumologica and the Societas Europaea Physiologia Clinicae Respiratoriae.

CAMEROON

Diana's three-day trip with Charles to Cameroon in West Africa in March 1990 is chiefly remembered for the red-carpet gaffe and an astonishing series of snubs to the royal couple. The omens were ominous from the start, the Prince and Princess arriving at the capital Yaoundé on March 21 after their five-day tour of Nigeria amid a dispute over whether their visit was official or not. Buckingham Palace said it was; the Cameroon Government said it wasn't. Dancers waiting to welcome them at the airport didn't even know in advance who was arriving. Then the official greeting got off on the wrong foot, when the Princess was shoved *off* the red carpet by Cameroon officials and forced to walk round the back of the guard of honor, while Prince Charles strode on ahead. This is apparently normal form in Cameroon, where polygamy is common (in Gerald Durrell's memorable Cameroon book *The Bafut Beagles*, the Fon of Bafut, a local grasslands tribal king, had innumerable wives) and where the spouses of visiting VIPs have to put up with the indignity of being diverted "backstage" while the men receive all the pomp and ceremony of reviewing the troops. However, this was hardly a suitable welcome for the Princess of Wales. Diana's bodyguard Ken Wharf leapt forward and remonstrated vigorously, after which the Princess was guided back through a gap in the ranks onto the red carpet, by which time she was scarlet with embarrassment herself. A walkabout was promptly canceled, and Charles and Diana headed off in an official car to the state guesthouse to freshen up and on to a reception at the British Ambassador's residence—the Cameroon President Paul Biya not receiving them until almost six hours after they had arrived in the country.

Biya had met the Queen in London in 1985 and apparently was miffed that Her Majesty was not making the visit instead.

This perplexed Palace officials, since Charles and Diana had been invited on the tour by the Government of the Republic of Cameroon in their own right, not as substitutes. However, the hiccups continued. In an "unprecedented" fashion, the President had decided to cancel the agreed-upon after-dinner speeches and the customary toast to the Queen at a first-night banquet at the Unity Palace in Yaoundé. Then, after feverish diplomatic protests about protocol behind the scenes, he changed his mind. All of this struck a curious chord in view of the President's desire for Cameroon to join the Commonwealth. A spokesman for the British Embassy, which had apparently read Biya the diplomatic version of the riot act, was quoted as saying, "We had a word with the President and told him we were worried," adding, "The red carpet incident was rather tatty and awkward, I admit, but that's the way they do things here."

Before the banquet, however, Prince Charles finally had an audience with the President at the Unity Palace, where gifts were exchanged, while Diana had tea with Biya's wife and chatted to her through an interpreter. (French, which is not the Princess's best subject—see EDUCATION—is the main language in that region of multilingual Cameroon.) Then Diana went on to visit the Special School for Children with Deficient Hearing, the only school for deaf children in the country. There an eight-year-old child told her, "Bienvenue Altesse à notre école"—French for "Welcome Highness to our school"—and Diana replied, smiling, "Even I can understand that."

That evening, Charles, who is normally a stickler for punctuality, pointedly arrived with Diana five minutes late for the banquet, which meant that the President and his wife had to wait ten minutes, since they had turned up (post-wigging) five minutes early. However, Biya led Diana, who was sporting a strapless gown, into the Unity Palace. And during the speeches, Charles told the President that "the eyes of the world" were on Cameroon and its rain forests and that Britain would help Cameroon to preserve its "priceless natural heritage."

The following day, they flew to Bamenda to see a hydroelectric project and to visit the local prison. At the prison reform school, the Centre for the Rehabilitation of Delinquents, Diana met a sixteen-year-old youth who'd been sent there for two years after being caught stealing a bicycle. She giggled when she spotted the name on his identity tag—Innocent—and asked, "Is that your real name?" "Yes it is," he said. "So you are Innocent," the Princess said, laughing. "He may be Innocent by name, but not by nature," an officer commented afterward.

On the royal yacht *Britannia*, the Brits had their own problems. The air conditioning broke down in stifling 49° C (120° F) heat after thousands of three-foot killer jellyfish got sucked into the cooling vents underwater. As a result, Diana revealed, the heat was so unbearable that neither she nor Charles slept for two nights. According to someone who attended an official dinner on board for Cameroon VIPs, it became "a nightmare," with sweat dripping from everyone present.

Diana flew straight home at the end of the tour to see Fergie's second baby, Princess Eugenie, who had just been born. Charles stayed on an extra day to visit the Korup rain forest—one of the last great rain forests in Africa but threatened by European timber firms—where he posed for pictures in his safari suit on a 110-meter (120-yard) suspension bridge built over the river Mana by Operation Raleigh, with which he has been connected. However, during a trek through the jungle, apart from soldier ants which threatened to crawl up his leg, he did not spot any of the wild animals he'd hoped to see because the heavy presence of armed security guards had frightened them all away. "That's what usually happens," he said dejectedly before leaving for a private two-day visit to Tunisia, an engagement in Italy, and a couple of days' sketching near Rome.

Among the gifts given to the couple in Cameroon—which is a marvelous country with splendid people, despite the odd behavior of its President and officials—was a carved wooden rocking horse for William and Harry. Back home at Kensington Palace, Diana got hooked on the 1990 World Cup, in which the Cameroon team, the Indomitable Lions, finally put African soccer on the world map. After raving about England's thrilling win against Belgium, which qualified them to play against Cameroon in the quarterfinal, she declared, "I shall be there watching England play Cameroon on TV." No doubt she cheered like millions of other Brits when England won, only to lose by a penalty shoot-out in the semifinal.

CANADA

Such was the welcome when Diana made her first tour of Canada with Prince Charles in June 1983 that local psychiatrists compared "Di-mania" to the Beatlemania of the sixties. The only difference, they suggested, after a crowd of seventy thousand turned out to cheer, chant, and scream at St. John's in New Brunswick, was that whereas Beatle fans identified themselves with teenage rebellion, the Princess as an idol represented a longing for traditional values of morality, stability, and family closeness. Charles's public comments about adding to the family produced ribald jokes when the royal yacht *Britannia* arrived in Conception Bay. But Diana wasn't amused by the over-the-top behavior of Canada's longest-serving provincial Premier Richard Hatfield, known as Disco Dick, at an official dinner in New Brunswick. After blushing at a love-song serenade to her by a pop group, she heard Hatfield make an effusive "toast of love" to her instead of a formal speech. "I've never been so embarrassed in my life," she confided later. It was no joke in Halifax either when a local newspaper broke the royal rules by reporting private remarks made by the couple at a reception. See PRESS. And Diana was livid in Newfoundland when a television boom microphone was pushed out of a crowd, close to her legs, during a visit to a national park. According to her Press Officer, burly Canadian ex-professional soccer player Victor Chapman (see STAFF), a former employee of the Canadian Prime Minister Pierre Trudeau (whom she charmed at a barbecue north of Ottawa), she resented any attempt to record her walkabout conversations with the people. Chapman declared, "The Princess was very upset, furious in fact, and said she would kick away anymore boom mikes she sees near her legs."

However, the tour had many happy moments too. The highlight came in Edmonton, Alberta, where for a gold-rush era barbecue party and raunchy sing-along led by a bosomy brunette billed as Klondike Kate, backed by her scantily clad blond Klondettes, the royal pair had to dress in Victorian costumes. Diana looked terrific, but felt uncomfortable, in a whaleboned floor-length salmon pink Thai silk and cream lace dress, complete with bustle, which had apparently been worn by actress Francesca Annis when she played Lillie Langtry, the mistress of an earlier Prince of Wales (later Edward VII, Charles's great-great-grandfather) on television in the series "Lillie." Charles was done up in a rig which included a frock coat reminiscent of the one worn by great-great-grandpa for a visit to Canada in 1860, plus spats and a cane; he seemed somewhat self-conscious. The impression remained as the bawdy songfest got under way in a marquee in the grounds of Fort Edmonton, which had been converted into Kelly's Saloon. Diana shrieked with laughter, waved a blue cotton napkin over her head, clapped and joined in gustily with all the old music hall songs, smiling to encourage her husband when the 850 guests were told to stand, hold hands, and sway in time to the music. And when Klondike Kate chorused, "Isn't it true, a good man is hard to find?," while the other women yelled back "Yes!," the Princess grinned, shook her head firmly, and said, "No." In fact, though the royal couple hadn't expected the event to be quite their scene, it turned out, as Diana said later, to be "a hoot." It was also in Edmonton, where Prince Charles opened the World University Games, that crowds sang "Happy Birthday" to mark her twenty-second birthday. Though the tour was a huge success, Diana missed Prince William, who had his first birthday while they were away. A cake with a single candle was kept for a joint celebration on their return, the Princess declaring that going home to William was her "perfect birthday present."

On their return visit to Canada in April to May 1986, the couple made a hectic tour of British Columbia. In the city of Prince George, at the opening of an arts festival, Prince Charles made his famous philosophical speech in which he said:

> I rather feel that deep in the soul of mankind there is a reflection as on the surface of a mirror, of a mirror-calm lake of the beauty and harmony of the universe. But so often that reflection is obscured and ruffled by unaccountable storms. So much depends, I think, on how each one of us is introduced to and made aware of that reflection within us. So, I believe we have a duty to our children to try and develop this awareness, for it seems to me that it is only through the development of an

inner peace in the individual, and through the outward mani-
festation of that reflection, that we can ever hope to attain the
kind of peace in this world for which so many yearn. And we
must strive if we can to make living into an art itself, although
it will always remain a tremendous struggle.

In Vancouver, they opened Expo '86 and watched dancing by
Musqueam Indians. After touring overheated pavilions, Diana
fainted and fell into Prince Charles's arms, prompting queries
from the Press and the firm denial from the Palace: "The Princess
is not pregnant." But she *was* very tired and had to go straight on
to the tour of Japan. See JAPAN.

The Princess is Colonel-in-Chief of the Princess of Wales's
Own Regiment in Canada and Patron of Canadian Red Cross
Youth Services.

CHILD ACCIDENT PREVENTION TRUST

The Princess has shown "tremendous commitment" to the aims
of the Child Accident Prevention Trust, whose General Secretary,
Louise Pankhurst, said, "I think this is because the Princess is
herself a young mother and is able to communicate her natural
concerns on this subject." The Trust believes that "anything she
says publicly on child safety will be heeded"; therefore, Diana's
involvement as Patron since March 1988 has been "extremely
helpful." More than two million children are killed or injured
each year in Britain in accidents which need not have happened.
The organization, which became an independent charitable trust in
1981, aims to stop these tragedies by encouraging research into
the causes of childhood accidents and seeking methods of prevention.

In October 1988, attending the Trust's annual general meeting in London, Diana discussed ways of preventing burns, scalds,
poisoning, suffocation, and other accidents, and she met several
children who'd been accidentally injured at home. They included
three-year-old Gemma Dunkley, scarred after tipping a kettle of
boiling water over herself, to whom the Princess gave a teddy
bear, and nine-year-old Catherine Hogan, who presented Diana
with a bouquet. Catherine told her that she had spent more than

a month in the hospital after breaking her elbow in a fall down the stairs at her home. "I hope you are all better now," Diana said. Another child, three-year-old James Sweet, had injured his chest and nose falling through some glass panels while he played. His father told Diana that James was "lucky to be alive." While she was there, the Princess was delighted to be given a Gordon the Gopher cuddly toy each for William and Harry by Ian Scott, a council member of the British Toy and Hobby Manufacturers Association, and remarked that her two sons knew Gordon the Gopher from BBC Television's "Going Live" program. See TELE-VISION. In her speech at the annual general meeting, Diana said:

> As a mother of two small and rather inquisitive boys, I know how easy it is for accidents to happen. All of us must be aware of the safety of our children in the home, in the street, in the car [see MOTORING], and in play generally.
>
> As I am sure you do not need reminding, Christmas is fast approaching and the shops will be filled with many tempting toys. I would ask everyone who is buying something for a child this Christmas, however small, to look at it very carefully to ensure it is totally safe—because for a child, objects which we, as grown-ups, take for granted can become a *major* hazard.
>
> The work of the Child Accident Prevention Trust is vital and needs our maximum support, and I am so pleased to have been able to attend today's meeting.

In a foreword to the Trust's 1988–89 annual review, she wrote:

> Tragically, accidents are still the commonest cause of death among toddlers and young children. And all too often these accidents could have been prevented, with careful attention from adults—not only parents—but designers, planners, and manufacturers.
>
> I have seen some of the terrible results of accidents to children—the pain and suffering they endure, as well as their families.
>
> The Trust is a scientific advisory organization which is dedicated to reducing the number of accidents to children. It is a voluntary organization and needs continued support for its vital work.

As Patron of the Child Accident Prevention Trust I believe
it makes sense to commit resources to prevention rather than
pay for the consequences.

CHILDREN

Diana's love of children has been obvious since her childhood.
See FAMILY, EDUCATION, and JOBS. "She always loved babies,"
her father, Lord Spencer, said. Astrologers have predicted that
the Princess will have three or four children (see ASTROLOGY),
but in March 1990, she declared that she wanted five. At a
reception on board the royal yacht *Britannia* during her visit to
Nigeria with Prince Charles, Diana told Daulla Bello, wife of
Nigeria's Chief Justice, who had eight children herself, "I'd like
three more babies—but I haven't told my husband yet. I think he
may find it a bit of a surprise. You see, I grew up in a family of
four, but I would like one extra. I think five children make the
perfect family."

Like her mother before her, Diana became pregnant very
quickly after her wedding but suffered badly from morning sickness. "Nobody told me I would feel like this," she wailed sadly on
one engagement. See HEALTH and FOOD & DRINK. There has
always been a prospect that she might have twins, since there are
twins in her family background. See AMERICA. However, when a
traditional Morris dancer in Chesterfield offered Prince Charles a
pig's bladder, claiming it would bring Diana twins, the father-to-
be refused the gift, saying, "You can keep the bloody thing."
Throughout her pregnancy, Diana was under the care of the
Queen's gynecologist George Pinker.

Prince William was born at the Lindo Wing of St. Mary's
Hospital, Paddington, London, at 9:03 P.M. on June 21, 1982. He
weighed 7 pounds, 1½ ounces, had blue eyes, and cried lustily.
Prince Charles, who had been present at the birth, described the
experience as "rather a grown-up thing." Diana, who holds strong
views on childbirth, was adamant that she wanted to return home
with her baby as quickly as possible and not remain in the hospital
for the forty-eight hours which many British doctors feel is appropriate after a baby has been born. Since she was "in very good
health" and leaving the hospital early posed no medical problems,
George Pinker agreed. She left the hospital with baby William and

Diana and Prince William. (Snowdon/Camera Press London)

Prince Charles only twenty hours, fifty-seven minutes after the birth, wearing a maternity frock and knee socks. Prince William was christened William Arthur Philip Louis (see NAMES) by Dr. Robert Runcie, Archbishop of Canterbury, in the Music Room at Buckingham Palace at twelve noon on August 4, 1982. He was forty-four days old, wore the special royal christening robe, and bawled his head off to such an extent that he was nicknamed the Prince of Wails. Diana had to put her little finger in his mouth to calm him down and keep him quiet. For godparents, see FRIENDS. William's parents and grandparents of course were "potty" about him, Diana declaring, "It's amazing how much happiness a small child brings to people." At the age of five months, William learned to spit and Diana revealed that she was "getting the full benefit of it." But Charles was around too and very involved in the business of fatherhood, changing diapers, bathing the baby (see BATHS & BATHROOMS), mopping up dribbles from his chin, and waving toys to attract his attention when photographs were taken. At six months, during a Press photo session, William won over cameramen by wrapping a tiny finger around theirs in a baby handshake. He had a healthy appetite and loved putting things in his mouth, including his Queen Buzzy Bee toy which had loud clacking wings. As Diana later remarked, he liked anything which made a noise. He also liked breaking things and flushing objects down the lavatory. Before he was one year old, Prince William accompanied his parents on Diana's debut foreign tour to Australasia in 1983. See AUSTRALIA and NEW ZEALAND. He had cut his first tooth at Christmas 1982, and by the time of the trip he had at least six teeth. He also had lots of blond hair and could smile, laugh, gurgle, and say "Yaya," his earliest public attempt at saying "Mama" or "Dada." In New Zealand, he had a celebrated crawlabout on a rug in Auckland in front of fifty Press and TV cameras, demonstrating that he could stand on his own feet, with help from his parents, before toppling over a moment or two later. He also attempted his first steps. At home, an adventurous and very active little lad, he kept trying to climb up the stairs and at least once caused a security alert by inquisitively pressing an alarm button. Charles and Diana, who were traveling to Canada on a prearranged tour, had to miss his first birthday. See CANADA. Diana hates being parted for any length of time from her children and misses them terribly when duty takes her abroad. But she telephones them from wherever she is and takes along a photograph of them in a silver frame, which is always propped up at her bedside.

The second stage of what Charles called "the royal breeding program" was soon under way. Again following the example of her mother, deliberately or otherwise, Diana had her second child two years after her first. Prince Harry was delivered by the same doctors in the same wing of the same hospital where William had been born. He arrived at 4:20 P.M. on September 15, 1984, weighing 6 pounds, 14 ounces. Once again, Prince Charles was present at the birth, and once again Diana left the hospital with the baby within twenty-four hours of the delivery. St. Mary's had been the hospital chosen when Princess Anne broke the tradition of royal babies being born at home, hospital facilities being considered safer. Prince Harry was the ninth royal baby to be born there under the care of Mr. Pinker, who has since become Sir George. Prince Harry was christened Henry Charles Albert David at St. George's Chapel, Windsor, on December 21, 1984, like William by Dr. Runcie. The two boys are lively, healthy lads, though William has proved quite a handful at times, and his first nanny, Barbara Barnes, left her job at the Palace after Prince Charles allegedly decided that his first son and heir needed firmer discipline. See STAFF. Harry is quieter and less boisterous.

In no time at all, it seemed, the two boys had grown and were off to Mrs. Mynors's nursery school in Notting Hill—where William fell for a little girl named Eleanor Newton, who said he'd told her, "If you don't marry me, I will put you in my jail"—and then on to Wetherby. In September 1989, visiting a social services center in St. Albans for families with emotional or financial difficulties, Diana told parents that she had taken both of her sons to school that morning (Harry, by then aged five, had recently joined William at Wetherby) and remarked, "They are growing up too fast," a feeling many mothers would recognize. When she spotted one child in the center's sandpit hitting another child over the head with a spade, she commented, "They are all like that, aren't they?"

Prince Charles has made comments suggesting he feels that small boys can be a pain in the neck on occasion (see MARRIAGE), and even Diana welcomes brief breaks from them. During a visit to Durham in September 1987, when someone remarked that it was a shame her two sons were not with her, the Princess grinned and replied, "I don't think so. It's rather nice being away from them for a while." Asked by a pensioner in 1989 whether Charles looks after the children when she's away, Diana produced another grin and said, "Sometimes." In July 1990, shortly before William was due to start his first term away at boarding school at Ludgrove School near Wokingham, Berkshire, she revealed how busy her sons were keeping her at home. The household was "taken over" that year by their fad for the Teenage Mutant Ninja Turtles while Charles was nursing his broken arm. The Princess told well-wishers, "It's school holidays with a vengeance!"

But she was born to be a mother. She has taken them on outings to see Santa, to a circus, to Alton Towers Leisure Park in Staffordshire, to the amusements and rides at Thorpe Park in Surrey, and even to ride the bumper cars as they did on a fun day out at Durdham Downs Fair in Bristol. Stallholders could hardly believe their eyes as the Princess of Wales and her son and heir giggled and squealed as Harry and a dectective crashed their car into Mum's. "What you notice," said one fairground lady, "is how much she loves her boys."

Since Diana wants five children, the delay before having her third child seems curious. Whatever the reason, members of the public who asked when she would have her next child tended to get the defensive reply that she wasn't a machine. "I'm not a production line, you know," she declared in 1985. Which didn't, of course, stop Press speculation. See CANADA, ARAB GULF STATES, and MARRIAGE. Was there perhaps some problem? In her biography *Princess*, Ann Morrow claimed that Diana had found it more difficult to conceive the second time "and used the 'temperature test' which helps indicate when a woman is most fertile." Whatever the situation, many were surprised by reports in 1991 that Diana had revealed she was "sticking to two" children (which may have been prompted by Charles's concerns about world overpopulation—he likes to practice what he preaches). But she soon set the record straight. "Contrary to what you may have heard," she declared that March, "I'd like lots and lots more children." In London a few days later, touring the Hospital for Sick Children, of which she is President, she was asked by the father of a sick baby girl whether she would like a daughter. Diana replied, "Yes, I would love one," but added, smiling, "I wonder if the world is ready for another me."

With her great commitment to family life, the Princess has become particularly concerned about the problem of child abuse. During visits to the headquarters of Childline, whose chairman is

"That's Life" and "Hearts of Gold" TV presenter Esther Rantzen (see TELEVISION), she has sat alongside counselors at the twenty-four-hour-a-day phone lines which sexually abused children can call for help. She has also made a large personal donation to the charity.

Diana has made the world of children and the issues, problems, or illnesses which can affect them a major part of her public work. See BARNARDO'S, BIRTHRIGHT, CHILD ACCIDENT PREVENTION TRUST, HOSPITALS, THE MALCOLM SARGENT CANCER FUND FOR CHILDREN, THE NATIONAL MENINGITIS TRUST, NATIONAL RUBELLA COUNCIL, ORCHESTRAS, PRE-SCHOOL PLAYGROUPS ASSOCIATION, and RED CROSS. She is also involved with work for children abroad and has had a children's health camp named after her at Rotorua in New Zealand. See PRESIDENCIES & PATRONAGES.

COLLECTIONS

Diana loves frogs, and the theme is spread throughout her homes and even to her car in the form of the frog mascot which Prince Charles gave her as a twenty-first birthday present. A cushion on one of their sofas bears a frog with the legend, "It's no fun being a prince." She likes to buy gifts and playthings for the children from a shop called Frog Hollow, close to Kensington Palace, which specializes in toy frogs. Doing some Christmas shopping there in November 1988, she laughed when she spotted a cuddly green frog for £4.95, bearing the embroidered invitation, "Kiss me, I'm a prince," and said, "I must have this!" She also bought an inflatable frog soap boat and a dozen frog-shaped bubble bath sachets as stocking fillers. Diana has a running joke with Charles about frogs, based on the fairy tale about the girl who kissed a frog and it turned into a prince. Visiting Glasgow in November 1985, Charles burst out laughing when he saw a poster of a huge toad with the message, "Before you meet a handsome prince, you have to kiss a lot of toads" and revealed, "My wife is always teasing me about that." On their tour of Nigeria in March 1990, when he spotted a frog in the Governor of Lagos's fishtank, he couldn't stop himself from telling Diana, "Look at the frog!" and pointing out the plastic toy which kept opening and closing its mouth by means of a current from miniature waterwheels. On an earlier tour in Australia in 1983, Diana hooted with laughter when a little boy waved his Kermit, the frog hand puppet, to attract her attention, and she walked off with him hand in hand. Kermit is one of her favorite "Muppet Show" characters (see TELEVISION), and she does a noted impersonation of his would-be paramour, Miss Piggy.

As a child, the Princess's father said, "she loved her soft toys nearly as much as she loved babies." She still does. Various soft cuddly toys, including her toy frogs, sit on Charles and Diana's four-poster bed, alongside Charles's threadbare childhood teddy bear, which, according to author Andrew Morton, his valet tucks in every evening to await Charles's arrival at bedtime, making sure teddy's paws are under the sheets so they don't get cold. Packed in a shirt bag amid the luggage for overseas visits, the teddy bear travels almost everywhere with the Prince, except on trips Charles makes as Colonel-in-Chief to his regiments, teddy's bearing being somewhat less than military. When Charles suddenly found himself unexpectedly in the hospital after breaking his arm playing polo in 1990, the *Sun* newspaper promptly delivered a substitute teddy bear to keep him company and cheer him up. Charles's teddy is so old and worn now that the Queen Mother had to patch him up.

Anyone who thinks hanging on to a childhood toy is soppy might bear in mind the investment potential. In May 1989, Alfonzo, a red-haired teddy bear dressed in Russian costume which was made for Princess Xenia, a cousin of Czar Nicholas II, by the famous German firm of Steiff between 1906 and 1909, was put up for auction at Christie's in London. The teddy bear, which had once accompanied Princess Xenia on a visit to Buckingham Palace in 1914, was expected to fetch between £2,000 to £3,000. Instead, Alfonzo went to Oxford antique dealer Ian Pout for £12,000—a record price until a 1927 Steiff teddy called Edward T went for a staggering £55,000 four months later at Sotheby's. The mystery buyer of Edward T, which had sat in an attic and never been cuddled by a child, turned out to be a rich American who wanted it as a thirty-fifth wedding anniversary present for his wife, who was the same age as the bear. The auctioneers' doll expert, Bunny Campione, revealed that American collectors had been forking out thousands for the "right" bear since Sotheby's first teddy bear auction in 1982, when the top price was £360, adding, "There is a huge teddy bear cult in the United States. Businessmen take them to work in their briefcases."

Though Fergie is the teddy bear collector of the Royal Family (she is said to have hundreds, plus a teddy bear brooch which she has worn on public engagements, and reportedly spent a tidy sum on a teddy bear for Bea), many of the royals are devoted to their childhood teddies, some of which were put on display awhile ago at the Teddy Bear Museum in Stratford-upon-Avon. The Queen Mother was given one of the first teddies ever made, and she still has it. Princess Margaret and Princess Anne still have theirs. Princess Alexandra's teddy bear was left behind during a royal tour of the Far East, and it had to be flown home by the Burmese Air Force. And Prince Andrew was accompanied throughout the Falklands conflict by Bruno, the teddy bear mascot given to him by his sweetheart Koo Stark, which he kept close by in his helicopter. The last Prince of Wales, later Edward VIII, chose a teddy bear as the emblem of his love affair with Thelma "Toodles" Furness, the woman who introduced him to Wallis Simpson, for whom he gave up his throne. When Diana was given a white toy bear named William in February 1990 by a little boy at London's Royal Marsden Hospital, of which she is President, she had to ask for a second one, for five-year-old Prince Harry, to make sure there wouldn't be ructions between her two sons. "Thanks, but I must have two," she said. "Otherwise there'll be a terrible row back home." Another of the £12 bears, symbols of a fund-raising campaign, was produced and she said happily, "That will be all right now. Thank you very much." In April 1990 Sean Connery and his wife Michelene presented her with two toy bears in Russian naval uniform for her sons at the premiere of Sean's film *The Hunt for Red October*, in which he plays a Soviet submarine captain.

Apart from frogs, the Princess also collects charming but expensive little hand-painted enamel boxes made by Halcyon Days, the London-based royal warrant holders and suppliers of *objets d'art* to the Queen, Prince Philip, the Queen Mother, and Prince Charles. She gives specially designed ones, usually bearing her initial or cypher, as personal gifts. One went to the fashion designers David and Elizabeth Emanuel, who also collected the boxes, as a token of thanks for making her wedding gown. Another, bearing her cypher within an oval cartouche surrounded by the symbolic flowers of the United Kingdom—roses, daffodils, thistles, and shamrocks—was donated for an auction to help raise funds for Help the Aged in Canada. She has also made donations of carriage clocks made by Halcyon Days, including one which was auctioned for £9,000 for the English National Ballet. She gave another one decorated with her initial *D* in gold as a personal gift to Mrs. Babangida, wife of the President of Nigeria, during the royal tour there in March 1990.

Prince Charles collects antique lavatories and lavatory seats, which he displays in special "throne rooms" at Kensington Palace and Highgrove. He has a collection of books about old lavatories, and he had a lavatory seat slung around his neck in a jokey naval farewell ceremony years ago when he left his ship HMS *Bronington*.

COOKING

When she was seventeen, Diana took Elizabeth Russell's ten-week cookery course in Wimbledon, southwest London, and later cooked and served food for private dinner parties. See JOBS. She is said to be a very good cook. Since her marriage, she has given several of her favorite recipes to books for charity. One, for borscht, the Russian soup made with beetroot, she gave to help raise funds for the Duke of Beaufort's hunt, with which Charles goes hunting. See SPORT. On that occasion, she apparently forgot to say how much beetroot and so on would be needed and how she personally prepares the soup. However, for later recipes, she did. The Princess has a sweet tooth and loves to make homemade fudge. Here's the recipe, which she donated to children's cook-books, including one in aid of the National Society for the Prevention of Cruelty to Children (NSPCC), the Church Army, and a Ladies' Circle in Middlesex which was raising funds to buy dogs as companions for the deaf. (Diana is linked with several organizations for children and the deaf. See CHILDREN and DEAF.)

Diana's Homemade Fudge: Gently stir 4 tablespoons of water, 2 cups of sugar, and ¼ cup of butter in a large nonstick saucepan until the sugar has dissolved. Pour in the contents of one large can (10 ounces) of condensed milk, bring to the boil, then simmer on low heat for about half an hour until the mixture thickens and browns, stirring occasionally. Remove the pan from the heat, beat the mixture well, and pour into a greased pan. Once it has set, cut into squares and eat!

The Princess's recipe for watercress soup has also appeared in several books, including one to help pay for repairs to a church in Cambridgeshire, the BBC's *Food Aid Cookery Book* in aid of famine relief in Ethiopia, and another in aid of the NSPCC. TV chef Glyn Christian reckons it is "superb." Want to try it? Here's what to do:

Diana's Chilled Watercress Soup: Melt 2 tablespoons of butter in a saucepan on low heat and stir in ¼ cup of flour for about two minutes. Add 1 pint of warm chicken stock, stirring until creamy, plus two bunches (6 ounces) of washed fresh watercress, and cook for about 20 minutes until soft, stirring occasionally. Remove the soup from the heat and once cooled, liquidize [puree in a blender] and chill. Before serving, add a half-pint of table cream. This amount should serve about three people.

Another of the Princess's recipes, for leek-and-noodle casserole, was sent to the pupils in Class 1 of Grove Junior School in Pembroke for their healthy eating project in 1986. Opinions on the casserole, once made, were divided. Fourteen of the schoolchildren loved it, fourteen didn't, some suggesting that the whole-wheat noodles it contains reminded them of worms or rubber bands. Most (no surprise) said they'd really rather eat french fries. However, it's regularly on the menu at Kensington Palace because it's one of Prince Charles's favorite dishes. If you'd like to reach your own verdict, here's what to do:

Diana's Leek-and-Noodle Casserole: Boil 14 ounces of whole-wheat noodles until soft in salted water with a little oil, then drain. Sauté 4 or 5 leeks, washed and cut into half-inch chunks, in a large pan in a small amount of oil; then add a pinch of curry powder and a little vegetable stock. Cook until softened but not browned. Put the noodles and leeks, in alternate layers, into an ovenproof casserole dish, cover with grated cheese, pour table cream over the top, and bake for about 20 minutes in a hot oven until crisply golden.

Like most busy moms, Diana often buys convenience foods, including hamburgers for the children, and has confessed that she finds pizzas useful to pop in the oven. See SHOPPING and FOOD & DRINK.

Diana's father, Lord Spencer, and her father-in-law, Prince Philip, are both expert barbecue chefs, and Prince Charles says he enjoys nothing more than food sizzling away on a barbecue grill outdoors. Though he and Diana tend to entertain their guests indoors, they have a barbecue on their roof garden at Kensington Palace where on summer evenings their royal neighbors might catch a mouth-watering whiff as chef Charles prepares food like barbecued salmon steaks, corn on the cob, and baked potatoes wrapped in foil. The royals also love having picnics.

COURTSHIP

Prince Charles is Diana's distant cousin through several relationships. He is her seventh cousin once removed through William Cavendish, 3rd Duke of Devonshire; tenth cousin twice removed through King James I in three different ways; eleventh cousin through Queen Elizabeth of Bohemia; eleventh cousin once removed through a different line of descent from King James I; and fifteenth cousin once removed through King Henry VII in at least four different ways. However, they barely knew each other as children, despite the fact that Diana was born at Park House on the Queen's Sandringham estate in Norfolk. She was, therefore, literally the girl next door. Prince Andrew and Prince Edward, with whom she grew up, were nearer her age than their eldest brother. Prince Charles and Diana actually first set eyes on each other when she was three years old. According to her nanny, Diana was sitting on the floor of the nursery at Park House, dressed in a smock, when Prince Charles, then aged sixteen, put his head around the door.

Thirteen years later in 1977, when Diana herself was sixteen, they met in a plowed field close to Nobottle Wood during a shoot at Althorp. Charles had been invited by Diana's eldest sister Sarah, who was his girlfriend at the time, and it was she who introduced them. Diana recalled later that her first thoughts about the Prince, who was then Britain's most eligible bachelor with a dashing "Action Man" image, were that he was "pretty amazing." He later recalled, "I remember thinking what a very jolly and amusing and attractive sixteen-year-old she was. I mean, great fun—bouncy and full of life and everything."

Having developed a schoolgirl crush on Charles, Diana must have felt it keenly when he and Sarah joined the Duke and Duchess of Gloucester on a skiing holiday at Klosters in Switzerland while she was feeling miserable at finishing school nearby. See EDUCATION. However, Sarah made it clear to journalist James Whitaker in an interview for *Woman's Own* that her relationship with the Prince, whom she regarded as the "big brother" she never had, was platonic. She added, "I wouldn't marry anyone I didn't love, whether it was the dustman or the King of England. If he asked me, I would turn him down." Charles took this blow to his ego on the chin and went on to new pastures. He seemed to have an endless stream of girlfriends, usually slim, long-legged blonds, who were known as Charlie's Angels. After Diana and Sarah were invited by the Queen to join a shooting party at Sandringham in January 1979, Charles started asking Diana out, purely as a friend, to the opera or the ballet or to even out the numbers at dinner. She watched him playing polo with his team, Les Diables Bleus, at Midhurst in Sussex. She was a royal guest at Cowes. She was a guest at Sandringham in February 1980. She visited Balmoral, ostensibly to stay with her sister Jane, whose husband is one of the Queen's senior aides. See FAMILY. And they began to realize there was something more in the relationship. Charles was fishing for salmon in the river Dee at Balmoral, with Diana watching him from the bank, when she was spotted by the

Press. Royal reporter Harry Arnold broke the news in the *Sun* on Monday, September 8, 1980, with a story headlined, "HE'S IN LOVE AGAIN! Lady Di is the new girl for Charles." See PRESS.

To describe the early relationship between Charles and Diana as a romance might not be strictly true. Although Diana followed him around like some lovesick puppy and was clearly head over heels in love with him, Charles seemed to be letting his head rule his heart, as he had previously said he must when choosing a bride. See MARRIAGE. Asked on their engagement if they were in love, she confirmed it without hesitation while he merely said, "Whatever that is." The twelve-and-a-half-year age gap between them may also have played its part in their differing responses. Diana was an innocent teenager, who had filled her head with the stuff of romantic novels while at school and had never previously had a serious boyfriend. Charles, on the other hand, was old for his years, had gone the course with innumerable girls, and was well aware that his days of bachelor freedom were numbered. He had to marry and produce an heir, and the oft-repeated public question of when was he ever going to find a suitable bride and get married had grown louder and more insistent.

Although she had once had eyes for Prince Andrew, her childhood playmate, Diana had said long ago, according to one friend, that her ambition was to become a dancer or the Princess of Wales. However, a career as a dancer had gone by the board when she grew too tall. See DANCING. Prince Charles's valet Stephen Barry (see STAFF) claimed later that Diana set out to get the Prince and did. Charles needed a bride who was virginal, from the right sort of family, knew the royal ropes, and was likely to be a good child-bearer and mother. The Queen Mother and her friend Lady Fermoy, Diana's grandmother, apparently agreed that Diana would be ideal, though suggestions that it was an arranged marriage have been denied. See MARRIAGE.

As luck would have it, the timing was perfect, too. Charles's passionate affair with the fiery Anna Wallace, nicknamed Whiplash Wallace, with whom he was hopelessly in love, had ended abruptly and acrimoniously over what she apparently regarded as his neglect of her while he circulated at the Queen Mother's eightieth birthday ball at Windsor Castle in June 1980. She allegedly told him, "Don't ever ignore me like that again. I've never been treated so badly in my life. No one treats me like that—not even you!" At a later ball, held by Lord Vestey at Stowell Park in Gloucestershire, it is said she left early after Charles kept dancing with Camilla Parker-Bowles. See FRIENDS. Almost immediately afterward, Anna married someone else. Charles was in the doldrums, and here was Diana, this lovely, sweet-natured young girl who was clearly besotted with him. What man could resist?

Once news of his interest in the teenage Lady Diana Spencer broke, droves of reporters and cameramen dogged their steps, camping outside her London flat at Coleherne Court and the Young England kindergarten where she worked, and followed her wherever she went. See PRESS. The bicycle on which she had previously rode around London was no match for this kind of pursuit, so she switched to a car, courtesy of her mother, and became very adept at little tricks like zipping through traffic lights just before they turned red, leaving her Press pursuers stuck behind her, or putting luggage in a decoy car before speeding off to some secret rendezvous with Charles in another. See MOTORING. Sometimes his valet Stephen Barry drove her. Further privacy for the couple was provided by the Queen Mother at Birkhall in Scotland and by Lord Mountbatten at his home, Broadlands, in Hampshire. See HONEYMOON. Despite the best efforts of the Press, whom the royals love beating, the cameramen never once got a photograph of Charles and Diana together.

But the Press and the public, who had fallen for Diana in next to no time, had to wait for a long nail-biting period to discover officially whether the Queen's son and heir had done the same. Charles went off on tour to India, then relaxed in Nepal. He trekked for three days in the Himalayas, no doubt mulling over the prospect of marriage with Diana. At Sandringham for the New Year, 1981, the Royal Family were besieged by the Press, hoping to catch a glimpse of Lady Diana. The Queen became livid. See PRESS. But Charles had finally made up his mind. He told his parents, and Diana was invited to Sandringham, arriving and leaving in secret. Charles went off for his annual skiing holiday in Switzerland, still leaving the Press and public none the wiser.

He had first raised the question of marriage, in a roundabout way, just before Christmas 1980 as he and Diana stood in "a cabbage patch"—the vegetable garden at Bolehyde Manor, the seventeenth-century home of his old friends Andrew Parker-Bowles of the Household Cavalry and his wife Camilla. He said something on the lines of, "If I were to ask, what do you think you might answer?" and Diana apparently giggled. He actually popped the question on February 4, 1981, two days after his return from Switzerland, after a candlelit dinner in the blue sitting room of his apartment at Buckingham Palace. Charles knew that Diana was due to go to Australia on a vacation with her mother and stepfather. He thought the forthcoming separation would give her the chance to weigh up the pros and cons of marriage to the heir to the throne, and all which that would entail, and to decide "if it was all going to be too awful." At least one of his former girlfriends, Lady Jane Wellesley, had balked at the prospect of leading a royal life. Indeed, the Queen Mother, who had been a virtual second mother to him in childhood when his parents were away on tours abroad, had turned her husband down several times before agreeing to his proposal. Diana, however, needed no time whatsoever. The minute Charles asked, "Will you marry me?," she said "Yes" immediately. "It's what I want," she said later. "I never had any doubts about it." When Charles telephoned her father to ask formally for her hand with the words, "Can I marry your daughter? I have asked her and very surprisingly she has said yes," Lord Spencer simply said, "I'm delighted. Well done," commenting later, "I don't know what he would have done if I'd turned him down."

At Coleherne Court, Diana's simple and very private announcement "I'm engaged" brought screams of delight from her flatmates Ann Bolton and Virginia Pitman. See TELEVISION. Nineteen-year-old Carolyn Pride was in the bathroom at the time and had to hear the glad tidings through the door. Diana giggled as the girls ran around excitedly, laughing and shouting and opening a bottle of champagne to celebrate. The three flatmates, who had heard Prince Charles's voice on the telephone when he rang for Diana but had never met him (see NAMES), kept the news secret until the official announcement three weeks later. They were guests at the wedding, though Diana was not allowed to have a wedding-eve hen party with them, as she had hoped, nor to have any of them as her bridesmaids. The royal strictures had already begun.

The official announcement was released from Buckingham Palace at 11:00 A.M. on Tuesday, February 24, 1981, and read, "It is with the greatest pleasure that the Queen and the Duke of Edinburgh announce the betrothal of their beloved son the Prince of Wales to the Lady Diana Spencer, daughter of the Earl Spencer and the Honourable Mrs. Shand Kydd." An hour later, wearing her sparkling sapphire-and-diamond engagement ring and matching blue silk suit (see JEWELRY and FASHION), Diana posed with Charles for engagement photographs on the garden steps at Buckingham Palace. See BEAUTY SECRETS. They laughed and looked, as Diana herself said, "blissfully happy." Earlier, sitting on Charles's sofa in the room where he had proposed, they gave an intimate five-minute TV interview which was seen by five hundred million viewers around the world. See TELEVISION. Charles declared that he was "absolutely delighted and frankly amazed that Diana is prepared to take me on." Diana's sister Sarah, who had originally brought them together, remarked happily, "They are both over the moon. He met Miss Right and she met Mr. Right. They just clicked." See WEDDING, HONEYMOON, and MARRIAGE.

$\mathscr{D}$

DANCING

Diana admits to being "obsessed" with dancing—as Charles is about playing polo—and loves tap dancing, jazz, and ballet. She used to dance regularly, telling TV interviewer Sir Alastair Burnet that she thought it "vital to switch off for one or two hours every week." According to Fred Astaire's biographer, Tim Satchell, she gave Prince Charles a pair of tap shoes "so that he could join her in her practical enthusiasm for Astaire's dancing." Prince William and Prince Harry, whom she also hoped would learn to tap, started dance classes. The Princess "always" wanted to be a ballet dancer and started taking lessons herself when she was only three and a half. At school she was still so "mad keen" that in addition to the usual dance classes, she took extra lessons. See EDUCA-TION. On school expeditions, which she rushed to join, she saw *Sleeping Beauty*, *Giselle*, and *Coppélia*, and she would wait for hours if necessary by the stage door with other fans afterward in the hope of getting an autograph from a favorite dancer. See AUTOGRAPHS. She loved *Swan Lake* so much that she saw it over and over again. Her ambition to become a professional dancer, which experts say she has the talent to have achieved, never changed, but she grew too tall. "I overshot the height by a long way," she said. "I couldn't imagine some man trying to lift me up above his arms."

However, dancing remains her "absolute passion." In her single days, she took tap, jazz, and fitness classes at the Dance Centre in Covent Garden, and joined adult classes at the Vacani School of Dancing where she worked. See JOBS. Until fairly recently she still had regular lessons when time permitted. When she was living at Buckingham Palace, she took hour-long ballet lessons twice a week in the Throne Room, wearing a black leotard, from Wendy Vickers and Lily Snipp, her dance teachers at West

Diana is ready for a night of dancing. (Glenn Harvey/Camera Press London)

Heath. Elderly Miss Snipp, who has since died, also gave her piano lessons. She recalled, "She just lived for ballet and was completely dedicated. . . . Her lessons helped her get away from the pressures of being a member of the Royal Family." Diana would round off each session by tap-dancing to songs like "Hello Dolly" and the Fred Astaire favorite "Top Hat, White Tie and Tails." After moving to Kensington Palace, she continued dancing in her sitting room, as she had previously done at Althorp, where she used to tap-dance on the checkered black-and-white marble floor of the Wootton Hall, the grand entrance hall, and at Coleherne Court. In 1983, she arranged six weeks of lessons at the studio of Dame Merle Park, Principal of the Royal Ballet and Director of the Royal Ballet School. In 1988, before she had a video made of herself dancing as a gift for her husband (see VIDEOS), she had tips from award-winning choreographer Gillian

Lynne. And for two years she had regular private lessons from Anne Allan, dancing in a pink leotard behind drawn blinds at the dance studios of the English National Ballet (ENB) near the Royal Albert Hall. Allan, a Scot and former ballet mistress with the London City Ballet, had worked with dance star Wayne Sleep and on the Andrew Lloyd Webber musicals *Cats* and *Phantom of the Opera*. Unfortunately, those lessons ceased when Allan moved back to Scotland, and the Princess found she no longer had time anyway to continue—a great pity, especially if dance classes really did help her to cope with the inevitable strains of royal life and to relax. Indeed, with neither Diana nor Charles able to let off steam by following their particular passions after Charles broke his arm playing polo in 1990, one couldn't help wondering whether the double loss would bring them closer together—or send royal aides running for the hills.

The English National Ballet was formerly called the London Festival Ballet and is also known as the Nutcracker Ballet because of its traditional performances of *The Nutcracker* at the Royal Festival Hall every Christmas. Since 1976 its Patron had been Princess Margaret, another great ballet fan. Diana took over as Patron in August 1989, shortly before the controversy which erupted when Pamela, Lady Harlech, former London Editor of American *Vogue*, became Chairman and Peter Schaufuss, nicknamed the Dancing Dane, was fired from his post as Artistic Director. Schaufuss, aged thirty-nine, who had made his name dancing with the Bolshoi and Kirov ballets, had four offers within a week and promptly signed a five-year contract with the Deutsche Oper ballet in Berlin, reportedly being followed to work in Germany, where dancers can earn double, by ten leading ENB dancers. Diana was put on the spot in public over the controversial sacking at the ballet company's fortieth anniversary gala at the Royal Albert Hall in March 1990. She was standing on stage with founder-President, Dame Alicia Markova, as Lady Harlech praised the spirit of the company when someone in a grand tier box suddenly shouted, "How about a tribute to Peter Schaufuss?" and some of the 2,500-strong audience burst into applause. According to *Daily Mail* gossip columnist Nigel Dempster, the Princess "turned quickly aside, withdrawing behind a neutral wall of royal discretion." *Mrs.* Schaufuss, the Australian ballerina Janette Mulligan, mother of their one-year-old daughter, was among the dancers who performed that evening.

At the ball which followed, Diana danced too, being swept on to the dance floor for a quickstep by forty-six-year-old Hungarian-born Ivan Nagy, whose appointment as the new Artistic Director had just been announced. Afterward, somewhat flushed, the diminutive five-foot-four-inch Mr. Nagy, who had made his reputation in the West with the New York City Ballet and has danced with prima ballerinas Natalia Makarova and Margot Fonteyn, was quoted as saying of the Princess, "She's wonderful. She's a natural." *And,* which would no doubt have thrilled the aforementioned ladies, "She is the most light-footed dancer I have ever partnered." But it wasn't a wild, dazzling display, like Diana's *Saturday Night Fever* disco-dancing with John Travolta at the White House in November 1985. See AMERICA. Or a performance, like the stunning surprise routine she did on stage at the Royal Opera House at Covent Garden a month later with dance star Wayne Sleep, much to the astonishment of the audience and, in particular, Prince Charles—who, according to Sleep, "nearly fell out of" the royal box but, being "a great sport," was "very nice about it afterward." They did a three-and-a-half-minute routine which included soft-shoe tapping and high kicks, at one point Diana doing high kicks over the head of Wayne, who is eight-and-a-half inches shorter, to Billy Joel's "Uptown Girl," one of her favorite records. See FAVORITE THINGS. Wayne, whose six scissor-legged entrechats in the air beat Nijinsky's by one, making *The Guinness Book of World Records*, and who is the only dancer to have performed *Swan Lake* with both Nureyev and the Goodies, telephoned the steps to Diana, who practiced solo. They later had just one rehearsal. Even so, on the big night the Princess—whom he says is very supple, agile, and graceful, and loose with lots of rhythm—was "brilliant," and they had eight curtain calls. Wayne, the son of a dockyard clerk who was named after a cowboy in a book once read by his mother, says, "Diana is a true performer. When she was dancing with me that one time, she was electric." At his home in Kensington, he has some joke mugs showing a leotarded Diana saying, "Let's Dance. Yah!" He thinks

Diana, who wore a tight-fitting white dress with a swirly skirt for their memorable *pas de deux*, bought some herself one Christmas as novelty gifts.

Those who have partnered Diana on the dance floor include Tom Selleck, Neil Diamond, Clint Eastwood, Gregory Peck, and Christopher Reeve. See AMERICA. At the Diamond Ball in London in December 1990, the Princess, wearing an emerald-and-diamond choker and a slinky green sequined gown with a slit skirt, invited TV star and ex-MP Robert Kilroy-Silk to partner her in a jitterbug to the Glenn Miller classic "In the Mood." It was the first time for at least five months that Charles and Diana had attended an evening function together in Britain. Although the Prince danced until almost midnight with other women, including Lady Tryon, Chairman of the Ball Committee (see FRIENDS), according to Ashley Walton in the *Daily Express*, he did not dance, or even sit at the same table, with his wife. Guests had paid £100 to £1,000 to attend the ball, which raised more than £130,000 for the charity SANE (Schizophrenia, A National Emergency), of which Prince Charles is Patron. Friends stressed, Walton reported, that the Prince and Princess, last known to have danced together (cheek-to-cheek) at Charles's fortieth birthday party two years before, felt duty-bound to spend their time with guests rather than together. However, this did nothing to quash the rumors which had arisen again that summer that they were leading "separate lives." See MARRIAGE. And neither did the charity's refusal to confirm or deny that they didn't dance together, an official saying, "That's a personal question we're not allowed to answer."

According to other reports, the royal couple did dance together a few evenings later at the Buckingham Palace ball, which celebrated four royal birthdays: the Queen Mother's ninetieth, Princess Margaret's sixtieth, the Princess Royal's fortieth, and the Duke of York's thirtieth. But they left separately in different cars within half an hour of each other. Though Charles and Diana danced several times in public in earlier years, he does not seem to share her enthusiasm for dancing. He has admitted that when they have to lead off the dancing on an empty dance floor with everyone watching, his heart sinks.

The Princess is also Patron of the London City Ballet (LCB), started in 1978 by its South African–born Artistic Director Harold King, which she has fought long and hard to help keep above water against pressing financial odds. King, who had previously worked with Rudolf Nureyev, had to "beg, borrow, or steal" basic sets and costumes for the company's first full-length production, having ambitiously chosen to tackle the world's most popular ballet, *Swan Lake*. By 1990, when the company finally found a permanent home at Sadler's Wells, the LCB had become one of the top six classical ballet companies in Britain with an annual turnover of over £1 million. From its humble beginnings, with four staff and a handful of dancers who performed to taped music, it had grown to a staff of twenty-two, with thirty-four dancers (increased to forty-seven for performances on vast stages, as in Japan) and nineteen musicians, giving more than two hundred performances a year around Britain and abroad.

In February 1984, Diana flew to Oslo for a gala performance of the company's second full-length work, a ballet of *Carmen*, choreographed and produced by Harold King. See NORWAY. She deliberately delayed the announcement that she was expecting her second child until her return to Britain, shrewdly aware that this would maximize publicity for the ballet company for whom she had just made her first solo official visit abroad. (Her first actual foreign trip as the Princess of Wales was a private one. See MONACO.) In 1990 she agreed to make another trip, to Washington, D.C., that October, to help raise desperately needed funds for the company which, unlike the English National Ballet, did not receive revenue funding from the Arts Council and had to survive on box-office receipts and sponsorship, mainly from London-based businesses. According to Harold King, the LCB was in an "extremely perilous" financial position. Of the Princess as fundraiser he said, "She's made it known: 'Please, if you're going to involve me in any London City Ballet events, capitalize and maximize the financial benefits for the company.' We rely very much on her to help us raise money, which she seems so happy to do, which is great. She has never let us down." Proceeds, hoped to be a million dollars, were to be shared by the Washington Ballet, Grandma's House (a Washington pediatric center which cares for babies with AIDS), and the LCB. See AMERICA.

Diana's commitment to the company, of which she became

Patron in 1983 after attending rehearsals, was also shown in a foreword she wrote in September 1989 for the company's 1989–90 brochure in which she said:

> Last year was an important landmark in the history of London City Ballet when the Company celebrated its 10th anniversary. The measure of what has been achieved during that time should not be underestimated and, despite challenging odds against its survival, London City Ballet has flourished artistically.
>
> I have watched the Company's development year by year with increasing pleasure and I am delighted that the passing years have done nothing to diminish the marvellous spirit of enthusiasm of everyone involved with the Company.
>
> London City Ballet brings great pleasure to audiences throughout the United Kingdom and abroad and I look forward to working with the Company to ensure a successful and secure future.

The Princess has gotten to know the dancers during her visits to rehearsals and performances, though she has never joined their dance classes. "And I don't blame her, because all the dancers would probably be ogling her," Harold King said. "She told me she doesn't have time to dance anymore, and that's sad because the Princess loved her dancing. Whenever she comes in to us she just watches. But what she really enjoys is going around the studios, squatting on the floor and talking to the dancers. She seems to get a buzz out of that. She's interested in their problems, the injuries—what hurts, what doesn't hurt—and worries about the fact that we tour so much, how tired they get." She frequently lunches with LCB bosses to discuss the company's problems, held a party at Kensington Palace for all their sponsors, where she made a point of meeting every single sponsor in the room, and even asked to attend a fund-raising greyhound race at Wembley Stadium—having never been to one before—where, out of the blue, a man walked up to her table and offered her a brand-new Jaguar XJS, the same car she herself drove, to raffle for the LCB. See SPORT.

"As a person I think she's great, wonderful," Harold King said.

And it's also been wonderful seeing her blossom. Because when she first became Patron, she certainly didn't have the confidence that she has now. I think even speaking to the dancers and line-ups after the performance seemed to un-nerve her slightly. Whereas now she simply *sails* through, asks all the right questions, says all the right things, has *tremendous* confidence. So it's been lovely seeing her grow up at the same time as we've grown up. It's been a side-by-side thing. She's a remarkable woman. She's got a wonderful personality and she just radiates beauty. I've seen men absolutely *floored* by her because she's so beautiful. The Princess is the one who's really put us on the map and helped us survive. When I started the company in 1978, I didn't believe it would last that long unless the Arts Council rallied around and gave us the revenue funding that we desperately need. When the Princess became Patron in 1983, we were really struggling and dancers weren't being paid properly, we couldn't afford to use an orchestra and all sorts of things like that. From the time that she became Patron, the sponsorship took off. So that gave us new life, really. I can't think how the Princess could do more for us. She's our guardian angel. I mean, without her London City Ballet wouldn't be here now.

The London City Ballet was somewhat bizarrely in the news in December 1989 when the *Daily Telegraph* reported that a dressmaker had dropped a claim for £1,200 against the company for four tutus she had made for its two principal ballerinas for a production of *Swan Lake* the previous year. The company had refused to pay for them on the grounds that they didn't fit and were too-too revealing. Harold King claimed later, "The tutus were baggy around the waist and the knickers were too high. The bodice was too short on one of the ballerinas so that when she bent backward, her boobs popped out. Our wardrobe mistress was in a panic when she saw them. She had to hire some more from the Royal Ballet, and eventually we had others made."

During the case at Westminster County Court, the judge studied a photograph of the offending tutus which, according to the *Telegraph*, showed "a ballerina's left breast popping out of one of them" (see X-RATED). The ballerinas wore them in court to show him how "unsuitable" they were. The dressmaker said she had been ill and had therefore had to cancel a third fitting before finishing the tutus.

In July 1990, Harold King—who receives Christmas cards from Diana, who also attended his fortieth birthday party and bought him a pale yellow cashmere sweater—heard that Dame Margot Fonteyn, seriously ill, was in Britain from Panama for medical tests. He also learned that Dame Margot, a Patron of the International Spinal Research Trust, of which Diana is Royal Patron, was longing to have a chat with the Princess, who was a fan of hers, but had never had the chance. So he rang the Palace, and the Princess and the former prima ballerina ended up having tea together at Claridge's, accompanied by Harold, his ex-wife Marian St. Claire, principal ballerina of the LCB, and her new husband Michael Beare, the company's rehearsal director. "I thought the Princess would stay half an hour, but she was there chatting to Margot for an hour and a half," Harold said. "It really made Margot's day. It was a real mutual admiration society, and they both seemed thrilled to have met. It was absolutely super." Sadly, Dame Margot died in 1991.

In March, the month after her death, it was announced that despite healthier box-office receipts and thriving sponsorship, the London City Ballet could no longer continue its thirteen-year struggle to survive without Government revenue via the Arts Council and would close in June 1991. Diana was said to have anxiously followed the events in the days leading up to the announcement. A Buckingham Palace spokesman was quoted as saying, "She is acutely aware of the problems besetting London City Ballet and has expressed her deep concern."

At the end of March, Harold King said:

It costs £1.7 million a year to run London City Ballet. We take approximately £700,000 a year at the box office and raise in the region of £500,000 in sponsorship, so there's a shortfall of

£500,000. The Arts Council are still considering giving us proper revenue funding, but unless they come up with the money, which they say they don't have, we'll have to close. Diana, who came in yesterday to see the dancers and watch rehearsals, had already told me that she would try and speak to the Arts Minister, Tim Renton, and put in a word for us. We've been told he's been bombarded with letters and petitions from our audiences and ballet schools and even ballet companies. The thing which really got people going was a letter written to *The Times* by Dame Ninette de Valois [the prima ballerina who founded the Royal Ballet]. She has also given us a ballet of hers, *The Rake's Progress*, if we survive. So there's a lot going on and there may still be a chink of light. It would be ridiculous to fold after thirteen years. We're on tour twenty-six weeks a year, and we're doing the Arts Council a huge favor—we're making ballet accessible to places and tax-payers who wouldn't get to see ballet. If we fold, who else is going to do those venues? And how are those people going to see ballet unless they're prepared to travel miles? We just hope there'll be a last-minute reprieve. [There was.]

DEAF

Diana learned sign language to communicate after becoming Patron of the British Deaf Association (BDA) in February 1983. (They had got in early and asked her to become Patron as far back as April 1981, when she was still Lady Diana Spencer.) She used the skill in September 1987 to tell students at Durham University who were training to teach the deaf, "My name is Diana. I live in London." The following July, when five-year-old Michael Gleason asked, "Is that the Princess?" when she walked into his classroom during a visit to a school for the deaf in Newcastle upon Tyne, she replied in sign language, "Yes, I'm the Princess of Wales." But she used the skill most publicly in August 1990 when she replied in sign language to a message of welcome when she attended the centenary congress in Brighton of the BDA, for whom she has made many visits and attended fund-raising events and premieres, including that of the James Bond movie *A View to a Kill*. Late the previous year, she presented the Young Deaf Achiever 1989 award in London to twenty-eight-year-old Catherine Clough, Britain's only deaf teacher of children who can hear, at an event organized by the deaf-blind consortium Deaf Accord, which includes the BDA. Catherine specifically wanted to teach nondeaf children but had a hundred job applications rejected before she succeeded, finally becoming art teacher at Stantonbury School in Milton Keynes. She wept with joy and relief when she learned she had got the job, and Diana herself was moved to tears when she heard how success finally came after years of study, struggle, and frustration. The Princess told Catherine's mother, "I know how proud you must be. If my children make me as proud, I will be the happiest woman alive." Diana has visited the deaf on tours abroad. See CAMEROON.

Diana's concern for the deaf was shown in a speech she made at the launch of the BDA's centenary year at the Mansion House in London in February 1990, when she said:

Today we are celebrating a hundred years of the British Deaf Association, an organization which from its birth has been run for deaf people by deaf people. Today its role is more important than ever, especially to the seven million Britons who suffer some form of hearing loss.

To many of those seven million people, the BDA is the key to their relationship with the hearing world. It is the BDA who have taken a leading part in explaining the positive contribution deaf people are making to society. Even more important, they aim to make clear how much society has yet to benefit from the deaf community's enormous untapped potential.

Because deafness is invisible, it is all too easy for this potential to be overlooked by the hearing world. And, with so many good causes competing for attention, it is hard to be sympathetic to a handicap which you can't even see; hard to imagine the frustration felt by deaf people whose intellectual and physical talents are so often obscured by communication problems; and harder still to imagine the loneliness of deaf children, 90 per cent of whom have parents who can hear.

To those of us fortunate enough to have our hearing, and to have children who can hear, this centenary should prompt us to try and imagine life without hearing. Because unless we make this effort, we will never fully understand the crucial importance of charities like the BDA.

As someone who can hear, I ask those of you who are deaf to be patient as I briefly mention aspects of deafness which, with a little imagination, we can all understand.

For example, communication is a gift which, unlike the rest of us, few deaf people are able to take for granted. The BDA has done much to promote the special culture represented by all forms of deaf communication, especially British sign language. But whichever medium is used, the message is the same: the deaf community wants to play a full part in society.

Sadly, society seems reluctant to play its part. Access to education, employment and recreation is slowly improving for those suffering other forms of handicap. But for deaf people, many special obstacles remain. Low educational standards, restricted training opportunities and prejudiced employers all conspire to limit the deaf person's enjoyment of full membership of our community. No wonder that some deaf people feel like strangers in the hearing world all their lives.

It would be wrong to finish on this unhappy note. Deaf people are not asking for sympathy, only for a fair chance to live and contribute as full members of society. The BDA already operates many schemes to help deaf people overcome everyday difficulties, and indeed would like to operate many more. Many of you, to my admiration, have already conquered disability and discrimination to succeed in a silent world.

The BDA believes the hearing world should listen to the story of this success, and in so doing learn how much more could still be achieved.

I wish the association all the strength and resources it will need in this vital task, and hope the rest of us will get the message loud and clear.

In 1985, the Princess also became Patron of the Commonwealth Society for the Deaf and attended a charity lunch given by the society at the Fishmongers Hall in the City of London. The following year, she asked to visit the office to meet the organization's staff, officers, and its specialists who volunteer to work abroad. "This gave us some encouragement," said Leon Yow of the society. "Having asked her to preside over a major charity fashion show for the society which clashed with another, she nominated us as beneficiaries of the 1989 British Council Awards

Show at the Royal Albert Hall. We received good exposure and an addition to our funds. The fact that HRH The Princess of Wales is our Patron has undoubtedly given the society, in the public eye, the stamp of approval, but it would be something to look forward to and we would dearly love to have our Patron present at one of our major events." Perhaps by the time this book is published, that may have happened.

DRUGS

The worldwide problem of drug addiction, particularly among young people, is one that deeply worries Diana, and she is connected with several drug organizations. During her brief visit to Washington in 1985, she went to Springfield, Virginia, with the First Lady, Nancy Reagan, to see an American drug rehabilitation program called Straight. In Britain she signed her name to the national "Just Say No" antidrug campaign. See TELEVISION. Her brother, Viscount Althorp, made a nationwide antidrug appeal on television following the drug-linked death of his friend, Olivia Channon. The Princess has also urged pop stars she has met to help in any way they can. In April 1990, opening the annual drug conference of the Association of Chief Police Officers of England, Wales and Northern Ireland, held in Hutton, Lancashire, she said in a speech, "You do not have to be an expert to see that drug abuse destroys the user—slowly and painfully, physically and mentally. And it does not take an expert to realize that drug-related crime poses a frightening threat to our society. . . . Cutting supply is important but . . . also notoriously difficult. So is catching traffickers . . . increasingly the emphasis must be placed on finding—and funding—ways to reduce the *demand*."

Diana became Patron of the Institute for the Study of Drug Dependence in 1989, its twenty-first anniversary year. Its Director, Jasper Woodcock, said, "We were amazed and delighted at our good fortune. The Princess has made the drug problem one of her particular concerns, and we are very glad of that support." The Institute is Britain's national resource organization which provides backup for professionals dealing with drug users. It does research, runs an information service, and produces publications like handbooks for family doctors, training material for youth workers, and educational material for teachers to use in schools. Diana is also Patron of the Freshfield (drug counseling) Service at Truro in Cornwall. She has been to a reception there and a team meeting at which, according to the Administrator, Steve Large, "She displayed a good working knowledge of drugs and the problems surrounding them, and funding issues. There's no doubt that she's done her homework and knows a great deal about the subject." The service was set up in 1984 in response to demand in Cornwall, which despite being a favorite vacation spot has the same problems as anywhere else. It deals with about two thousand people a year including drug users, their families and friends, and people who phone for advice. But by far the most work the Princess does in the drug field is for Turning Point. See TURNING POINT.

In 1988 American narcotics agents in Miami discovered masks of Charles and Diana on a plane smuggling in cocaine. The masks had been placed on stands to make it look as if the aircraft were carrying passengers.

$\mathscr{E}$

EDUCATION

Diana "adored" her school days, though she was never a scholar and fell well behind her sisters and brother in terms of academic achievement. She began her elementary schooling at home at Park House under her governess Ally, Miss Gertrude Allen, who had taught her mother years before. In January 1968, after her mother left home (see FAMILY), Diana, then aged six, and her young brother Charles were enrolled at Silfield, a private day school seven miles away in King's Lynn, where the uniform was red and gray. Charles proved the academic one, but Diana was a trier. See ZOO. She was also a cheerful, though mischievous, little girl who loved helping out those in the nursery class.

After Silfield, she was sent to Riddlesworth Hall boarding school, a two-hour drive away from home, at Diss in Norfolk. She was nine years old and arrived for the Michaelmas term, in September 1970, with a goodie box containing chocolate cakes and her trunk full of school outfits from Harrods, all labeled with her name. The winter uniform was again red and gray, and gloves and sensible black shoes had to be worn for church on Sundays. During the summer months, the girls had to wear a panama hat with a turquoise dress made, of all things, of wool which made their skin itch. At first Diana was very homesick, but she had friends there and also Peanuts, one of her pet guinea pigs (see STAFF), which she kept in one of the hutches at the school's Pet's Corner, with mice, hamsters, and rabbits belonging to other pupils. During her three years at Riddlesworth Hall, she was visited separately on alternate weekends by her mother and father, who would arrive bearing treats of Twiglets, cream eggs, and gingersnaps. Schoolchums remember her as a high-spirited girl who enjoyed playing pranks. The school games in summer were swimming and tennis, for which the Princess retains a passion (see

SPORT) and in winter, netball and field hockey. Swimming was Diana's forte: she competed in internal and external swimming matches, and her team won the Parker Cup in her final year. Rather than ride (there was a choice), she chose to dance. She learned Scottish dancing and natural movement, and she loved ballet so much that she took extra lessons. See DANCING. Academically she didn't shine, but she was awarded the school's Leggatt Cup for helpfulness.

One of her classmates, her neighborhood childhood friend Alexandra Loyd, who had also been with her at Silfield, later became one of the Princess's Ladies-in-Waiting. In April 1989, sixteen years after they'd left Riddlesworth Hall, she accompanied Diana on a return visit when the Princess opened a new mixed prepreparatory department for children aged from four to seven. Full of nostalgia as she toured one of the dormitories where she had slept, Dormitory Three, Diana revealed some schoolgirl memories (see BEDS & BEDROOMS and BATHS & BATHROOMS) and remarked with a grin, "They have not changed the wallpaper, I see." To make her feel at home, the current headmistress, Mrs. Patricia Wood, put up a photograph of the class of 1971, showing Diana and Alexandra as schoolgirls—the young Diana barely recognizable wearing her hair in pigtails. "The Princess seemed quite shy when she arrived but she really enjoyed her visit," Mrs. Wood said afterward. "We could hardly tear her away from the little ones and she remembered so much about her time here, even remarking, 'It still smells of floor polish.' " Her former headmistress, Miss Elizabeth Ridsdale, known as Riddy, recalled Diana as "a decent, kind" little girl. "Everyone seemed to like her . . . ," she said. "What stands out in my mind now is how awfully sweet she was with the little ones."

In September 1973, Diana arrived as a pupil at West Heath, a boarding school at Sevenoaks in Kent, where in differing ways her two older sisters had both made their mark. Sarah had excelled at riding and the piano, had performed in the school plays, and passed 6 GCE O levels (General Certificate of Education, Ordinary level) before being booted out for misbehavior. Jane, who had played on the school's lacrosse and tennis teams, had already passed 11 O levels and was about to tackle her As (Advanced level). And she was a prefect. During her four years at West Heath, Diana adored playing tennis, won several cups for swimming and diving, was a member of the lacrosse and field hockey teams, and again took extra ballet lessons, plus classes in ballroom and tap dancing. In 1976 she won the school dancing contest, judged by Betty Vacani. See JOBS. She also took up the piano, proving to have talent. See MUSIC. Academically, however, it was the same old story. She didn't pass a single O level, which was put down by one friend to the fact that they spent "all" their time reading hundreds of "slushy" romantic novels by Barbara Cartland "when we were supposed to be doing prep." See BOOKS and FAMILY. Diana also used to read the Court Circular in the *Daily Telegraph*, which outlines the public engagements of members of the Royal Family (it was in 1977, while she was a schoolgirl at West Heath, that she was introduced to Prince Charles at Althorp—see COURTSHIP), and spent a lot of time weeding, which was a punishment for misbehavior such as talking after lights out. Among her worst subjects were French, mathematics, and needlework. See ARTS & HANDICRAFTS. Having failed her GCE exams in English Language, English Literature, Geography, and Art, which she took in June 1977, Diana remained at the school until Christmas for a second attempt. In her last term before leaving in December 1977, she became a prefect and won the Miss Clark Lawrence Award, which may have consoled her once it became clear that she had failed her O levels for the second time. The award, given on occasion to a pupil whose efforts have "gone unsung," was for services to the school. When Diana won it, she told the headmistress, Ruth Rudge, that it was "one of the most surprising things" that had ever happened to her. Her lack of academic achievement cut deep, but she knew there was hope. According to one report, she cut out and kept an article she read on "successful gifted failures."

Less than four years later, Diana became the Princess of Wales, and there was a big welcome for her in November 1987 when she returned to the school with her sisters to open the Rudge sports hall, named after the headmistress, where she told the assembled staff and pupils in a brief speech:

I am delighted to have this opportunity to revisit West Heath and to pay tribute to Miss Rudge. I do, however, find it rather daunting to be standing up and speaking in front of so many—not least my past headmistress—as I feel sure that there are more practised and certainly better speakers than I in the audience. [See SPEECHES.]

My years at West Heath were certainly very happy ones. I made many friends whom I often see and in spite of what Miss Rudge and my other teachers may have thought I did actually learn something—though you would not have known by my O level results!

I cannot think of a better and more lasting memento to Ruth Rudge's years at the School, both as teacher and headmistress, than this magnificent Hall. Perhaps now, when future generations are handed out punishments for talking after lights, pillow fights, illegal food, they will be told to run six times round this Hall. It has to be preferable to the lacrosse pitch or weeding the garden—which I became a great expert at! It gives me great pleasure to open the Hall and to wish Miss Rudge every happiness in her retirement. After 37 years teaching at West Heath—it must be well deserved.

When Diana left West Heath, she was sixteen years old. She did not wear makeup, she had never been abroad, she had never even flown in a plane. More to the point, her French wasn't good and she had never had to stand on her own feet without the company or support of either family or friends. However, after Christmas 1977 she was sent to a finishing school called the Institut Alpin Videmanette at Château d'Oex near Gstaad in Switzerland, arriving months after most of the others girls, who had started in September. Diana met Sophie Kimball (see FRIENDS) and learned to ski, but she broke the rules by speaking English much of the time instead of French and was miserably homesick. After six weeks she decided she had had enough and returned to London. See JOBS.

F

FAMILY

If one thing has affected Diana's family (motto: "Dieu défend le droit") more than anything else, it is love. And like the Royal Family, with its various romantic goings-on, the Princess's would provide more than enough material for one of those glossy TV soap operas she so enjoys watching. Diana's parents married at Westminster Abbey at the biggest society wedding of 1954. The Queen and Prince Philip, the Queen Mother, and Princess Margaret were among the 1,500 guests. The eighteen-year-old bride, the Honorable Frances Roche, was the younger daughter of the 4th Baron Fermoy. See AMERICA. The bridegroom Johnnie, aged thirty-two, was then the dashing Viscount Althorp, heir to the 7th Earl Spencer. The couple began their family immediately, Diana's eldest sister, Sarah, being born nine months after the wedding, in March 1955. A second daughter, Jane, followed in 1957. In January 1960, a son, John, was born but died within ten hours. When Diana was the next baby to arrive, on July 1, 1961, her parents were so looking forward to a son that they hadn't even chosen a name for a girl. Diana weighed 7 pounds, 12 ounces. According to her father, "She was a delightful child, and as a baby she could have won any beauty competition." A son and heir, Charles, finally arrived in 1964. Ironically, Diana was the only child who did not have a member of the Royal Family as a godparent. The Queen Mother had become godmother to Sarah, the Duke of Kent godfather to Jane, and the Queen herself became godmother to Charles. Diana's godparents were John Floyd, who had been to Eton and Sandhurst with her father and later became Chairman of Christie's the auctioneers; Alexander Gilmour, her father's cousin and half-brother of the former Lord Privy Seal, Sir Ian Gilmour; Lady Mary Colman, a relative of the Queen Mother, wife of the Lord Lieutenant of Norfolk, and a former

Diana arranges her schedule to spend as much time as possible with her children. (Jim Bennett/Alpha)

Extra Lady-in-Waiting to Princess Alexandra; Sarah Pratt, who lived at Ryston Hall, Downham Market, close to Diana's childhood home, Park House, on the Queen's Sandringham estate in Norfolk; and Carol Fox, another neighbor who lived at Anmer Hall, which later became the home of the Duke and Duchess of Kent.

Until she was six years old, Diana's family life was normal and unbroken. Then, in the autumn of 1967, half the family disappeared. That September Diana's two elder sisters went off to boarding school. And in November her mother left home, having fallen in love with married wallpaper heir Peter Shand Kydd. That Christmas the nanny whom Diana and her brother Charles had shared for the previous couple of years also left. Although Diana's mother presumably expected to gain custody of her children and has always remained close to them, her departure was regarded as a scandal. Fuel was added to the flames in April 1968 when Peter Shand Kydd's wife, Janet, divorced him, citing Frances as "the other woman." The case was uncontested. That December, when Frances sought to divorce Johnnie on the grounds of cruelty, he did contest and was eventually granted a divorce on the grounds of his wife's adultery with Peter Shand Kydd. Frances lost custody of her children, and Peter lost custody of his. Frances found herself shunned by some people. Few married women, especially with children, go off with another man unless their marriage has long been unhappy—the departure from a husband being a symptom rather than the cause of marital breakdown. And although there was clearly another side to the story, it is one which Frances has never made public. Her second wedding, a quiet register office ceremony in 1969, was very different from her first. She and Peter Shand Kydd moved away to the south coast, later dividing their time between farming in Scotland near Perth and on the Isle of Seil (where Frances Shand Kydd breeds Shetland ponies and had a gift shop in Oban) and their thousand-acre sheep station in New South Wales, Australia. Diana's secret vacation in Australia in 1981, shortly after Prince Charles proposed to her, was the first time she had ever been there with them. See AUSTRALIA.

Few children emerge from a broken home unscathed, and the young Diana was deeply distressed by her parents' separation and divorce and the battle for custody. She coped with courage and only occasional tears, but nothing was ever quite the same again. Further fundamental changes in the children's home life were on their way and a whole series of adjustments had to be made. Having "lost" their mother, in 1975 they lost their grandfather when the 7th Earl Spencer died. They also lost their home at Park House. Their father, having succeeded to the earldom, inherited the family stately home, Althorp in Northamptonshire, and they then moved there. The following year further adjustments were required, on both sides, when Diana's father, now the 8th Earl Spencer, married Raine, the formidable daughter of romantic novelist Barbara Cartland, whose books Diana was devouring by the hundreds and mooning over at boarding school at West Heath. See EDUCATION and BOOKS. Raine, the mother of three sons and a daughter, had been married to the Earl of Dartmouth until she fell in love with Johnnie. No doubt it was a difficult time for all concerned.

When Diana had problems, she took them to her grand-mother Ruth, Lady Fermoy, who had become an Extra Woman of the Bedchamber to her friend the Queen Mother in 1956 and a Woman of the Bedchamber in 1960, recently succeeding Lady Angela Oswald as Lady-in-Waiting to the Queen Mother. Diana's father, Lord Spencer, had been an Equerry to King George VI from 1950 to 1952 and to the Queen from her accession to the throne on the death of her father that year until 1954. Having lived on the Sandringham estate, Diana and her family had had regular contact with members of the Royal Family, particularly the Queen's younger sons, Prince Andrew and Prince Edward (who were nearer Diana's age than Prince Charles or Princess Anne), and Princess Margaret's children. The family's royal connections were further strengthened by Diana's older sisters. Sarah, a red-head and the most extroverted of the girls (who had had a lively but troubled youth during which she had left West Heath school under a cloud and later developed anorexia), had made headlines, before her marriage to Neil McCorquodale in 1980, when she emerged as the latest in Prince Charles's long line of girlfriends. In fact, it was while Sarah was dating the Prince, in 1977, that she introduced Diana to him. And in 1978, Jane, Diana's other sister, married Robert Fellowes who had a key position at Buckingham Palace as Assistant Private Secretary to the Queen, becoming the Queen's Deputy Private Secretary in 1986 and her Private Secre-tary in the autumn of 1990 on the retirement of the Queen's long-term right-hand man, Sir William Heseltine. Jane and her husband, now Sir Robert, live at Kensington Palace, and Diana visited them there and at Balmoral when they followed the Queen to Scotland in August. Diana was at Balmoral when she was spotted with Prince Charles and their relationship became public knowledge. See COURTSHIP.

After the royal wedding, Diana's stepgrandmother, Barbara Cartland, declared of the royal match, "Just like a Barbara Cartland novel, dashing and adored, the Prince of Wales fell in love with the sweet, gentle, shy little girl who loved children. They were married in 1981 and the whole world prayed that they would live happily ever after." However, the flamboyant, larger-than-life Miss Cartland, always a vision in pink outfits, false eyelashes, and diamonds, was noticeably absent from the wedding at St. Paul's Cathedral, the rumor being that the Queen did not want her to attend. True or not, it was a sad omission because she is a splendid soul with her heart in the right place who talks a lot more sense than she is sometimes given credit for. But as you'd expect from such a woman, she put a brave face on it and graciously swept aside any embarrassment. For years she has been a superenergetic campaigner for purity, honey, health foods, and vitamins. A remarkable woman and no shrinking violet, Miss Cartland's list of achievements is the longest entry in *Who's Who*, dwarfing Mrs. Thatcher's. One of Miss Cartland's most devoted fans was the late Earl Mountbatten of Burma (whom she called "darling Dickie"). In the 1991 New Year Honors List, Miss Cartland, then aged eighty-nine and just completing her 530th novel, was made a Dame of the British Empire. One of her more surprising fans is Colonel Qaddafi of Libya.

Diana's great love of children and empathy with them probably stems from early childhood when she took her young brother, Charles, under her wing. The son and heir her parents had longed for after the tragic death of their first son four years before, Charles was born at the London Clinic in May 1964 when Diana was almost three. Flags flew at Althorp, where the 7th Earl still reigned, and at home at Park House in Norfolk the entire household celebrated. From the beginning Diana played mother hen, bossing him around in the nursery and helping the nanny look after him. In childhood, the royal children to whom he was closest were Princess Margaret's son David, Lord Linley, who broke his pop-gun, and daughter Lady Sarah Armstrong-Jones. After school at Silfield (see EDUCATION), Charles went on to Maidwell Hall, a boarding school near Northampton. From 1977 to 1979, he was a Page of Honor to the Queen, his godmother. He continued his education at Eton, where he learned to play the bagpipes and coedited the school newspaper, The Eton Chronicle, and at Magdalen College, Oxford, where he gained a degree in history. During his high-spirited undergraduate years, gossip columnists found him good fodder. But his nickname, Champagne Charlie, went back much further to childhood when, at the age of eight, he drank the dregs from empty champagne bottles at his grandfather's eightieth birthday party at Althorp and, a little bit tipsy, had to be carried to bed.

In 1986 Charlie got a job based in London as a £35,000-a-year television reporter for the American NBC morning news show Today. One of his TV assignments was to report on the wedding of Prince Andrew and Fergie. He dropped a clangor in his report by telling twelve million viewers that Fergie's father, Major Ronald Ferguson, had once romanced his mother, Frances. But apart from one revealing comment (see STAFF), he has remained very discreet about Diana, the older sister with whom he still enjoys a gossip. "I could make a fortune writing a book about Diana," he once admitted, "but of course I never would. I am so proud of her, the way she has handled everything. She works so hard." He doesn't envy her her royal role, knowing what she has to "put up with."

Viscount Althorp will one day inherit Althorp, about sixteen thousand acres of land, and be worth around £15 million. But after the arrival of his stepmother, Raine Spencer, changes were made at the stately home. However, Raine, who has been much criticized outside the family, not least for the changes to Althorp (one critic likening the redecorated stately home to "the inside of a summer pudding"), *has* managed to keep the place going. In 1982, nine years before the 1991 public controversy on the subject in Britain, the *Daily Mail* quoted her as saying,

> If you believed everything you read in the newspapers, you would think I married [Johnnie] for his money and that we were selling off all the family treasures to keep me in my old age. I sound like a monster. But I can't be that much of a monster, can I? Would such an idiot or such a monster be asked by the Government three times to prepare reports for them? People don't realize I've been in public life for 26 years. . . . We do everything we can to keep [Althorp] going and all we get back is a pittance—6,000 visitors a year at £1 a head. Of course, we had a bit of luck with Diana . . . but all the extra visitors have cracked the library ceiling.

Charlie expected to marry young. "All my sisters did—it's a family habit," he said in 1984. "I am very impetuous when it comes to matters of the heart. I'm a romantic and can fall head-over-heels in love very easily." Which is exactly what he did. Around May 1989, then twenty-five, Charlie met ex-*Vogue* model Victoria Lockwood, aged twenty-four, and they fell for each other hook, line, and sinker. After a whirlwind six-week romance, he proposed on bended knee and bought her an 1850 ruby-and-diamond engagement ring with two hearts entwined beneath an earl's coronet, estimated to be worth between £10,000 and £30,000. Genealogist Harold Brooks-Baker told the *Sunday Times* that the fact that Charlie, who was "descended from one of 153 landed families in Britain dating back to William the Conqueror," had chosen to wed a middle-class girl was "a knife in the back of class distinction." Diana, who had been critical of some of her brother's former girlfriends, met the "deliriously happy" couple at Kensington Palace and gave her approval. "All the ones in my family who matter adore her," Charlie declared. But his American TV boss, NBC executive Karen Curry, warned, "Look out—he's married to his job. Victoria should expect lonely nights as he rings from various corners of the world." And one of his close friends was quoted as saying, "[Charlie] really doesn't get on at all well with Raine Spencer. That will make things a bit fraught at the wedding since they will probably get married in a church near Althorp and hold the reception there."

Sure enough, the wedding took place in September 1989 at the twelfth-century church of St. Mary the Virgin in Great Brington, Northamptonshire, near the family stately home. Chief among the guests, who arrived under umbrellas in a steady downpour, were Charles and Diana, Frances Shand Kydd (who had recently separated from her second husband and who in 1991 was reported to have married champagne expert Marie Pierre Palmer), and Barbara Cartland, as always in shocking pink. Summer sunshine would have added to the fun of the eighteenth-century-style wedding. The bride arrived seventeen minutes late in a horse-drawn 1760 coach escorted by four "cavalier" horsemen styled after the Three Musketeers, complete with stuck-on mustaches. (Prince Harry, aged five, was a pageboy dressed musketeer-style as well.) But the bride's long dark hair went lank in the damp weather, and her unusual gold silk wedding gown provoked savage comments from the Press, who thought it resembled a "designer dishcloth" or "an old pair of curtains." Finally, Charlie's car broke down in the rain on the way to the airport to catch their honeymoon flight, and it had to be towed back to Althorp. The laugh that Charlie had raised at the wedding reception shortly beforehand was also of a watery nature. According to one report, in his speech he consoled the bride's parents by saying that they were not losing a daughter, they were "gaining Raine."

In February 1991, Diana's brother confessed that in March 1990, six months after his wedding, he had had a one-night stand in Paris with an old flame, glamorous thirty-one-year-old divorcée Sally Ann Lasson, a columnist for the society magazine *Tatler* and also a cartoonist. It happened, Viscount Althorp said, when his marriage was going through an "extremely unpleasant patch." But he had made it up with Victoria, who was quoted as saying, "We are together and will continue to be so." Charles and Victoria's daughter Kitty was born in December 1990. *Daily Mail* gossip columnist Nigel Dempster, who broke the story, quoted Althorp as saying, "I have caused my wife more grief than I would wish her to have in a lifetime with me. I accept full responsibility for the folly of my actions. Now, a month after the birth of our baby, we are deeply in love and our marriage is the most important thing in our lives. Victoria is profoundly upset, but has asked me to say that our marriage will not be destroyed by a woman who belonged to our unhappy past." Diana's brother made his public confession after learning that Sally Ann had sold her kiss-and-tell memoirs to a Sunday newspaper, the *News of the World*. See GULF WAR. Later the *Tatler* announced that it had "ended its association" with her. In March 1991, Althorp revealed that he was also changing jobs: having resigned from the NBC "Today" program, he had "several things lined up in British television." His departure from the American show had no connection with the publicity over his extramarital fling.

Someone once remarked that Raine Spencer is not so much a person as "an experience," and certainly she doesn't produce lukewarm responses. Even her name allegedly prompted resentful chants, when she moved into Althorp, of "Raine, Raine, go away." Comments she is alleged to have made about her stepdaughters include the following. On Sarah: "Sarah is okay while she sticks to hunting and shooting, which is all she cares about." On Jane: "Jane's all right just as long as she keeps producing more children. That's about all she is good for." And on Diana: "How can you have an intelligent conversation with someone who doesn't have a single O level? It's a crashing bore"; and "If you said 'Afghanistan' to Diana, she'd think it was a cheese." Raine admitted that the problems of inheriting stepchildren, which so many stepparents and stepchildren go through, have at times been "bloody awful." See RELATE. She was quoted as saying, "Sarah resented me . . . and Jane didn't speak to me for two years."

Then in September 1978, Lord Spencer went into a near-fatal coma after suffering a severe stroke. Raine took charge and moved mountains to get him whatever was needed. Jean Rook of the *Daily Express* quoted her as saying, "I'm a survivor, and people forget that at their peril. There's pure steel up my backbone. Nobody destroys me, and nobody was going to destroy Johnnie so long as I could sit by his bed—some of his family tried to stop me—and will my life force into him." She refused to let him die, and he survived. "Raine saved my life," Lord Spencer declared later. "Without Raine I wouldn't have lived to see Diana married, never mind walking up the aisle of St. Paul's. Raine sat with me for four solid months, holding my hand and even shouting at me that I wasn't going to die because she wouldn't let me." He finally came around to the sounds of his favorite opera. See MUSIC and

WEDDING. Even so, Raine told Jean Rook, "You're never going to make me sound like a human being, because people like to think I'm Dracula's mother." She was, she said, "absolutely sick of the Wicked Stepmother lark."

After Diana became engaged to Prince Charles, Lord Spencer remarked, "Sometimes I feel very worried, as if I'll never see her again—later, yes, but not for the first few years, when I'll be watching her, like everyone else, on telly." But that didn't prove the case. See MARRIAGE. One of Lord Spencer's proudest moments was when he watched Diana receiving the Freedom of the Borough of Northampton, her home stamping ground, in June 1989. Later he remarked, "Someone said to me recently that the two most famous people in the world are the Pope and my daughter. I am so proud." But he worries about her too. See PUBLIC ENGAGEMENTS.

FAMOUS RELATIVES

Diana has numerous famous relatives, including, of course, Prince Charles himself (see COURTSHIP) and her stepgrandmother, Barbara Cartland, the world's most celebrated romantic novelist. See BOOKS and FAMILY. Her cousins past and present, distant or otherwise, include: King Juan Carlos of Spain; the Aga Khan; United States Presidents George Washington, Calvin Coolidge, and Franklin D. Roosevelt; British Prime Ministers Sir Winston Churchill and Sir Alec Douglas-Home (now Baron Home of the Hirsel); Oliver Cromwell; Bismarck; Lawrence of Arabia; film stars Humphrey Bogart, Olivia de Havilland, Rudolph Valentino, Lee Remick, Orson Welles, and Lillian Gish; tycoon Nelson Bunker Hunt; heiress and jeans designer Gloria Vanderbilt, who attended the banquet given by the Reagans for Charles and Diana at the White House (see AMERICA); writers Samuel Pepys, George Sand, Jane Austen, Louisa M. Alcott, Erle Stanley Gardner, Ralph Waldo Emerson, George Orwell, Virginia Woolf, Graham Greene, Lady Antonia Fraser (wife of Harold Pinter), Harriet Beecher Stowe, and Washington Post Editor in Chief Ben Bradlee; portrait painter John Singer Sargent; philosopher Bertrand Russell; and Lord Lucan, the missing British peer involved in the world's most baffling high-society murder case who was a pal of the Princess's friend, Nicholas Soames, an MP and an Extra Equerry to Prince Charles. See FRIENDS. Five of Diana's ancestors were the mistresses of kings: Arabella Churchill of King James II; Frances, Countess of Jersey, of King George IV; and Barbara Palmer, Duchess of Cleveland; Louise de Keroualle, Duchess of Portsmouth; and Lucy Walter were among the many mistresses of King Charles II.

FASHION

Entire books have been written about Diana's clothes sense. Suffice it to say that she has not only brought youthful elegance and chic to royal dressing (which had always been safe rather than sensational), and introduced fun and style in her off-duty gear, but she has single-handedly revitalized the British fashion industry. Trends she has set, which earned her the accolade from the United States of being the world's most influential woman of fashion, have included blouses with frills or neck ruffles; crinoline gowns; picture sweaters like the famous one depicting sheep from Warm & Wonderful (see SHOPPING); sailor collars; polka dots; the Cossack look; anklets worn with a skirt; two-tone court shoes; flats and low heels; baggy-leg boots and cowboy boots; hats (in particular, veiled hats, "flying saucers," and baseball caps); and stockings of all descriptions, including colored, patterned, and fishnet tights, black nylons with seams and others with bows, tassels, or other decorations at the heel; and more—without even mentioning her pearl choker necklaces and hairstyles, which have been copied by women worldwide. See JEWELRY, BEAUTY SECRETS, and SPORT. In 1989 she gave calf-length culottes the royal seal of approval when she donned a bright red pair to take the children to school and a pleated pair, also in red, to visit HMS Cornwall that October. See ARMED FORCES.

To suggest that any woman in her position with the funds and access to top designers could look the same would be missing the point. Diana's style did not come with her fame and fortune: she was a trailblazer fashionwise long before the royal wedding. Remember the bachelor-girl knickerbockers? She had a sense of color and a clever knack of knowing what would go with what to

Diana's natural flair for fashion is admired throughout the world. (David Parker/Globe Photos)

produce an effectively simple but stylish look without being fussy or contrived. Her dress sense was one of the first things Prince Charles noticed about her and approved. Even at school, doing weeding as a punishment for some misdemeanor in a pair of jeans, her headmistress at West Heath, Miss Ruth Rudge, noticed a "distinction" about the way she dressed. Of course, she's had her disasters, but that was only to be expected. One minute she was an unknown teenager, cycling around London and helping at a kindergarten; the next she was having to dress for photo sessions, public engagements, and televised events watched by millions. How would *you* cope if you had to dress as if you were going to a wedding several times a week? See QUOTES. Diana's engagement suit, blue to match the oval sapphire in her engagement ring, was bought ready-made from Harrods. That choice, and others later, was influenced by her mother, Mrs. Frances Shand Kydd, who also led her to milliner John Boyd, who has since made many of the Princess's hats, including the tiny head-toppers with veils and bows which were such a feature of her wardrobe during her 1983 tour of Australia and New Zealand. She takes a size 7½ hat. See QUOTES. She also had help early on from staff at *Vogue* magazine, where both her sisters had worked. She'd slip in to their office via a rear entrance and strip down to bra and panties to try on clothes selected for her by Editor in Chief Beatrix Miller and Deputy Fashion Editor Anna Harvey. Nowadays designers turn up at Kensington Palace with their fabric samples and sketches to discuss the outfits she will need, for example, for forthcoming tours overseas.

Quite apart from color, style, and the need to keep certain parts of the body covered to avoid offending custom in various countries (which can mean having to wear calf-length high-necked dresses with long sleeves), skirts can't be too short because she doesn't want children or photographers peering up them, and sleeves can't be too tight or she'd risk tearing the seams when she reaches up or over to shake hands or accept flowers from people in the crowds. She now also avoids low-cut gowns which display cleavage. See X-RATED. Wind is her great enemy, but she has her skirts weighted to avoid embarrassing displays, and her hats incorporate a special device to anchor them down.

Apart from the visits from her designers, the Princess also likes to shop for herself. The very successful white dress with red dots which she wore in Japan in May 1986 came off-the-rack from a boutique called Tatters on London's Fulham Road. She has visited the ready-to-wear shop of Prince Charles's Australian designer friend Lady Tryon, called Kanga (for kangaroo) after his nickname for her, and has worn several of her designs. She has also bought off-the-rack clothes by Jaeger and Miss Antoinette, and she regularly shops for herself and the children at branches of the Italian fashion chain Benetton. See SHOPPING. She wears British dress sizes 10 or 12, depending on the maker.

Her designers are the *crème de la crème*: Catherine Walker, the ultradiscreet French-born head of the Chelsea Design Company; Victor Edelstein, creator of some of her most lovely evening dresses; her friend Bruce Oldfield, a guru of glamour (see BARNARDO'S); Belville Sassoon, whose exquisitely made clothes and fairy-tale gowns would make any woman wearing them feel like a princess; David and Elizabeth Emanuel, now apart, who made her breathtaking ivory silk wedding dress; Yuki, who designed the sapphire blue gown she wore for an audience with Emperor Hirohito of Japan in Tokyo; Hachi, who designed that now very familiar slinky white beaded off-one-shoulder number which she wore twice to James Bond film premieres (see MONEY); Gina Fratini; Jasper Conran; Donald Campbell; Jan Vanvelden; Bill Pashley; David Neil; Caroline Charles; Rifat Ozbek; Arabella Pollen; Benny Ong; Jacques Azagury; Murray Arbeid; Anouska Hempel; Zandra Rhodes; Roland Klein; Alistair Blair; Graham Wren; Paul Costelloe . . . the list goes on and on. Plus, of course, her milliners, headed by Philip Somerville and including John Boyd, Viv Knowlands, Frederick Fox, Marina Killery, who made Diana's first Cossack-style fake fur hat—the Princess avoids wearing real fur—worn in December 1984 in Shrewsbury; and Graham Smith of Kangol.

Although she is so feminine, the Princess likes dressing up as one of the boys. She got the white tuxedo worn with a white blouse, black trousers, and black satin bow tie, which she wore to a rock concert in Birmingham in 1984, from designer Margaret Howell. Three years later, she turned up at a charity do at London's Hippodrome nightclub in a black tuxedo with a fuchsia bow tie and cummerbund made by Catherine Walker. She also wore the black tux again for a charity evening at Wembley Greyhound Stadium in 1988, together with a green silk waistcoat from Hackett, the London menswear shop. See DANCING. She has even had

her own versions of male military uniforms made up. See UNI-
FORMS.

On her tours, Diana makes a point of making diplomatic
fashion gestures when she can, usually on the first day. On her
early tour of Wales, she wore the Welsh colors of red and green;
in Japan in 1986, the red-dotted white dress in tribute to the
Japanese flag; in Nigeria in March 1990, a Catherine Walker dress
in the national colors of green and white. The same applies, where
possible, at single engagements at home. For a concert given by the
National Children's Orchestra, of which she is Patron (see OR-
CHESTRAS), Diana deliberately wore a dress in exactly the same
cherry red shade as the outfits worn by the musicians. Which all
goes to show how much advance planning goes into her choice of
clothes. Though in private she wears garments by famous foreign
designers like Valentino (and very sexy some of them are said to
be), in public she flies the flag by almost always wearing British
designs. However, tact overseas pays dividends too. Since she
wants to create a good first impression, on the first day of a visit
abroad she occasionally wears an outfit from that country. At a
reception in Berlin in 1987, she wore a yellow-and-black woolen
coat from Escada, a German fashion house. And in Paris in 1988,
she arrived flatteringly dressed in Chanel.

Public engagements pose a problem because the Princess
needs so many clothes. And that puts her in a catch-22 situation.
Diana hates suggestions that she's a fashion shopaholic who
spends fortunes on clothes (see MONEY), though Charles, who is
as thrifty as the Queen, has been said to blanch at some of her
bills. The Princess herself says that clothes are not her big thing,
whatever people think. See QUOTES. However, her name is syn-
onymous with fashion. She needs new outfits, especially for her
visits and tours overseas where crowds become very disappointed,
as they did in Australia, Italy, and Japan, if she doesn't turn up in
something stunning which has never been seen before. The only
way she can win is to pack a judicious mix and alternate something old with something new, which is what she generally does.
Perhaps to make up for any earlier disappointment, or carping
from the fashion critics, she often chooses to turn up on the last
evening of a visit or tour in something new and spectacular as a

finale—as she did in Australia when she first wore that slinky Hachi sheath, the sexiest garment ever seen on a member of the British Royal Family.

The Princess has umpteen pairs of shoes, in bright colors as well as the more serviceable black to match her more vibrant outfits. Apart from having shoes specially made for her at Rayne, she's also bought shoes from Hobbs, Charles Jourdan, Manolo Blahnik, Midas, Russell & Bromley, Harrods, and branches of Bertie's in London. She has a habit of slipping her shoes off whenever she gets the chance, under the table at restaurants, for instance. See ITALY. But when her feet ache on duty—and she's frequently on her feet all day—that's not always possible. So she's come up with a clever idea to ease the strain. When she thinks it will be necessary, she sets off for an engagement with *two* pairs of shoes, plus handbags, all of which coordinate with her outfit. One pair of shoes she wears on her feet: the other is kept in reserve by her Lady-in-Waiting, who also keeps track of the extra handbag. And when Diana's feet get hot or tired, she simply slips on the cool, fresh pair of shoes and switches handbags. See JAPAN. This ploy, however, does not always go without a hitch. During the welcoming ceremony for her old friends the King and Queen of Spain, who were on a state visit to Britain, Diana, presumably in some discomfort, was seen mouthing, "Where are my other shoes?" The message got passed from the Crown Equerry to her Lady-in-Waiting, but no extra pair turned up; whether or not they had accidentally been left behind, she just had to grin and bear it. Once home, Diana kicks off her shoes and makes a point of pampering her feet. See BEAUTY SECRETS.

Gloves were once considered obligatory for ladies in the Royal Family and for women about to be presented to them. In fact, in Austria years ago, one girl borrowed a huge pair from a hotel commissionaire, who unfortunately had fingers like bananas, rather than miss shaking hands with the Queen. Princess Michael of Kent allegedly wrote to the organizer of one charity event, even in recent times, insisting that ladies who were due to shake her hand should wear gloves. Though other royal ladies still regard them as part of their outfits, Diana does not like wearing gloves, possibly because she was forced to wear them to church as a schoolgirl. See EDUCATION. Even when her aides have advised her that it might be wise to wear them (as, for example, for a Naval encounter at sea which meant gripping wet, slippery rails), it was noticeable that she didn't. However, she carries gloves about at Royal Ascot, where the Royal Enclosure rules demand them, and sometimes wears warm gloves for cold-weather days or long satin or taffeta ones for very dressy evening events. Even then, she has managed to be different and visually exciting. In 1986, for a ball in London, she wore one red and one black long satin evening glove with a sensational flamenco-ish red-and-black gown by Murray Arbeid, which looked stunning.

And what does she wear underneath? The Princess buys slinky silk underwear and teddies in soft pastel shades from shops like Fenwicks, Liberty's, Bradleys of Knightsbridge, Night Owls on Fulham Road, where she shopped for part of her trousseau, and Janet Reger. Other Reger fans include Fergie; Jerry Hall, who likes frillies in bottle green and coral-and-black; and Joan Collins, who prefers classic plain black. Diana has apparently also obtained uplift from Balance Bras, who make brassieres for the Queen Mother and Princess Margaret. She likes lightweight white, lacy bras, as the Press cameras recorded when her beige top sagged revealingly as she bent down to accept a posy of flowers from a child in south London in July 1989. In private, it seems, she doesn't always wear one—at least according to disc jockey Martin Milsome, who watched her boogying at the Casa Antica nightclub at Klosters one year in a sexy white blouse and tight leather pants. He was quoted as saying, "She was definitely not wearing a bra. Several guys were very turned on by her and, if she wasn't a princess, I'm sure they'd have chatted her up." Prince Charles, whom she has got wearing boxer shorts, likes lovely lingerie. In February 1987, he picked up a pair of frilly white pant slips, designed by a fifteen-year-old schoolboy who had been assigned to a textile firm to study industry, and remarked, "That's a nice bit of stuff." In 1989, as a thank-you to Charles, he was presented with a silk and lace teddy for Diana by Christine Arthurs and Janet Downend, whose Cinderella Underwear company in Derbyshire, specializing in making camisoles, pant slips, and negligees, got off the ground with £3,000 from the Prince's Youth Business Trust. When the weather's cold, however, Diana wears cozy thermal underwear. When she opened the new Parkhead psychiatric hospital in Glasgow in 1989, Betty Ramsay, aged fifty-five, who had stood shivering outside in the cold for two hours to see her, shook her hand and remarked, "My, your hands are warm!" Diana replied, "I'm lovely and warm. I was expecting Scottish weather so I'm wearing thermal underwear." To another frozen housewife in the crowd, the Princess said, "Haven't you got your thermals on?"

To look through her fashions of the past ten years is to see Diana coming totally into her own. In her early years as a princess, anxious, unsure, and eager to please, she tended to wear possibly what she thought she should wear, what her mother and other older advisers suggested. Many of her outfits then were fussy and aging. And the overall shape, given those little hats perched like nests on top of her head, wasn't always flattering. But now she has the measure of herself and dares to be different: her own woman in fashion terms as well as personally. Though she still has the odd miss (see ITALY and SPAIN), more often she scores a hit. In recent years, with the invaluable help and encouragement of her brilliant top team of Catherine Walker and Philip Somerville (Somerville designs each hat shape to complement Catherine Walker's dress design, using the same fabrics or colors in both), Diana has gone for a total look which is absolutely hers: a sleek, svelte, V shape tapering down from a wide-brimmed Somerville hat, with great simplicity of line and cut and absolutely no fussy detail, in one, two, or at the most three plain but very striking colors. Ultimate chic and absolutely unbeatable. The new look was exemplified by the sensational red-and-pink outfit which she wore in Dubai in March 1989, and the red, purple, and cream one which she rewore at Royal Ascot in 1990. Simplicity, style, and elegance. Diana has them all and whatever the cost, wherever she goes, they put her very clearly in a class of her own. But what *do* they do (or fail to do) with royal ladies' hemlines, especially on coats? I know the hems of quality garments aren't supposed to be pressed, but sometimes they look *terrible*.

FAVORITE THINGS

Diana's favorite things, past and present, in no special order include:

Authors:
◆ Dame Barbara Cartland
◆ Barbara Taylor Bradford
◆ Colleen McCullough
◆ Danielle Steele
◆ Daphne du Maurier
◆ Mary Stewart
◆ Jeffrey Archer

Classical composers:
◆ Rachmaninoff
◆ Grieg
◆ Schumann
◆ Tchaikovsky
◆ Mozart
◆ Verdi
◆ Dvořák

Colors:
◆ pink
◆ red
◆ purple
◆ yellow
◆ blue

Dancers:
◆ Mikhail Baryshnikov
◆ John Travolta
◆ Wayne Sleep
◆ Dame Margot Fonteyn
◆ Fred Astaire

Fashion designers:
- ◆ Catherine Walker
- ◆ Victor Edelstein
- ◆ Bruce Oldfield
- ◆ Bellville Sassoon

Film stars:
- ◆ Clint Eastwood
- ◆ Robert Redford
- ◆ Michael Douglas
- ◆ Tom Selleck
- ◆ Roger Moore

Food:
- ◆ shepherd's pie
- ◆ kippers
- ◆ plaice
- ◆ chicken
- ◆ pasta
- ◆ fruit
- ◆ vegetables
- ◆ salad
- ◆ pizzas
- ◆ bacon sandwiches
- ◆ Chinese carryouts
- ◆ Twiglets

Hymn:
- ◆ "I Vow to Thee My Country"

Jewels:
- ◆ sapphires
- ◆ fun fake jewelry

Makeup:
◆ Colourings
◆ Clinique
◆ Christian Dior

Milliner:
◆ Philip Somerville

Nightclub:
◆ Annabel's

Opera singers:
◆ Dame Kiri Te Kanawa
◆ Luciano Pavarotti

Pop bands and stars:
◆ Supertramp
◆ Dire Straits
◆ Kid Creole and the Coconuts
◆ Genesis
◆ Spandau Ballet
◆ 10 cc
◆ Neil Diamond
◆ Barry Manilow
◆ Michael Jackson
◆ Diana Ross
◆ Tina Turner
◆ Phil Collins
◆ Eric Clapton
◆ Paul Young
◆ Jean Michel Jarre
◆ Bryan Ferry
◆ Elton John

Radio station:
◆ Capital Radio, London

Records:
◆ "Dreamer"—Supertramp
◆ "Breakfast in America"—Supertramp
◆ "Uptown Girl"—Billy Joel
◆ "Chain Reaction"—Diana Ross
◆ "Can't Smile Without You"—Barry Manilow
◆ "Dancing in the Street"—David Bowie and Mick Jagger
◆ "Once Upon a Long Ago"—Paul McCartney
◆ "Mull of Kintyre"—Paul McCartney
◆ "Cracklin' Rose"—Neil Diamond
◆ "Sweet Caroline"—Neil Diamond
◆ "True"—Spandau Ballet
◆ "One More Night"—Phil Collins
◆ "Your Love Is King"—Sade
◆ "Two Young Lovers"—Dire Straits
◆ "Love of the Common People"—Paul Young
◆ "Annie I'm Not Your Daddy"—Kid Creole and the Coconuts
◆ "Don't Go Breaking My Heart"—Elton John and Kiki Dee
◆ The *Top Gun* theme

Restaurants:
◆ San Lorenzo
◆ Launceston Place
◆ Ménage à Trois
◆ Green's Champagne, Oyster Bar & Restaurant
◆ Harry's Bar

Scents:
◆ Miss Dior
◆ Diorissimo
◆ Passion by Annick Goutal

Sweets and chocolate:
◆ cream eggs

◆ fruit pastilles
◆ toffees
◆ Opal Fruits
◆ wine gums
◆ Mars bars
◆ Kit Kat bars
◆ Yorkie bars
◆ Lindt chocolate
◆ Bendick's Bittermints
◆ homemade fudge (see COOKING)

Television programs:
◆ "Blind Date"
◆ "Bread"
◆ "Brookside"
◆ "The Clothes Show"
◆ "Crossroads"
◆ "Dallas"
◆ "Dynasty"
◆ "EastEnders"
◆ "Home and Away"
◆ "Neighbours"

Theater show:
◆ *Phantom of the Opera*, starring Michael Crawford

TV snack:
◆ eggs Benedict

FIJI

The royal couple's shortest official overseas visit to date was to Fiji in November 1985. The Royal Australian Air Force jet taking Charles and Diana for their tour to Australia had stopped at Fiji to refuel on the way out; it returned them for the one-hour visit on the way back, en route to Hawaii. Without even leaving the airport tarmac, Prince Charles inspected a guard of honor of red-jacketed Fijian soldiers in white skirts with zigzag hems. He and Diana then sat in a native pavilion, built for the occasion, to watch some plump, grass-skirted Fijians performing a dance of welcome, ending when they prostrated themselves at the royal feet.

FOOD & DRINK

As a child, the school meal Diana loved best was shepherd's pie, the British beef-and-onion pie topped with mashed potatoes. She also adored baked beans, and at West Heath school she used to eat up to *four* bowls of All-Bran for breakfast! She still likes All-Bran and baked beans, plus foods like spinach quiche, egg dishes, cheese soufflés, salads, baked potatoes in their jackets, and sorbet rather than a heavy pudding. She and her family eat lots of garden-fresh vegetables, including carrots, zucchini, cabbages, potatoes, peppers, and turnips which avid gardener Charles grows at High-grove. At Kensington Palace they even grow tomatoes on their roof garden. Diana didn't eat pasta at the time of their Italian tour (see ITALY), but it later became such a favorite that the royal couple hired a special pasta chef. See STAFF. Gourmet Charles likes filled pasta: ravioli and agnolotti; Diana, ribbon pasta like macaroni and spaghetti. And before her pasta lunch, the chef's Warm Scampi Salad starter: fresh boiled scampi served on lettuce with grapefruit and orange segments. But the biggest pasta fan in the family is William.

Being environmentally aware and health-conscious, they like food to be fresh, organic if possible, and unadulterated. Diana likes Earl Grey tea with lemon (the Queen drinks tea without milk or lemon). The Princess also buys noncaffeine herbal teas, including lemon verbena, from suppliers like Culpeper in London. See SHOPPING. Charles doesn't drink coffee. Diana drinks decaffeinated. Though they are *not* vegetarians, the Prince eats less meat than he once did. They both prefer to avoid red meat and pork. According to Brian Hoey in *The New Royal Court*, Charles refuses to have any meat in his homes from animals reared with artificial stimulants like growth hormones. Diana prefers fish anyway. See MONEY. (None of the Royal Family use fish knives and forks, which are considered middle-class.) One of Charles's favorite dishes is smoked salmon with scrambled eggs. They believe in balanced eating and at home eat light meals based on fruit and vegetables, chicken, fish, and seafood, including salmon, lobster, crab, and prawns. The Princess, a good cook, has revealed several of her recipes. See COOKING. In October 1990, a seed company named a runner bean the Lady Di. See NAMES.

There have been constant stories about Diana being "fussy" about food and just picking at it. But she prefers not to eat while traveling by air. And she "loathes" being watched while eating in public, so sometimes she eats in private or at home before a formal meal. Like most of the royals, she prefers plain cooking to the fancy stuff that tends to be served at banquets. One of her pet hates is having mountains of food served up for her. She would much rather have something *light*. If she's at some stand-up buffet reception, as she herself has pointed out, she often ends up chasing a piece of chicken around a plate because it simply isn't possible to eat and talk to all the people being introduced to her at the same time. So assumptions that she has a poor appetite (see HEALTH) are off base. She has been known to eat a double helping at an official dinner (see FRANCE), and once declared, "I have an enormous appetite, despite what people say, and so has William. He takes after his mother." She has even been said to have secret binges, raiding the fridge at night.

Given a choice when she eats out privately, the Princess often chooses a light appetizer like avocado pear, then Dover sole or some other fish dish or pasta for the main course, and a creamy pudding like crème brûlée or a sorbet to finish. At the Commonwealth Games village in Edinburgh in July 1986, when she had a self-service cafeteria meal which she ate with a plastic knife and fork, she selected an orange and litchi fruit cocktail, cold Scotch salmon with salad, crème caramel, and a glass of grapefruit juice. She often drinks mineral water with meals. But those who prepare food for the Princess on royal visits should remember that you can have too much of a good thing. At a clinic for alcoholics which she visited in Rotherham, South Yorkshire, in October 1987, Diana spotted the salad lunch which was being made for her and groaned, "Oh, no! Everywhere I go, they give me salad." At official dinners, particularly on overseas tours, where Diana can find herself facing unfamiliar local delicacies like Arabian roast sheep with the head and eyes intact, oysters and other shellfish tend to be kept off the menu to avoid the risk of laying the royals low with gippy tummies.

In her single days in London before her marriage, Diana didn't eat breakfast or a balanced diet, but domesticity and motherhood changed that. On the 1983 tour of Australia and New Zealand, when she had whole-wheat toast and honey, the chef at one stop sent out for Special K and All-Bran after a valet passed on a message that she'd like cereal as well. She has talked of eating "my Weetabix" (a wheat, cookie-like cereal) and is said to like Harvest Crunch. She also enjoys Alpen Cruesli, muesli with corn and barley, and William and Harry like Weetabix Weetos, chocolate-flavored wheat hoops. Diana is also reported to like breakfasting on pink grapefruit and yogurt. Charles, it has been claimed, has had special muesli imported from Australia. In London in March 1988, when Charles asked a building site cook what he cooked for breakfast and was told, "Sausage, bacon, egg, beans, and tomato," he joked, "It is probably better than we've had." He loves sausages, provided they are additive-free ones using only the best, natural ingredients. In 1989 he was reported to get sausages delivered every week from butcher Michael Newitt's shop at Thame in Oxfordshire, specializing in several varieties, including pork, beef, and wild boar!

Charles takes some of the organic fruit and vegetables grown at Highgrove up to Scotland to eat on vacation. Lovage, which he also grows, is a good savory addition, he reckons, to soups and stews, and he is also said to have tried making nettle soup and dandelion wine. Guests are sometimes lucky enough to be given gifts of produce from the royal garden. When billionaire Armand Hammer (see AMERICA) visited Highgrove, Charles gave him boxes of fresh strawberries, adding, "I picked them myself this morning."

Despite their health-conscious eating, the royal couple also treat themselves sometimes to rich, fattening foods, convenience foods, and even junk foods. Among Charles's favorite fattening treats are chocolate cake and bread-and-butter pudding, which was a favorite of Diana's too as a child. She adores bacon sandwiches (see QUOTES), likes eating pork pie with Branston pickle, apparently loves fish-and-chips wrapped in newspaper (Charles used to have them from a local chip shop when he first acquired Highgrove, before cooking facilities were installed), and has a passion for pizzas. (British chips are a larger, softer version of french fries. What Americans call potato chips, the British call crisps.) She enjoys Chinese and Indian curry carryouts and also hamburgers, revealing in October 1986, "I've got into the habit of sending out to McDonald's for hamburgers for the boys. The trouble is I often end up eating them myself!" See RESTAURANTS.

During her first pregnancy, she developed a craving for kippers (strong-smelling dried, smoked herring, popular at breakfast), which she said "stank out" Kensington Palace and made everyone "glad when William was born." "I like plaice," she said, visiting Newlyn's new £1 million fish market in Cornwall in July 1988, "but kippers are my favorite. I ate them all the time when I was pregnant." And guess what she likes to dive into when she returns home from an official engagement? Custard. She once told Cliff Richard, "It's so nice to get home and have a bowl of custard."

Diana's sweet tooth could, of course, cause weight problems. In her single days, Diana practically lived on Mars bars. She also loves Kit Kat and Yorkie bars, fruit pastilles, and Opal Fruits. She loves chewing toffees while watching tennis at Wimbledon. See FAVORITE THINGS. But because she takes regular exercise (see HEALTH and SPORT), she manages to stay slim without having to go on diets, which she has said she couldn't keep to anyway. In June 1988 as she tucked into a packet of potato chips (crisps) saying, "Salt and vinegar [flavor]—lovely!" she told Press reporters, "You keep writing that I'm on a diet, but I'm not."

Flour milled from organic wheat grown on the Duchy of Cornwall Home Farm at Highgrove is used in the Highgrove Stoneground whole-wheat bread sold by the Tesco supermarket chain. The Duke of Cornwall's Benevolent Fund benefits from sales, which began in July 1990. Charles also supplies Tesco with "stress-free" lamb, reared humanely and on a vegetarian diet, on Duchy of Cornwall land treated with a minimum of fertilizer. (The Prince is the Duke of Cornwall.) Cuts of the "traditionally reared prime Cornish lamb," packed in green biodegradable trays marked with the Duchy of Cornwall crest, went on sale for a trial period in March 1991 at stores in Truro, Cornwall, and in Sandhurst, Berkshire. Despite the fact that they cost about 15 percent more than ordinary lamb, they were snapped up by eager shoppers—the Sandhurst branch selling 240 pounds of lamb in a couple of hours. In Truro, one man bought £30 worth, declaring, "You only have to look at it to see how good it is." The Prince is also helping design a new supermarket on the outskirts of Dorchester, Dorset, for Tesco. Tesco, quite separately from that and the royal bread and lamb sales, is raising £1 million for the charity Birthright, of which the Princess is Patron.

Before Charles and Diana's visit to Brazil in April 1991, Brazilian chefs who had been hoping to serve spicy local foods like Feijoada (prepared with garlic, onions, black beans, and pork) were reportedly asked by Palace aides to serve plainer food instead. The Brazilians were apparently told that the Princess has an allergy to hot peppers and spices. Generally speaking, the Royal Family tend not to eat garlic on public occasions, presumably in order to remain nice to be near.

As for drinking alcohol, some people—including Louis, the manager at Annabel's, London's most exclusive nightclub and a royal haunt, who can reel off what members of the Royal Family like to drink there: Princess Anne, Coca-Cola; Prince Charles, frozen daiquiri—have asserted that Diana "is teetotal." The Palace doesn't go that far but says she "doesn't like alcohol." At the other extreme, however, there have been newspaper claims of her dragging Charles into a pub at closing time, gasping for a glass of wine after an evening in a hot theater, and even jokingly suggesting to Fergie and friends at Royal Ascot in 1987, "Let's get drunk!" *That* story prompted Press questions about whether she was hitting the bottle. The Princess showed that the royals can answer back when they want to when she used a speech she was making, after being granted the Freedom of the City of London the following month, to deny it. Thanking her hosts for the great honor and the delicious veal lunch, she added, " . . . and the wine—well, I am sure that too is excellent. But contrary to recent reports in some of our more sensational Sunday newspapers, I have not been drinking and I am not, I can assure you, about to become an alcoholic." She was once said to favor Pimms, not realizing it contained alcohol. In Germany, she grimaced after sipping a glass of beer she'd been given. And at a banquet in Indonesia in November 1989, she was seen declining a glass of bubbly, explaining to President Suharto, "I don't like champagne." Prince Charles never drinks red wine. Diana once liked white wine. She and Charles serve German white wine and his favorite champagne, Bollinger, at their dinner parties—but never spirits, which neither of them drinks. Diana often has mineral water or fruit juice instead. While she was probably never much of a drinker, it seems she no longer touches a drop. In May 1991 at a center for reformed alcoholics in south London, she was reported to have said, "I don't drink at all. But I understand the pressures. I'm constantly being offered drinks at parties and social functions, and I know how difficult it is to resist."

FRANCE

The French adore Diana. Her beauty. Her elegance. Oh la la! She might almost be French! Diana's big year for France was 1987 when she went there three times. The first trip, that February, was when she and Charles traveled to Toulouse for the launch of the A320 airbus. In May they were on the Riviera for the Cannes Film Festival, which the Princess enjoyed so much that she wanted to stay longer. (Charles had a nice time too, sitting next to a James Bond film beauty.) For the screening of a British entry, *The Whales of August* (should have been Waleses, right?), she wore a pale blue silk chiffon gown with a matching piece around her throat by the French-born Catherine Walker. One of her disasters was the striped puffball dress she wore for an appearance on the balcony of the Hôtel de Ville, the local town hall. Four months later, they returned to visit Caen, where she wore a chic new Rifat Ozbek suit in red and black with a matching Spanish-style hat with snood by Philip Somerville. But the big trip came in November 1988, when the royal couple made a five-day visit to Paris and Blois.

Diana, conscious that some of the world's most fashionable

and discerning eyes would be on her, pulled out all the fashion stops. They arrived in style at Orly airport, Charles piloting the plane, Diana flattering her hosts by dressing for the first time on an official engagement in French clothes: a red Chanel coat, designed by Karl Lagerfeld, and matching Chanel hat with jaunty black feathers. See FASHION. For President François Mitterand's state banquet at the Élysée Palace, she wore a new ivory duchess satin gown and bolero, decorated with gold and silver beads, by Victor Edelstein, which she wore again the following year in New York. Other outfits making their first appearance on the tour included a red-and-black silk, off-one-shoulder gown by Catherine Walker which she wore to a dinner at the British Embassy in Paris; and one of Catherine's most stylish designs ever, a sleek and ultrasimple cream coatdress with a stand-up collar, large black buttons, and long black velvet sleeves which Diana sported at the Hôtel de Ville. Jacques Chirac, the Mayor of Paris, who formally received the royal couple there, told the blushing Princess through an interpreter (French is not her strong point—see EDUCATION), "Your charm and elegance have already seduced the French people." One of her most stunning hats was the wonderful black one with the face veil by Viv Knowlands which she wore with a simple black coat, and a spray of red poppies, for the Celebration of Armistice ceremony at the French National War Memorial in Paris.

Another somber part of the tour came when, in what HIV pioneer Professor Luc Montagnier described as "a highly symbolic gesture," Diana visited the laboratory at the famous Pasteur Institute where he first isolated the AIDS virus. (Profits from the auction of the fabulous £7 million collection of jewels owned by the Duchess of Windsor, who lived and died in Paris like the Duke, which raised £31 million, went to the Institute to further AIDS research.) See HIV. However, there was fun too, feasting in a country renowned for its gourmet delights. Diana and Charles dined on a romantic *bateau mouche* trip down the Seine. At one dinner she sat next to former French Premier Raymond Barre, who revealed later that she'd had a double helping of *pâté de foie gras* as a starter—her own and then *his*, which he had left because he was dieting. See FOOD & DRINK. And at a banquet at a magnificent château in Chambord, the Princess so enchanted France's handsome (and happily married) Cultural Minister Jack Lang that in a lyrical speech he declared she had such "wonderful blue eyes they would inspire a poem." With typical Gallic charm, he promptly invited her back for a private visit.

FRIENDS

Friends have always been very important to Diana, and many she met in childhood or at school remain friends to this day. Among them are Mary-Ann Stewart-Richardson; Caroline Harbord-Hammond; Sarah Robeson; her mother's godchild, Theresa Mowbray; Sophie Kimball; and Alexandra Loyd, daughter of the Queen's Land Agent at Sandringham, and Laura Greig, who are both now Ladies-in-Waiting to the Princess. See STAFF and RESIDENCES. Diana's BFs, or best friends, also include her flatmates at the time of her engagement: brigadier's daughter Ann Bolton, who settled on a 300,000-acre spread in Queensland, Australia, after marrying rancher Noel Hill in 1983; interior designer Virginia Pitman; and Carolyn Pride. Carolyn is a godmother to Prince Harry and Diana attended her wedding to brewery heir William Bartholomew of Juliana's Discotheque. Diana also attended the church blessing after Virginia married banker Henry Clarke in 1991.

Ex–King Constantine of Greece, a godfather to Prince William, is a great friend. They've all been on holiday together in Majorca. Charles and Diana visit him and his wife at their London house in Hampstead Garden Suburb, and they were among the many European royals who attended the exiled former monarch's glittering fiftieth birthday party at Spencer House in London in June 1990, for which relatives and others were estimated to have stumped up £250,000. See RESIDENCES. Sir Laurens van der Post, another of William's godfathers, is the elderly author and explorer who has encouraged Charles's interest in anthropology and has been his long-term guru. Diana finds him "fascinating," though she allegedly once declared that having to sit through dinners with some people wasn't so much a case of being a hostess as "a hostage."

Norton Knatchbull, Lord Romsey, another godfather to William, is a second cousin to Prince Charles, the son of Lord Bra-

Diana exchanges notes on motherhood with Christina Wildenstein, wife of Charles's fellow polo player, Guy Wildenstein. (Glenn Harvey/Camera Press London)

bourne, and grandson of the late Earl Mountbatten (Charles's favorite "Uncle Dickie" and "honorary grandfather" who was murdered by the IRA). He and Charles both went to school at Gordonstoun, and the royal couple spent the first part of their honeymoon at the Romseys' home, Broadlands in Hampshire. See HONEYMOON. A film producer like his father (Lord Brabourne's movies include *Sink the Bismarck, Murder on the Orient Express,* and *Tales of Beatrix Potter*), Lord Romsey is also a Director of Diana's favorite pop music station, Capital Radio in London. See RADIO. Lady (Penelope) Romsey, a former girlfriend of Prince

Charles, who is godfather to the Romseys' son Nicholas, has links with Birthright, of which Diana is Patron. See MARRIAGE, PRESS, and BIRTHRIGHT.

William's godmothers are Princess Alexandra, always one of the royals' favorite royals; Lady Susan Hussey, a Woman of the Bedchamber to the Queen, an old friend of Prince Charles, and the wife of Marmaduke Hussey, Chairman of the Board of Governors of the BBC, a former Director of Times Newspapers Ltd., and Chairman of the Board of Governors of the Royal Marsden Hospital, the famous London cancer hospital of which Diana is President; and Diana's friend Natalia, or Tally, who is married to Gerald Grosvenor, the Duke of Westminster, Britain's richest man. Diana is godmother to their second child, Lady Edwina Louisa Grosvenor. Until their quickie divorce in March 1990, the Duke's sister, Lady Jane, was married to Guy, the Duke of Roxburghe, who is said to be the richest man in Scotland. Indeed, their combined fortune when they married was reported to be over £300 million. Lady Jane is the sister of Lady Leonora, former wife of the Earl of Lichfield, who took the official photographs at Diana's wedding. The Duke and Duchess of Roxburghe entertained Charles and Diana at their hundred-room Georgian Scottish mansion, Floors Castle, set in sixty thousand acres near Kelso—where Prince Andrew took Koo Stark fly-fishing in 1982 and later proposed to Fergie. The Roxburghes' daughter, eight-year-old Lady Rosanagh, was a bridesmaid at the Yorks' wedding, and Lady Jane is godmother to Princess Beatrice.

Two of Prince Harry's godparents are Prince Andrew and Princess Margaret's daughter, Lady Sarah Armstrong-Jones, both of whom have been friends of Diana since childhood. Lady Sarah was also the maid of honor at Diana's wedding. Lady Vestey, another godmother, is the wife of meat tycoon Lord (Sam, nicknamed Spam) Vestey; they live in Gloucestershire not far from Highgrove. The two other godparents are also friends: Gerald Ward and the artist Bryan Organ. See ARTS & HANDICRAFTS.

Friends from Charles's side include former "Goon Show" stars Spike Milligan, Sir Harry Secombe, and Michael Bentine; plus millionaire racehorse owner Hugh van Cutsem, the Prince's racehorse trainer Nick Gaselee, and David Hicks, the interior designer, each of whom has a child who acted as a wedding attendant on the royal wedding day. Several of the Prince's long line of former girlfriends were, incidentally, also at the wedding. However, Charles's married women confidantes—fashion designer Lady (Dale) Tryon, the wife of an Old Etonian banker, who keeps the Prince's photograph on the grand piano at her country house near Salisbury; and Camilla Parker-Bowles, the wife of Princess Anne's former escort, Andrew Parker-Bowles—found themselves in the cold during the early years of the royal marriage. But three months after the royal couple chatted briefly to Lady T at the premiere of *Out of Africa* in March 1986, the Princess lunched with her and has since sported several of Lady Tryon's designs. Camilla was at a wedding ball the royal couple attended in 1987, and in October 1990 she and her husband were among friends who joined Charles during his long Scottish holiday at Balmoral and Birkhall. See FASHION and MARRIAGE.

Other friends—or Throne Rangers, as the group around Diana are sometimes called—include Humphrey Butler and Willy Von Straubenzee, who both used to shoot at Althorp; Old Etonians James Boughey, Simon Berry of the St. James's wine merchants family, and Harry Herbert, plus his sister Carolyn, the offspring of Lord Porchester, the Queen's racing manager; George Plumptre, who has written about royal gardens; City businessman Mervyn Chaplin; and property developer Ben Holland Martin. Those with whom Diana socializes seldom escape the attention of the Press. Brewery heir Peter Greenall, a former champion National Hunt jockey, who went with a skiing party to the Casa Antica nightclub at Klosters, found himself in the newspapers in 1987 after disco-dancing there with Diana. According to the club disc jockey, she turned up apparently bra-less in a sexy white silk top and black leather trousers (see FASHION) and had "the time of her life," having left Charles behind in the royal chalet to have a quiet evening without her. Financier Charles Carter found himself besieged by the Press after he danced several times with the Princess at the Guards' Polo Club during a party prior to Fergie's wedding. One Old Etonian friend, James Gilbey of the gin family, who works at a Saab car showroom, found himself front-page news after Diana allegedly nipped out, without her detectives, to visit him one evening at his London home. The reason for her visit, apparently, was that he wanted some personal advice; Diana, being something of an agony aunt, kindly offered a shoulder to cry on. See MARRIAGE. Another friend, whisky heir James Teacher's wife Chloe, who was in a coma with critical head injuries after a riding accident (she had been thrown and kicked in the head by a horse in November 1988 while out with the Quorn hunt) was visited in the hospital several times by Diana and also by Prince Charles. In May 1989 Chloe was featured in a *News of the World* story headlined, DI'S MIRACLE SAVES COMA PAL, which claimed that Diana's visits had helped coax her from her coma. See HOSPITALS.

Kate Menzies, daughter of wholesale and retail newsagent millionaire John Menzies, has watched tennis at Wimbledon with the Princess and is also one of her partners at the Vanderbilt tennis club at Shepherd's Bush, where Diana plays regularly. Another tennis partner is Julia Dodd Noble, known as Crown Jools because she is also a friend of Fergie. Yet another tennis-playing friend is Antonia, the Marchioness of Douro—daughter of the late Prince Frederick of Prussia and wife of a member of the European Parliament—who is Chairman of the Guinness Trust, of which the Princess is Patron. Antonia and her husband, who is heir to the 8th Duke of Wellington, have entertained the royal couple on the family estate in Spain. See SPAIN. Charles Swallow, co-owner of the Vanderbilt, who has played in doubles matches with Diana, is also a friend. He has been to Kensington Palace for lunch, and she bought him a sweater with a tennis racket motif for his fiftieth birthday. See SPORT. The American-born Queen Noor of Jordan, who plays at the same club, is another friend of Diana's. She and King Hussein invited Charles and Diana on a private vacation to Jordan, and they have been guests at Kensington Palace. So have pop tycoon Richard Branson and his then bride-to-be Joan Templeman, who were invited to dinner as a thank-you for letting Diana take William and Harry on holiday to his private island in the Virgin Islands. The King and Queen of Spain, at whose palace in Majorca Charles, Diana, and the children have spent summer seaside vacations, are also great friends, though they did not attend the royal wedding. See HOLIDAYS and WEDDING.

Lulu Blacker and Major Hugh Lindsay, of the 9th/12th Royal Lancers, were the two friends whom Diana and Fergie prodded with their umbrellas in some horseplay at Royal Ascot in June 1987, which lost them both brownie points. Lulu, then girlfriend of the Duke of Marlborough's heir, Jamie Blandford, a former drug addict, reportedly revealed the following month that she had experimented with drugs, saying, "I've tried all kinds of drugs myself." The Princess, of course, campaigns strongly against them. See DRUGS and TURNING POINT. Major Lindsay, an Equerry to the Queen, was the friend who died tragically in the avalanche which almost killed Prince Charles too when they were skiing in a party at Klosters in March 1988. Another friend, Patti, wife of the Prince's friend Charles Palmer-Tomkinson, was injured and spent a long time in the hospital recovering. The tragedy was deeply distressing for them all. Major Lindsay and his wife Sarah had been married for less than a year and were expecting their first child, a daughter named Alice. Prince Charles became her godfather, and the royal couple were a great support to Sarah, who eventually went back to her job in the Press Office at Buckingham Palace. In his spare time, Major Lindsay had sung with a rock group called Sweatband. His place with the band was taken by a schoolmate of Diana's, Baroness Izzy Van Randwyck.

A friend from the Princess's single days who also had a tragic accident, but who survived and has been in a wheelchair ever since, is Andrew Widdowson. He danced with the young Diana at the Argyll Ball near Oban in Scotland, but later he became paralyzed after a rugby accident. Diana wrote him get-well letters and invited him to the royal wedding. He called her "the girl with the golden hair." Andrew, who is a math teacher at a school in Essex, where he also coaches the rugby team, has helped raise funds for the International Spinal Research Trust, of which the Princess is Royal Patron.

Another friend from the days before her marriage is Rory Scott, who himself married in 1990. Diana, who met him through her sister Jane, who was a flatmate of his sister Henrietta, has always loved washing and ironing and used to do his shirts for him. The Princess has lunch with friends like Caroline Twiston-Davies and photographer Terence Donovan, who was spotted exchanging a friendly kiss with Diana outside one restaurant and was a guest at the wedding of her brother, Viscount Althorp. See FAMILY. Another friend is hairdresser Nulah Burgess. The Princess was almost prevented from visiting her in July 1987, after Nulah had given birth to a baby daughter, when she arrived after visiting hours at St. Helier Hospital in Carshalton, Surrey. She was told by twenty-two-year-old nursery nurse Juliet Higgans, who failed to recognize her, "You can't come in. It has gone four o'clock." Among those who have entertained the royal couple are David Frost—also a friend of the Yorks—and his wife Lady Carina Fitzalan-Howard, daughter of the Duke of Norfolk. Frostie has helped raise funds for Birthright, whose other supporters include Fergie's comedian friend Billy Connolly. Connolly's other half, actress Pamela Stephenson, was involved in the policewoman prank on Prince Andrew's stag night. See UNIFORMS. Other friends include dress designer Susie Murray-Phillipson, whose wedding to Alex Dolby in Uppingham, Leicestershire, in September 1988 was attended by Fergie, Viscount Linley, Diana, and her sister Lady Jane Fellowes. In February 1989, Diana and a girlfriend lunched at Green's in Mayfair with Princess Anne's friend, Lieutenant-Commander Timothy Laurence, an Equerry to the Queen, who made headlines after personal letters he had written to the Princess Royal went missing. Another friend, from Diana's school days, is Sue Fenwick. At the church blessing at Waltham-on-the-Wolds, Leicestershire, in July 1989 following her register-office wedding to property developer Jonathan Harrington, Prince Harry, clad in tartan, was a pageboy.

Sir Winston Churchill's grandson, the Honorable Nicholas Soames, Tory Member of Parliament for Crawley since 1983, is an old-established friend of the Prince. A seventh cousin to Diana once removed, the portly Soames was an Equerry to Prince Charles from 1970 to 1972 and has since been an Extra Equerry. The Prince was best man at his wedding in 1981 to Catherine Weatherall. During that same fateful ski trip to Klosters in March 1988 when Major Lindsay died, Catherine fell for Pimlico antique dealer and former British Olympic skier Piers von Westenholz. The Soames' marriage has since ended, though Diana still counts both of them among her friends. Nicholas Soames, son of the late Lord Soames, was a friend of the missing British peer, the 7th Earl of Lucan, who disappeared after the murder of his children's nanny in 1974. He has been sought by police throughout the world, alive or dead, ever since. Lord Lucan was condemned by an inquest jury in his absence in 1975, but the authors of two books on the case since (including my own) believe he did not commit the murder. Lucan, nicknamed Lucky, is or was a second cousin to the Princess once removed; and a close friend of William Shand Kydd, half-brother of Diana's former stepfather, Peter Shand Kydd, and brother-in-law of Lucan's estranged wife, Lady Lucan, who was injured on the night of the murder and accused Lucan of being the attacker.

One friend who found himself the victim of rumor and gossip connecting him with the Princess was tall, dark, handsome Old Etonian merchant banker Philip Dunne, son of the Lord-Lieutenant of Hereford and Worcester, a godson of Princess Alexandra, and a bachelor with a reported reputation as a lady-killer. Bespectacled Dunne, who looks like *Superman* star Christopher Reeve, skied with the royal party in Klosters early in 1987. Later the Princess stayed with a group of friends at his family's stately home, Gatley Park, near Leominster, Herefordshire, while his parents were away skiing in the French resort of Meribel and Prince Charles was abroad. Dunne turned up in the royal party at Royal Ascot that June. And at the wedding reception of Bunter, the Marquess of Worcester, and actress Tracy Ward—where Prince Charles reportedly spent time deep in conversation with Camilla Parker-Bowles—the Princess allegedly danced over and over again with Dunne, ran her fingers through his hair, planted a kiss on his cheek, and kept on boogying until dawn despite the fact that Prince Charles left at 2:00 A.M. Since gossips were already suggesting that the royal marriage was on the rocks and that the couple were leading separate lives (see MARRIAGE), it did not take much of a leap of the imagination for them to suggest that the Princess was smitten with the good-looking Philip. In June 1987, after several tabloid newspapers wrongly identified him as the mystery man who had been photographed head-to-head with the Princess at a David Bowie concert at Wembley, Dunne issued a statement through his solicitor saying the stories were "totally false": it wasn't him and he wasn't there. In fact, Dunne's girlfriend at the time was photographer Katya Grenfell, daughter of the late Lord St. Just and ex-wife of Sir Ian Gilmour's conductor-son, Oliver. Katya produced a book of photographs of nude people called *Naked London* and was once reported to have been included by a snob magazine in a list of blue-blooded Brits who allegedly didn't wear panties. She and Philip, who was allegedly spotted lunching with the Princess at the Ménage à Trois restaurant, apparently had long discussions about the gossip linking his name with Diana's.

In February 1989, the Princess flew back from her triumphant solo visit to New York in time to be among the guests when Dunne, aged thirty, married Domenica Fraser, daughter of former Rolls-Royce Chairman Sir Ian Fraser, at Brompton Oratory in London. Diana went on to the wedding reception at the Reform Club, driving herself there in her sporty Ford Cosworth while other guests were disgorged from a couple of blue double-decker buses. Prince Charles spent that afternoon a hundred miles away with the Duke of Beaufort's hunt. Camilla Dunne, Philip's sister, who is known as Millie, is among the ladies who lunch with Diana. See RADIO. The Princess also attended her wedding. Millie and Philip's mother, Henrietta Dunne, is a first cousin of Susanna Swallow, the wife of the co-owner of the Vanderbilt Racquet Club, where the Princess plays tennis. See SPORT.

The friend who was mistaken for Philip Dunne by the Press at the David Bowie gig, where he and Diana were in a party which also included Viscount Linley but not Prince Charles, was bachelor Life Guards officer Major David Waterhouse. He is a nephew of the Duke of Marlborough and an old friend of Fergie, and he rode in the Household Cavalry escort for Fergie's wedding procession. Far from being head-to-head with Diana because they were whispering sweet nothings, he explained later, "it was the only way we could talk and hear each other because the music was so loud." He was quoted as saying, "The Princess had a wonderful time, but it is ridiculous for anyone to suggest that she is having an affair with Philip Dunne, myself, or anyone else." Diana enjoys playing bridge with her friends (she was President of the British Bridge League's 1989 World Junior Championships) and also likes poker. It was after a bridge supper at the London mews home of Kate Menzies, which Waterhouse attended, that a further story arose. In November 1987 the *News of the World* published claims by a freelance photographer that after the Princess had left the house, he had taken photographs of her larking around in the mews with Waterhouse but that he had been persuaded to hand over the film after demands from her bodyguard and impassioned and tearful pleas from Diana herself. Major Waterhouse denied the story, declaring that he had left the mews house earlier than the Princess and adding, "The only people with her as she left were her detective and her hostess." He was quoted as saying, "All this speculation about us is nonsense. The stories are a fabrication, and it's appalling the way the Princess is being persecuted." Kate Menzies, who runs a catering company and is a friend of Lord Linley, dismissed suggestions that the royal marriage was crumbling and was quoted as saying, "It's nonsense, but it's impossible for me to say more in case I am misinterpreted or misconstrued. I am sorry, but I feel it would be wrong of me to speak about any of my friends." In December 1988, Diana was reported to have attended a performance of *Sleeping Beauty* given by the Royal Ballet at Covent Garden in a party of five which included Major Waterhouse, who was then thirty-four and coming to the end of a one-year Staff College course in Camberley before being posted to Wiltshire. In March 1989, he was reported to have joined Diana and two more of her friends, Michael and Julia Samuels, who live near Kensington Palace, for supper and a visit to the Princess's local cinema, the Odeon in Kensington, where they all watched Tom Cruise and Dustin Hoffman, a friend of the Yorks and winner of the Best Actor Oscar that year, in *Rain Man*. In August 1990, Waterhouse was also reported to have visited Diana at Highgrove, though as a friend there was no reason why he shouldn't, if the story were true. See MARRIAGE and GULF WAR.

Being a friend of the Princess may be wonderful. But there are many drawbacks. New friends have to be vetted by MI5, domestic intelligence, unless they are known to the family; and wherever Diana goes, there is a detective in tow. Her time and freedom are restricted, which means it is difficult, if not impossible, to make spontaneous last-minute plans to see her. There is the Press attention and publicity to cope with. And above all, friendship with a member of the Royal Family, if it's to last, demands total discretion. If friendships wilt under these strains, it is perhaps not surprising. Unfortunately, it is part of the price Diana has to pay for being the Princess of Wales.

G

GERMANY

Diana's first trip to West Germany was in October 1985 when she made a two-day solo visit to the 1st Battalion of the Royal Hampshire Regiment, nicknamed the Tigers, of which she had recently become Colonel-in-Chief. See ARMED FORCES. A special bathroom with brass fittings and pink wallpaper was reportedly prepared for her at the Wavell Barracks, next door to Spandau jail where Rudolf Hess, Adolf Hitler's former deputy, was still imprisoned. And the whole regiment, serving and retired, voluntarily contributed to buy her a unique jeweled regimental brooch, a replica of their cap badge but with diamonds, emeralds, rubies, and pearls set in gold. "It is beautiful. How generous everybody is," she said. During the visit, wearing a black-and-yellow track suit and plimsolls, Diana drove a fifteen-ton FV 432 armored personnel carrier with a 30-mm cannon backward, forward, and around a corner of the parade ground, at one point forcing an army instructor to leap out of the way. (He still reckoned she deserved ten marks out of ten and said she had "learned very quickly.") "I enjoyed it. . . . I would love to do it again," Diana declared, telling Press cameramen who'd photographed her progress, "I thought you were pretty brave standing there!" See MOTORING. But she blushed when ten of the soldiers abseiled down ropes from two hovering helicopters, their faces smeared in brown and green camouflage, to present her with a box of chocolates and a single red rose.

Diana returned for her first state visit to the Federal Republic of Germany with Charles in November 1987, when all eyes were focused extra sharply on the royal couple following stories that their marriage was on the rocks. See FRIENDS and MARRIAGE. In Berlin the Princess made a point of wearing a German-designed coat. See FASHION. They went on to Bonn, where a twenty-five-year-old girl in the crowd asked the Princess, "May I kiss you?" and was told, "No, but you may kiss my husband." (She did, leaving lipstick on his cheek.) At a government ball, Diana appeared for the first time in public in her fabulous sapphire-and-diamond jewels from the Sultan of Oman (see JEWELRY), which stunned observers reckoned must be worth at least £500,000. At Cologne, Charles saw restoration work on the cathedral. And at Munich, the Princess jokingly pretended to thumb a lift, spotting an ambulance with its blue light flashing and saying, "That will do. I will go in that," after a stream of official cars went without her. They saw *The Marriage of Figaro* at the Munich State Opera. And they were given a private lunch by Prince Franz of Bavaria, head of the Wittelsbachs, the Bavarian Royal Family, who showed Diana the portraits in the famous Gallery of Beauties at Nymphenburg Palace. Prince Charles had told Herr Franz-Joseph Strauss, the Bavarian Prime Minister, "Were it not for the Act of Settlement [see STAFF] . . . the present head of the Royal house of Bavaria would probably have a better claim to the British throne than myself."

Before and after Christmas 1990, Diana made trips to Germany to visit families of British servicemen sent to the Gulf following Iraq's invasion of Kuwait. Charles visited the troops in Saudi Arabia. See GULF WAR.

THE GUINNESS TRUST

Diana is Patron of the Guinness Trust, a charity for people in housing need and a registered housing association. Her friend and tennis partner Antonia, the Marchioness of Douro, is Chairman. See FRIENDS. The Trust was founded in February 1890 with an endowment of £200,000 (the equivalent of about £15 million today) by Edward Cecil Guinness, the first Earl of Iveagh. During the past century it has provided housing, says Diana, for "many thousands of people . . . often when few other affordable alternatives were available." The Earl was the great grandson of Arthur Guinness, who established the Guinness Brewery in Dublin in 1759, though the Trust nowadays has no connection with the brewery company Guinness Plc. The charity now provides more than ten thousand homes throughout England, with plans for two thousand more by 1993. It is also involved with a plan to build a detoxification unit, day center, and hostels for homeless people with alcohol and drug problems at the Smithfield Centre in Manchester, in partnership with Turning Point; in renovating a rundown residential district at Teesside; and with a self-build plan in Tower Hamlets, London, to help the young unemployed build their own homes. The Princess, who became the Trust's first Patron in April 1987, has made several visits a year to its projects and attended its one hundredth birthday lunch in 1990. In a recent foreword to one of the charity's publications, she wrote, ". . . homelessness has again become a major problem and one that may take many years to solve. It is therefore very important that organizations like The Guiness Trust continue to have the resources they need to make progress in housing homeless and disadvantaged people."

Charles and Diana are both very concerned about the homeless, including people who sleep in boxes on the streets in "cardboard cities." But some feel they should do more. In March, when Charles ran into a demonstration against homelessness during a visit to Manchester, someone yelled, "Why don't you let the homeless live in your palaces?" "We are trying to do something about it, thank you," he retorted.

GULF WAR

The Princess became very involved in the crisis which followed the invasion of Kuwait by the forces of Iraq's military dictator Saddam Hussein in August 1990, and the war which ensued when he refused to get out by the January 15, 1991, deadline. Diana gave great comfort and support to families of soldiers, sailors, and airmen involved in Operation Desert Storm, who made her their favorite wartime pin-up.

Though it wasn't a religious Muslim-Christian conflict, strong feelings were aroused around the world. Back in September, the month after the invasion, Diana increased her understanding of the Muslim mind by attending two lectures on the "positive aspects" of Islam at the Royal Anthropological Insti-

Visiting with families of the British soldiers serving in the Gulf War. (Erma/
Camera Press London)

tute, of which she is Patron, in London. Professor Akbar Ahmed
of Cambridge University, an expert on Islamic affairs, also gave
her a copy of his book *Discovering Islam*.

Aware of the overwhelming support in Britain for the Allied
forces of many United Nations countries under the command of
U.S. General "Stormin' " Norman Schwarzkopf, it was reported
in London at the end of January that the Queen wanted members
of the Royal Family to avoid fun and games. A senior Buckingham
Palace aide was quoted as saying, "For the duration of the war,
you will not see any of the royals at play. They understand the
sensitivity of people at a time like this, and they know they ignore
it at their peril."

Less than two weeks later, however, on February 10, fierce
criticism of the Royal Family's war effort was voiced in the leader
column of the prestigious Establishment newspaper, the *Sunday
Times*. It blasted Fergie, who'd come back from yet another skiing
vacation and had been photographed enjoying a "high-spirited"

dinner at a London restaurant; Prince Andrew, who'd been golfing in Spain; and Lord Linley, who'd gone off on a vacation to
Mustique in the Caribbean, shortly after the *Sun* pictured him on
the front page at a fancy dress party, "wearing red lipstick and
holding on to various males in drag."

The leader column declared, "This country is at war, though
you would never believe it from the shenanigans of some members
of Her Majesty's clan . . . [who] carry on regardless with their
peacetime lifestyles, parading a mixture of upper-class decadence
and insensitivity which disgusts the public and demeans the monarchy. The Queen should put a stop to it. . . .Their behaviour at
a time of national crisis is helping to undermine the very role of
the Royal Family."

Buckingham Palace hit back with a list of royal engagements
carried out to support the troops and their families, which *Sunday
Times* Editor Andrew Neil said "entirely vindicated" his newspaper's stance. A Sky TV poll of more than 2,750 viewers showed
that 83 percent were "disgusted" with the behavior of some of the
younger royals.

Though not royal, even Diana's brother, Lord Althorp, had
been mentioned in the leader, having had an extramarital fling
with a girl whose kiss-and-tell memoirs had recently made headlines. See FAMILY. Diana herself, however, was specifically ex-
cluded from the *Sunday Times* criticism. Some royals, said the
leader, "notably the Princess of Wales," had been "seen to do
their bit."

Just before Christmas she had gone to Germany, where she
visited families of British servicemen who had been sent to the
Gulf. Prince Charles flew to see the troops in Saudi Arabia. In
January she returned to Germany, traveling to RAF Bruggen, the
British base on the German-Dutch border, to comfort the wives
of Tornado pilots and navigators involved in the conflict who
were anxiously awaiting news of their loved ones. The Princess
told them that she had been glued to the television coverage of the
war—"I stay up all night," she said—and declared, "I think your
husbands are wonderful. It's one thing to train for the job, but
quite another to do it." Eager to talk to as many of the wives as
possible, she ran forty-five minutes over her schedule. Among

those she met and talked to at length was the wife of an RAF flier who had failed to return from a bombing mission over Baghdad on January 23. The wives described the royal visit as "a great morale booster," one of them saying, "It's nice to know someone cares."

Back in the U.K., Diana and Charles went to the Devonport naval base at Plymouth to visit the families of sailors serving in the Gulf. She visited one of her regiments, the 13th/18th Royal Hussars at Assaye Barracks at Tidworth, Hampshire. And in Hull, touring sheltered accommodation run by the Sailors' Families Society, she said that the troops' wives had been doing "a terrific job. They have had a hard time over the past few weeks." She also revealed that she found the Gulf TV coverage "very addictive" and admitted, "I have been getting up early. . . . I was up at 5:00 A.M. watching."

Wanting to let the troops know that everyone at home was thinking of them, Diana wrote an open letter to them from Kensington Palace, which was published in *Soldier* magazine, *Navy News*, and *RAF News*. It read:

> A message written to the thousands of you in the Gulf from the safety of my home in London can all too easily sound remote or condescending. But I do want you all to know just how <u>much</u> you are in our thoughts and prayers.
>
> In the last few weeks I have been lucky enough to meet some of the families and friends you have left behind at Hohne and Paderborn Garrisons and RAF Gutersloh and Bruggen in Germany, and Royal Navy Devonport, Plymouth. They are all bearing up remarkably well: I was immensely proud to be able to see so many of them, if I may say so, you can be equally proud of the support they are giving you. I was also pleased to be able to visit the Postal and Courier Depot Royal Engineers, Mill Hill, to see how they are coping with the thousands of letters and parcels that are being sent to you.
>
> Like everyone else following events in the Gulf hour by hour on the television screen, on the radio and in the newspapers, I am full of admiration for the extraordinary professional way in which you are all doing your jobs: utterly determined to do what is asked of you to the best of your ability yet never

losing your essential humanity and sense of proportion. I know
that this is the result of years of training, hard work, and
consummate self-discipline. But I would just like you to know
that <u>none</u> of us back home underestimates the difficulties and
anxieties which you are experiencing, or the size of the task
ahead of you.

Good luck and God speed.

Diana.

The conflict was expected to be over quickly. "I've got a
skiing holiday booked for the first week in April and I'm bloody
certain I'm going on it," Brigadier Patrick Cordingley, Commander of the Desert Rats, was quoted as saying. Thanks to the
high-tech equipment, the brilliant tactics of Stormin' Norman,
and the bravery of the men and women under his command, it
was.

Even then Diana continued her visits, taking in RAF Finningley, Doncaster, South Yorkshire, and RAF Scampton, Lincolnshire, plus the 16 Air Defence Regiment Royal Artillery at Hems-
well, Lincolnshire, accompanied by one of her Ladies-in-Waiting,
Viscountess Campden, and her Equerry, Squadron Leader David
Barton, RAF.

At RAF Finningley, the Princess committed a faux pas when
she praised the new British Prime Minister John Major, saying,
"He has been doing a wonderful job as Prime Minister. It was
hard for him, particularly taking over at the time he did, and both
running the country and conducting the war. I could not have
done that." Members of the Royal Family are supposed to keep
out of party politics. But Diana may have been following the lead
set by Prince Charles, who had just sparked another controversy
by saying he backed proportional representation, which is Liberal
Democrat policy.

At RAF Scampton, the Princess had her *third* comedy duo
exchange with *Sun* photographer Arthur Edwards. See PRESS and
JAPAN. Arthur, aged fifty, whose hair is thinning, noticed Diana's
new, shorter hairstyle and remarked, "If you have your hair
cropped any shorter, you will look like Sinéad O'Connor,"
referring to the skinhead Irish singer. "At least I've got some
hair!" the Princess responded.

Also in March, Diana visited Gulf servicemen's families at
RAF Locking, Weston-super-Mare, and at 29 Transport and
Movements Regiment, Royal Corps of Transport, at the Duke of
Gloucester Barracks in South Cerney, near Cirencester, Gloucestershire. She sympathized with one wife who revealed that her
husband had been sent to the desert only five days after their
wedding, saying, "You haven't had much of a married life yet."
Trips to RAF Leuchars, in St. Andrews, Fife, in Scotland, and to
families of the King's Own Scottish Borderers at Redford Barracks in Edinburgh were among other visits she made.

Because of the war, Charles and Diana's February visit to
India was called off, and their state visit to Brazil in April was
initially in doubt. (Visits to Britain were also affected. Shirley
MacLaine and Meryl Streep reportedly stayed away from the
London premiere of *Postcards from the Edge*, which Diana at-
tended.)

However, the Queen and Prince Philip's May visit to the
United States went ahead. The Queen had a special meeting with
General Schwarzkopf, on whom she conferred an honorary
knighthood, like that given to former President Ronald Reagan.

The portly Gulf hero, who allegedly said he'd like Robert
Redford to play him in the movie of the war, had never been to
Britain. But toward the end of March while he was still in the
Gulf, his wife, Mrs. Brenda Schwarzkopf (who'd been visiting
bases in the United States) took in Buckingham Palace during a
sightseeing trip around London. She had flown in, on her first trip
to Britain, with Norman's elder sister Sally at the invitation of the
Daily Star national newspaper, to collect one of its Gold Awards
on behalf of her husband. She vowed to take Norman with her on
her next trip to the U.K., where she fell for the red tunics of the
Beefeaters at the Tower of London. "Perhaps I ought to take one
home for Norm," she said. "He'd look really neat in it." At the
Georgian restaurant at Harrods, she ate traditional British roast
beef and Yorkshire pudding, likening the latter to an onion pop-
over. Harrods, the Top People's store and one of Diana's favorite
shops (see SHOPPING), donated £200 worth of vintage champagne
for the couple's celebration on General Schwarzkopf's return
home to Florida. In July 1991, the General paid a four-day visit to

Britain, where he visited SAS heroes who played a key role in the war, and where in a survey he was voted the man British women would most like to meet, after Kevin Costner but before Tom Cruise or Richard Gere.

Two of Diana's friends who served with the forces in the Gulf War were Major David Waterhouse (see FRIENDS and MARRIAGE) and his fellow Life Guards officer, Millfield-educated polo player Major James Hewitt, known as Winkie. Hewitt is said to have given riding lessons to Diana and Prince William while stationed at Combermere Barracks, near Windsor Castle, and to call the Princess by the nickname Dibbs. See NAMES.

HAWAII

Fifteen American secret service agents were sent over by President Reagan to help the Hawaii Five-O security teams guard Charles and Diana in November 1985 when they had an eighteen-hour rest break in Hawaii en route to Washington from their exhausting two-week tour in Australia. The royal couple stayed at the $1,400-a-night presidential suite at the Kahala Hilton (see BATHS & BATHROOMS) where Diana, who was "shattered," was heard playing the grand piano before zonking out on the seven-foot-square bed. Next morning they dived into a paradise breakfast of tropical fruit served in pineapple shells before heading off to a millionaire's £3 million beachside bungalow, used as a setting in the "Magnum, P.I." TV series, to sunbathe for hours by the pool. "Magnum" star Tom Selleck, who later attended the Reagans' banquet at the White House for the royal pair with his English-born girlfriend, Jilly Mack, was in Hawaii when he received the coveted invitation. See AMERICA. Charles went surfing later on Sandy Beach, nearly losing his oversize shorts in the breakers, which prompted one female onlooker to remark, "Now I know what Diana sees in him." And there was another saucy moment when a girl offered the Prince a traditional Hawaiian garland of flowers, saying, "Can I give you a lei?" (which is pronounced "lay"), and he replied, laughing, "Oh, why not?" A picture of Diana posing po-faced with her husband against a background of palm trees (see PRESS) gave quite the wrong impression. Out of sight of the cameramen, the royal couple apparently larked around happily as if they were on a second honeymoon.

HEALTH

Diana had mumps and chicken pox as a schoolgirl, and she broke her arm when she fell from her pony. See SPORT. She suffers from morning sickness when pregnant. "Nobody told me I would feel like this," she said the first time around. The second time she confessed, "I haven't felt well since Day One. I don't think I'm made for the production line . . . but it's all worth it in the end." When she was first pregnant with Prince William, she fell down the stairs at Sandringham, but neither she nor the baby was injured. After William's birth in 1982, she lost so much weight that people feared she might have anorexia nervosa, the eating disorder previously suffered by her eldest sister Sarah. But this was denied. See MARRIAGE and FOOD & DRINK. In November 1990, visiting the Eating Disorders Association in Norwich, where she met eight women with eating problems, the Princess urged the public to take the plight of anorexia nervosa sufferers more seriously and said, "It is not about women being silly."

Being catapulted from teenage obscurity to royal life placed Diana under considerable stress. Rushing around on official engagements, especially abroad, can make her tense. And she has admitted feeling claustrophobic amid the vast crowds who gather to see her, though less so when Charles is with her. But she stood up remarkably well to her first six-week-long overseas tour of Australasia, though her tours since have been very much shorter. "The Princess is amazing—she has so much stamina," said her personal doctor on that tour, Royal Navy surgeon Commander Ian Jenkins. "After the official engagements, the rest of the royal party fall into the backs of waiting cars and [collapse]. We go fast asleep. But the Princess just seems to go on and on. She has no health worries on this trip—she is marvelous."

However, Diana suffers badly from jet lag and from extremes of heat and cold, which may mean she has low blood pressure. In June 1984, pregnant with her second son, she was overcome by heat watching Verdi's Aida at the Royal Opera House and was taken home early. In Canada she fainted after visiting overheated and poorly ventilated pavilions at Expo '86. In Spain's scorching temperatures she became unwell visiting Salamanca. And during the sizzling summer of 1990, just before temperatures soared up to 37° C (99° F), among the highest ever known in Britain, she commented, "The weather is lovely but I just can't stand it when it's this hot."

A radiant mother-to-be. (Richard Slade/Camera Press London)

She also suffers from back trouble, believed to have been caused by the way she used to pick up William and Harry, taking their weight on her hips. She is reported to have regular lumbar massage and exercise from a private Harley Street physiotherapist who calls at Kensington Palace. See BEDS & BEDROOMS. Diana's backache was noticed during her visit to Vienna in April 1986, when she was seen in obvious pain, holding her spine. Prince Charles referred to the problem at one official event when they both sat on low children's chairs and he was overheard to remark, "If we sit here much longer, we'll both have backache." Diana's troubles with her back, and probable sympathy with about twenty-three million other Brits (more than half the adult population) who have similar problems, may have encouraged her in 1990 to become President of the General Council and Register of Osteopaths, and Patron of the Anglo-European College of Chiropractic. The College, based in Bournemouth in Dorset, is the only internationally recognized school for chiropractors in Britain and Europe. In addition to its training courses, it has a clinic for up to two hundred outpatients a day, most of whom seek relief from chronic back pain. (A recent survey by the British Government's Medical Research Council found that chiropractic is more effective for back pain than conventional hospital outpatient treatment.) Diana recently revealed that she has received chiropractic treatment for her back for seven years.

The Princess hates having injections (see NATIONAL RUBELLA COUNCIL) but is required to for overseas tours. After the yellow fever, typhoid, and cholera jabs he and Diana were given before touring Nigeria and Cameroon in March 1990, Prince Charles said he felt like "a pin cushion." The royal couple also had to take antimalaria pills. And as an extra safeguard, medics on board the royal yacht Britannia were reported to be carrying an "AIDS kit of frozen plasma" because of the increased risk of catching AIDS through infected blood supplies in Africa, where AIDS is rampant and is widely thought to have originated. See HIV.

In March 1989 there was some mystery when the Princess (who is an Honorary Fellow of the Faculty of Dental Surgery of the Royal College of Surgeons of England) went into the King Edward VII Hospital for Officers in London, allegedly so that she could have four impacted wisdom teeth removed by her personal dental surgeon, John Simons. The reason for doubt was that a few days later, with no sign of the facial swelling which normally follows such an operation, she appeared at a Help the Aged lunch at Claridge's and apparently had no problem tackling a four-course meal which included smoked salmon, trout, and fillet of lamb with roast potatoes. One top dental surgeon was quoted as saying, "It's absolutely unbelievable. Most people wouldn't be able to eat solid food for at least a week." Gossip columnist Chris Hutchins suggested in Today that Diana had actually had the mercury amalgam fillings removed from her teeth, and replaced with white polymer ceramic composite fillings, on the advice of the Queen who, he claimed, had suggested that Diana study reports on the effects of mercury poisoning on health. (Many people in Britain have fillings containing mercury, which is toxic, and which the antimercury lobby believe can adversely affect health, especially if a person's immune system has already been compromised by other factors.) Buckingham Palace dismissed Hutchins's claims as "absolute nonsense," but the Queen and Prince Charles are well ahead of the field in terms of their knowledge and use of homeopathy and other alternative forms of medicine. It would be surprising if they weren't aware of the mercury fears and debate. Charles, who has even awarded a Royal Warrant to a homeopathic firm to supply remedies for livestock on his Duchy of Cornwall farms, told the Royal College of General Practitioners on video in July 1990 (see VIDEOS) that he was "saddened" by the mistrustful attitudes of doctors to complementary medicine. "What I am in favor of," he said, "is the harnessing of the best aspects of ancient and modern medicine to contribute toward the most effective healing of the patient's mind and body."

Charles was praised by hospital doctors in Cirencester for the way he faced the first operation on his right arm, broken playing polo in June 1990. But Diana later joked at a Buckingham Palace garden party that he was "a bad patient," adding, "But then so are all men . . . well, at least 75 percent of them." In October 1990, when Diana revisited flood victims in Towyn, North Wales, and was asked how Charles was, she said, "He's looking much better. He is going fishing and golfing and other things that men do. He would like to get back on his horse." And she indicated that she couldn't prevent him from rushing his recovery. "Like most men, he does what he wants to do. He's doing what he shouldn't do half the time," she said. See MARRIAGE.

The Princess goes to health clubs and farms. She once spent two nights at Champneys health farm in Hertfordshire, naughtily taking several Kit Kat bars in with her. She reportedly had aromatherapy massages with essential oils of geranium and rose at Ragdale Health Hydro. See BEAUTY SECRETS. While at Sandringham, she and Fergie have nipped off for a swim at the local

Knights Hill Health Club. And at Balmoral, they have both taken their children to splash around and swim in the tropical indoor pool at the nearby Craigendarroch Country Club. In September 1990, Diana joined the LA Fitness club in Old Isleworth, Middlesex, to get superfit after reading in *You* magazine of its new American exercise system, pioneered there by instructor Carolan Brown and called Steps. After that news leaked out, it was reported that Carolan was giving the Princess private instruction at Kensington Palace instead. Diana's exercise routine to keep fit and stay trim, apart from swimming and regular games of tennis (see SPORT), also includes doing a daily two-mile walk at home on a treadmill and jogging.

HELP THE AGED

Though Diana is always associated with her love of children, she also shows great care and concern for elderly people. As a member of the Voluntary Service Unit during her final year at West Heath school (see EDUCATION), she used to spend one afternoon every week helping an old lady who lived near Sevenoaks. In 1985, she became Patron of Help the Aged, which was founded in 1961 to help improve the quality of life of frail, isolated, and poor elderly people in Britain and abroad with fund-raising and aid programs and by promoting a better awareness and understanding of their needs. In practical terms, it raises and grants funds toward community-based projects, housing, and overseas aid. It has given more than six thousand grants to local neighborhood projects and community organizations to develop day centers and luncheon clubs, provided some 760 minibuses to ferry elderly people about, and supplied more than fourteen thousand domestic emergency alarm units to improve security at home. With fund-raising assistance and donations, it supports hospices and day hospitals, and it has established a network of sheltered housing projects and registered residential care homes. Among its projects abroad, through its HelpAge International program, the charity supports health care campaigns and gives the elderly emergency relief in times of disaster. The Princess has made at least twenty-seven visits to Help the Aged projects in Britain and others abroad. See

HONG KONG and THAILAND. In January 1990, when she visited elders of the Shia Muslim Senior Citizens Association, which has been helped by the charity, at the multipurpose Husaini Shia Islamic Centre—the first of its kind in the world—in Stanmore, Middlesex, Diana made a point of covering her head to show respect for traditional custom.

HIV

Diana's top priority has always been to be a good wife and mother, but her concerns about children, family life, and indeed marriage are very much reflected in her public work too. She has also chosen to be particularly involved, through various organizations, with the disabled, deaf, blind, elderly, and homeless. More surprising, however, is the work she has taken on to help with the problems of drug addiction, alcoholism, and mental illness—fields not normally associated with royalty—and in particular the pioneering action she has taken internationally to counteract worldwide ignorance, prejudice, and fear about HIV (or AIDS) and leprosy. Indeed, nothing demonstrates more clearly her personal courage and compassion or the way she has brought royalty closer to the people and literally in touch with today's world. Perhaps her greatest and most natural quality is that she spreads happiness, and the dark recesses where people hunger for kindness or relief from some so-far incurable disease are where joy and understanding are needed most.

Though AIDS has been dubbed a modern form of "plague," the Princess has demonstrated personally, as she has done with leprosy, that the disease, however devastating, does not render sufferers untouchable and, by implication, that it is an added cruelty for them to be shunned. In 1987, proving that AIDS cannot be passed on by casual contact, Diana shook hands with patients when she opened the AIDS unit of Middlesex Hospital in London. The fact that she did so without wearing gloves, one of them commented later, "meant more to me than anything." In November 1988, she attended a charity auction at Christie's of works donated by some of Britain's top painters and sculptors, which raised more than £450,000 for a new AIDS center. In February 1989, she shook hands and chatted with AIDS patients

Diana comforts an AIDS patient at St. Stephen's Hospital in London. (Globe Photos)

at a special hospice at Mildmays Mission Hospital in east London, the first of its type to open in Europe. One of them, Shane Snape (whom she had first met when he worked as a nurse in the AIDS unit of Middlesex Hospital two years before), commented afterward, "She is doing as much for AIDS sufferers as a nurse or doctor." The same month, during her solo trip to New York, Diana earned wide praise for cuddling children dying of AIDS at Harlem Hospital. See AMERICA. And that July, she opened a new AIDS center in south London, where she sat in on a counseling session with a male AIDS patient and learned that women who get AIDS by having sex with men receive even less sympathy than male sufferers. The Princess took this to heart, remarking several times that she was surprised that the problems faced by women with AIDS had not received more attention, declaring, "I think it is terrible what they have to go through." Jonathan Grimshaw, Director of the center, who had discovered five years before that he was HIV positive himself, revealed after the visit, "The Princess was genuinely moved by the difficulties facing patients." Among many other visits connected with AIDS, in July 1991— shortly after becoming Patron of the National AIDS Trust—Diana revisited the HIV wards at Middlesex Hospital with First Lady Barbara Bush. (President Bush was in London for economic summit talks.) When an AIDS patient, Steve, asked Diana why she was always involved "with the deaf and the sick," she replied movingly, "Anywhere I see suffering, that is where I want to be— doing what I can." Prince Charles's former valet, Stephen Barry, who left his job shortly after the royal wedding, died of AIDS-related pneumonia at age thirty-seven in 1986. His friend Richard Mosselman, who had nursed Barry through his last two years, died from AIDS three years later at the age of twenty-three. See AUTOGRAPHS, HEALTH, LEPROSY, STAFF, and X-RATED.

HOLIDAYS

Royal holidays are traditionally spent with the Queen: Christmas and Easter at Windsor, the New Year at Sandringham, and the summer holidays at Balmoral in Scotland. (However, Christmas has been spent at Sandringham in recent years because of refurbishment at Windsor Castle.) The ten weeks a year Prince Charles takes off also include a week's annual skiing in Klosters in Switzerland. The differences between Charles and Diana are never emphasized more than at vacation times. He is a countryman who loves the rain and finds simple country pursuits at wet, windy Balmoral bliss. She prefers sunshine and sophisticated London life and would rather be lunching with girlfriends at San Lorenzo, shopping at Harvey Nichols, and going to the ballet or opera. He likes activity holidays, painting, sketching, or fishing. She likes to laze around on a beach with a good book, sunbathing and swimming. As a child, Diana's family had a beach hut at the seaside in Brancaster in Norfolk, where they'd go in the summer. She still prefers bucket-and-spade holidays, where William and Harry can build sandcastles while she works on her tan. So the couple compromise. Charles joins his wife and children on seaside holidays in Majorca, where they have stayed for several years with

King Juan Carlos and Queen Sofia of Spain at Marivent Palace, their summer home on a hilltop overlooking Palma, where they play ping-pong in the evenings and listen to music. The King, then aged fifty-two—who dived fully clothed into the sea to rescue two drowning girls in the Bay of Palma in July 1990—loves teasing William and Harry and put a blow-up Loch Ness monster in the pool for them that year, which they loved.

For the rest of the summer holidays, Diana and the children go with Charles to Balmoral, where they stay at a lodge called Craigowan on the estate. They are also reported to have bought a cottage in the hills above Royal Deeside in 1987. They have also vacationed on the car-free Scilly island of Tresco, where they all go cycling. Charles owns the island, as Duke of Cornwall, which he leases to his friend Robert Dorrien-Smith and his wife Lady Emma, and has a small holiday house on St. Mary's called Tamarisk. At other times, the royal couple each do their own thing. Charles has gone off milking cows, fishing, sketching, painting, and communing with nature in the Kalahari desert. See MARRIAGE. In May 1989 he visited archaeological sites in Turkey. That January Diana took the children on holiday to Necker, tycoon Richard Branson's private seventy-four acre island in the Caribbean. In April 1990, while Charles was salmon fishing in Scotland, she returned to Necker in a seventeen-strong family party which included her mother, her sisters and their children, and her brother and his wife. The Balinese-style main house there came complete with ten bedrooms (and mosquito nets), bamboo furniture, a bamboo-framed TV with 102 channels, piano, snooker table, Jacuzzi, freshwater swimming pool, tennis court, naked statues, and a staff of nineteen. Other celebrities who have found privacy on the paradise island include Steven Spielberg, Harrison Ford, John Hurt, Paul McCartney, Bryan Ferry, Phil Collins, Robert De Niro (who had caviar flown in), Richard Dreyfuss (who raided the fridge), Annie Lennox (who sang Christmas carols with the cook), and Princess Stephanie of Monaco. But even paradise can prove uncomfortable for Diana. "Five days in that heat was too much," she said later. See HEALTH. She also hates being pestered by Press cameramen while she's on vacation. See PRESS.

Honeymoon

After their wedding, Charles and Diana boarded a special three-coach royal train to travel the eighty miles from London to Hampshire, where they spent the first night of their honeymoon at Broadlands, the home of Lord and Lady Romsey (see FRIENDS) and the former home of Lord Mountbatten, where the Queen and Prince Philip had begun their honeymoon thirty-four years before. As the bride and groom began to relax and unwind from the pressures of the wedding, Charles was soon out fishing for salmon on the river Test, which runs through the six thousand acres of land around the house. After a couple of days of seclusion, Charles flew them to Gibraltar, in an RAF Andover, to meet the royal yacht *Britannia*. Practically everyone in Gibraltar had decided to give the newlyweds a send-off to remember. About thirty thousand people lined the two-mile route waving Union Jacks, throwing confetti, and cheering as the royal couple drove in an open Triumph Stag to the dockyard. There they boarded the yacht for a cruise of the Mediterranean. Successfully evading Press cameramen, Charles and Diana swam, snorkled, scuba dived, sunbathed, windsurfed, had beach barbecues, and relaxed for two perfect weeks. The yacht made secretly for the Algerian coast, then on to Tunisia, Sicily, and the Greek islands. Nine years later, in March 1990, American psychic Sandra Leigh Serio reportedly claimed that the Prince and Princess were Greek sailors in an earlier life and that "their honeymoon cruise of the Mediterranean was a reenactment of their previous existence."

Be that as it may, *Britannia* then sailed to Egypt, land of mysteries, treasure, and fabulous sunsets, where at Port Said they invited Egyptian President Anwar Sadat (who was shortly after assassinated) and his English-born wife Jihan for dinner on board. Then they continued via the Suez Canal to the Red Sea, where sailors on *Britannia* caught a ten-foot shark close, but fortunately not close enough, to where they were swimming. Too soon the cruise was over. The Sadats saw them off when they boarded an RAF VC 10 at the military airfield at Hurghada to fly to Scotland, joining the Royal Family for several weeks at Balmoral, where during a honeymoon photo session for the Press teams they'd managed to dodge (except at Port Said, where they'd posed for photographs), the couple looked very together and relaxed. As for married life, "I can highly recommend it," Diana revealed happily. During the honeymoon, the Princess developed a passion for Pimms. And that, she indicated with a twinkle, wasn't all . . . See BEDS & BEDROOMS, MARRIAGE, and FOOD & DRINK.

HONG KONG

The massacre of Chinese students taking part in the peaceful prodemocracy demonstrations in Peking's Tiananmen Square in June 1989 forced the cancellation of Charles and Diana's planned six-day tour of China. It also heightened anxieties among Hong Kong's six million residents as to what the future might hold for them after Britain hands the colony back to the People's Republic of China in 1997. Fears became fury when the British Government then refused to grant up to 3.2 million Hong Kong Chinese the right to live in Britain. Another controversy about the plight of fifty-six thousand Vietnamese boat people held at camps in the colony, who were threatened by Britain with forcible repatriation, cast further doubt on the wisdom of the royal couple's planned three-day visit to Hong Kong in November 1989. In the end, however, despite the threat of anti-British demonstrations, it went ahead. In Hong Kong the Prince had to steer clear of political controversy in his speeches. But he was reported to have expressed deep concern privately about the fate of British passport holders in the colony. And it was claimed that he and Diana wished to meet the boat people but were banned from seeing them. On the surface, the royal visit to Hong Kong, the eleventh richest economy in the world, took place as if none of these issues were festering beneath. Indeed, far from making the couple the focus of their anti-British anger, the people gave them a surprisingly warm welcome, cheering and clapping (not normal custom for the reserved Chinese) and pushing against crash barriers to spot Di On Na Wong Fei (shortened affectionately to Wong Fei), meaning Diana, royal concubine.

Charles and Diana flew in after dark from Indonesia, seeing the glittering lights of Hong Kong from the harbor as they crossed in the Governor's launch to Queen's Pier, where they were greeted with a twenty-one gun salute and a spectacular welcoming ceremony which included a traditional lion dance and a laser light show. The Princess, wearing a sensational Catherine Walker silk suit in red, cream, and purple with a sarong skirt and a pagoda-ish Philip Somerville straw hat, was especially enchanted by the kindergarten tots. Next day, at a local youth branch of the Red Cross, she watched a demonstration of first aid and heard the children sing. Later, during a visit to HMS *Tamar*, the naval shore base where the royal yacht *Britannia* was berthed for the royal visit, she laughed as, one after another, five fragrant garlands of flowers were placed over her head by Nepalese girls related to Gurkha officers stationed there. But a huge row erupted when it was discovered that a Chinese photographer clicking away from an overlooking skyscraper had bypassed blanket security to photograph Diana having her early morning swim in a pool at the base. The London-based Rat Pack (see PRESS) went crazy trying to buy up the pictures, showing the Princess doing backstroke in a red one-piece swimsuit. They finally went to the *Daily Star* for £25,000, which splashed them on the front page and center-page spread. In a story headlined "DI IN PERIL," *Star* reporter Hugh Whittow claimed that the camera could have been a sniper's gun. And that Diana had been left vulnerable to a bullet from hitmen allegedly hired to kill her by Triad godfathers (organized crime figures) angry that their crime empires would suffer once China regains Hong Kong. Security was tightened even more, producing further trouble when television news crews walked out, claiming they were unable to film Diana watching the Royal Marines band on the deck of the *Britannia* from the only spot nervous cops allowed them to use their cameras.

But the Princess carried on with her program regardless, visiting a drug addiction center on Shek Wu Chau island for two hundred youths withdrawing from heroin. She attended a gala concert by the British Bach Choir with Charles, who has sung with them (see MUSIC) to mark the opening of the new Cultural Centre, a huge pink concrete building on the Kowloon shore from which one of the world's most magnificent views could be obtained had they installed windows. Prince Charles, well known for his opinion on modern architecture, avoided giving his verdict on the much-criticized building, nicknamed the Ski Jump. But he did break one royal rule. See AUTOGRAPHS. During their brief stay, as Patron of Help the Aged, Diana showed her sympathy and concern for Hong Kong's seven thousand homeless old folk by visiting a home at Chak On Estate which provides shelter for about nine hundred elderly people in need and runs a home-visiting program. The home is supported by the charity's sister organization in the colony, Helping Hand, which was also pioneering a project through which the local authorities would pay for places for elderly people in its care homes. Despite the problems in Hong Kong and the fears expressed beforehand, the visit went surprisingly well and proved a personal success for the royal couple. Saying she wished she could have stayed longer, Diana flew home alone, the *Sun* bestowing on her the headline "KONG-QUEROR DI." Prince Charles sailed off on the *Britannia* for a private visit to islands in the South China Sea to film more of his BBC documentary on the environment. He had visited Hong Kong ten years before, but what he had seen on the tour with Diana had left a strong impression. "It is impossible not to be impressed by the vigor and resourcefulness of the people of this city," he said. "It is these qualities which are the real guarantees for Hong Kong's prosperity in the years ahead."

HOSPITALS

Links between the Royal Family and the world-famous Great Ormond Street Children's Hospital in London go back to its humble beginnings about 140 years ago. In Dickensian times, children in Britain worked up chimneys, down the mines, and in factories. In 1850, for fear of infection, no hospital would admit the twenty-one thousand children, all under age ten, who ended up dying in their poverty-stricken hovels or in the street. Then, in 1852, Dr. Charles West opened the Hospital for Sick Children, as it is correctly called, at 49 Great Ormond Street. The hospital, the first of its kind in the country, had just ten beds. The first Patron was Queen Victoria, and one of its original supporters was Charles Dickens, whose reading of A *Christmas Carol* raised sufficient funds to buy the house next door and double the number of beds. In 1937, the copyright for *Peter Pan* was bequeathed by Sir James Barrie to the hospital which now, much expanded, has a Barrie Wing and a Peter Pan Ward. Today Great Ormond Street is Britain's major children's hospital and, as it says, "a major centre of paediatric medicine, a pioneer in many areas of child care, a training ground for doctors and nurses throughout the UK and overseas, and a beacon of hope for thousands of children and their parents." The current Patron is the Queen, the hospital has 348 beds, and it admits about twelve thousand baby and child inpatients and sees around fifty thousand outpatients each year from all parts of the world. The hospital's motto is "The Child First and Always."

When he was eleven years old, Prince Charles was rushed to Great Ormond Street in a dramatic four-hour dash as a "blue light special" with appendicitis. "When we got there from my school in Newbury, the thing was about to explode," he recalled. "But I was looked after very well, particularly by the nursing staff, who spoiled me rotten, and I did not want to go home." It was a case of like father like son in 1988 when Prince Harry went in overnight for a hernia operation. And in 1991 when William was rushed in for an operation after his skull was fractured in an accident at school.

With Charles, Diana was Joint Patron of the Wishing Well Appeal, named after a well which once stood on the grounds. The Appeal, to raise £42 million to secure the future of the hospital by redeveloping it, was launched by the Prince to the public by satellite TV broadcast from Highgrove in October 1987. Diana visited the hospital that December when, with Jimmy Tarbuck dressed as Santa Claus, she distributed presents to young outpatients, making national headlines and further increasing publicity. A reception the royal couple hosted gained the support of the Navy, Army, Air Force, and organizations like the Rotary, Round Table, Women's Institutes, Scouts, Guides, and the police and fire departments. And they made personal donations themselves, as did the Queen, the Queen Mother, Princess Margaret, and Prince Michael of Kent. The Appeal, whose brilliant teardrop logo appeared on forty million of Diana's favorite Mars bars among other items (see FAVORITE THINGS), had tens of thousands of supporters, became the largest and most successful appeal of its kind ever mounted in Britain, and reached its target of £42 million by January 1989, a year ahead of schedule. One contributor, ten-year-old Joanne Morris from Twickenham, even raised £27 from a bout of chicken pox when she was sponsored for the number of spots she got. In June that year, a special service of thanksgiving was held at Westminster Abbey, with music before and after played by the band of the Royal Hampshire Regiment, of which Diana is Colonel-in-Chief. See ARMED FORCES. The service was attended by the Prince and Princess who, according to the Chairman of the Appeal, amiable former Agriculture Minister James Prior, had "taken a very personal interest in the progress of the Appeal by attending events and supporting us whenever possible." In a letter from Kensington Palace after the target was reached, Charles and Diana wrote:

> We have watched not only as Patrons, but also as parents, the astonishing progress of the Wishing Well Appeal since our initial involvement in 1986.
> It has given us tremendous pleasure to find that the Hospital has a special place in the hearts of so many people in the United Kingdom and also in many parts of the world. That the target has been reached in much less than the anticipated two years is the best indication of the affection the nation has for this special Hospital.
> The success of the Appeal is due to a wonderful community effort, with thousands contributing generously of both their money and their time. We are proud to have been part of such an exciting venture and would like to offer our appreciation and congratulations to everyone concerned.

In 1990 Diana became President of the Hospital for Sick Children. She is also President of the Royal Marsden Hospital, the famous London cancer hospital; and Patron of the National Hospitals for Nervous Diseases, now renamed the National Hospital for Neurology and Neurosurgery, where her father, Lord Spencer, was treated after his near-fatal stroke in 1978 (see FAMILY); and Patron of the Trust for Sick Children in Wales, set up in 1984, whose projects include raising money to build accommodations for parents of sick children in hospitals in Wales.

She regularly visits hospitals and hospices, and she has been credited with near-miraculous curative powers. In 1985, thirteen-year-old Lindsey Elliott, who was hospitalized in deep shock after her mother, aunt, and uncle had perished in the Boeing 737 blaze in Manchester, hadn't opened her eyes for days. But when Diana approached her bedside and began talking to her, she did. In 1989 Diana's friend Chloe Teacher, in a coma after a riding accident, said visits from the Prince and Princess had helped her make an amazing near-total recovery. See FRIENDS. And consultant Peter Gautier-Smith, of the National Hospital's rehabilitation homes, has been quoted as saying that Diana "seems to have extraordinary healing powers. You could almost compare it to the laying-on of hands. She has a miraculous effect on people. The uplift which the Princess gives can sometimes do more good than any doctor."

In September 1990, the Princess visited patients at Queen's Medical Centre, Nottingham, where Prince Charles was recovering from a second NHS (National Health Service) operation on his right arm. See SPORT. Among them was twenty-three-year-old father of two Dean Woodward, in a coma on a life-support machine since a road crash, whom she visited four times. During one visit she hugged his mother, Ivy, and spent forty-five minutes at Dean's bedside, sharing his family's tearful vigil. Dean's uncle, Terry Woodward, said later that Ivy was "convinced that Dean's grip in her hand tightened" when Diana touched him. "I cannot believe what she has done for us," he said. "She shook all our hands and was so reassuring. We thanked her for her support and she just blushed. She's one hell of a woman. You usually see the royals on TV and think they are untouchable, but she's the most human woman I have ever met. I was never a royalist before, but I definitely am now. There was something magical about it. She has been sent by God as far as I'm concerned. She is an angel." Dean came out of his coma after four weeks at the end of September, when his father John, an ex-miner, said, "What the Princess has done is a miracle. She came to us when we thought everything was hopeless. I thought Dean was going to die. I'm sure the Princess has helped save my son's life." Diana, who had sent Dean's mother a bouquet, taken her sons to meet the family, and made regular phone calls to encourage them, was "delighted" at Dean's recovery and visited him after he left the hospital.

The Princess was very sorry to hear of the death in August 1990 of twenty-one-year-old cancer victim Mandy Turner, who had spent her final months raising £1 million toward a hospital body scanner and died within days of reaching the target. Diana had sent her a message of support that July, and, with the Duchess of Kent and Mrs. Thatcher, was among the first of thousands to send messages of condolence. Just before her death, Mandy won first prize in the YMCA/BBC Radio 4 *Today* program's Best of British Youth awards.

Diana's help to the sick was acknowledged, though sent up, on TV's "Drop the Dead Donkey" comedy series about television journalists, in which one character remarked, "I thought the story on Princess Diana's verruca [wart] was a great comfort to verruca sufferers." In Truro, Cornwall, last year, the Princess launched the Dump 1990 Campaign urging people to get rid of old and unwanted medicines left around at home, which cause about 2,500 accidental deaths every year.

HUNGARY

Mikhail Gorbachev's *perestroika*, the falling of the Berlin Wall only a few months before, and the decline of communism throughout Eastern Europe were the prelude to Charles and Diana's historic four-day official visit to Hungary in May 1990. It was the first ever made by members of the British Royal Family to a Warsaw Pact country, and they were given an ecstatic and emotional welcome after flying in forty-five minutes late from London due to an "electrical fault" in the plane. At Ferihegy airport in Budapest, when the Hungarian national anthem was played for the first time in public since Hungary broke free of its communist shackles and held free elections, the emotion proved too great for some to conceal. Zsuzsa, the sixty-four-year-old wife of Hungary's first non-communist leader, President Arpad Goncz (a writer who had been imprisoned after the 1956 anti-Soviet revolution for more than six years), wept openly and clutched Diana's hand. That evening, Charles referred to his Hungarian great-great-great-grandmother, Claudine, Countess Rhedey, of whom he had been given a portrait, saying, "I am enormously proud of the Hungarian blood which courses somewhere in my veins." He declared, "Our visit comes at an extraordinary and challenging moment in your history. Having watched, powerless and desperate, as you endured your tribulations for the past forty years, our hearts leapt with joy when you finally cast aside the remnants of your chains." The next day, standing alongside a statue of Karl Marx at the University of Economics, he made a passionate speech against communism, speaking of the Soviet Union's seventy years of "horrendous totalitarianism." Going around a market, seeing the tourist sights and a fashion parade, visiting a film set, watching dancers in traditional costume and displays of bareback riding and whip cracking in the countryside, visiting a peasant farmhouse, meeting the crowds—many of the men gallantly kissing her hand—Diana quickly sensed the excited jubilation of the people. She commented, "It's almost spiritual. The Hungarians are elated to be free." The royal visit, said the President, would be "a great help to the new democratic Hungary."

On the final day Diana visited the famous Peto Institute, which for forty years has achieved miracles for handicapped children brought by their parents from all parts of the globe, often when local doctors have claimed nothing more can be done to help them. Their success was epitomized by nine-year-old Dawn Rogers from Carlton, Nottingham, who can now write, speak English and Hungarian, feed herself, and even walk—as she proved to the Princess by stepping toward her. Only three years before, having sacrificed everything to raise the funds for her treatment, Dawn's parents had taken her to the Institute from England as a quadriplegic spastic in a wheelchair who couldn't even hold up her head. Tears came to Diana's eyes as she heard that and similar stories, confessing that she found it all "absolutely heartbreaking" but "very moving." In her first investiture, on behalf of the Queen, the Princess pinned an honorary Order of the British Empire (OBE) insignia to the lapel of Dr. Maria Hari, the Institute's Director, and told her, "It is the Queen's wish that I give you this OBE. She hopes that my being here will help the Institute." Dr. Hari remarked later that the Princess was "exceptional" with children and would make a good Peto conductor (their word for instructor) herself. The immense contribution the conductors make was made clear again by the devastation felt in Hungary and Britain two months later when one of the Institute's most experienced conductors, Hungarian Mrs. Erzgebet Kameniczki, a thirty-five-year-old mother of two who was on holiday with British families involved in the Peto program, slipped during a clifftop walk at Land's End and plunged 150 feet to her death. She had joined the Institute, founded by Dr. Andras Peto, more than ten years before. In 1989 she had spent six months helping at a British school funded by the Foundation for Conductive Education, a Birmingham-based independent national charity set up in 1986 to bring Peto's work to the U.K. Impressed by the work she had seen in Hungary, in December 1990 Diana visited the school, the Birmingham Institute for Conductive Education, which teaches children and adults with cerebral palsy and Parkinson's disease to lead independent lives without wheelchairs or major artificial aids. She also became Royal Patron of the Foundation.

9

INDONESIA

Indonesia, a Muslim democracy of 180 million people, had its first contact with the British when Sir Francis Drake's ship, the *Golden Hind*, sailed in more than four hundred years ago. In November 1989, the country welcomed Charles and Diana on their first official visit, a late replacement for their canceled trip to China. See HONG KONG. It was in Indonesia, at the start of their Far East tour, that Diana first showed her courage and compassion in the face of leprosy, demonstrating publicly by shaking hands with lepers that the disease does not make them untouchable. Dr. Maartin Teterissa, Director of the pioneering Sitanala Leprosy Hospital on the edge of the jungle fifteen miles from Jakarta, which aims to cure and rehabilitate patients, said later, "Her visit means everything to me. And not only me but all the five hundred thousand lepers in Indonesia. It will show the world that this disease is not as frightening as they think." Diana had particularly asked to visit the hospital and, sweltering in 94° F, she met and shook hands with about 100 of the 550 patients, helping to break down stigma and prejudice. Accompanying news teams flinched at the sight of the patients' suffering and their cruelly disfigured limbs. The Princess did not, though she could not fail to be upset. It was the children's ward which touched her most. The patients were so young. "She did so much more than she had to," said a doctor there. "She need only have shaken their hands and moved on, but she sat on their beds and listened." She watched a couple of children playing chess and outside joined a game of bowls. She bowled two woods up the green after saying, "I don't want to make a fool of myself," and she raised both hands in delight at her success with the second. See SPORT. As she left the hospital, Dr. Teterissa said, "The Princess has done an enormous service to the world's fifteen million leprosy sufferers by demonstrating that the disease is fully curable by drugs, and that it is contagious only through many years of constant and prolonged contact." See LEPROSY.

Although the royal couple began their five-day visit at the start of the monsoon season, and there was a tropical downpour as they flew toward Jakarta, President Suharto had brought in a Rain Mover, his personal pawang, to ensure dry weather for their arrival at Halim military airport. (It had poured on the Pope, so this time they took no chances.) The pawang was reported to have fasted for seven days and prayed around the clock, along with other pawangs, in preparation. And sure enough, by the time the royal VIPs flew in, the clouds had cleared. (It works the other way too. I've seen Hopi Native Americans, whom Charles admires, produce rain for their own reservation, which stopped short of the Navajo land next door. Incidentally, one of Charles's childhood playmates, the Honorable James Lascelles, son of the Queen's cousin, the Earl of Harewood, and thirty-second in line to the British throne, is married to a beautiful Native American named Shadow. They live with their daughter Tanit and son Tewa among members of the Isleta Pueblo and Choctaw tribes in Albuquerque, New Mexico.) Diana looked cool and delicious in a cream silk suit and one of Philip Somerville's wondrously flattering matching hats. Jakarta schoolchildren presented her with a bouquet of orchids and sweet-scented jasmine, and they garlanded Charles with white jasmine and red roses, the national colors of Indonesia.

During their official welcome at the presidential palace, Instana Merde, jet-lagged after their sixteen-hour flight from London in a Royal Air Force DC 10, the Prince told the President, "Excuse me if I fall asleep tomorrow morning" [when they were due for a further meeting]. He added, "I think all planes should be fitted with bunks because the best way to travel is to sleep to adjust to the time delay." The royal couple had been briefed on the country while in London by Charles's old friend, Sir Laurens van der Post, who was Lord Mountbatten's Military-Political Officer attached to 15 Indian Army Corps in Java, one of the Indonesian islands, around 1945. The Prince discovered more on the second day of the visit, when Diana went to the leper hospital, at a lunch with Indonesians of his own generation who are experts in various fields. Such meetings, where Charles can meet tomorrow's leaders and learn more about their part of the world, have become a regular feature of his tours. That evening, Diana giggled at the British Ambassador's reception where a model of London's Tower Bridge, carved in ice, forgot its stiff upper lip and melted in the heat as her husband began a speech. "I feel very strange about addressing you all in front of a collapsing Tower . . . ," he joked. "I suspect it may have been staged deliberately." There was a display of traditional dancing later, after the presidential banquet, where Diana refused champagne (see FOOD & DRINK) and Charles grinned as they were serenaded with a memorable version of "Colonel Bogie" by a bamboo band.

The next day they flew on to Yogyakarta where Charles wanted to see the world's oldest and largest Buddhist temple, Borobudur, which has become the national symbol of Indonesia. Elephants dragged two million blocks of gray stone to the site for the temple to be built around A.D. 750. It has 504 statues of Buddha, some protected by stupas (bell-shaped domes in stone latticework), and carvings, depicting scenes from Buddha's many lives, which stretch for about four miles. The temple was lost for centuries under volcanic ash until it was rediscovered in 1814 by Sir Stamford Raffles, the British administrator who had taken part in the capture of Java from the Dutch three years earlier and who, while Governor of Sumatra, founded Singapore in 1819. Charles, who takes a deep interest in archaeology and Buddhist philosophy, climbed about a hundred steep steps to the top of the temple and reached inside one stupa to touch the hand of a "magic" statue of Buddha which is said to grant one wish. Press photographers, who always like an action replay for their cameras, asked him to do it again and the Prince laughed, saying, "You can only do it once. You only have one wish." At Yogyakarta, the royal couple also visited the Karaton, the ornate eighteenth-century Javanese palace of the Sultan of the province, Hamengku Buwono X, and his beautiful Queen Hemas, who sat with them in the jasmine-scented Golden Pavilion to see a traditional performance by court entertainers. The humidity was killing, and Diana sat discreetly blowing air from the corner of her mouth on to her face to try and cool down as she and Charles watched a shadow puppet show and a stylized two-hundred-year-old classical dance by exotically dressed Javanese girls playing two warrior princesses vying for the love of the same king. A gamelan orchestra played, which may have been of particular interest to Charles (who, like many keen gardeners, talks encouragingly to his plants) since gamelan music is said to make flowers grow faster.

Another highlight of the tour, given his concern for the environment and the fact that many forest areas have been lost in Indonesia, was a visit to the Wanagame Reforestation Project where a whole new rain forest has been planted and grown on once-barren land. He was accompanied by Dr. Emil Salim, a world authority on the tropical rain forest and Indonesia's Environment Minister, whose views turned out, reportedly, to coincide with those of Professor Timothy O'Reardon, Charles's environmental adviser from the University of East Anglia. Souvenirs he came back with when he was reunited with his wife included some honey from a stall for himself, a fan, and some eucalyptus oil for her. The final day was spent in Jakarta, where Diana met children at the British School, joined Charles at a theme park called Taman Mini where tourists can get a taste of Indonesia's twenty-seven provinces, and attended a ladies' lunch where, according to an aide, she was "impressed" to find that "women play such an important role in Indonesia, unlike many other Muslim countries." Charles's last visit was to a rat-infested shantytown in the densely populated Grogol area beside a hideously polluted river used by the poor, barefooted people for sewage, drinking water, and washing. He pressed a button to officially open a water-purifying plant, a British project and a world first, and presto—clean, healthy water on tap! A successful end to a successful visit before he and Diana flew off on the second stage of their Far East tour. See HONG KONG.

INTERNATIONAL SPINAL RESEARCH TRUST

Part of Diana's work for the disabled is done through the International Spinal Research Trust, whose sole purpose is to find a cure for paraplegia. A paraplegic is paralyzed from the waist down as a result of injury to the spine. There are thought to be about thirty-five thousand people with spinal injuries in the United Kingdom alone. The shocking fact is that the average age at which these injuries occur is nineteen. Young, active people who are injured riding, swimming, playing rugby, or in industrial or car accidents can find they must spend the rest of their lives in a wheelchair in conditions, says the Trust, which can be more confining, horrible, and barbaric than those in prison. Apart from immobility, incontinence, and lack of, or reduced, sexual function, side effects of the injury can result in further illness which the Trust declares "makes life a constant struggle against death." Those who know term paralysis an "endless, tormented nightmare," and there is no remission until a cure can be discovered. Thus the Trust. It was founded in 1981 by Stewart Yesner, who broke his neck in a car accident in Zambia when he was seventeen.

The Princess's first engagement for the Trust came in 1986, three years before she became Royal Patron, when she greeted the three youths who had taken part in the Great British Push, pushing themselves in their wheelchairs the length of Britain from John O'Groats to Land's End, which took forty-two days and helped raise funds of £500,000. They went to Kensington Palace to meet her. In 1989 Diana launched a second Push, from Edinburgh to London, inviting the charity to lunch with her at the Palace after the finish. "She actually threw a party there for all our supporters and everyone involved, and it was the first time one had taken place at the Orangery," recalled Trust Secretary Mrs. Valerie Dunk. It was a hot July day and William and Harry arrived too, in Bermuda shorts—William toting a gift which he gave to a child in a wheelchair. "The Princess shows great concern and real understanding for people in wheelchairs," Mrs. Dunk said. "She knows about spinal injuries because she opened the spinal unit at Stoke Mandeville Hospital."

In July 1990, Diana wrote a foreword to a Trust brochure in which she said she had always been "deeply impressed" by the "courage and cheerfulness" of the many victims of spinal cord injury she had met. "Though confined to wheelchairs," she wrote, "they set the rest of us a tremendous example of physical and spiritual perseverance. The work which the Trust sponsors bears the hopes of many such brave people. Although much remains to be done, in recent years these hopes have moved closer to fulfillment. As Patron, I offer my encouragement to all who are working to achieve this aim, which needs—and deserves—all our support."

Among those who have helped raise funds for the Trust are Diana's former dancing partner, Andrew Widdowson (see FRIENDS), and his mother, Felicity, who is a friend of the Princess's mother, Mrs. Frances Shand Kydd. After seven-year-old Lerona Gelb was paralyzed in a car accident in 1988, her mother Susan, from Whetstone, north London, asked how she could raise funds. It was suggested she start with a coffee morning. Instead, a week later she had booked the London Palladium, where a host of stars, including Wayne Sleep, appeared in *Lerona's Celebrity Spectacular* in October 1990, which Diana attended, raising £125,000! Patrons of the Trust include the very rich Duke of Buccleuch, who became paralyzed after a riding accident while out hunting but has apparently managed to shoot grouse since from a chair strapped to a Land Rover; and until her recent death, Dame Margot Fonteyn, whose late husband, Roberto Arias, was paralyzed after being shot in a Panamanian assassination attempt. See DANCING. In 1991 Diana also became Patron of the Association for Spinal Injury Research, Rehabilitation and Reintegration.

ITALY

Diana's plans to meet the Italians were subject to some delay, but since Italians love *bambini*, they no doubt understood. Having canceled at the last minute from a grand dinner which the Italian Ambassador, Signor Andrea Cagiati, and his wife were due to give for her and Prince Charles in November 1981, it was announced the following day that Diana was expecting her first child. And in February 1984, the royal couple's proposed visit to Italy that October was canceled the day after it was announced because by then she was pregnant again! The tour of Italy, one of Prince Charles's favorite countries, was rearranged for the spring of 1985. Just prior to the seventeen-day tour, journalists and diplomats from five out of six nations voted the Princess the most popular Briton abroad, which must have given her a considerable boost after a long break from international duties while she devoted herself to motherhood.

Choosing a wardrobe for the Italian Job posed a few prob-

Diana arrives at the Vatican for a private audience with the Pope. (Glenn Harvey/Camera Press London)

lems, not least because of Diana's scheduled first audience with the Pope. For him women are traditionally expected to wear black and be veiled. But even the Queen had fallen afoul of Italians in 1961 because the black lace Norman Hartnell dress she'd worn at the Vatican had a scooped neckline. For her return visit in 1980 she took three possible choices for safety, finally wearing an outfit by Hardy Amies. However, when a female journalist rang the Vatican in January 1984, before the original planned visit, to ask what form of dress Diana would be expected to wear, a Papal spokesman was reported to have made the memorable reply, "Well, as long as she doesn't clash with the Pope, dear. He will be all in white, long dress, long sleeves." For the rest of the trip, Diana was expected to lay on a virtual fashion firework display since Italy is one of the world's leading fashion centers and the Italians like their clothes feminine, chic, and sexy.

Since Italy is also the land of handsome dark-haired Romeos who have a hard time keeping their hands to themselves when they see some luscious foreign blond, the pistol-packing guards on duty were apparently primed to make sure no local Latin lover managed to pinch Diana's bottom. Similarly, the paparazzi, the stop-at-nothing Italian photographers, were warned not to pester her or treat her like a movie star by a British Embassy official who declared, "Lay off the Princess or you'll be in trouble." During the visit, the royal couple stayed with eighty-one-year-old author and aesthete Sir Harold Acton, one of the greatest authorities on Italian Renaissance art, at La Pietra, his villa near Florence, frequently visited by D. H. Lawrence, Somerset Maugham, and, more recently, Princess Margaret, who had given a party in his honor at Kensington Palace.

The tour, which also included Sicily, began in Sardinia in late April 1985 where Charles and Diana met the *Britannia*. Diana's cruise into La Spezia naval base on the second day, wearing a Catherine Walker cream navy-striped coatdress and jaunty nautical hat, got her off to a good start in Italy. She also made her mark when she insisted on going with Charles—who as a Royal Navy Commander had been given security clearance, which she as a civvie had not—to see a frigate's NATO control room, bristling with top-secret antimissile devices. After a hurried discussion, Italy's Defense Minister, Giovanni Spadolini, agreed, declaring later, "If you tell an English princess she can't do something, then she will insist on doing it! There is a trace of your Queen Elizabeth in her. She took an acute interest in all the technical stuff." Below deck in the galley of one of the ships, Diana asked for the recipes for the mayonnaise and béchamel sauce the cooks were preparing, but she refused their offer of pasta, saying, "If I eat this sort of food I'll get fat—I'll explode." In fact, pasta later became one of her favorites. See FOOD & DRINK. After lunch, when she asked for capuccino (coffee with milk instead of the traditional Italian black espresso), the other ladies present tactfully followed suit. But Italian journalists made amused comments later about Charles having to roll up his spaghetti with the aid of a spoon and about Di slipping her shoes off under the restaurant table, which she often does. See FASHION.

At La Scala in Milan that evening to see Puccini's opera
Turandot, thousands cheered the couple's arrival and the audience
gave them a standing ovation. But Diana, who had been expected
to wear some devastating new evening number, turned up in her
Victor Edelstein pink chiffon gown with shoestring shoulder
straps which she'd worn two years before in Brisbane, Australia,
and in Canada. As in both those countries (Australian fashion
critics had called her clothes "dowdy and frumpy"), the knives
came out. "She looked like a salesgirl from a department store,"
sniffed one onlooker. "We wanted something more sophisticated," declared another. In the four tons of royal luggage which
had traveled to Italy on the royal yacht, Diana had taken a reported seventy-five outfits, so there was no lack of choice. But she
was so miffed at a report that she'd spent £100,000 on her tour
wardrobe (some said it was "nearer £15,000"—she apparently
only pays wholesale price anyway) that she left the new stuff in
the trunk. As a result she was tagged "second-hand Rose," which
didn't thrill her either. See MONEY. Back in Britain, a spokesman
for fashion designer Jeff Banks, a presenter on "The Clothes
Show," one of Diana's favorite TV programs (see TELEVISION)
was quoted as saying, "These things cost so much money that the
British taxpayer will appreciate Princess Diana wearing clothes
more than once." Also in the luggage, according to one report,
was a last-minute load of new bras from Fenwicks, ordered late
for some reason and which, since Diana's bra size wasn't given in
the rush, turned up in various shapes and sizes. Another near-
farce had occurred at the Circolo Della Caccia, the most exclusive
club in Rome, where a thousand VIP members were allegedly
invited to hobnob with the royal couple at a club banquet until
some unfortunate realized that only 250 could be seated and the
rest (750) had to be promptly uninvited.

Being driven around in a Maserati, Charles and Diana were
enjoying the tour. "When they are in the car, they're always
laughing. They're always lighthearted," the driver said. "They are
a really happy couple." In romantic Florence, one of Prince
Charles's favorite cities in Italy, where the weather was balmy, and
magnolia, bougainvillea, azaleas, and apple blossom were in full
bloom, they visited the Santa Croce monastery, saw Leonardo da

Vinci's *Last Supper*, and spent so long discussing the paintings at
the Uffizi Gallery that the visit was prolonged by half an hour.
Charles was in his element, and Diana was learning more all the
time, becoming in the process more of a companion for her
husband in his intellectual pursuits. Not that she has ever pretended to be an intellectual—far from it. When he ducked under
an arch in a garden in Florence and warned, "Mind your head!,"
she replied with a grin and one of her self-deprecating remarks,
"Why? There's nothing in it." See QUOTES. Count Emilio Pucci,
who gave a grand dinner for them, said of the Princess, "She
descended on Florence like a beautiful living portrait. . . . She has
brought us a real breath of spring."

Meanwhile, Italy's most wanted man, Red Brigade terrorist
Vittoria Antonini, was seized with a cache of weapons and ammu-
nition. In the full-scale alert which followed, Charles and Diana,
twenty-five miles away on a visit to Rome, found themselves
surrounded by a hundred extra Italian cops, some carrying submachine guns. That day the Princess wore a Tommy Cooper–style
fez and a curious Bruce Oldfield suit which some thought fitting,
others ill fitted. At the Bambino Gesu (Baby Jesus) Hospital on
Vatican land high over the city, which Diana asked to visit, she
greeted the children in Italian with "*Buon giorno*" and "*Come sta?*"
("Good day" and "How are you?"). When one urchin in the
crowd asked, "Is it true you have a crown?," she replied, "Yes, but
I have left it behind today." In the leukemia ward, Dr. Lidia Russo
noted, "The Princess was very sad when we talked about how long
the children needed treatment. She asked a lot of technical questions about their condition and treatment. You can see she has
worked with children. When she is with them she shows real
compassion—*simpatica*." At the Vatican, the royal couple had a
forty-five-minute private audience with the Pope, for which Diana
wore a Catherine Walker long-sleeved, calf-length black lace
dress, without a scoop neck, and a matching black lace veil.
Charles, it was claimed, wanted to have a private Mass with the
Pope, but the Queen allegedly vetoed the idea. See STAFF. After
touring St. Peter's Basilica and seeing the Sistine Chapel, they
traveled thirty miles to visit the beachhead at Anzio.

They sailed into Venice on the *Britannia*, Diana snapping

away with her camera. Crowds at St. Mark's Square gave them a tumultuous welcome. They saw the golden mosaics at St. Mark's and were taken on a private tour of the Doges' Palace. On a motor launch ferrying them to lunch on the island of Torcello, there was a momentary distraction when an armed guard fell off the back. On splashdown he struggled about manfully holding his submachine gun above the waves until he was picked up thirty seconds later. Back on the royal yacht, Charles declared that he and his wife would treasure the memories of the tour—the most enjoyable and exciting visit he could remember. To TV cameras, reading in Italian from a note hidden behind her evening bag, Diana said, "My husband and I are very happy to be here" and commented on "how kind and wonderful the Italians have been to us. They have made us feel so much at home." The following day Prince William flew in with Prince Harry on an Andover of the Queen's Flight to spend three days cruising with their parents around the southern tip of Italy.

Though the tour was a great personal success for Diana, in fashion terms it was an equally great flop. Shortly after, the glossy American fashion magazine W put her at the top of its "fashion victims" of 1985 list. Conceding that she "looks terrific" in the casual off-duty clothes she wears to watch polo or go shopping, the magazine said, "But as the recent Italian tour shows, when Di is on duty she exhibits all the symptoms of being a 23-year-old fashion victim, a sufferer of the all-too-woman disease of grabbing at every new look and trend, whether it suits her or not. . . . There are some good designers in Britain. But some of the others should stick to dressing the Queen Mother, not turning a ravishingly pretty princess into a middle-aged frump." Singled out for a special raspberry was the oversized Emanuel green-and-black check coat complete with vast padded shoulders and a huge collar which Diana had worn in Venice for her brief trip down the Grand Canal with Charles in a gondola. Out of earshot, people in the crowd had actually burst out laughing when they saw the outfit, worn with a ludicrous outsize hat. British journalists reckoned the Princess "looked like a cross between the Three Musketeers and Coco the Clown." Two royal aides thought it was "bloody awful." In W's view, it had "all the visual appeal of a horse blanket." But Carlos an De, as the Italians called them, had made their mark, even if some of the clothes hadn't.

Diana's sister Jane spent six months studying art and the history of art in Florence after leaving school at West Heath. Prince Charles loves sketching and painting in Italy, where some of his work has been exhibited. See ARTS & HANDICRAFTS and MARRIAGE.

In February 1992, the Princess made a flying visit to Rome to meet the ailing Mother Teresa, who was there convalescing.

9

JAPAN

"Japan sounds a fascinating place," said the Princess, six months before her whirlwind six-day visit to the Land of the Rising Sun with Charles in May 1986. As their arrival approached, fever-pitch "Di-mania" gripped Japan, where the royal wedding had been watched on TV by even more people than in Britain. Shops and entrepreneurs eager to earn extra yen did a roaring trade in Charles and Di windup dolls, T-shirts, clothes, hats, shoes, posters, Diana porcelain figures, dial-a-Diana-wedding-commentary phonecards, memorial stamps, copies of Diana's jewelry (£40 for an initial *D* pendant, £800 for a pearl necklace), and commemorative platinum medals costing up to £1,200. A Tokyo restaurant offered diners "Diana domburi," a tasty rice dish topped with fried chicken. Dozens of magazines featured Diana on the cover, unlikely articles inside instructing pint-sized brunette Oriental charmers how to look like the statuesque blue-eyed Princess. Hairdressers offered look-alike blond Diana haircuts. A previsit claim in one magazine that Charles towered eight inches above his wife (see BEAUTY SECRETS) owed more to local preference than fact, Japanese gentlemen preferring their ladies short. Television stations ran hour-long documentaries on the Princess and an animated cartoon version of the royal romance called "Diana Monogatari." Prize-giving TV game shows expected contestants to know so much about her from the torrent of publicity that they were expected to answer questions like, "What was the name of Diana's pony?" (The answer is Romany—see SPORT.)

Part of the fascination perhaps lay in the accessibility and informality of the British royals compared to their Japanese counterparts. Until only about forty years before, ordinary mortals prostrated themselves before Emperor Hirohito as a living god, and anyone who suggested he wasn't divine could be thrown into prison for a decade. Though the war changed much, mystique is still preserved about the Imperial Family. So the imminent arrival of Charles and Di, and the hullabaloo surrounding their visit, allowed the Japanese people to indulge their yearning for everything they could learn about life among the royals. The fact that you could speak to a British princess personally, even shake the royal hand, seemed astounding. And since she had once been photographed on a visit to Wales wearing a Sony hat, the welcome was assured. However, the tremendous media coverage brought criticism from Prince Mikasa, aged forty, a nephew of Emperor Hirohito, who declared that the Tokyo Press were portraying the Princess "as if she was a sort of fashion model or a famous actress coming to Japan" when she should be shown as the future Queen who "is also leading a crusade against narcotics."

Charles and Diana flew in to Japan after a thirteen-hour flight from Canada, where Di had fainted (see CANADA) and had had a backache. As she emerged from the jet, pale and subdued, her smile for the two hundred cameras was weary. The couple were met at Osaka airport by Japan's most eligible bachelor, twenty-six-year-old Prince Hiro, then second-in-line to the Chrysanthemum Throne (named after the sixteen-petal family crest) after his father, fifty-two-year-old Crown Prince Akihito. They had met Prince Hiro before as a student in Britain, where he was at Oxford University for two years. On his last visit to the U.K. Prince Charles had taught Prince Hiro salmon fishing. To his anxious inquiry, Diana told Prince Hiro she felt "okay." However, they were glad of the chance to recover from the flight at their temporary home, the palace in Kyoto where ten thousand people gathered outside to greet them, before the arduous schedule starting the next day. Charles relaxed by sitting alone in the palace gardens, sketching a bridge spanning water, and absorbing the beauty of the scene.

Diana was to carry out twenty-nine engagements during the six-day tour, some days on duty for up to twelve hours, much of the time on her feet. The first full day alone in Kyoto, the ancient capital in the south of Japan—where a hundred thousand people crammed the narrow streets in temperatures around 24° C (75° F), chanting "Diana! Diana!"—she visited three temples, a museum, a garden party, and the Japan British Society before attending a Foreign Ministry dinner. In sparkling form, she delighted the crowds by wearing a stunning white silk dress with large red dots—a symbolic homage to Japan's national flag. See FASHION. Like VIP tourists, they drank bitter bright green tea, whisked into a froth at a shortened version of the famous Japanese tea ceremony, and visited monasteries and the old castle of Nijo, where ten girls in kimonos played the Beatles' song "Hey Jude" on traditional thirteen-stringed lyres called kotos. Diana was presented with a kimono herself, an orange silk affair decorated with Japanese flowers and cranes, which she decided to try on, much to the delight of the accompanying Press cameramen, who promptly applauded. The kimono was so long that she nearly tripped over the hem, but she did a little geisha shuffle-walk in it, giggling with her husband. On various occasions during the tour she had to take off her shoes, revealing polished toenails, to go barefoot Japanese-style. To keep her feet cool that day, she also swapped her shoes. See FASHION. At the twelve-course Foreign Ministry banquet, she sat at a low table wearing a pale pink evening dress with pearls dripping from the zigzag sleeves and hem, and was entertained by dancing geisha girls. The menu included whitebait garnished with lily bulb and ginkgo nuts, white rice with the eyes of scallops, and grilled duck. Diana revealed next day that she enjoyed raw fish and coped well with chopsticks, which she had used throughout.

The tour continued with visits to factories, a church, a department store, and Honda showrooms, and an open-car drive through Tokyo to the Akasaka Palace, during which more than 150,000 almost hysterical fans thronged the streets to see the royal couple—the biggest turnout they had ever had in a non-Commonwealth country. The crush of the crowds was so great in places that the crash barriers had to be held fast by the blue-uniformed, black-booted police, some of the seven-thousand-strong royal visit squad, who had to push against the barriers with all their might from the curb. Later Diana received an honorary membership medal of the Japanese Red Cross Society, and she sat barefoot in the annex of the Akasaka Palace watching demonstrations of doll making and ikebana, the Japanese art of flower arranging which dates from the seventh century, when flower arrangements were placed as offerings in Buddhist temples.

The Princess had particularly asked to see sumos fight and seemed fascinated, laughing and talking excitedly to Charles and deluging the interpreter with questions, when they watched four titanic bouts of sumo wrestling at the sumo stadium in Tokyo. Meeting two of the vast, pot-bellied sumo wrestlers backstage afterward, who were still sweating from the near-naked bout but now had their masses of flesh suitably covered, Diana blushed bright red, giggled, and said, "You really made our trip." She prodded one of them, giant five-hundred-pound Salevaa "Sally" Konishiki, in the stomach with her index finger to see how much of his massive pot belly was muscle. Her action so astounded the Japanese, to whom sumos are national heroes, that a VIP business-man asked her at an official lunch later, "Did you *really* poke a sumo in the stomach?" Six-foot-two Hawaiian-born Sally, aged twenty-two, was famed as the biggest sumo wrestler in Japan, with a sixty-eight-inch chest and a sixty-five-inch "waist." He revealed that he had been besotted with Diana for two years and that meeting her had been "nerve-racking but wonderful." "A girl like her is very hard to find," he said. "But if she was my wife, I would want her to put on more weight." (He has since married.) When Diana asked what sumos eat to get so huge, she was told rice and stews of fish and meat. "But that sometimes isn't enough," said Sally, who is known as the Dump Truck. "I like to eat chili hot dogs, pizzas, and Kentucky fried chicken. I can eat a lot of hot dogs. This business makes one very hungry."

The following day when Charles made a speech to the Na-tional Diet, the first made to the Japanese Parliament by a foreign royal, Diana wore a new crushed coral silk suit with a cream silk blouse and a small cream and coral hat, pleasing Japanese fashion commentators who had been disappointed that more of her outfits weren't getting their first public airing in Japan. But during a half-hour visit to a Kabuki theater, the tiring schedule seemed to be telling on her. Despite chuckling at some of the stylized acting, at one point she appeared to nod off to sleep. On the last day of the tour, the royal couple visited a television station in Tokyo where they watched the filming of an episode of a twelfth-century soap opera called "The Legend of Benkei," a tale of jealousy, treachery, and love involving a warrior monk, his half-brother, and two women. See TELEVISION. Diana was fascinated; but as she later confessed during an audience at the Imperial Palace with Emperor Hirohito (who had just celebrated his sixtieth year on the Chrysanthemum Throne), she was tired out. Not that she looked it. For the audience, after which the Emperor and other members of the Imperial Family were hosts to the couple at a magnificent court banquet, Diana wore a sapphire blue evening dress by the Japanese designer Yuki, set off with her fabulous sapphire-and-diamond jewelry and a stunning headband which she'd had made from a diamond watchstrap, the clock face replaced with a large central sapphire. See JEWELRY.

But dedicated royal-watcher James Whitaker of the *Daily Mirror* (see PRESS) was worried. As Charles and Diana flew home to Britain two months before their fifth wedding anniversary, he sounded an alarm claiming that she was in danger of burning herself out and that she needed a vacation from royal duties but wouldn't get one. He declared that Diana had often been "bad-tempered" in Japan with the hordes of Japanese cameramen who never left her alone. Charles had compensated for her "boredom," he claimed, by becoming increasingly animated. "He is a tower of strength to her," Whitaker wrote. "No woman could have a more caring and understanding husband, but even the Prince cannot paper over all the cracks that have begun to appear in his wife's persona." Diana's father was also to become concerned that the work load of her public duties might affect her health. See PUBLIC ENGAGEMENTS and MARRIAGE.

In November 1990, a year after the death of Emperor Hirohito, the Prince and Princess returned on a five-day visit to Japan for the £50 million enthronement of his son Akihito as the 125th Emperor. A row broke out at home when they and their entourage of fifteen flew to Tokyo in a chartered 360-seat Boeing 747 jumbo jet, costing taxpayers an estimated £500,000, because the RAF VC-10 due to take them was involved in the Gulf crisis and there were no seats on scheduled flights.

They attended a Remembrance Day service at the Commonwealth War Graves cemetery near Yokohama, where Diana comforted a war widow who collapsed, and Charles made his first salute since breaking his right arm. See HEALTH and SPORT. At the ancient enthronement ceremony, Diana was placed seventy-first in the pecking order amid about 2,500 guests, though her

Japanese fans who crowded the streets made it clear she took top billing with them. (American Vice President Dan Quayle was placed ninety-sixth until he was moved to a front seat.)

In Tokyo the Princess visited the National Children's Hospital, attended two banquets, and stunned Tokyo society in the sexy, off-the-shoulder fuchsia gown she wore at a gala performance of Richard Strauss's opera *Salome*, given by the Welsh National Opera, of which she is Patron (see MUSIC), at Bunkamure Opera House. Two of her hats also caused comment: the veiled headband which she wore at the enthronement and a white hat bearing the rising sun national emblem, which she sported at the Emperor's garden party.

But the best comments came during a visit to a Honda car factory where the Princess saw the 212-mph Formula One McLaren-Honda Grand Prix racing car in which Ayrton Senna won the world championship. Recalling the warning Diana had received after speeding home on the expressway (see MOTORING), photographer Arthur Edwards from the *Sun* declared cheekily, "They'd never catch you on the M4 in that, Ma'am!" "I'll make the jokes, thank you, Arthur," she replied instantly. Two weeks later there was a sequel, during a public engagement back in Britain, when Diana spotted the cap Arthur was wearing in rainy Norwich and asked, "Are you wearing that hat for a bet, Arthur?" "I'll tell the jokes, thank you, Ma'am," he replied, grinning. See PRESS and GULF WAR.

JEWELRY

When Diana met Prince Charles, she had barely any jewelry apart from her gold initial *D* pendant necklace and her pearl choker necklace, which were gifts. Both became her trademarks. But since Charles sealed their match with that fabulous engagement ring, a large oval sapphire surrounded by fourteen diamonds (a ring which to the Prince's fury turned out to be featured in a Garrards' catalog, priced at £28,500), she has gained a virtual treasure chest of jewels. It was the Spencer family diamond tiara which she wore at her wedding, but her most beautiful one is Queen Mary's lovers' knot tiara with the teardrop pearls, which was given to her by the Queen as a wedding present. Unfortunately, it is heavy. In *The Royal Jewels*, Suzy Menkes reveals that when Diana has it placed in the afternoon and keeps it on through tea at Kensington Palace before appearing in it at some grand affair in the evening, she ends up with a headache. (We all have our crosses to bear.) Her mother lent her the pearl-and-diamond earrings Diana wore on her wedding day; her sister Sarah lent her the pearl choker in which she left for her honeymoon. The great sapphire surrounded with diamonds which made eyes pop at the White House banquet in 1985 was originally a brooch—a wedding gift from the Queen Mother—which Diana cleverly had mounted on a pearl choker. (She doesn't very often wear brooches.) Another incredible wedding gift came from the Crown Prince of Saudi Arabia: a beautiful sapphire-and-diamond pendant necklace, bracelet, earrings, ring, and watch—the last two of which she had made into the dazzling headband she wore in Japan in 1986. The headband she once wore to twirl around at a dance with Prince Charles in Australia, when her tiara had apparently been left behind, was an emerald necklace which had belonged to the stiff and starchy Queen Mary, who presumably twirled about in her grave. Among Diana's favorite treasures are the exquisite sapphire-and-diamond necklace, bracelet, and crescent-shaped earrings, made by Asprey, which were given to her by the Sultan of Oman during the royal tour of the Arab Gulf States in 1986. See GERMANY.

Charles's gifts to her have included a watch, which she wears in the daytime on her left wrist, and a gold charm bracelet, which she often wears on her right. Charles adds extra charms on special occasions, a royal custom started by Queen Victoria's consort Prince Albert. On her twenty-second birthday, Charles gave Diana a tiny gold wombat, after one of the nicknames they have for Prince William (see NAMES), to add to the bracelet. As his wedding present, he gave her an emerald-and-diamond bracelet and earrings, which she seldom wears because she is not keen on green, although she has worn more of the color lately. Sapphires are her stone, to match her eyes, just as Fergie likes rubies to match her red hair. Charles has designed some of the jewelry he has given his wife, including her most prized piece, a gold medallion which he gave her to mark the birth of their son and heir, simply inscribed "William" in Charles's handwriting. Another favorite is her Prince of Wales's feathers pendant necklace.

The Princess buys fun fake costume jewelry from Butler & Wilson on London's Fulham Road. Other clients include Madonna, Jerry Hall, Joan Collins, Faye Dunaway, Catherine Deneuve, and Dame Edna Everage. A huge £50 jeweled spider brooch and matching earrings Diana bought there proved such a hoot that she returned for two more matching sets, explaining they were for friends who would think them "a great joke." The bow-and-heart earrings she wore on the Italian tour in 1985 were said to have come from there, price £18.50. She was even reported to have nipped into the shop for a pair of red-and-black earrings to match one of her outfits en route to the airport for her trip to New York in 1989.

JOBS

After she left finishing school, Diana's first job took her to Headley in Hampshire for almost three months, where she worked as nanny to Alexandra, the baby daughter of Philippa Whitaker, sister of her friend Willy Von Straubenzee (see FRIENDS) and her photographer-husband Major Jeremy Whitaker. Back in London, she got temporary jobs as a baby-sitter and a domestic, through the employment agencies Knightsbridge Nannies and Solve Your Problems respectively. In September 1978, she went to cookery school, later preparing and serving food for guests at her sisters' parties and providing suitable fodder for other people's dos via another agency, Lumleys. See COOKING. Early in 1979 she became a £100-a-year student teacher at the dance studios of Miss Betty Vacani, whose school had taught generations of royal children to dance. She helped with various classes for children aged from two to nine and enjoyed dancing herself in the mothers' ballet classes. See DANCING. But as with finishing school, she suddenly quit (see EDUCATION) and in March went back to cleaning and baby-sitting. Some months later, she took a part-time job as a kindergarten assistant (see YOUNG ENGLAND KINDERGARTEN), where she still worked when her romance with Prince Charles became known. For a year she also earned extra money, through Knightsbridge Nannies, as a part-time nanny to a little boy named Patrick Robinson, the son of an American oilman who lived in Eaton Square. And to supplement her income further, also for a year, she worked as a charlady—dusting, washing the dishes, mopping, scrubbing, cleaning the lavatory and everything else three times a week at the Chelsea mews flat which her sister Sarah shared in London with Hamp-shire landowner's daughter Lucinda Craig-Harvey. Lucinda, a theatrical producer, commented, "She was very good. . . . I'd mark her a good eight out of ten." In November 1987, the Princess was guest of honor at the West End gala opening of Lucinda's production of The Importance of Being Earnest in aid of leukemia research. In January 1988, when Diana attended the launch with Lucinda of a foundation for young leukemia sufferers, she told guests, "I used to char for this lady." (In 1991 the Princess became Patron of the Leukaemia Research Appeal for Wales.) The Queen, incidentally, employs about fifty-eight house-maids to clean Buckingham Palace, which has more than six hundred rooms. Diana still loves cleaning and washing up.

Key Dates

1961

July 1 — Diana born at Park House, Sandringham, Norfolk.

Early education from governess Ally at home.

1967

November — Her mother leaves home in love with Peter Shand Kydd.

1968

January — Diana enrolls at Silfield school, King's Lynn.

April — Peter Shand Kydd divorced.

1969 — Diana's parents divorced.

Diana's mother marries Peter Shand Kydd.

1970

September — Diana goes to Riddlesworth Hall boarding school, Diss, Norfolk.

1973

September — Diana goes to West Heath boarding school, Sevenoaks, Kent.

1975

June — Diana's grandfather, the 7th Earl Spencer, dies.

Her father, Viscount Althorp, becomes the 8th Earl Spencer.

Diana becomes Lady Diana Spencer.

Family moves to stately home, Althorp, Northampton.

Dressed for a day at the polo grounds. (Glenn Harvey/Camera Press London)

1976
July 14   Lord Spencer marries Raine, the Countess of Dartmouth.

1977
November   Prince Charles is dating Diana's sister Sarah.

Sarah introduces Diana to the Prince at Althorp.

| December | Diana leaves West Heath. |

1978

January	Diana goes briefly to Swiss finishing school.
March	Diana returns to London.
	Later takes jobs as nanny, baby-sitter, and charlady.
April	Diana's sister Jane marries Robert Fellowes.
September	Diana takes three-month cookery course.
	Lord Spencer collapses with cerebral hemorrhage.

1979

January	Lord Spencer leaves the hospital.
	Diana and Sarah are guests of the Queen at Sandringham.
	Prince Charles starts asking Diana out as a friend.
	Diana works briefly at Vacani dance school.
July	Diana moves into her own flat at Coleherne Court in London.
	Diana vacations with Jane at Balmoral.
	Diana later starts work at Young England kindergarten.
1980 May	Sarah marries Neil McCorquodale.
June	Prince Charles's romance with Anna Wallace hits a rock.
July	Diana vacations with Jane at Balmoral.
	Diana's romance with Prince Charles begins at Balmoral.
September 8	Harry Arnold breaks news of royal romance in the *Sun*.
	Press besiege Diana for months at Coleherne Court.

1981

February 4	Prince Charles finally pops the question.
	Diana vacations in Australia with mother and stepfather.
February 24	Engagement officially announced.
March	Diana's first public engagement as Charles's fiancée.
July 29	Wedding at St. Paul's Cathedral.
October	Diana's first U.K. tour with Charles, in Wales.
November	Diana's first solo engagement as Princess of Wales.

1982

June 21	Birth of Prince William.
July 1	Diana's twenty-first birthday.
September	Diana attends Princess Grace's funeral, Monaco.

1983

March/April	Diana's debut overseas tour with Charles, in Australia and New Zealand.

1984

February	Diana's first solo official visit abroad, Norway.
September 15	Birth of Prince Harry.

1989

September	Diana's brother, Viscount Althorp, weds Victoria Lockwood.

1991

July 1	Diana's thirtieth birthday.
July 29	Charles and Diana's tenth wedding anniversary.

Kuwait & the United Arab Emirates

In March 1989, seventeen months before the invasion by Iraq's Saddam Hussein, Diana and Charles toured oil-rich Kuwait, going

on to visit Abu Dhabi, Bahrain, and Dubai. Their tour of the
Arab Gulf States three years earlier had been a success despite a
diplomatic row between Britain and Syria. This time the furor
over Salman Rushdie's novel *The Satanic Verses* had inflamed
feelings between Muslims and Westerners, and there was tight
security throughout the six-day tour, with machine guns much in
evidence as the royal couple arrived in Kuwait. To avoid offending
Arab custom, Diana remembered lessons she had learned for and
from the previous trip. Keep covered up, in high-necked, sleeved
outfits with long skirts or trousers. Don't kiss in public, as she
and Charles had done after a polo game in 1986 in Oman: even
"Mickey Mouse" cartoons get censored when Mickey kisses Min-
nie, a fact the Princess found privately amusing. Only eat food
with the right hand (the left is "unclean" because that's the one
used to wipe the bottom), and don't refuse any, though you can
leave it on your plate. Get ready to leave an audience or banquet
when the rosewater and incense appear. Never point the soles of
your feet toward anyone. And don't cross your ankles or legs
(which is apparently the equivalent of a middle-fingered insult in
the United States)—a rule she momentarily forgot during an
audience with the Crown Prince, who was reported to have turned
his head diplomatically while she remembered.

Earlier the royal couple had an audience with the Emir,
Sheikh Jaber al-Ahmad al-Sabah, known as Jaber III, head of a
dynasty which had ruled Kuwait for two centuries and one of the
world's richest men with reported earnings of £1 million a *minute*.
Despite his modest, even frugal, lifestyle compared with that of
some oil-state rulers, he has lavished fabulous gifts on the British
Royal Family (he is said to be forty times richer than they are).
Diana was expected to return from the trip with more dazzling
jewels tucked into her luggage.

In Kuwait she visited a center for handicapped youngsters
and the same evening, with Charles, attended a banquet given at
the Sha'ab Palace by the Crown Prince, Sheikh Sa'd Abdallah al-
Salim al-Sabah. The sheikh had been educated partly in the thoroughly unlikely setting of Hendon police training school in north
London, having begun his career with the Kuwaiti police and gone
on to head state security before becoming Prime Minister. For the

banquet Diana wore a pinky-lilac silk gown by Catherine Walker with a beaded and embroidered top. She went native next day by trying on a caftan covered in gold braid during a visit to the Kuwait Museum of Islamic Art.

Then it was off to Bahrain for lunch with the Emir and on again to Abu Dhabi, where she had to have dinner with the ladies while Charles dined in Arab style with the Crown Prince, men only. The British Press corps reckon the royals bring rain (see AMERICA, INDONESIA, NEW ZEALAND, and PORTUGAL); even in parched Abu Dhabi, it started to pour within minutes of their arrival. Heavy spots landed on the Princess's glorious pink-and-red outfit and matching hat, possibly the most striking ensemble ever created for her by her brilliant "Walkerville" team of designer Catherine Walker and milliner Philip Somerville. See FASHION. They watched camel racing at a track at Al Ain, Diana looking away at the ground as the boy jockeys, called rakbis, beat them to get them started. But the thrill of the spectacle once the races were under way soon got her excited. See ZOO. Then she visited a women's college before joining Charles, sheikhs, and Bedouin tribesmen for a magnificent picnic lunch at a desert oasis, sitting on cushions on the ground. Whole roast lambs, eyes intact, were laid out with rice, fish, curry (which she likes—see FOOD & DRINK), plus masses of salad and fruit, including peaches, melons, grapes, and strawberries. The Princess, wearing a cool blue-and-white top with white pants, rolled her eyes at the sight of so much food, which she tackled British style with a knife and fork as servants brushed sand off the tablecloths. After lunch, she and Charles climbed into Range Rovers and raced each other through the sand dunes. Then it was on to the final stop, Dubai, where Diana discovered during a banquet that her scheduled British Airways flight back to London would be three hours late. With typical Arab generosity, Sheikh Mohamed Bin Rashid Al Maktoum, the Defense Minister, offered her one of his family planes instead. So she flew home to the children in grand style in his Boeing 747 while Charles stayed on to visit his old ship HMS *Hermione*, which was in the Gulf, to play a game of polo (which he was banned from playing on security grounds, leaving him "deeply disappointed"), and to enjoy a private visit to Saudi Arabia to paint in the desert. The sixty-four-year-old Emir of Kuwait, the 13th Emir, fled to Saudi Arabia with his three wives, a fourth "semiofficial" wife, and his children, said to number more than forty, after the invasion of his country by Iraq in August 1990. See GULF WAR.

𝓛

Leprosy

On her tour of Nigeria with Charles in March 1990, as she had first done the previous year in Jakarta (see INDONESIA), Diana publicly demonstrated that leprosy, a horrifically disfiguring disease whose victims have been shunned and cast out by society since biblical times, can be confronted without panic or fear. She met lepers at a leprosy hospital, where among those whose hands she shook was a sufferer ironically named Lucky. And when she toured the leper colony, where the sufferers live in traditional African mud huts, she did not hesitate to shake hands with the chief of the colony, sixty-nine-year-old Bulama Duna, or his wife, Botul, though the chief's limbs were disfigured and his wife had no fingers. Following Diana's lead, Prince Charles shook the hand of a recovering patient at the hospital too. Kate Dawson, a British doctor who showed them around the hospital, said later, "The Princess helped so much. She has shown that lepers are not a risk to anybody." See NIGERIA. Diana made it clear that she intends to continue this work when she agreed to become Patron of the Leprosy Mission in Britain. In February 1992, she visited lepers in Calcutta. See HIV.

Letters

The Princess is an avid correspondent, surprising many people, including the American mother who once employed her as a nanny for her little boy (see JOBS), by the fact that she finds time to write. She even managed to send astonishingly prompt thank-you letters to personal friends and relatives for wedding presents when her honeymoon had hardly begun. Diana usually pens her mail in her sitting rooms at Kensington Palace and Highgrove. She sometimes has lapses with her punctuation and, like Prince Philip, with her spelling. Those close to her and Charles use a special

208

Left: Diana as a young girl. She was the only child in the family who did not have a royal godparent.

Below left: The famous picture of Diana with two of her kindergarten charges, taken in September 1980, when her romance with Prince Charles became known.

Below right: When Diana left Princess Margaret's birthday party at the Ritz in December 1980, she was still free to walk alone and to wear an ordinary coat over her gown.

The bridal party collapsed in giggles after po

he official royal wedding photographs in 1981.

The ultrafeminine Princess wore a pink and gold gown by her favorite designer, Catherine Walker, in this early photograph.

The Princess chose this trouser outfit for a lavish desert picnic in a Bedouin tent in 1986.

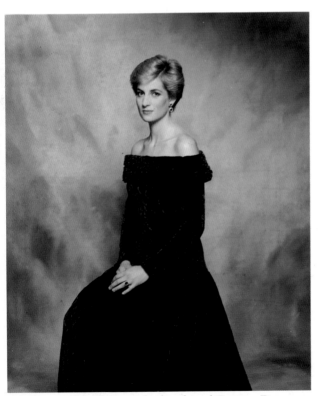

The Princess used Queen Mary's emerald necklace as a headband for dance in Melbourne in 1985.

A portrait of the Princess by her friend Terence Donovan taken in 1986. She wore the crushed velvet Bruce Oldfield gown at a banquet in Lisbon in 1987.

The royal couple in Kyoto in 1986. Diana wore her "rising sun" dress in symbolic homage to the Japanese national flag.

Flamenco-ish fashion flair at the America's Cup Ball in 1986. With her striking Murray Arbeid gown Diana wore one long black glove, one red.

Diana wore silk flowers in her hair to set off her exotic gown for a banquet in Bangkok in 1988.

Diana's top design team of Catherine Walker and milliner Philip Somerville produced this stunning pink and red outfit for her Arabian tour in 1989.

Top left: The Princess on the ski slopes at Klosters in 1988, shortly before the avalanche tragedy in which Major Hugh Lindsay was killed.

Top right: Tennis-mad Diana played a mixed-doubles match with champion Steffi Graf at the Vanderbilt Racquet Club in 1988.

Middle: A kiss at a polo match for the Prince and Princess of Wales.

The Princess has competed several times in the mothers' eighty-yard sprint held on Wetherby School Sports Day. In 1988 she won.

Casual chic: Diana wore a baseball cap, cowboy boots, jeans, jacket, and sweat-shirt for polo at Windsor with William in 1988.

Diana, her sons, and two bodyguards had fun getting drenched on the Log Flume rollercoaster during a day at Alton Towers Leisure Park in 1990.

Charles, Diana, William, and Harry enjoyed cycling together on a holiday at Tresco in the Scilly Isles in 1989.

Top left: Diana, in denims, drove an armored vehicle on Salisbury Plain during a day with the army.

Top right: The Princess had this outfit made specially for a 1990 dinner with the Royal Hampshire Regiment, of which she is Colonel-in-Chief.

Above: The Princess loves to sunbathe and swim, so prefers seaside holidays. This swimsuit started a new trend.

Right: The caring Princess took a young AIDS sufferer nicknamed First Lady for a drive in her official car during Diana's 1990 visit to Washington.

code when they write so that their letters go to the royal couple personally and don't get mixed up with the rest of the Palace mail. This code is thought to involve writing initials on the envelope, but they presumably have to be the *right* initials, in case you're thinking of trying to crack it!

Diana gets mail from, among others, people involved with and supporting the various organizations with which she is linked, including the Services. Shortly before she was due to revisit the frigate HMS *Cornwall*, of which she is sponsor, at Plymouth in October 1989, the crew sent her a snappy postcard from their travels which read, "Just a quick jolly to Paris while our ship is in Rouen. Looking forward to seeing you on our ship again." See ARMED FORCES. That card emerged when some of the Princess's private papers were mysteriously found dumped.

In October 1989, a make-believe letter to Prince William won seven-year-old Charlotte Overton-Hart a £400 top prize in a Royal Mail competition. Charlotte wrote, "Why is it that your socks stay up and mine fall down?" Answer: because royal nanny Olga Powell fixed elastic garters to them. She went on, "Perhaps your mummy always tidies you up before you go anywhere special. . . ." She was right about that. Diana once told William after he'd been playing, "You are not meeting your father looking like that!"

On occasion a letter to the Princess can produce surprising results. American Hope Manley, a fan of Diana since the royal wedding, wrote to Buckingham Palace explaining that she suffered from cystic fibrosis and saying, "I always dreamed of meeting Princess Diana, but I guess I'll never be able to. So could I have a picture of her instead?" Diana replied personally, sending Hope a Christmas card bearing a photograph of herself with Charles, William, and Harry which she signed, "With love from the four of us, Diana." But thirteen-year-old Hope's biggest thrill came when an American charity called Dreams Come True arranged to drive her "like a princess" in a long white limousine from her home in Allentown, Pennsylvania, to see Diana during her first solo visit to New York in February 1989. Hope's family accompanied her. She met Diana at a toy shop where Hope gave the Princess two red roses and was rewarded with a handshake and a chat. "It was wonderful," Hope said ecstatically, "and I'll never forget it." Indeed, it all went to show, said Hope's mother, Peggy, "that things you keep wishing for really can be yours."

Two letters from Diana's mother have made news. See PRESS and RADIO.

LONDON SYMPHONY CHORUS

Diana is Patron of the London Symphony Chorus (LSC), one of the world's leading amateur symphony choruses, which sings to professional standards at concerts in London and abroad and occasionally around Britain. The two hundred singers come from all walks of life and include housewives, lawyers, accountants, teachers, civil servants, publishers, journalists, architects, organ builders, and even an Undersecretary at the Treasury. The chorus was founded in 1966 by the London Symphony Orchestra (LSO), during a burst of enthusiasm when orchestras formed their own choirs to accompany them. Since 1976 the chorus has been independent, spreading its talents more widely, though the LSO remains its parent orchestra and provides most of its work. Solicitor David Leonard, Chairman of the chorus, reckons the LSC is the "hardest worked of all the British choruses," giving more than twenty concerts a year and making about five recordings, each of which takes three or four sessions, in the same period. The singers meet to rehearse around a piano in a huge gothic-looking hall at Bishopsgate, on average two evenings a week and on weekends when concerts are due. They sing everything from the classics to *Porgy and Bess*, and in July 1986 about fifty of them made a TV commercial with the LSO for North America. In full black evening rig, they gave what was virtually a concert performance of a "funny little jingle" for Diet Coke, which reached its climax when they had to hold up Coke cans with the labels face-forward. At concerts in Moscow, the chorus gave the first performance in the U.S.S.R. of *The Dream of Gerontius* and *Belshazzar's Feast*. The LSC has also appeared in France, Italy, Switzerland, and the United States.

Diana became Patron in 1988 and, according to David Leonard, who himself joined as a tenor about eleven years ago, has shown a "tremendous" interest. "She came to two rehearsals and five or six concerts in the first two years, which is quite something, really," he said. "A royal gala which she attended raised in excess of £80,000 each for the chorus and the British Lung Foundation, of which she is also Patron. The Princess has been a very big asset to us. She talks to the chorus members, and there's lots of interchange of ideas. She's easy to talk to and very encouraging." Prince William and Prince Harry both have blue LSC sweatshirts. See ORCHESTRAS and MUSIC.

ℳ

The Malcolm Sargent Cancer Fund
for Children

One of the first organizations for which Diana became Patron, in February 1982, is the Malcolm Sargent Cancer Fund for Children. It was launched in March 1968 as a memorial to the famous conductor following his death the previous October. Fans who'd attended his Promenade Concerts at the Royal Albert Hall approached his manager, Sylvia Darley, now the Trust's General Administrator, suggesting some kind of musical scholarship in his memory. But Sir Malcolm had instructed during the last days of his life that no musical memorial should be established in his name. However, he had a particular love for children and young people, and he himself had died from cancer. So Sylvia Darley began the Trust, at first using her kitchen table as an office. Since then, the charity has collected more than £14,858,000 and has given practical help and support to hundreds of youngsters, aged under twenty-one, at home and in the hospital, suffering from all forms of cancer, from leukemia to Hodgkin's disease. There is a network of over forty Malcolm Sargent social workers throughout the country who work in centers which specialize in childhood cancer. When the Trust first began, very few children with leukemia or cancer were expected to be cured of their disease; now at least half live long-term.

Since Diana became Patron (last year she also became Patron for the Fund in Australia), she has attended numerous concerts and other events in aid of the charity, including an Evening of Opera at the Duke of York's Barracks in March 1990 organized by her former flatmate, Carolyn Pride, and Carolyn's husband, William Bartholomew (see FRIENDS), in conjunction with the National Society for the Prevention of Cruelty to Children

(NSPCC). As a result of the Princess's encouragement and help, the charity, which receives no Government support, is now able to give £1 million a year to those children and their families, often in tragic and desperate circumstances, who need financial help. Gifts which have been given to the youngsters include a new flute, music and riding lessons, a pony, a rabbit, and a budgerigar. One little girl who had been chosen to present a bouquet to the Queen Mother at a concert, but who had lost her hair through chemotherapy, was bought a wig. To mark the charity's twenty-first birthday in 1989, it opened two staffed vacation homes—one by the beach in Jaywick Sands near Clacton in Essex, the other in Prestwick in Ayrshire—so that at a time of great stress for families, the children and their exhausted parents can relax. Diana visited both homes in September 1989 and has also visited the children themselves. "When the Princess makes hospital visits and meets the children and their parents in the clinics, she appears to be very much at home," Sylvia Darley said. "She is particularly sympathetic with parents who have the problems of a terminally ill child. At all fund-raising events, two of our children and their families always have the opportunity to meet Her Royal Highness—the boy presents the program and the girl gives the bouquet."

MARRIAGE

Prince Charles may have been the world's most eligible bachelor, but as husband material this enigmatic and complex man must have presented a major challenge. Though he is the best-prepared heir to the throne ever, his preparation for a happy, fulfilled life as a person, husband, and father could, from today's standpoint, have been bettered. He was a quiet, shy, serious boy whose parents were often absent on extended tours abroad or other royal duties. Charles talks of coming from a loving "close-knit" family, which it undoubtedly is. Yet even before she became Queen, according to Lady Longford in Elizabeth R, the time Princess Elizabeth kept sacrosanct to spend with her children was only half an hour in the mornings and an hour in the evenings. Charles's childhood was a lonely one dominated by nannies, granny, royal

A happy moment for Charles, Diana, and the boys aboard the royal yacht *Britannia*. (Glenn Harvey/Camera Press London)

servants, and bodyguards. During a schooling he partly hated, he was always different and other boys considered twice before befriending him for fear of it being thought they were sucking up. He had little experience of women until he was at college. And he had the kind of British upper-class upbringing in general which many people today would reject as unsound.

Traditionally, upper-class boys see little of their parents anyway, get most of their affection if they're lucky from nannies, and are packed off as soon as possible to boarding school until they are grown up, as if their parents never wanted them in the first place. Thus while they may have all the material benefits, they are deprived of what matters most: the constant loving parental care and attention which leads to emotional security, without which the rest of life can be a minefield. As adults, such men often retreat from deep emotional relationships with their own wives and children and continue to live much as they did as bachelors. Perhaps to make up for an emotional void, they frequently enjoy pitting themselves against the odds in thrilling but dangerous sports like racing, hunting, polo, the Cresta Run—and gambling. Scratch a gambler and you will often find a man who felt unloved as a child. Usually such men expect their wives to be decorative, provide offspring, and organize domestic and social arrangements but otherwise to do as they're told and fit in with the lifestyle the man has established for himself without complaint. The upper class, and the lower, are the last bastions of male chauvinism in Britain, and the Prince, despite having a great respect for women, is no champion of feminism. Although he is very sensitive and can be extremely kind, as a bachelor some of the treatment meted out to his girlfriends (who tended to be busty, long-legged blonds and were known as Charlie's Angels) was described as "cavalier." Furthermore, at thirty-two Charles still was a mama's boy who lived at home with his parents; expected to spend most of his vacations and all major festive occasions like Christmas, New Year's, and Easter with them, as he still does; and could deny his mother nothing. As if all that weren't enough—and none of this, of course, is his *fault* or indeed his mother's—he was also set in his ways and incredibly spoiled. A spoiled man is usually a selfish one, and that does not make for marital harmony.

The Prince's frustration, impatience, and flare-ups over unpunctuality, delays, red tape, or any job not done by his staff to perfection—an echo of the unreasoning tantrum of a child who can't have what he wants instantly—is fully understandable only when you realize that apart from blowing his nose, washing, going to the bathroom, making love, and reading his official papers, he has always had staff, servants, and bodyguards around to deal with virtually all the other basic necessities of life for him. And other essential matters like having to earn a living, which occupy the rest of us most of our lives, simply don't apply. He has not had to cope personally with the myriad dawn-to-dusk minor frustrations and irritations which ordinary folks accept as part and parcel of daily life. Which is not to detract from the difficulties and frustrations of the royal round or from his many admirable personal qualities. However, he does not have to rely on a morning alarm clock, run his bath, clean his shoes, iron his shirts, or get his own breakfast. He does not have to cope with missing a bus or a commuter train to work, being stuck for hours in rush-hour traffic, fearing the sack for being late, putting up day after day with a mind-mashingly boring job, standing in line for lunch

at the company cafeteria or for a bus home at the end of the day.
He is unlikely ever to be jostled by other commuters or mugged
or assaulted on the way home. When he gets home, he is unlikely
to find he's been burgled or that the gas, electricity, and telephone
have been cut off because he can't pay the bills. He is never going
to be at a loose end socially because no one wants to see him; the
rich, the powerful, and the famous are never going to ignore him;
and no cinema, theater, or opera house is ever going to tell him he
can't come in because the tickets have all been sold. He is never
going to be broke, evicted, homeless, collecting unemployment or
welfare, or in need of medical treatment yet unable to get a quick
bed in a hospital or sympathetic and competent medical advice.
His wife will never have to forgo dental treatment to buy the
children shoes; and his kids will never have to wear secondhand
clothes, go without food or vacations, or be poorly educated
through lack of cash. He will never yearn to see places abroad he
can't afford to visit, have to put up with a leaking roof he cannot
pay to be repaired, have to worry about meeting mortgage payments, or grieve that through lack of funds he was unable to
provide help for a dying relative or a friend in dire straits. Charles
may have to wait years to be King, but he is not confined through
lack of education, opportunity, or position to a mundane little
life. During his time on this planet he can enjoy a richness of
experience beyond the wildest dreams of other people. Despite his
self-doubts, he need never feel ineffectual or that he lacks the
influence to affect the lives of others for the good in a major way
denied to the majority. He simply never has to face the sort of
problems which beset most of us most of our lives. Even in the
most trivial ways he is catered for. According to Brian Hoey in
The New Royal Court, he doesn't even have to put a fresh blade in
his razor or take the top off his toothpaste.

While all this may seem enviable, being so dependent on
others can become destructive and even crippling in terms of self-
confidence, self-esteem, and a practical ability to take care of
yourself, as pop stars and people who come into a fortune and
surround themselves with gofers can find. The fact that Charles
has on occasion gone off to pitch in on a farm and milk cows may
be a recognition of the need to get back to the basics. But his

occupations away from his royal duties, which often separate him from Diana and the children (and which have left her a polo widow in summer and a hunting widow in winter), are also a retreat, an escape. Getting away from it all to paint, sketch, fish, hunt, play polo, or whatever fulfills a deep need in him. "If I didn't get the exercise or have something to take my mind off things, I would go potty," he has said. Of course, if most men took ten weeks' vacation a year, as he does, they'd probably also spend most of it fishing or doing their own thing and only a couple weeks with the wife and kids at Margate or Marbella. (Indeed, many more marriages would break up if they didn't, since family vacations are a prime time for marital strife.)

Yet even when Charles is technically home, he is sometimes not. When William and Harry were younger, he would escape from Kensington Palace to have lunch with the Queen Mother at Clarence House when he couldn't stand the noise the children made in the nursery. "I love William and Harry dearly," he has said. "But sometimes I just have to get away from home to get some peace." The separate bedrooms he has at the Palace and Highgrove *could* also be seen as a further refuge. See BEDS & BEDROOMS.

When faced with marriage or family problems, any wife must have the opportunity to thrash things out with her husband if harmony is to be maintained. But since Charles prefers to avoid confrontation—on the "anything for a quiet life" basis—that may prove problematical. The fact that he flies off the handle quickly doesn't help. And he is not a good listener ("She says I'm deaf," he's admitted) though fortunately Diana is.

Many mature women who know how difficult marriage and family life can be, even with a near-perfect husband, would run a mile from the prospect of matrimony with a man from such a background, however alluring his attractions, however great his personal virtues. But Diana was a naive, insecure young girl from a broken home, full of romantic notions, whose experience of men was nil. Her wedding had been a fairy tale; and as everyone knows from childhood, once Snow White and Cinderella married their princes, they lived happily ever after. The shock for Diana—not just of marrying into the Royal Family with its different culture, tradition, and requirements, or of being jettisoned into the brightest and most unrelenting media spotlight which has ever been trained on a public figure, but also of finding that the dashing Prince she adored was less than an ideal husband—may well have been profound. Like any young bride embarking on wedlock the first time around, she might have thought that the love of a good woman would do the trick and that she would be able to change anything about her husband she didn't like. As far as Charles's appearance was concerned, she was right. She soon got him into double-breasted suits, slip-on shoes, yellow sweaters, and boxer shorts. He even let her hairdresser do his hair. Diana also proved to have a subtle and very clever way of handling him, and, indeed, her notoriously difficult father-in-law, Prince Philip, who adores her and thinks his eldest son was incredibly lucky to have landed such a spouse. But a wife soon learns that leopards don't change their spots and that the husband she married for better or worse is the husband she's got.

The same applies, of course, vice versa. Over the early years, while Charles realized that Diana was no doormat but a force to be reckoned with, she came to realize that although, as she's said, she'd like to see more of him, he would be away doing his own thing a large part of the time and that this would probably never change. When she remarked to a journalist once that she and Charles would each be going their own way more often in the future, it may well have been a sign of her acceptance of the situation and a recognition of the fact that, like the wives of naval officers, long-distance truck drivers, royal bodyguards, and other regularly absent husbands, she needed to build a life of her own in addition to the one they shared. That does not mean that they lead totally separate lives, that the marriage is on the rocks, or that they are any less devoted to each other or their children.

The mistake we make is in looking at the royals from the wrong angle, assuming that they are like us—which they're not—and then concluding when they diverge from what we'd do that something must be wrong. Kings, princes, and aristocrats have always led selfish lives and gone off and done their own thing, leaving their wives to amuse themselves back at the palace or castle. From Charles's standpoint, going off frequently without

Diana and the children is perfectly normal behavior. As the Princess said with a certain resignation about something else in October 1990, "Like most men, he does what he wants to do," the key difference being that Charles has both the time and the means to do it. See HEALTH.

What *is* remarkable is not that the couple spend a considerable time apart or that they have separate bedrooms, but that Diana has been able to encourage Charles to help create the kind of real family life, normal to most of us, which he himself had never known. They have given William a close family upbringing unlike that of any previous heir to the throne. Both he and Harry seem happy and well adjusted. Although, according to Brian Hoey, Charles still doesn't understand Diana's unroyal but entirely natural "preoccupation" with the children (could he perhaps be a little jealous of it?), he has been far more involved with them than had previously been royal custom. "It isn't only a woman's job to bring children up, of course. It's a man's job as well," the Prince once declared. Not only did he see his sons being born, but he bathed them as babies, changed the diapers, and was so ready to impart wisdom on the business of babyhood that Diana suggested *he* could have the next one while she sat on the sidelines dispensing advice. See CHILDREN. The couple have a real home at Highgrove, as opposed to a house, where Charles has blossomed tending his garden. See RESIDENCES.

As for Diana herself (one way to assess a man and his marriage is to closely observe his wife over a long period, assuming no long-term illness or family crisis exists to distort the picture), it is clear that marriage, motherhood, and her public role as the Princess of Wales have been the making of her. How much of this is due to the Pygmalion-style, Professor Higgins–ish influence of her much older, more experienced, and better-educated husband can only be a matter of conjecture. But it was Diana herself who said at the start, "With Prince Charles beside me, I can't go wrong." Despite the way she teases him (she even giggled at him in public when on one royal visit he was given an ill-fitting protective hat to wear), she has always looked up to him almost as a hero. She has enormous respect for him. And it is inconceivable that she could have transformed herself to such an extent, and achieved such remarkable success, without his loving support and guidance.

The fact that Prince Charles and his wife would not live in each other's pockets and would spend considerable periods apart was in the cards long before he married, or indeed chose a bride. His life was mapped out; his work schedule and sporting and social fixtures were planned months ahead. They were so set in concrete and so time-consuming that he once remarked on the problem of finding *room* in his life for a wife and children. Which suggested on the one hand that he felt little need then for marital companionship. (Some have suggested that had he not been obliged to produce an heir, Charles might well have been content to remain unwed.) And, on the other, that any girl he chose would have to be prepared to fit in, make the minimum of demands, and not disrupt the status quo. In other words, be a mouse, but a fertile one.

He mused on marriage, the kind of girl who might be suitable, and the difficulties he faced in having to make the right choice. It had to be a marriage which would last. "If only I could live with a girl before marrying her. But I can't," he declared to British Pressmen in Delhi in the autumn of 1980, then aged thirty-two and already struggling to decide whether Diana was the right girl. "It's all right for chaps like you. You can afford to make a mistake. But I've got to get it right first time. And if I get it wrong, you will be the first to criticize me in three years' time."

A cool head was required. As he said on another occasion, "Whatever your place in life, when you marry you are forming a partnership which you hope will last for fifty years. So I'd want to marry someone whose interests I could share. A woman not only marries a man, she marries into a way of life, a job. She's got to have some knowledge of it, some sense of it, otherwise she wouldn't have a clue about whether she's going to like it. If I'm deciding on whom I want to live with for fifty years, well that's the last decision on which I want my head to be ruled by my heart." He also declared:

> I think an awful lot of people have got the wrong idea of what [marriage] is all about. It is rather more than just falling madly in love with somebody and having a love affair for the rest of your married life. Much more than that. It is basically a very

strong friendship. Creating a secure family unit in which to bring up children and give them a happy secure upbringing—that's what marriage is all about. I think you are very lucky if you find the person attractive in the physical *and* mental sense. . . . To me marriage seems to be the biggest and most responsible step to be taken in one's life.

Just before his investiture as the Prince of Wales, he had said, "When you marry in my position, you are going to marry someone who perhaps one day is going to be Queen. You have to choose somebody very carefully, I think, who could fill this particular role. . . . The one advantage about marrying a princess, for instance, or somebody from a royal family, is that they do know what happens. The only trouble is that I often feel I would like to marry somebody English, or perhaps Welsh. Well, British anyway." Friendship was important. "Essentially you must be good friends, and love, I am sure, will grow out of that friendship," he said.

Well, Diana was British, with more English blood than Charles himself. Her family, if not royal, were aristocrats who had served the Royal Family for many years; the Queen is her brother's godmother; and she had grown up mixing with royal children. Diana was never going to be awestruck or tongue-tied in royal company. As for being friends, that is how she and Charles had begun their relationship. Moreover she *wanted* to be the Princess of Wales and was head-over-heels in love with him. Early on, newly engaged, they declared that interests they had in common included dancing, fishing, music, opera, being outdoors, skiing, and walking, and that they shared a similar sense of humor. (They are also both vehement antismokers. Diana, who is Patron of the British Lung Foundation and of the Australian Council on Smoking and Health, even has a large "No Smoking" sign on the mantelpiece of her sitting room at Kensington Palace.) But dancing is much more her thing (he finds having to lead off the dancing at balls an embarrassment), fishing his. Since the disaster at Klosters (see FRIENDS), Charles has continued to ski there but at the time of writing Diana hasn't. And as for humor, she's said since their marriage that he never gets her jokes.

In some ways they are very different. He's a stickler for punctuality; like the Queen Mother, she is often late. He admits he is often indecisive; she usually knows exactly what she wants. (Except when she's deciding what to wear, when she'll sometimes ask his advice and then promptly wear something else.) She's obsessively neat and tidy; his study is said to be so cluttered you can hardly get through the door. He's strict with the children; she's more lenient. Both can be moody, but he can become angry quickly whereas she often takes a more relaxed view. He prefers the country; she prefers London. He likes action vacations; she likes to sunbathe and swim. He listens to serious stuff on BBC Radio; she tunes in to pop music on Capital Radio. He enjoys serious books and disapproves of the blockbuster novels and romances she loves. He gained a university degree; she failed her GCE O levels. Could they be partners on an intellectual level? And since Diana was only just twenty when they wed and Charles a prematurely aged thirty-two, how much of a problem would the age gap be? At the time of their engagement, the Prince brushed the matter aside. "It's only twelve years," he said. "Lots of people have married with that sort of age difference." In fact, Diana's mother had first married at eighteen, and there was a fourteen-year age gap between her parents. "I just feel you're as old as you think you are," Charles said. "Diana will certainly help to keep me young. . . . I think I shall be exhausted!"

Marriage to an exuberant young wife, and the birth of Prince William, did take years off the Prince, who seemed happier and more relaxed than he had been for years, if ever. But the age difference undoubtedly did tell. Though Charles and Diana have thrown parties at Kensington Palace for pop stars who've performed to raise funds for the Prince's Trust (see MUSIC), he has invariably seemed uncomfortable, for example, attending pop concerts with her, and she's taken to going with her brother or groups of friends. Similarly, Diana has left Charles behind for a quiet evening in a ski chalet on vacation while she's gone out disco-dancing with friends at a club.

On the other hand, Diana was young enough to be molded by her husband, and she says she has learned everything from him. She has also learned from his older friends like Sir Laurens van der Post and, as the years have gone by, from the work and expertise of numerous charities and organizations with which she is linked. Diana is no longer the unworldly girl Charles married but a mature woman who has gained a phenomenal amount of experience in the past decade, toured the globe, and conversed with world leaders. She can discuss in depth any number of issues, from drug abuse and AIDS to contemporary problems in marriage. Freelance royal correspondent Judy Wade, who has followed them around the world since 1983, says:

> She's very quick to suss [figure] people out and how to operate on them, like sheikhs or Presidents or whatever. She's good at people. She's always had a very quick intelligence, and now that she's had the sort of crash course on world politics and everything, she's got the education to go with it. She's a smart cookie. I think the age gap has shrunk amazingly, and that she and Charles share more now than they did ten years ago because she's grown up. Without pushing her, Charles has very subtly encouraged her, and as Harold Brooks-Baker once put it to me, the Prince has now got the wife that he always wanted.

Diana's interest in art, which Charles loves, seemed to surprise staff at one museum she visited (see SPAIN), despite the fact that Althorp has or had one of the world's greatest art collections. In October 1989 she got involved in another of her husband's great interests, anthropology, which he studied at Cambridge University, when she became Patron of the Royal Anthropological Institute in London. According to the Director, Jonathan Benthall, she is "already taking a lively interest in the Institute's work." On their Majorca holiday in 1990, the book she was photographed reading as she sunbathed in her itsy-bitsy red bikini on King Juan Carlos's yacht *Fortuna* wasn't one of her favorite romantic novels but a paperback entitled *The After Life*, which Charles might have encouraged her to read. A royal aide was quoted as saying, "The Princess is keen to understand and perhaps share the beliefs her husband often enthuses about." She doesn't like riding but has even tried hunting to help her understand his passion for the sport; and from the earliest days, she watched him play polo. See SPORT. People Diana works with marvel at the huge increase in her self-confidence in recent years; at her gift with people, whom she really listens to and draws out; at her ability to get to the heart of a matter; at her concentration and perception; and at the knowledge she has gained. Far from taking her charity duties lightly or casually, she gets deeply involved. And when family, friends, or staff have problems, she's usually there to help and offer comfort, advice, and a shoulder to cry on.

However, the Princess is not and never has been a mouse. She is very determined and very strong-willed. On one public engagement, she gave a hint of her steel when she advised some lovelorn girl with boyfriend problems, "Don't let him get away with a thing!" People have always had to take Diana on her own terms, and those who predicted on her wedding that she would be swallowed up by the Royal Family couldn't have been more wrong. Her father knew that. Lord Spencer said, "She is a very determined young woman. I know the royals can appear to swallow people up when others marry in, and the other family always looks as if it had been pushed out, but that could never happen with us. Diana would not permit it to happen, and she always gets her way." Her friends declare that she is still basically the same person she always was. If anything, she has changed the royals. Even the Queen dresses more prettily and greets children in crowds more warmly since Diana came on the scene.

But it wasn't all easy going. Diana had her own ways of doing things, which weren't always royal ways. In the early days at Buckingham Palace, when she went into a kitchen to snatch a bite to eat and chat to the cooks, as she'd often done at home at Althorp, the "Upstairs, Downstairs" divide was underlined and she was told that it wasn't her place. She apparently found some of the Palace courtiers infuriatingly "patronizing" in their early attitude toward her. See QUOTES. And when Charles or others expected her to fit in and do things the way they'd always been done or organized things for her without prior discussion, she made it clear that *she* hadn't agreed and expected to be consulted first. Another problem was that newlyweds require privacy to build an intimate relationship; but as Diana complained, she and Charles were never alone. There were always staff or bodyguards around, if not in-laws. Her natural ways—like fetching her own coat, washing dishes, or sitting on Charles's lap at the dining table—reportedly raised eyebrows within the Royal Family. She earned one of the Queen's frosty looks early on for giggling during the national anthem at the Braemar Games.

According to Prince Charles's former valet Stephen Barry, "There were no rows on honeymoon. They kept those for later." But when rows did erupt, they were often spectacular. Charles is also very strong-willed, and his temper can be "vile" and his anger formidable. The scope of their disputes even covered who they should shake hands with at some official reception. Years later, in a British TV interview, they even contradicted each other over whether they have arguments! See TELEVISION.

Although Diana has said that the Queen is the best mother-in-law in the world—and the Queen thinks that she is the perfect wife for Charles—the Prince's devotion to his mother, sometimes at Diana's expense, became one source of friction. According to Judy Wade, six months after the wedding, when the Princess was pregnant with William, Charles drove off to have lunch with the Queen's shooting party, leaving Diana shouting angrily from a window of Sandringham House, "That's right—go and have lunch with your mother and leave me here all alone!" Not satisfied with that, she then chased him in her Ford Escort, flagged him down, and leapt out to continue the row through the window of his Range Rover, demanding, "Why do you do this to me? Why can't we just have a meal alone together for a change?"

In the autumn of 1982 after William had been born, Diana risked her mother-in-law's displeasure by turning up late for an official engagement after another marital shouting match. On that occasion, the couple were due to join the royal party at the Royal Albert Hall for the annual Festival of Remembrance honoring Britain's war dead. However, exhausted from sleepless nights with baby William, Diana apparently wanted to beg off, and an almighty row ensued. Charles insisted that duty must be done, allegedly declaring, "My duty lies above my loyalty to you," and stalked off alone to the Albert Hall with the message that Diana wasn't coming because she wasn't well. Her chair was removed from the Royal Box, only to be brought back when she suddenly appeared, having dried her tears and decided she couldn't let people down. This left Charles with egg on his face leading, according to some reports, to a further fight at the back of the Royal Box. Diana's belated appearance also caused a serious breach of royal protocol since she had turned up *after* the Queen had arrived, which is never, ever done. Within nineteen months of their wedding, the *News of the World* was suggesting that Diana was on the verge of a nervous breakdown, or had already "freaked out," and that she and Charles were "bewildered and unhappy" knowing there was "no escape" from what the newspaper claimed had become "the world's most difficult marriage."

Early in 1983 in response to this story and others, a unique interview was obtained which provided the fullest, frankest account of the royal marriage which had ever been given. Published in the *Daily Star* to try to set the record straight, it still remains valid for the insight it gives. It came from someone who could (and can), unfortunately, only be identified as "a reliable source close to the Palace." This is a great pity because, as cynics know, the phrase "a Palace source" *could* mean a housemaid or dustman. In this case, however, I can personally vouch that the information came directly from a person of impeccable credentials and can be taken as the real thing. See PREFACE. In answer to questions, which were not dodged, the source said at the time:

> It's an extremely happy marriage and the occasional spats are few and far between. But they are spats with fireworks; it's a rumbustious marriage. From time to time, there may be ruster and buster but they wouldn't be human if they didn't have rows. But a row doesn't mean the end of the world. . . . There is an inbuilt tendency in male members of the Royal Family to be quick-tempered. They flare up suddenly but it only lasts thirty seconds or so. . . . The Prince and Princess of Wales are extremely attracted to each other and give every indication of being very fond of each other. Visiting them and Prince William at Kensington Palace, I have never seen a happier, livelier, or more jolly or amusing family. Anyone who thinks this is a problem marriage is off the mark. They get on extremely well.
>
> . . .
>
> Contrary to the gossip, the Princess does listen to Prince Charles; she doesn't ignore what he says. For the last eighteen

months, he's acted as her guide and mentor. . . . The couple are very happy. And the birth of Prince William has made Diana more secure in herself and serene. She obviously adores her son and takes the major part in looking after him. She doesn't leave it to the nanny. . . . She's in love with children, and the couple give every sign of wanting more. I expect them to have more children when they have got their major royal tours out of the way. The Princess is so happy being a mother.

Of Diana's debut overseas tour with Charles to Australia, which was due to take place that spring, and on which they broke with royal tradition by taking Prince William with them (some reports claiming that the Princess had put her foot down and refused to go without her baby), the source said:

There was never any question of Diana leaving her baby for such a long time to go to Australia. The Queen never tried to stop her taking William. It was assumed from the start that the baby would go with them. It was always planned they should go as a threesome. . . . Nobody's arm had to be twisted about this. The Royal Family don't work that way. Taking the baby will set a royal precedent, but methods of travel are so much better these days. It wasn't a question of Diana putting her foot down.

Nevertheless, she *has* got a strong will. I suspect she was always strong-willed. She hasn't changed since the wedding; she's just showing it more now. When she was a young girl she was understandably fairly shy. . . . She still is . . . in some respects. But the Royal Family feel she's done very well and they are extremely proud of her. If they had to give her an end-of-term report on her role as the Princess of Wales, the verdict would be "outstanding." She's new blood, and this has undoubtedly been beneficial to the Royal Family. And she is very popular. When Prince Charles arrives at a place, people say, "Where's Diana?" He replies, "Don't you want me?" He's enormously pleased he's chosen someone so popular, though he does feel a bit displaced. But there's never a spark of jealousy. Nor, despite the gossip, is there any jealousy from the Queen. The Queen and her daughter-in-law get on extremely well. . . . The Queen doesn't *need* to feel jealous. She rises above such things: the Queen is the Queen. She is delighted with Diana and very attached to her. If asked, the

Queen will give advice—but only if she's asked. Remember, she's a mother-in-law! I'm sure she's constantly asked for advice by the couple on a whole host of matters, everything from planning a state visit to dress for formal occasions. And, I presume, on private matters too.

People don't like an unblemished fairy story. People like to see warts even if there aren't any. But the Prince and Princess *are* happy. And like an ordinary family, though royal. Their apartment at Kensington Palace is homely, and the size of Highgrove is modest by royal standards. Prince Charles is seldom away from the Princess for any length of time. She's neither lonely nor bored. She has plenty of friends and plenty to do. . . . She enjoys watching him play polo, but she gets fed up with the photographers. The Press is the main strain in her life. She enjoys public occasions and meeting people. She enjoys it a great deal and there's no sign of stress. If there were only reporters there, it would be no problem. But she does feel harassed by Press photographers . . . and this feeling that she can't go anywhere without camera lenses trained on her. . . . The Royal Family are less worried about what is written or said about them than they are about the cameras. So much that is written in Britain and abroad is invented. To an extent they don't read it any more. You stop reading stuff that's rubbishy. The Princess barely looks at the papers now. When Diana was first confronted by the Press cameras before her engagement, it was new and relatively pleasant. . . . It was at that time she first started becoming aware of what was involved in becoming a member of the Royal Family. Now she must be the most photographed face in the world. I'm sure Jackie Kennedy and Brigitte Bardot would say that constant Press attention built up pressures in them too. The Princess cannot do anything without being photographed. And everything about her—her hemlines, her hairstyles, the rings on her fingers, whether or not she's breast-feeding—is scrutinized and picked to pieces, sometimes in a nasty way, sometimes not. On private occasions like her skiing holiday in the Alps with Prince Charles [one of the occasions she refused to pose; see PRESS], she was damned if she was going to have her picture taken. But the evening she came back, she was on duty again and she went to the Royal Academy and posed happy and smiling. On duty she will continue to be the sparkling Princess. But in private, like other members of the Royal Family, she's not prepared to pose for the cameras. . . . She can't understand why so many people want to take endless pictures of her. She's getting to hate the cameras. However, she will be able to deal with it extremely well, in public. She copes in her own way. . . . But a great deal of rubbish has been written about the stresses and strains. The reports have been greatly exaggerated. It would be a pity if a barrier was created between the Princess and the cameramen and Picture Editors. The Princess of Wales is going to be around a lot longer than them.

The source also exploded several myths:

◆ *That, according to an American psychiatrist, Diana was on the verge of a nervous breakdown.* "How any self-respecting psychiatrist could come to a diagnosis without seeing the patient is beyond me," he said. "Major life changes generally cause stress, but that doesn't automatically lead to a nervous breakdown. It's a question of whether the individual can cope with it or not. The interest in Diana has been universal and overwhelming. But she gives no indication of being anything but well balanced and well adjusted."

◆ *That she might be suffering from anorexia nervosa.* "Any talk of anorexia is rubbish, total nonsense. A woman changes after having a baby."

◆ *That she is a tyrant with her staff.* "I've never heard anything like that. They have a small number of staff and they are extremely loyal. Yes, her private detective did leave. But it's pretty difficult living a life with a shadow. You have to get on well in those circumstances." See ROYAL PROTECTION SQUAD.

◆ *That she had only visited her father, Lord Spencer, at Althorp once since the wedding.* "They have been to Althorp several times."

◆ *That Prince Charles was forced into an arranged marriage.* "There's no question of it being an arranged marriage. There's no way somebody like Prince Charles would do something he didn't want to do. An arranged marriage isn't a possibility in this sort of society. People don't behave this way. At one time people said there was going to be an arranged marriage between Prince Charles and Princess Marie-Astrid of Luxembourg. This was a complete myth. They had never even met."

◆ *That Diana had got rid of Charles's old friends.* "Well, I see plenty of Charles's old friends around, but I can't claim to have seen the old girlfriends. . . ."

◆ *And finally, that Diana rules the roost.* "They work as a team," the source said. "They both give and take. One time she does what he wants, then he does what she wants. There is certainly no one dominant partner."

(However, Charles was definitely the one wearing the pants in June 1987 at Smith's Lawn, Windsor, where he'd gone to play polo. He spotted Diana perched on his Aston Martin, delighting cameramen some distance away who, whether she realized it or not, were busy snapping shots of her legs. Apparently anxious that she might dent the bodywork, Charles ordered her to get off. He did it in a jokey, lighthearted way amid smiles, but it was noticeable that she sprang off instantly. If either of them does rule the roost, it is Charles rather than Diana.)

Despite the revelations, the rumors about the marriage did not cease; indeed, they probably never will. Before long Charles was being described as a "wimp," while Diana was alleged to have turned into a "little monster" and a shrew. The royal couple answered back in a British TV interview with Sir Alastair Burnet, aired in October 1985. See TELEVISION. Though the marriage can never have been easy, the couple seemed happy in Italy earlier that year. And relaxing in Hawaii in private that November, between visits to Australia, Fiji, and Washington, D.C., observers commented that they looked as if they were on a second honeymoon.

Then, around 1986, they seem to have hit a bad patch. That year the couple were in their fifth year of marriage, today's equivalent of the old seven-year-itch period, and Diana became twenty-five. Since the wedding, she had been occupied having babies and working hard at her royal duties, but the appeal of both appeared to have waned. She was very tired and not in top form. In Vienna in April, she had a backache and looked none too

thrilled at the way Charles allowed another woman to flirt outra-
geously with him in public. See AUSTRIA. In Canada shortly
afterward, Charles made his famous "reflection as on the surface
of a mirror" speech which got him labeled "a loony"; and the
Princess, who had looked "fed up" on occasion during the trip,
fainted at Expo '86. See CANADA. Denials that she was pregnant
again were swift. On the tour of Japan which followed, Diana was
at times "bad-tempered" and "bored," so unlike her usual sparkling self that royal correspondent James Whitaker warned that
she was in danger of burning herself out through overwork. See
JAPAN. At home, Charles was increasingly fed up with William's
bad behavior and declared publicly, "I have discovered I don't
like four-year-olds." There were differences of opinion about
William's upbringing between Charles and William's nanny, Barbara Barnes, and Diana was caught in the middle.

    That year seemed the most likely time, in theory, for Diana to
become pregnant again. She had followed the pattern set by her
mother, and indeed by the Queen, of marrying early, having her
first child as soon as possible, and giving birth to the second two
years later. In 1985 the Princess had declared on TV that she saw
her "most important" role not as being a world superstar but
being "a mother and a wife." See QUOTES. Had Diana continued
to emulate her mother, she would have produced her third child
three years after the second, in 1987, which meant conceiving
anytime from April 1986 onward. But far from doing that, she
soon made it clear that the arrival of a third child was by no
means imminent. For a woman who clearly loves children so much
and wants a total of five (see CHILDREN), her delay seemed
curious. Could she have hesitated knowing that her mother's ill-
fated third child had died soon after birth? Could she have been
put off by Charles's displeasure with William? Or, exhausted
from her tours and knowing that both children would be off her
hands to a degree within slightly over a year—William would start
at Wetherby in January 1987 and Harry at Mrs. Mynors's nursery
school that September—did Diana decide that, at twenty-five, her
youth was slipping away and it was time she had some fun?
Though Charles has many worthy qualities, he is also very serious. After meeting the couple for lunch in November 1984,
newspaper columnist and former Fleet Street Editor Sir John

Junor commented in his memoirs that the Prince seemed in "some danger of overwhelming his wife, and in even greater danger of boring her." Maybe what Diana needed was a long, lighthearted private vacation with him away from it all, just the two of them and no distractions. What she got was Fergie.

Diana's rebellious period, for want of a better phrase, coincided with the arrival into the Royal Family of the boisterous Sarah Ferguson, who married Prince Andrew in July 1986. The Princess had encouraged the romance. Before the wedding, she joined Fergie and her actress friend Pamela Stephenson for a fancy dress stunt in which they dressed up as policewomen in theatrical costumes, tried to gate-crash Prince Andrew's stag party, and ended up, still in disguise, at Annabel's nightclub in Berkeley Square. Skiing in Klosters early in 1987, Charles was clearly irritated when Fergie and Diana pushed and shoved each other in the snow like a couple of girls on a larky package tour in front of Press cameramen. And at Royal Ascot that June, where Diana was alleged to have joked to Fergie and her friends, "Let's get drunk!" (see FOOD & DRINK), the two of them earned more black marks for undignified behavior when the cameras caught them prodding two of their friends in the backside with their umbrellas. Whether Fergie was a bad influence on the Princess, as some claimed, or whether her sense of fun simply encouraged Diana to believe, wrongly, that she could goof off in public without damaging her own image or that of the Royal Family in general, has since been hotly debated.

But Fergie's arrival on the royal scene did seem to make Diana fear that her "rival" would knock her from the front pages. (It's interesting that Princess Anne got her act together after *Diana* first appeared on the scene.) Having once almost come to hate the ever-present cameras, Diana now told Press photographers almost plaintively, "You won't need me anymore, now you've got Fergie." That, of course, couldn't have been further from the truth.

However, whether or not world adulation had gone to Diana's head, it was clear that she got a kick from her celebrity. During those early months after the Yorks' wedding, she seemed keen to preserve her position as the world's most feted, photographed, and glamorous woman. In August, when she and Charles and the children had their first seaside vacation with King Juan Carlos of Spain and his family in Majorca, Press photographs were taken of Diana in a bikini, which apparently made Charles cross. That autumn at Balmoral, according to one report, she went out of her way to go where she and the children would be in range of the lurking Press lenses. After touring the Arab Gulf States in November—either demonstrating that she enjoyed wielding the power of her beauty or desperate to show that her appeal was undiminished—she proudly told journalists how she'd "turned on the full treatment" and "mopped up" the Arabs, who were "going gaga" and "falling over themselves" when they saw her. See PRESS. She was flirting with Pressmen in private; and on the following tour, to Portugal in February 1987, she flirted with the President, Dr. Mario Soares, in public. See PORTUGAL. It was not behavior likely to please a husband, though such tactics might well be employed by a woman determined to make her spouse take notice of her.

Charles had his own preoccupations. The month before, when he had been due to accompany Diana to see William off on his first day at Wetherby School (the same day that Nanny Barnes finally left royal service, Charles apparently having insisted on firmer discipline; see STAFF), he remained at Sandringham instead, allegedly "snowed in." (The trains from Norfolk to London were apparently running.) The same month Prince Edward quit the Marines. It may well have struck Charles that Edward could get out when he wanted to, but he couldn't. Edward went on to a show-business job, and Prince Andrew had his career in the Navy. But Charles still didn't have the job he'd been trained for. After half a lifetime waiting in the wings, and at an age when many men are approaching the peak of their careers, he still had no idea how many more years he'd be in limbo, neither one thing nor the other. Anyone who's ever been unemployed for longer than a few weeks knows how soul-destroying it is—especially for men, most of whom still define who and what they are by the work they do. It's a mark of the Prince's enormous commitment to duty that he does so much public work, including helping the underprivileged and racial minorities and campaigning for the improvement of the environment and modern architecture, when he could be spending the interim period, like Edward VII did before he became King, in riotous living, womanizing, and gambling.

Unfortunately, the difficulties Charles has faced trying to come to terms with his royal role can't have been helped by his lapse of imagination in apparently failing to recognize that in addition to the obligations, it also affords him glorious God-given opportunities which are simply not open to most other human beings. Instead, he once agreed with the daft comment of an air hostess who declared that he had the world's most boring job, and he has since talked of feeling "trapped." In addition, he seems none too keen on the idea of being King anyway. In Australia in 1983, when a little boy mistakenly called him "the King," Charles reportedly declared, "No, no, no. I am not King yet. And I am not sure that I think it will be all that good for me when I *am* King."

The Prince's internal turmoil over all this was bound to spill over into his marriage. If things weren't too hot at the time, it might explain why on the trip to Portugal in February 1987, Diana rubbed her stomach and volunteered the information to reporters, "By the way, I'm not [pregnant] at the moment." In March 1987 Charles vacationed without her in Gstaad with friends. After his six-day tour of southern Africa which followed, he went off again on a private trip into the Kalahari desert with Sir Laurens van der Post. In Spain in April, Diana made another curious comment when she told journalists, "I'm too busy to have any babies for at least a year. I have to go to Australia next January." And she added, gesturing toward her stomach, "You see, I'm safe." Charles went on from Spain to Italy, where his friendship with the lovely Contessa Fiammetta Frescobaldi sparked stories. See SPAIN. And after he and Diana visited Cannes in May, his lone trip to Birkhall in Scotland to spend several days fishing on the river Dee produced more "Charles goes off on his own again" publicity, which dismayed him.

There had also been reports about Diana's friendship with handsome Philip Dunne, who had skied with the royal party in Klosters early that year, played host to the Princess and other friends later at his family's stately home, Gatley Park in Hereford-shire, and was among the royal party at Royal Ascot that June. See

FRIENDS. The same month, Diana was photographed at a David Bowie concert with a group of friends which included another bachelor, Major David Waterhouse. That summer, when he wasn't away on one of his trips, the Prince seemed to be playing polo endlessly, most days of the week and weekends. And in July, Charles and Diana spent their sixth wedding anniversary apart. See ARMED FORCES.

That year, 1987, rumors that the royal marriage was on the rocks reached a climax. The clincher, or so it seemed, came in October when, after about thirty days apart, Charles flew down from Balmoral to join Diana in Wales to visit victims of floods in Carmarthen, then promptly flew back, alone, to Scotland. See WALES. The message seemed clear: it was the Prince's way of telling the world that he preferred his own company to his wife's, the marriage was a sham, and they were leading separate lives. What few thought until later was that Charles, who can be "perverse," simply wasn't prepared to stage some kind of romantic public performance to silence the gossip.

"If there's one thing he hates more than anything else in his life it's performing, like a dog jumping through hoops," former royal reporter Harry Arnold (see PRESS) says now. "It just drives him *mad*. He feels literally like a poodle in a cage. And so he's very likely to turn his face away from her, and the second they're alone, give her a kiss. And they'd both laugh and say, 'Well, that's got them all going again.' " At the time, however, it appeared from news reports that Diana and her prince had not lived happily ever after and the fairy tale was over. Or *was* it?

That there were, and probably still are, strains on the Prince and Princess and their marriage is clear. But to conclude that their relationship is therefore kaput is unrealistic. The truth of the matter, according to those who should know, is that it was the long-running marriage-on-the-rocks story, put out by journalists hampered by too little information, which was the sham. According to Judy Wade,

> It was totally manufactured by the Press, but I think they sincerely believed it. There was nothing much happening to write about, and somebody counted up the number of days

that Charles and Diana had spent apart and turned this into a huge drama. I think they just thought they'd found something new. It was only what the couple had done every year since they were married, but nobody had noticed before. If you looked carefully at the marriage, there were no signs that it was really in trouble, but the Press decided it was. One story which has now become gospel was that the Queen gave Charles and Diana a ticking-off and told them they must sort out their marriage and make it look good. I have several excellent sources who see the couple every day and they were adamant that that *never* happened. And they documented it for me by showing me what their movements were that night. There was another story about David Waterhouse being photographed leaving Kate Menzies's mews home with Diana and her pleading for the film. [See FRIENDS.] I rang Waterhouse the next day and he told me he wasn't even there then. I was in Wales on the flood story and Charles and Diana were friendly, walking along together and chatting, and when they got into the back of the car, they cuddled up together. Charles went back to Balmoral because that's what he always planned to do. He always spends October there looking after the estate. In the photographs that were published of the couple in Wales, they did look sad, but that was because they were hearing sad stories from people who had lost their homes in the floods. The truth didn't come out, which makes me so cross, and this is why Charles is so bitter about the Press.

(Another example of photographs not revealing the full truth was when Charles was photographed hugging his friend Penny Romsey while on vacation in Majorca. Lord Romsey, Penny's husband, who was with them there, then revealed that Charles was actually comforting Penny after the devastating discovery that one of her children had been diagnosed as having cancer.) See HOLIDAYS and PRESS.

It was on the royal tour of Germany in November 1987 that lovey-dovey stories were filed about Charles and Diana, finally putting an end (for the time being) to the marriage-on-the-rocks saga. Harry Arnold, one of the leaders of the Rat Pack Press corps at the time, recalled, "James [Whitaker] and I, I tell you, we made a decision to stop that crazy snowball rolling on forever. It was driving us mad. And it was a snowball. And there was very little basis to it. You know how rumors start. It's almost like a hula-hoop craze. One person starts and everybody's on to it. No one likes stories about couples being quite happily married, which I think they are. Or being happily married, having their rows occasionally, but still staying together. They like them to be having affairs and all this sort of thing. I believe none of the stories about affairs, liaisons, rendezvous. I think they're all utter bollocks."

So what *was* going on in 1987? Something seemed off-key. Why was Diana flirting on tour in public with the President of Portugal? Was it because Charles wasn't paying her enough attention? "She was flirting a lot," said Judy Wade,

but she hates touring now, finds it extremely boring, and sometimes she'll do something to liven it up, or send it up, or to cause a little bit of a ripple. She's magic with men. I've seen her operate on the Rat Pack. She flirts with her eyes with men. But flirting with public figures was all sort of 1987-ish, and I haven't seen her do that on a tour at all since then.

People who see Charles and Diana at home say they're always very affectionate to one another and they seem like any normal married couple. She'll go out at midnight to meet him back from a foreign trip. I do think sometimes she gets fed up; all wives get fed up. But these things blow over. Early on she had a lot of adjustments to make to the confines of royal life. Things like you can never go to your own family for Christmas, you must go to his. She railed against all these things at the beginning and thought, like all young wives, "Oh I'll change that." I'm sure they haven't got an idyllically blissful marriage—who has? But I don't think it was ever as bad as people have painted it. I think they're as happy as anybody is after ten years. I think they have hiccups every now and then. But Charles is such a genuine person and so serious and well meaning. He is not the type of man who would ever betray a woman. He's almost a spiritual type of person.

But I should think it's very difficult to be married to him. He was very set in his ways and doesn't see why he should change for Diana. And he does insist on certain things. So she just uses womanly wiles, and she has got around him a lot. He's made this vast concession of going to Majorca every year to please her. But he gets carried away with his schemes and projects, and when he's involved with something, doesn't quite seem to know that his wife and children are around. You know, typical man—can only think of one thing at a time. But whenever Diana has talked to the Press about Charles, she's always sounded terribly impressed by him, like a little fan almost. She thinks he's wonderful. I think they're more settled now than they have been for a long while. But I suspect he'd have been a very difficult patient with his broken arm, because he's the sort of man who gets very frustrated. [See HEALTH.]

He gets cross quite easily if something goes wrong. I was in Africa with him once, we were away a long time, and he'd come out in the morning sometimes and his staff would say, "Oh Christ, he's in one of his moods." But twenty minutes later, he's forgotten he's cross. He's one of those people who forgets to be mad. I saw him once when he lost at polo and Diana was with him, and he was really in a foul mood because he knew he could have won. And she *ignored* it. She kept telling him funny things and acting totally normally as if he wasn't glowering at everybody, and in ten minutes he was over it. His moods never last long and I think she thinks, "Oh this is going to blow over." She's got this beautiful way of handling him. Kevin Shanley, her former hairdresser, who really saw them in their home, said Charles came into Diana's dressing room one morning and was stomping up and down, complaining about something, and she said, "Oh, good job it's nothing serious." And it's a wonderful way of bringing it down to size.

So what about Diana doing her own thing and meeting friends of her own age at the home, for example, of her pal Kate Menzies? See FRIENDS. "I just think she desperately needs a kind of mental and emotional bolt-hole [oasis] where she can go and be the girl she was," Judy said. "When you see her in public, she's putting on this performance, she's being the Princess of Wales. But the real Diana is an outrageous, jokey person. With the Rat Pack she's hysterical, saying all these outrageous things and saucy lines and coming back with quick repartee. She can't be like that in public—when she is, she gets reprimanded for it. So she needs a place to let her hair down and people to be normal with. It's a kind of winding-down thing, and she needs that."

Charles needs to wind down, too. And with ten weeks' vacation a year, he has more time than most men to vacation with his wife and children *and* take extra trips to paint or fish or trek through the Kalahari desert without them. Although Brian Hoey claims Charles *has* now come to terms with his royal role, it's only when he's off fishing, trekking, hunting, or playing polo that he can get completely away from his official papers and the telephone. Diana seems resigned to the fact that he needs plenty of space alone. More than anything else, he perhaps dreads the further confinements on his life once he becomes King. Judy Wade said, "After my book *Inside a Royal Marriage* was published, I gained fresh information. It's not his wife, it's his life that's the problem with Charles." She claimed:

> He does not want to be King. He wants his life to go on the way it is now, and it's inevitable that it won't. He doesn't want to go and move into Buckingham Palace—everybody in the Royal Family loathes the place—and he doesn't want to give up Highgrove, but it's too small for a king and he'll have to go to Windsor. He doesn't want it all to change and it's going to and he dreads the day. And so he's had to come to terms with all this and it's very hard. That's why he kept running away and having these little think-ins in the Hebrides and elsewhere.

According to friends mentioned in Penny Junor's biography of the Prince, the couple *did* have problems late in 1987, which may mean after the Press brouhaha was over. Either way, it adds significance to the fact that early in 1988 Diana first became interested in the marriage guidance work of RELATE, in which she quickly became deeply involved, despite having turned down an invitation from them two years previously. She has since become Patron of RELATE, and it is one of her most-favored organizations. See RELATE.

In October 1990, when the couple were apart for about six weeks during the Prince's regular long autumn vacation in Scotland (see FRIENDS), some newspapers again interpreted this as a sign that they were leading "separate lives." This took no account of the fact that Diana had the children to look after when they weren't at school, and her public engagements to carry out—and indeed some of *Charles's* while his broken arm mended. (Duty was also given as the reason the couple reportedly didn't dance together when they attended the Diamond Ball that December. See DANCING.) A further Press claim that Charles was moving his office base to Highgrove while Diana stays in London, that the couple were on their way to a "weekend marriage," was denied as "untrue" by the Palace. No doubt other rumors will arise in the future.

But whatever difficulties she and Charles have individually and as a couple, and despite the odd bad patch every marriage goes through, I find it inconceivable that over so many years Diana could give such a convincing impression of being a contented wife and mother if in truth she were desperately unhappy and unfulfilled. That level of misery, which any normal woman feels when her marriage *is* doomed, cannot be concealed for long, particularly by someone like the Princess who wears her heart on her sleeve. One of the most telling remarks she has ever made came in Wales in March 1990 when the royal couple made another visit to comfort and cheer refugees, this time from the flooded village of Towyn. See WALES. Trefor Vaughan, a local man greeting them on his seventy-third birthday, reminded them that he had met them both before in Rhyl in 1982. Diana, joking, pointed to Charles and declared, "Yes—ten years later and I'm still stuck with him!" In my view that remark, made in public, could only come from a woman who is confident of her relationship and sure of her man. "Charles deserves a medal for putting up with me," she says, knocking herself too. In fact, the Princess is said to have commented after their marriage that for the first time in her life, she felt secure. In 1991, the year of their tenth wedding anniversary, that did not appear to have changed. According to an article by Andrew Morton, published in the April issue of *Good Housekeeping* magazine, Diana told a friend, "People jump to conclusions so easily. It is so easy for people to judge my marriage, but they don't understand me or my husband. . . . Whatever people may think and say, I am very happy, thank you very much

With William, Diana looks on as Charles pursues his passion for polo. (Alan Davidson/Globe Photos)

. . . don't worry about me, my marriage is fine."

Whatever the future holds, Diana said long ago, after her own experience of being a child from a broken family, that once she was married she never wanted to be divorced. See QUOTES. She has had ten years' experience of marriage and has gained extra knowledge and skills from RELATE. Whatever problems lie ahead—and no one knows how much longer Prince Charles will have to kick his heels as King-in-Waiting—she is likely to use it all, plus her considerable resources of courage, resilience, and determination, to ensure that the children's family life and her marriage remain intact.

But are so many periods apart wise? Genealogist Harold Brooks-Baker has been quoted as saying, "The Prince sees more of his wife and children than any other Prince of Wales in history." But this *wasn't* an arranged marriage, and repeated long separations don't wash with today's public. There is no doubting Charles's wish to serve his country, his fine qualities, or his immense good works over many years. But in an age when one of the key roles remaining to the Royal Family is to provide a focus of family unity for the people it serves, he would do well to devote more time and attention, and visibly so, to his wife and children. If he doesn't, people may begin to doubt whether the monarchy will have a future under Charles III.

MONACO

The Princess's first lone journey abroad after her marriage was a sad four-hour visit to Monaco in September 1982 to attend the funeral of Princess Grace. Diana had met the former Hollywood film star at her first public engagement with Prince Charles as his fiancée. It was the night in March 1981 when Diana wore that breathtaking strapless black evening dress. See X-RATED. According to the book *The Bridesmaids—Grace Kelly and Six Intimate Friends* by Judith Balaban Quine (Weidenfeld, 1989), the author, who was a bridesmaid at Grace Kelly's wedding to Prince Rainier, claims that as the flashbulbs popped around her, Diana realized that she would never be a private person again. She looked so alarmed that Princess Grace took her into the ladies' room, where Diana clung to her for comfort and sobbed, "What shall I do?" "Don't worry, dear," Princess Grace replied, putting her arms around her. "It'll only get worse"—a response which apparently put Diana back on course. Princess Grace and her son, Crown Prince Albert, who stood in for Prince Rainier, were later among the guests at Charles and Diana's wedding in July 1981. Diana represented the Queen at the funeral following Princess Grace's untimely death in a car accident just over a year later.

MONEY

The British Government pays certain members of the Royal Family under what is known as the Civil List. The Civil List payments for 1989, 1990, and 1991, with the percentage increases from 1990 to 1991, are cited in Table 1.

TABLE 1: CIVIL LIST PAYMENTS FOR 1989, 1990, AND 1991
AND PERCENTAGE INCREASES

	1989	1990	1991	1990–91 rise
The Queen	£4,658,000	£5,090,000	£7,900,000	55%
The Queen Mother	£404,000	£439,500	£640,000	46%
Duke of Edinburgh	£225,300	£245,000	£360,000	47%
Duke of York	£155,400	£169,000	£250,000	48%
Prince Edward	£20,000	£20,000	£100,000	400%
Princess Royal	£140,400	£154,500	£230,000	49%
Princess Margaret	£136,700	£148,500	£220,000	49%
Princess, Alice, Duchess of Gloucester	£55,400	£60,500	£90,000	50%
Duke of Gloucester	£110,000	£119,500		
Duke of Kent	£148,500	£161,500	£630,000	45%
Princess Alexandra	£141,600	£154,000		
Total:	£6,195,300	£6,762,000	£10,420,000	

Payments to the Dukes of Gloucester and Kent and to Princess Alexandra, which are refunded to the Treasury voluntarily by the Queen from her private resources, were fixed at £630,000 between them annually from 1991. All the 1991 sums will stay frozen for ten years under a new plan announced by Mrs. Thatcher in July 1990. Prince Edward, who got a whopping 400 percent rise in 1991, had not, unlike the others, received any increase for the previous three years. But most intriguing perhaps is the similarity between the sums paid to the Princess Royal (Princess Anne), the workaholic of the family, and those paid to the Duke of York and Princess Margaret, who do far fewer public engagements. See PUBLIC ENGAGEMENTS.

Though provision has been made via the Civil List for Princess Diana to receive a pension of £60,000 should she become widowed, she and Prince Charles, who have an estimated annual salary bill for staff of more than £250,000, are *not* on the Civil List. They get their income tax-free from the revenues of the Duchy of Cornwall, about a quarter of which Charles voluntarily gives to the Government in lieu of tax. Before his marriage, he gave the state about half. In 1988, the 128,000-acre Duchy was reported to have made over £2 million for the first time, giving the Prince a reported £3,000-a-week pay rise. In 1989, he was reported to have had an increase of £4,808 a week when profits rose to £2,515,925. In 1990 the Duchy made an extra £600,000, bringing the annual total for the first time to over £3 million.

Many people quibble about Civil List payments, especially pensioners and others struggling to survive on about £50 a week. In March 1990, a survey in *Woman's Own* magazine revealed that three-quarters of those who responded thought that the royals on the Civil List got too much money, only a quarter believing they were "worth every penny." The Queen is the richest woman in the world with assets estimated at £6,700 million, and she does not pay income tax. (Though public demands that she *should* pay have recently become persistent. More than 70 percent of people questioned in two opinion polls felt she should. And a move to make the Queen pay income tax, which her advisers said could mean she'd have to sell Balmoral, her Scottish home, was introduced in the British Parliament in July 1991. It did not become law.) But, people ask, why should she need subsidizing? In fact, she doesn't touch a penny of the money personally. The Civil List allowances are used by the royals to cover the cost of performing their public duties, the major part going to pay hundreds of royal staff—though wages and salaries are notoriously low. Since employees are taxed on PAYE (Pay As You Earn), the Exchequer gets much of it back anyway.

The actual cost of the British monarchy was expected to total £56 million in 1990—more than £1 million a week—since the Civil List covers only a fifth of the expenses, the rest coming from taxpayers via public departments, in addition to further sums paid personally by the Queen and by those royals who are not on the Civil List. According to royal expert Brian Hoey, writing for the

Daily Express's "Money Page" at the time of the March 1990 increases, here's who pays some of the extra bills:

◆ Official overseas tours, plus banquets for visiting heads of state (at around £8,000 per banquet): paid for by the Foreign and Commonwealth Office.

◆ Telephone calls and upkeep of Buckingham Palace, Kensington Palace, St. James Palace, the Palace of Holyrood House, Windsor Castle, and Hampton Court (but not the upkeep of Balmoral or Sandringham, which the Queen owns personally): paid for by the Department of the Environment.

◆ Running costs of the Queen's Flight (two helicopters and five planes) and Her Majesty's yacht *Britannia*, which had a £22 million refit in 1987–88: paid for by the Ministry of Defence.

◆ Royal Protection Squad: paid for by the Metropolitan Police, who keep the detectives who work as royal bodyguards on their payroll whether their duties are at home or abroad.

◆ Official royal mail: free. The Royal Mail absorbs the cost, without passing it on to other customers, because the amount of official royal correspondence is only a tiny fraction of the 60 million letters which it deals with every day.

In October 1990, a report by the Royal Trustees gave a detailed breakdown of spending beyond the Civil List, providing the first insight into the Queen's Household expenditure in more than six years. The figures in Table 2 are from this report. When this paperback edition went to press, these were still the most up-to-date figures available.

Despite these enormous sums, the Queen's thrift is well known. Her penny-pinching instincts were naturally passed down to her children and reinforced, as Princess Anne once implied, smiling cannily, by the fact that they had "a Scottish nanny." So if Diana wants to stay on the right side of her husband, she probably has to watch the pennies too. She frequently wears outfits which "work" for her time and time again. At Royal Ascot, for which she used to have new outfits or hats made specially, none of the outfits she wore in 1990 was new. She even wore the same slinky Hachi gown for two James Bond film pre-

TABLE 2: THE QUEEN'S HOUSEHOLD EXPENSES (EXCLUDING SALARIES)

	1983	1989	1990 (estimate)
Domestic expenses:			
Royal kitchens	£158,463	£185,750	£200,783
Royal cellars	£24,588	£66,420	£71,250
Furnishings	£123,183	£160,154	£180,557
Laundry	£27,986	£57,770	£63,700
Flowers	£37,838	£34,683	£37,950
Livery	£45,732	£78,353	£88,100
Royal garden parties	£149,986	£195,457	£213,650
Sandringham & Balmoral	£5,253	£17,039	£19,000
Horses & carriages:			
Purchase	£3,162	£9,588	£16,000
Upkeep & repair	£118,867	£139,546	£149,025
Cars:			
Purchase & hire	£25,865	£33,713	£37,042
Upkeep & repair	£42,802	£22,597	£36,275
Office expenses:			
Data-processing equipment	£75,801	£261,779	£123,150
Stationery & supplies	£173,925	£190,840	£138,900
Newspapers	£7,459	£13,054	£13,532
Insurance	£13,652	£23,545	£29,000
Other:			
Chapels Royal	£30,715	£2,316	£5,350
Royal gardens, Windsor (net receipt)	(£26,631)	(£8,228)	(£30,000)
Travel	£33,027	£45,602	£50,840
Official presents	£6,984	£37,114	£34,000
Donations, cups, & prizes	£4,728	£8,449	£9,500
Allowances & gratuities	£27,130	£21,212	£30,933
Rent & rates	£1,537	£1,984	—
Royal Library, Windsor (net receipt)	(£9,080)	—	—
Sundry expenses	£60,680	£79,774	£88,630
Total:	£1,163,652	£1,678,511	£1,607,167

Expenditure borne by Governmental departments:

Marshal of the Diplomatic Service	£21,546	£49,364	£53,807
Overseas visits at the request of Government departments	£409,800	£418,600	£580,000
Expenditure on palaces occupied by the Queen & residences occupied by members of the Royal Family	£10,678,000	£21,095,000	£25,560,000
Gentlemen-at-Arms & Yeomen of the Guard	£29,000	£52,000	£48,000
Official travel by train including maintenance of the Royal Train	£389,000	£851,000	£1,426,000
Royal Train renewal programme	—	£1,384,000	£850,000
Central Chancery of the Orders of Knighthood	£114,780	£187,216	£190,000
Royal Yacht	£8,905,000	£6,998,000	£9,272,000
Queen's Flight	£4,763,000	£6,229,000	£6,745,000
Royal flights in civil aircraft	£1,061,000	£800,000	£825,000
Equerries	£69,000	£205,000	£192,000
Publicity services (COI)	£159,000	£324,851	£376,000

mieres, first for *Octopussy* in 1983, then again six years later for *Licence to Kill,* by which time Timothy Dalton had replaced Roger Moore as 007. (It was on the set of Dalton's first Bond film, *The Living Daylights,* at Pinewood studios in 1986 that the Princess was urged to break a movie prop bottle, made of sugar glass, over Prince Charles's head—and she did!) Like the Queen Mother, she has alterations made to get more wear from some of her clothes, for example making sure that long-length outfits designed for her tours to Arab countries can be shortened later for general use.

Diana can be surprisingly concerned about the cost of food, once asking if she and Charles could "afford" to have lobster. See FOOD & DRINK. And dinner parties at Kensington Palace tend to be modest. You don't have to be royal, or rich, to offer guests soup, fish or chicken, and fruit salad. Candles are said to be popped in the fridge for a couple of hours before candlelit meals so that they burn longer. They save money by taking their own picnics to the opera. See MUSIC. And Charles apparently insists on having his hankies washed at home to save them getting lost in the royal laundry and having to buy more.

The Queen is the only member of the Royal Family who never carries cash, and Buckingham Palace says it is "unusual for close members to carry credit cards." Diana banks with Coutts, bankers to the Royal Family. When she is shopping or at a restaurant, she usually has the bill sent to Kensington Palace for payment. However, she has sometimes used an Access or a Duchy of Cornwall American Express card. But on one occasion, when she borrowed a credit card from one of her bodyguards to pay for some clothes, there were blushes all round when the available funds didn't cover the bill. In the *Woman's Own* magazine survey mentioned earlier, 74 percent of those who responded thought Diana sometimes spent too much on clothes. (How much she *does* spend on them has never officially been revealed.)

MOTORING

Diana is an excellent driver, and according to a member of the royal staff, she is "twice as good at handling a fast car as Prince Charles." But that may be little consolation to angry motorists who have protested at her antics on expressways, or to villagers near Highgrove who claim that her tire-scorching expeditions shatter the rural calm. "When she gets behind the wheel, she likes putting her foot down," said one. Diana is not alone as a royal speedfreak. Prince Michael of Kent was banned for two weeks and fined £100 in July 1990 for doing 103 mph in his Aston Martin on the M4 expressway in Wiltshire that April. That October, Princess Anne was banned for a month and fined £150 for breaking the speed limit twice in a week on a 60-mph road near Stow-on-the-Wold, driving at 77 and 90 mph in her blue Bentley Turbo. Viscount Linley has been caught speeding several times. In 1985, after Diana was clocked doing 96.1 mph on the M4 returning to Highgrove, Scotland Yard stepped in and asked her detectives, Graham Smith and Allan Peters, to discreetly warn her to slow

Diana in the driver's seat. (Richard Slade/Camera Press London)

down. See JAPAN. And in October 1990, she was warned again after speeding along Kensington High Street to the Palace at 55 mph—nearly twice the speed limit—on a Monday morning with her detective. Her motoring has been noted by Charles, who commented to businessmen during a visit to Vancouver that she seemed to think her marriage to him was "a good excuse" to run "through red lights." Diana's response was to turn red and glare.

But she has admitted cheekily using bus and taxi lanes to drive through London traffic, particularly the restricted slip road around the back of Trafalgar Square. And she recalled an occasion when a cabbie drew level with her car and began protesting about women drivers, only to say "Sorry, Ma'am" once he recognized her. In June 1986 London cabbie Mike Hanness told of twice running across Diana while driving his taxi behind Harrods, the first time almost literally when she stepped out of a car straight into his path. "I didn't half give her some verbals. I told her she was a stupid cow," he said. "I tell you, mate, she came very close to being killed." It was only when she "blushed scarlet and kind of muttered apologies" that he realized who she was. About a year later, he said, again behind Harrods, he got into one of those traffic jams "where you and the other driver wave each other on, and then move on together. . . . We stopped an inch away from a collision," he recalled, "and would you believe it, I saw it was Di! 'Hello, luv,' I said. 'It's me again, remember?' 'Yah, I remember you,' she replied. 'Gosh . . .' " Another taxi driver, Cockney Jimmy Ward, aged thirty-five, took advantage of being stuck alongside the Princess's car in a London traffic jam to wink at her. When she wound down the window, he invited her to attend a charity party given by cabbies for seven hundred needy children in February 1989, which she did. "She's so sweet," he said.

Diana regularly parks illegally on double yellow lines, which infuriates her husband, and was once told off for doing it at Cirencester in Gloucestershire by meter maid Pat Wright. When pop stars Matt and Luke Goss of Bros turned up late for a charity lunch in March 1989, wailing that their big blue Merc had been given the boot, Diana replied,"I'm so sorry. I know all about that." In fact, her bodyguards prevent her own car from being given the boot, wherever she's parked. It was reported that in May 1987, as the Princess was going to a public engagement in the center of London, her £25,000 chauffeur-driven Jaguar, followed by a police backup car, allegedly broke the law three times by ignoring a "No Entry" sign, mounting a sidewalk, and parking for eighty minutes on double yellow lines, forcing other traffic to reverse into busy Regent Street. "If they had been ordinary cars," a passing police officer was quoted as saying, "they would have been clamped [given the boot]."

There have been persistent stories of Di giving her detectives the slip in order to go out driving, sometimes alone at night. It was once claimed that she had been spotted in the early hours of the morning driving a Ford Escort near Sloane Square. And in April 1987 it was claimed that, driving alone late in a sporty black Escort turbo, she had been chased through London streets at 70 mph by a carload of leering Arabs in a powerful white Golf GTI. Both claims were denied, police alleging that the driver wasn't Diana but a "look-alike." See ROYAL PROTECTION SQUAD.

The Princess has a frog hood ornament on her car and listens to music while she drives. See COLLECTIONS. Prince Charles, who likes listening to opera when he's driving, has a polo player hood ornament. Fergie has an owl given to her by Prince Andrew, and the Queen has a figure of St. George and the dragon.

Diana crashed her second car, a blue VW Polo, coming out of a side turning in 1980. In December 1985, her car was bumped in the parking lot behind her favorite store, Harvey Nichols in Knightsbridge, where, accompanied by her detective, she had been doing some Christmas shopping. As they were about to pull out, another woman apparently backed her car into Diana's. The detective got out and checked the bodywork, and Diana declared, "No damage." The woman motorist made off, no doubt highly embarrassed. In November 1988, the Princess and Michael Heseltine could have ended up bumper to bumper when they both drove up late for a charity auction at Blenheim Palace. As he drove one way around the inner courtyard, Diana, driving her Jaguar, came around the other. Mr. Heseltine was ordered to give way to her by an official who stood on a wall and bellowed, "Stay there!"

In March 1990, Diana took part of an antiterrorist driving course at the Metropolitan Police Driving School at Radlett airfield in Hertfordshire after asking to see the kind of training given to royal chauffeurs and backup protection squads. She sat grinning beside instructor Sergeant Clive Pouncey as he sped off in a pacey red Range Rover and slammed on the brakes to avoid a mock "hijackers' roadblock" on the disused runway. When she took the wheel herself, she had the car swerving, reversing, and doing U-turns at high speed. She also had to drive slowly between a narrow line of cones, turn the Rover around when it was boxed in, and reverse through three gates. While she did it, she was chased by superdriver Police Constable Anthony Leonard, who did everything he could to make her blow her cool by sounding his horn and flashing his lights. He didn't succeed. "I did my best to harass her," he said afterward, "but she stayed calm and at the end she gave me a wicked grin!" Sergeant Stephen Mead commented, "The Princess of Wales would be cool, calm, and collected in a terrorist situation. She is a good driver and with further training would be able to get herself out of an attack." Speeding and getting praised for it made a nice change for Diana. "It was thrilling!" she said.

Like other members of the Royal Family, Diana can lease cars rather than buy them. Cars she has driven over the years include:

◆ Her mother's Renault 5, after she learned to drive with the British School of Motoring on Fulham Road (she passed her driving test at the second attempt).

◆ A Honda Civic, which her mother bought her.

◆ A pale blue VW Polo, the one she crashed, which her mother also bought her.

◆ A brand-new red Mini Metro, registration number MPB 909W, a further gift from Mum, in which Diana raced off, pursued by the world's journalists, to secretly rendezvous with Prince Charles in their courting days. In January 1981 a policeman found it unlocked and left a note on the windshield saying, "Please lock up in future or your vehicle may be stolen." The Metro was described as being in "good condition, one careful lady driver" when it was bought for £3,700 later by company director Roger Holmes from Bromley in Kent.

◆ A silver-gray Ford Escort 1.6 Ghia, registration number WEV 297W, which Diana drove from May 1981, shortly before her wedding, until August 1982, shortly after the birth of Prince William. The car had thirty-seven thousand miles on the odometer when it was sold in 1987 to John Gibson of Leeds, who used it to drive to work; his wife, Rosemary, also used it to do the shopping. Gibson had no idea it had belonged to the Princess until a friend showed him an old newspaper picture of Diana in it. In March 1988 it was snapped up for more than twice the £2,875 he'd paid. A month later, dubbed the Fairy Tale Car, it appeared as the major prize in a contest organized by the *Daily Mail*. (The tabloid had previously run contests for some of the Duchess of Windsor's jewels and the Duke of Windsor's 1936 black Buick, which, the newspaper trumpeted, had "figured prominently" in the Abdication crisis.)

◆ A black Ford Escort 1.6 Ghia, registration number BJN 17X, which Diana leased from the Ford Motor Company from April 1982 until September 1983. It was bought for £3,700 seven months later, from a dealer in Torquay, by John and Caroline Glanfield from Plymouth. They didn't at first know that Diana had driven it. That car too was a newspaper competition prize.

◆ A 114-mph Ford Escort Cabriolet.

◆ A £10,432 black Ford Escort RS Turbo which could reach 60 mph in 7.8 seconds and had a top speed of 126.2 mph.

◆ A £28,000 XJ40 3.6 Jaguar, lent to her for a couple of days from launch day in October 1986, when she was chauffeur-driven in it, wearing a midnight blue dress, to a gala performance of Andrew Lloyd Webber's *Phantom of the Opera*, thrilling a Jaguar spokesman who declared, "We are absolutely delighted that she has shown such an early interest—even her outfit matched the car! Most members of the Royal Family already lease our cars, and we hope and confidently expect that her gesture of support tonight will continue the tradition."

◆ A Ford Sierra Sapphire Cosworth.

◆ And the car with which she was generally associated, her 145-mph green Jaguar XJS. In October 1988, Diana was driving the green Jag off the busy M4 toward Kensington Palace when she was allegedly spotted talking on her car phone for several minutes, risking being charged with driving without due care.

The following month, visiting a factory in Telford, Shropshire, which produces car phones and other electronic equipment, Diana quizzed technician Nick Spencer about eavesdroppers, perhaps thinking of a call between James Whitaker of the *Daily Mirror* and Fergie's father, Major Ronald Ferguson, which had been tapped by another newspaper. "The Princess asked how easy it would be to tap into a car phone conversation," the technician said. "I told her it could probably be done by anybody with a good scanner. But then I suggested that her frequencies are probably special ones and more difficult to detect. I don't know if she was thinking about the Press listening in, but she did seem reassured by what I told her." See AUSTRALIA.

In March 1989, Diana was criticized for allowing four-year-old Prince Harry to sit between her knees in the driving seat and apparently steer the car in a public park. A year later, Charles was criticized after letting Prince Harry sit on his lap behind the wheel of a Range Rover while Charles guided it around the private roads

of the royal Sandringham estate in Norfolk on New Year's Eve
1990—the same day Diana caused a security scare by going off
alone. See ROYAL PROTECTION SQUAD. Diana was also chastised,
as Patron of the Child Accident Prevention Trust, by a road safety
liaison officer for the under-five-year-olds in Essex for letting
William and Harry "fool around in the back of her car" instead of
using child seats and safety belts.

In August 1990, when Viscount Linley drove up to Clarence
House for the Queen Mother's ninetieth birthday party in a new
Mercedes-Benz 500SL, Diana exclaimed, "You're driving my car!"
She had borrowed one from the German company for a week,
loved it, and wanted to keep it—so much so that she eventually
sold her personal Jag. And in January 1992, using her own private
funds, she leased her dream car—a 156-mph, £72,310, metallic-
red, soft-top, two-seater Mercedes-Benz 500SL—as a "personal
runabout." This unleashed fierce criticism from politicians and
recession-hit car workers in Britain, since senior members of the
Royal Family are expected to fly the flag by driving only cars
made in Britain. Unlike Fergie, Diana is not known for public
insensitivity. So her determination to have the Merc at all costs
really dented her image. Especially at a time when millions of
citizens were in debt and many thousands were having their homes
repossessed because of mortgage arrears. It was a clear demonstration of the Princess's willfulness. However, the Palace said she
would continue to use a Jaguar, "by and large," for public engagements. (Princess Anne ordered an £80,000 yacht at around the
same time, but at least she ordered it from a British boat builder.)
Of course, Jaguar is now owned by Ford of America anyway.
Charles's most beloved car is the Aston Martin the Queen gave
him for his twenty-first birthday. In 1986 he was given an
£80,000 convertible Aston Martin by the Sultan of Oman, whom
he and Diana visited. See ARAB GULF STATES. Prince William is
reported to have a miniature electrically powered Jaguar XJ-SC,
rumored to have cost almost as much as a full-sized car.

In addition to cars, the Princess has driven various other
vehicles. In August 1988, she and about thirty pals, including
Viscount Linley, spent more than £1,000 on a night's hush-hush
go-cart racing in Clapham, south London, where they sped
around the track at 35 mph. Diana beat three other girls in a

women's race, winning a trophy. She also beat a senior instructor and her three detectives, prompting instructor Martin Howell of Playscape Racing to comment, "The Princess is a very good driver." In May 1989, she drove a ninety-six-seat double-decker bus during a tour of a bus factory in Falkirk, Stirlingshire, taking off across the factory yard after remarking to the driver, "You're brave to let me behind the wheel." She also drove an FV 432 armored personnel carrier, with a little help, during a visit to the Royal Hampshire Regiment. See GERMANY.

MUSEUMS & EXHIBITIONS

Diana is Patron of the Natural History Museum, which is visited by 180,000 schoolchildren a year. Prince William and Prince Harry have been there on a school trip. And Mum popped into the museum with them on a private visit to see "Dinosaurs Live!," a major show featuring robotic dinosaurs. One of the little princes was later spotted clutching a small toy dinosaur of his own. The museum, which is close to Kensington Palace, is the first national museum in Britain to have a royal Patron. Diana took on the role in 1989, and in February 1990 she officially opened the museum's Activity Centres, based in a new purpose-built block. The Centres provide educational services for visiting families and schoolchildren; they include a Discovery Centre where children aged 7 to 11, curious to find out about natural history for themselves, can discover how fish float, how we move, and why the tortoise didn't win the race, by experimenting with "hands-on" displays. That October, Diana was present at the launch of the museum's Development Appeal, when she was presented with a print of a salmon-crested cockatoo, one of the world's most endangered species.

The Princess is also Joint Patron, with Prince Charles, of the EUREKA! project, initially called the Children's Museum Ltd. A collection of exhibitions rather than a museum, EUREKA!, based in Halifax, West Yorkshire, will be a new kind of leisure and learning center, a living "encyclopedia" of the everyday world, where visitors can learn how things are made and how they work. The themes of the major exhibitions will be "Living and Working Together," "You and Your Body," and "Creating and Inventing."

Half a million visitors of all ages are expected to visit EUREKA! annually after it opens in 1992.

Diana is an Honorary Family Member of the Friends of the Imperial War Museum. In July 1990 at Spencer House (see RESIDENCES), she presented the Building of the Year Award jointly for two buildings, including a new gallery created from a former courtyard at the museum.

MUSIC

Diana loves music and comes from a musical background. Her maternal grandmother, Ruth, Lady Fermoy, was a concert pianist before her marriage. As the young Ruth Gill from Aberdeen, she had studied at the Paris Conservatoire under Albert Cortot. She launched the annual Festival of Music and the Arts at King's Lynn in Norfolk, for which the Queen Mother became Patron. Diana was first photographed in public, at the age of twenty months, at the ceremony in March 1963 when Lady Fermoy was made a Freeman of the Borough of King's Lynn in recognition of her work in music and art in West Norfolk. Both Diana's sisters, Sarah and Jane, excelled as pianists. When Diana herself finally took up the piano at school at West Heath, somewhat belatedly at the age of fourteen, she made "phenomenal progress." Her headmistress, Ruth Rudge, commented, "Everyone wished that she'd begun to play earlier." There was always a piano around for Diana to play. At Coleherne Court, her flatmate, Carolyn Pride, who was studying at the Royal Academy of Music (of which Diana later became President) had a piano. And the Princess has a grand piano at Highgrove and another at Kensington Palace, which Prince William and Prince Harry were once seen thumping unmelodically in a British TV film. The Royal Family love sing-alongs around the piano. At Christmas Diana and Princess Margaret play, Diana often choosing numbers from Andrew Lloyd Webber's hit musicals.

Diana demonstrated her skill as a pianist for the first time in public when she and Charles visited an arts college in Melbourne during their 1988 visit to Australia for the Bicentennial celebrations. Professor Henri Touzeau, the seventy-eight-year-old music teacher who had taught Charles the cello when he was at school in

Australia, had suggested that the Prince might show his prowess. A string had broken during Charles's previous public recital, and he confessed he'd been a "very bad" cellist anyway. He eventually gave a short demonstration on fifteen-year-old student Adam Merangue's cello. Diana watched, amused, until the Professor gestured toward the piano and declared, "I know you play too. Would you like to play a few notes?" Not looking as if she much relished the idea, Diana sat at the keyboard and played a few bars of one of her favorite pieces, Rachmaninoff's *Piano Concerto No. 2*. The moment she finished, the professor grabbed her and bestowed a kiss, at which Diana said, "Oh, Gawd!," blushed, and shot toward the door past her husband, who said, "Well done!" The professor was overjoyed. "I think she is lovely," he said. "She is a very, very talented player, and a very warm player. When I was standing beside her, I could feel the warmth of her body. She is very accomplished. She shows great musical ability, and she is very sensitive." The Princess is Patron of the Newport International Competition for Young Pianists in Gwent. She is also Patron of Swansea Festival of Music and the Arts, and Joint Patron, with Prince Charles, of Chester Music Festival. Like her husband, who's been known to weep during the *Symphonie Fantastique* by Berlioz and also adores Bach, Mozart, and Schubert, Diana loves classical music. Her favorite composers are Rachmaninoff, Grieg, Schumann, Tchaikovsky, Mozart, Verdi, and Dvořák.

Her love of pop music is better known. Her portable radio at home is tuned to pop music on Capital Radio (see RADIO). She drives to music, and she has been known to sail along corridors at Buckingham Palace and to go for walks with her Sony Walkman clamped to her head so that she can have music wherever she goes. Since she was a teenager, Diana has been a great fan of Neil Diamond. When she first met him after a concert in Birmingham in 1984, she told him, "I've always wanted to see you. I wanted to see you seven years ago at Woburn Abbey but my father wouldn't let me. Well, he can't stop me tonight, can he!" Neil, who has met her several times since, says, "You can't help but be entranced by Princess Diana. She's spectacularly beautiful, very charming, and I think everyone who has met her personally falls in love with her a little bit, including myself." See AMERICA. Diana's favorite pop group, from the time she was a thirteen-year-old schoolgirl at West Heath, was Supertramp. See FAVORITE THINGS. She adores Kid Creole and the Coconuts and once told the group's leader, August Darnell, "I have all your albums at home, and I know the words of all your songs." She has a large record collection, and several stars have presented her with their latest releases. Lionel Richie gave her an entire set of his albums in 1987. In July 1989, soul star Mica Paris said that the Princess had asked for her latest album on compact disc, adding, "She told me that vinyl records are now old hat. She said that she wants to listen to my album on her new portable CD player."

Though Charles often looks out of place at some of the pop concerts his wife loves (and they've both taken ear plugs with them), he is a great fan of the Three Degrees, whom he invited to his thirtieth birthday party at Buckingham Palace. He loves Diana Ross, has a large collection of Barbra Streisand albums, which he is said to play "endlessly," and made a point of catching Gladys Knight performing live during one trip to America. He and Diana have held parties in the drawing room at Kensington Palace for pop stars who have performed at concerts in aid of the Prince's Trust, at which the Princess has danced while Elton John has played the piano.

Like Charles, despite stories to the contrary, Diana loves opera. So does her father. In fact, her stepmother, Raine, kept playing a recording of Lord Spencer's favorite opera, Puccini's *Madame Butterfly*, to help bring him out of a coma after his serious stroke in 1978. See FAMILY. When she's free but Charles isn't, Diana takes parties of friends to the opera at Covent Garden on her own. She was there with a girlfriend for *La Bohème* on the day in June 1990 when Charles broke his arm playing polo, and she left early, in some agitation, to drive to the hospital to see him. See HEALTH. That December, the Princess became Patron of the American Friends of Covent Garden—the current U.S. Ambassador's wife is usually President—which raises funds for the Royal Opera House. At home the couple have recordings of all Mozart's operas. When they go to the Royal Opera House, according to James Whitaker in the *Daily Mirror*, they save money by eating their own picnic supper. A Palace van arrives earlier carrying cold salmon and salad, and they tuck into it there in a private dining room using silver and gold royal cutlery, bone china, and crystal glasses, also from the Palace. See FOOD & DRINK and MONEY. Their favorite female opera singer is New Zealand–born Dame Kiri Te Kanawa, who sang at their wedding—though they missed that performance because, as Charles said later, they were "busy signing the register at the time." They are also huge fans of the great Italian tenor Luciano Pavarotti. On Pavarotti's return to Covent Garden, after a six-year absence, in March 1990 for a revival of Donizetti's *L'Elisir d'Amore*, for which the audience paid up to £98 a seat, Diana and Charles turned up to hear him with four friends, arriving in a Palace minibus ten minutes before the curtain rose. Greeting them afterward, Pavarotti remarked, "I am very touched. We have the royal guests. What more could I ask?" In August 1990, Diana and her mother, Mrs. Frances Shand Kydd, flew to Italy to hear Pavarotti in a sell-out performance of Verdi's *Requiem* at the ancient Roman amphitheater in Verona. The Princess told him afterward, "It was absolutely marvelous, really unforgettable. I was so profoundly moved." And in July 1991, with Prince Charles and about one hundred thousand other fans, Diana got drenched at Pavarotti's free open-air thirtieth anniversary celebration concert in London's Hyde Park. Despite the deluge, it was a huge success. Pavarotti dedicated his first encore to the Princess and kissed her hand later.

In October 1982, Diana became Patron of the Welsh National Opera (WNO), founded in 1946, which began as an amateur group of music-loving miners, shopkeepers, and others in 1943 and became fully professional thirty years later. It was one of the first patronages she chose to take on after her marriage and the first to demonstrate her link with the Welsh as the Princess of Wales. In March 1984 she opened their new £350,000 rehearsal rooms and restaurant in a building named after her opposite the WNO headquarters on John Street, Cardiff, where, pregnant with Prince Harry, she was greeted by sixty children singing and waving daffodils. She has attended performances in Cardiff and London. And in February 1989 she made her first major solo overseas trip to New York to attend a royal gala benefit performance of Verdi's opera *Falstaff* at the company's U.S. debut at the Brooklyn Academy of Music. See AMERICA and JAPAN. In 1991 the princess also became Patron of the British Youth Opera.

Though Diana herself has not performed as a singer in public since her marriage, Carolyn Pride and the Duchess of Kent sing with the Bach Choir (see HONG KONG), as has Prince Charles, the choir's President, who sang in the *Messiah*. In July 1983, Diana was in the audience at the King's Lynn Festival when the Duchess and Carolyn, both sopranos, took part in a performance of Verdi's *Requiem*. At school at West Heath, Diana was said to be "a gifted soprano with a fine middle-range voice." But reported rumors that she would appear as a featured vocalist with a choir in a performance of Elgar's *The Kingdom* at London's Barbican in June 1989 proved unfounded. She did, however, sing "Just One Cornetto" (from a TV commercial for ice cream) from the Glass Coach on her wedding day. See WEDDING.

Charles and Diana's sons both gave solo performances at Wetherby School's carol concert at St. Matthew's church, Bayswater, in December 1989. Prince Harry (who also sang solo in 1990 and 1991) gave a rendition of "Rudolph the Red-Nosed Reindeer," and William, then aged seven, sang a chorus of "Gloria in Excelcis Deo"—to proud beams from Mum and their grandmother, Mrs. Shand Kydd. In April 1986, Diana heard the first performance of a prize-winning lullaby for Prince Harry sung at a concert in Cardiff. She told the schoolboy composer, fourteen-year-old Phil Boyden from Gwent, "It was wonderful. Thank you for writing it." Phil was then a violinist with the National Children's Orchestra, which played at the concert and of which the Princess is Patron. A copy of the score of the lullaby was reduced in size and presented to her. The young princes have attended Fun with Music classes run in London by Ann Rachlin, who takes pupils down the river in a barge in the summertime, playing Handel while telling them about the life and work of the composer. See LONDON SYMPHONY CHORUS and ORCHESTRAS.

𝓃

NAMES

Diana was given her middle name, Frances, after her mother. She was the Honorable Diana Spencer until her father, then Viscount Althorp, succeeded to the earldom. As the daughter of an earl, she then gained the second courtesy title Lady Diana Spencer. (The Honorable is a courtesy title too.) When the Press and public first started to call her Lady Di (hardly an uppercrust nickname, though it was affectionately meant), her mother recoiled. "I shudder when I hear it," Mrs. Shand Kydd said. "No one in her life has *ever* called her Di." Diana hated the nickname, once informing a crowd, "My name is Diana." (She also can't bear it when Americans refer to her husband as "Chuck," a name she'd never call him in a million years.)

She became Her Royal Highness The Princess of Wales on her marriage to Prince Charles, when Buckingham Palace was at pains to point out that her name is not Princess Diana nor even Diana, Princess of Wales, but The Princess of Wales. However, for such a young, warm, and friendly royal, this has always seemed too formal; and the incorrect but popular name Princess Diana has stuck the world over. On her marriage, Diana also took on all of her husband's titles except that of Great Steward of Scotland for which, says David Williamson, CoEditor of *Debrett's Peerage*, there is no female equivalent. Her full titles are, therefore: Her Royal Highness The Princess of Wales and Countess of Chester; Duchess of Cornwall; Duchess of Rothesay, Countess of Carrick, and Baroness of Renfrew; and Lady of the Isles. See RADIO. When speaking to the Princess, she should be addressed first as "Your Royal Highness" and then as "Ma'am" (pronounced "mam"). Prince Charles is addressed first as "Your Royal Highness," then as "Sir." The Queen and Queen Mother should be addressed as "Your Majesty" the first time, then "Ma'am."

Prince William—christened William Arthur Philip Louis—took his last two names from his grandfather, Prince Philip, and from Prince Charles's "honorary grandfather," the late Earl (Louis) Mountbatten of Burma. David Williamson suggests that he may have been named William after the late Prince William of Gloucester, adding, "Arthur is one of Prince Charles's names and was also one of the names of his grandfather King George VI, named after Queen Victoria's third son, the Duke of Connaught, who received it in honor of his godfather, the Duke of Wellington." His young brother, christened Henry Charles Albert David, was named Henry because both his parents like the name and because there is no other Henry in the Royal Family. He was the first royal baby to be christened Henry since King George V's third son, who became the Duke of Gloucester. The last king with the same name was Henry VIII. The name Charles is, conveniently, both a royal and a Spencer name; Henry shares it, of course, with his father and his uncle, Viscount Althorp. Albert was the name of the Queen's father, George VI, who was christened Albert and known by that name, or Bertie, until he came to the throne; it was also the name of Queen Victoria's consort, Prince Albert. He was given the final name David after David Bowes-Lyon, the Queen Mother's favorite brother, who was Prince Charles's great-uncle. For all that, Charles and Diana call William by the nicknames Wills and Wombat, and Henry has been known as Harry since birth.

Nicknames given to Diana by people who know or knew her include Thicky Spencer, as she was allegedly known by some of her contemporaries at school, and the Landlady, which her flatmates at Coleherne Court used to call her. Her old friends have long called her Duch, for Duchess. Some friends call her POW, as in Princess of Wales and POW! Princess Anne was once reported to call her the Dope because of her giggles. Diana's stepmother Raine, referred to as Come Dancing by her stepchildren and more widely by the nickname Acid Raine, used to call Diana the Fawn. Diana's names for Charles, though they usually call each other darling, include Fishface.

The Royal Family have always liked nicknames. The Queen is Lilibet to immediate members of the family—and was Aunt Lilibet to Diana as a child—though Prince Philip is reported to call the Queen Cabbage and Sausage. Princess Michael of Kent is known as MC, for Marie-Christine, and Our Val, as in Valkyrie. Then there's Gramps for Prince Philip; Blob for Prince Andrew, who is called H in the Navy, short for HRH; Margo for Princess Margaret; Pud for Princess Alexandra; Maou for Prince Michael of Kent; and Pooh for Lord Nicholas Windsor. King George V's son Harry, the Duke of Gloucester, was affectionately called Potty and Glossipops. Names given them by the satirical magazine *Private Eye*—Brenda for the Queen, Cheryl for Diana, Brian for Charles, and so on—are also said to be popular at the Palace, where nicknames extend to some of the staff too: Bobo for the Queen's dresser, Margaret MacDonald, who has been with her since childhood, and Mossy for her Woman of the Bedchamber, the Honorable Mary Morrison. Who originally coined the name Fog for Captain Mark Phillips, allegedly because he's "thick and wet," is not clear. But Princess Michael of Kent got her nickname Princess Pushy from the Press, as did Fergie (Duchess Dolittle) and Princess Anne, who before her transformation and reincarnation as the Royal Family workaholic, was termed Princess Sourpuss. Tim Graham, one of the top cameramen covering the royals, is called Squirrel. See STAFF and ROYAL PROTECTION SQUAD.

The royals often use pseudonyms when they want to be incognito. Charles entered a painting later hung at the Royal Academy calling himself Arthur George Carrick, a mix of two of his names and part of one of his titles. When he was courting Diana, he'd ring under a different name as a cover-up. Before their marriage, when the Emanuels wanted to preserve secrecy about Diana's wedding gown, she was booked in for fittings under the name Miss Deborah Smythson Wells. And when a secret record request was played for the Princess on Capital Radio (see RADIO), she was referred to in code as Charlie's Angel, Prince William and Prince Harry being called the Little Goblins. Because of her record requests from Kensington Palace, she was also nicknamed Disco Di from KP.

THE NATIONAL MENINGITIS TRUST

Charles and Diana's country house, Highgrove, stands in Gloucestershire, where in 1985 there was growing concern about the rising number of cases of meningitis in the county. That year, a group of worried parents who had direct and sometimes tragic experience of the disease set up the Meningitis Trust. At the time, they found themselves facing many mysteries with few answers. Though meningitis had been a serious notifiable disease since 1912, there was no publicly available information about its severity and aftereffects. Officialdom offered little advice or support. By 1986, similar outbreaks beyond Gloucestershire made it clear that the problem the Trust had to tackle was widespread, so it became a nationwide organization adding the word *National* to its title. Research revealed that outbreaks occur in the U.K. every ten to fifteen years. During an outbreak year, there are estimated to be at least five thousand cases of bacterial meningitis in England and Wales alone, resulting in about five hundred deaths and one thousand patients left permanently handicapped with problems like deafness, brain damage, or sometimes loss of limbs. Figures showed that the number of cases had increased dramatically during both World Wars, in 1959, 1974-75, and from the mid-1980s onward. In 1988 there were more reported cases than for over thirty years. Bacterial meningitis, which requires urgent treatment, is caused by very common germs (carried by one in ten people at the back of the nose and throat, in most people perfectly harmlessly), which are passed on through close contact like kissing, coughing, or sharing a cup. Why they cause illness in some and not others is not yet known. Cases of viral meningitis, which is less serious, went almost totally unreported but are thought to affect more than ten thousand people a year. The Trust, which is wholly dependent on voluntary contributions, dedicated itself to raise funds for research of the disease, to support sufferers and their families, and to increase public awareness about meningitis in the hope that early diagnosis would save lives.

Diana became President in August 1989, giving a "great boost" to morale and fund-raising efforts. The Trust's Helen Buttery feels that she may have been influenced to take on the role by the fact that although the charity has flowered into a national organization, it "has retained the personal touch—many of the founder members are parents whose children suffered meningitis, and many are still on the national committee. The Princess has always shown a great interest in children's charities and although meningitis can affect people of any age, those most at risk are young children and teenagers.'' The Trust now has over sixty support groups around Britain and a twenty-four-hour support and information service based at its head office in Stroud, Gloucestershire. In February 1990, Diana visited staff and voluntary committee members and saw their work firsthand. Five hundred fans braved the rain to see her at the head office, where she was presented with armfuls of flowers by twelve children who had suffered the illness. She also took home Trust sweatshirts for William and Harry. Trust Chairman Mrs. Sue Neale, whose eleven-year-old son Adam recovered completely from meningitis, says, "We entered the 1990s with a renewed determination to conquer this terrible disease, and we are extremely grateful for the support and encouragement of the Princess of Wales in our efforts to achieve that goal.''

NATIONAL RUBELLA COUNCIL

Diana's concern to protect unborn children from the effects of rubella (German measles) was voiced in a speech she made in Oldham in Greater Manchester, as Patron of the National Rubella Council, to mark National Rubella Week in November 1987. Urging "all women to seek protection against the risks of catching rubella," the Princess said:

> It is so important to ensure that women everywhere understand why rubella protection is necessary. Too many women in this country are still not protected against the risk that rubella (German measles), if caught in pregnancy, can result in a child being born deaf, blind, or mentally or physically handicapped. The risk is preventable by having a simple blood test to establish immunity followed, if necessary, by an injection. We must take the opportunity of Rubella Awareness Week to save children from serious handicap and their families from untold distress.

Diana meets many handicapped children in her work, sympathizes deeply with the difficulties and problems they and their families face, and feels very lucky that William and Harry were born so fit and healthy. The Council, which has now changed its name to Child 2000—The National Council for Child Health, was founded in 1983 and consists of eleven voluntary organizations concerned with the effects of rubella, together with the Health Education Authority and the Health Departments of England, Wales, and Northern Ireland. Its primary objective is to increase immunization against rubella. To that end, Diana visited the Peartree Clinic in Stevenage, Hertfordshire, in October 1988 to mark the beginning of a new immunization program called MMR (measles/mumps/rubella) with a Government target of immunizing up to 660,000 children a year. But though her heart was in the right place, the Princess winced and turned her head away after watching toddlers getting their jabs. In fact, she gave her Palace aide a wigging, demanding, "What on earth have you set this up for? You know I can't stand injections!" She told one mother that she had been apprehensive about Harry having the injection but felt a lot better afterward. She revealed to another that William had been "ill off school for a couple of days, but it was nothing serious." And according to a third mother, "She said that if either of her boys were ill, she let them get into bed with her, even though she wasn't supposed to." It has been reported that Prince William was inoculated against whooping cough when he was three months old. See BIRTHRIGHT and HEALTH.

NEW ZEALAND

Bolstered by the success of her month's debut overseas visit to Australia, Diana flew to Auckland in April 1983 on the second leg of her Australasian tour with Charles and baby William. It was just as well that she felt more assured because in New Zealand, frequent rain and the odd gale dampened spirits. The two-week visit was also marred by several incidents, including protests claiming that the Treaty of Waitangi in 1840 had unfairly ceded sovereignty of Maori tribal homelands to Prince Charles's great-great-great-grandmother, Queen Victoria. Maori demonstrators were at the airport, protesters poured quick-setting cement down lavatories, and there were stink bombs at the St. James Theatre,

Before leaving New Zealand, Diana is treated to a traditional farewell from Maori girls. (Lionel Cherruault/Camera Press London)

where the royal couple attended the New Zealand Ballet Company's gala performance of *Coppélia*. One Maori bared his bottom at them before being arrested for insulting behavior; and his companion, named of all things Diana Prince, got charged with assaulting a police officer. Further protests came from antimonarchists and IRA supporters. In Pupuke, where they were deluged by rain while watching children canoeing, Charles commented, "I feel as though we are walking around under a permanent rain cloud" (see KUWAIT & THE UNITED ARAB EMIRATES), and Diana was made even wetter when she was soaked in the spray made by a boy jumping into a pool. (The brass band played "Raindrops Keep Falling on My Head," and she laughed.) After a wet walkabout, their car wouldn't start because of ignition trouble. In Wellington the accompanying British Press corps protested that facilities for coverage had been restricted to local journalists. And when the Prince and Princess climbed into a giant war canoe at the end of the tour, so many half-naked Maori warriors jumped in with them that it shipped water and nearly sank. The warriors, about eighty of them, some with tattooed faces, paddled the 117-

foot canoe on a fifteen-minute trip across the Bay of Islands to the Waitangi Treaty Ground. There Prince Charles, confronted by more protesters holding banners which declared that the treaty was "a fraud," urged "a fresh spirit of respect" and encouraged "the people of two races and two cultures to come together as rational human beings."

There were, of course, lighter moments on the tour, which also took in Wanganui, Gisborne, Tauranga, Dunedin, and Christchurch. Diana, hesitant at first, but with tuition from her husband, soon became an expert at the hongi, the nose-to-nose rub used as a traditional form of greeting by the Maoris. She tried it for the first time, amid giggles, at Eden Park sports stadium in Auckland, where they were greeted by a crowd of forty-five thousand, mainly children, and saw displays of singing and dancing. Watching her first traditional Maori "challenge," during which a boy playing the "chief" stuck out his tongue to "frighten strangers" off and then charged at them with his spear, the Princess backed off anxiously, declaring, "Goodness, I thought he was going to stab me!" Then they all dissolved in laughter. At Wanganui Collegiate boarding school, they had a reunion with Prince Edward, a tutor and housemaster there at the time, who welcomed them wearing his Maori ceremonial feathered cloak as an honorary chieftain of the Ngati Awa tribe. "Good Lord, it must be a fancy dress party. What have you come as?" Prince Charles said, roaring with laughter and teasing his brother when they arrived in a Rolls-Royce. "What the hell is it you are wearing? It looks like a blanket!" At Government House, Auckland, where he'd been based with Nanny Barnes throughout the tour, Prince William had a celebrated crawlabout on a rug on the lawn before the cameras. See CHILDREN. And at Wigram airbase, where the royal couple watched a display of aerial acrobatics by a team from the Royal New Zealand Air Force, Prince Charles, a pilot himself, told Diana, "I'd love to have a go at that!"

There were serious moments too. They attended a commemorative service in Auckland on April 25, ANZAC Day, which is the anniversary of the landing of the Australian and New Zealand Army Corps at Gallipoli in 1915 and remembrance day in Australasia for the dead of both World Wars. The Prince, in full

Naval uniform, took the salute as the dwindling ranks of Gallipoli veterans marched past. And at a state banquet he took the opportunity to thank New Zealanders for the wholehearted help and support they gave Britain during the more recent conflict in the Falkland Islands. "It is so easy to compromise on principle, but the New Zealand people keenly felt on that occasion a year ago that every now and then a stand had to be made," he said. "The knowledge that you were sharing our anxieties really did help to render more bearable the sacrifices some were called upon to make."

When they waved good-bye, William flew home with Nanny Barnes while Charles and Diana flew to Bermuda for ten days' vacation before final preparations for their eighteen-day tour of Canada. The Princess is International President of Barnardo's, New Zealand, and Patron of the Princess of Wales Children's Health Camp at Rotorua, the New Zealand College of Obstetricians and Gynaecologists, the Royal New Zealand Foundation for the Blind, and the Variety Club of New Zealand.

NIGERIA

Diana had been hailed as a role model in Nigeria, where the President's wife, Maryam Babangida, was urging downtrodden African women to "develop their own innate talents." The enthusiasm of the crowd which surged forward as the royal couple arrived for their five-day tour on March 15, 1990, produced chaos at hot, dusty Lagos airport. Security broke down, and armed police were urged by a royal bodyguard to hold the crowds back. Not that everyone knew who they were, a Lagos taxi driver inquiring later whether the VIPs who'd arrived were the son and daughter-in-law "of Margaret Thatcher." Throbbing African drums, tribal dancing, and a nineteen-gun salute greeted the couple before their drive into Lagos, Diana almost getting into a security car by mistake for the official limousine. It was the first British royal visit to Nigeria since the Queen's 1956 tour and Diana's first trip to Africa. As a typical compliment she wore a cool Catherine Walker silk dress in the national colors, green and white. That evening she and Charles dined at a welcoming banquet given by the military ruler, President Ibrahim Babangida, whom she had first met on his state visit to Britain the previous year. The unaccustomed menu featured stuffed rams' heads and bison, and Diana ate very little.

Sweltering in 38° C (100° F) heat and intense humidity the next day, the royal couple visited the Governor of Lagos, Colonel Raji Rasaki, who presented them with gifts which included a four-foot-high "talking drum." "Do you dance to it or send messages?" Charles asked and was told the latter, handy in view of Nigeria's quirky telephone system. Charles gave Colonel Rasaki a silver paperknife bearing the Prince of Wales's feathers, apologizing for his gift being so small in comparison (which British royal gifts abroad often are). See COLLECTIONS and MONEY.

At Lagos University Teaching Hospital, the Princess almost toppled over in the heat as people came forward eagerly to greet her. She was clearly distressed by the plight of some of the tots in the children's ward, which takes only the most seriously ill. Infant and child mortality is a major problem in Nigeria. To help, the royal couple presented gifts supplied under a £6 million grant from Britain—£600,000 worth of medicines, plus a lifesaving £5,000 incubator. Diana was particularly moved by the sight of a severely burned six-month-old baby who had fallen into a cooking fire. After being presented with a bouquet by another patient, an eight-year-old girl who had been saved by the hospital from almost complete paralysis and death, one of the Princess's aides commented, "Such a morning makes the Princess realize how lucky she was with her own children."

That day Diana accompanied President Babangida's wife to a Rural Women for Better Life fair where they watched an open-air display of tribal dancing, which the dance-mad Princess enjoyed so much that she asked for an encore. It was 43° C (110° F) in the shade. Perspiration ran down Diana's nose under the blazing African sun. Sitting on a dais for over an hour, there was no awning to shield her (though she had apparently been promised one) and the Princess seldom wears a sunhat. Nevertheless, she kept up the good work, chatting to children wearing traditional dress and intricate, highly decorative, braided hairstyles at Tafawa. As always, Prince William and Prince Harry were never far from her mind. "I miss them. I hate leaving them when I go away," she said that evening during a champagne reception on board the royal yacht *Britannia* for the President and his wife and 350 other VIPs. She also revealed that she secretly wanted three more babies but hadn't yet told her husband. See CHILDREN.

Apart from problems with the heat and humidity, the Princess was upset on the tour when she discovered that disabled people and beggars had been moved out of one town she visited to avoid "offending" her, and some of the visits were heartbreaking, even traumatic. But as always, she showed concern, sympathy, and goodwill. At the Molai Leprosy Hospital at Maiduguri, the capital of Borno State in northern Nigeria, Diana met patients and shook hands with leprosy sufferers, as she had done the previous year in Jakarta. Charles, coming face to face with the horrific effects of leprosy for the first time, was visibly shaken but followed his wife's lead and shook hands with a recovering patient himself. At the leper colony which they visited, the Princess met the chief, shook hands with him and his leper family, and squatted down to see into the mud hut where they live. See LEPROSY.

Arriving at the airport, the couple had been greeted by the unlikely wail of Scottish airs on bagpipes, taught to the local kids by a top British Council official based in the area. The heat at Maiduguri, a remote spot a few miles from the rapidly encroaching sub-Sahara desert, was getting to Prince Charles too. During a visit to the British Voluntary Service Overseas center there, he was told that the age limit for voluntary workers was fifty-five and remarked, "I suppose the heat might finish them off. I am feeling pretty old myself." He revealed that he had considered doing voluntary work in the Third World, though he said he would probably miss soft beds and hot water, adding, "The problem was that the only skill I had to offer was teaching people to write speeches." Diana visited the palace of the local sheikh, the sixty-six-year-old Shehu of Borno, who had four wives and umpteen children. She kneeled respectfully to give a signed photograph of herself, Charles, and their children to the Yagumsu, the number one wife, during the exchange of gifts. Before they left Maiduguri, the couple wilted in 43° C (110° F) heat for about ninety minutes while two thousand horsemen, their mounts festooned in silver, staged a durbar (official assemblage) outside the palace. (There were thirty thousand horses at the durbar when the last Prince of Wales visited Nigeria in 1925.)

At Enugu, in Anambra State, Diana was helpless with laughter at the antics of an acrobatic team of young tribal dancers. And she collapsed in giggles when two men struggling to present her and Charles with a massive gift from the State Governor—a five-foot-high mirror in a vast iroko wood frame—were practically felled by the weight. Flying on to the next stop, she blushed scarlet at the three-foot-high dance mask worn by a tribal dancer who greeted them at Port Harcourt, which bore what the *Sun* reporter described as "two bonking figures . . . meant to represent her and Charles." After she'd sneaked a second look, an official was quoted as saying, "It was just a dance of welcome. Everyone makes love—even royal ladies and gentlemen."

On the final day of the visit, before going on for the second stage of the West African tour (see CAMEROON), the couple drove to meet dozens of tribal chiefs who had gathered at the farming village of Umuagbai near Port Harcourt, where they toured a farm and saw how the women extract oil from nuts and prepare cassava to be cooked. At a traditional weaving center, where Diana met a woman who was weaving a loincloth, a village elder suggested she might like to try her hand. The Princess, who didn't make her mark as a needlewoman at school (see ARTS & HANDICRAFTS) got down on her knees to help, saying, "Well, I'll try, but I'm not very good," dashing off only when nature called. "Gosh," she said suddenly, "I absolutely must go to the loo [bathroom]!" "She wouldn't make much of a living at weaving if she had to do it full-time. She is too slow," one villager remarked of her efforts. "But she didn't make a fool of herself either." The last event of the tour was a sort of regatta, Nigerian-style.

There were some odd off-stage happenings during the trip. In Lagos, where the military governor had recently declared that "Jungle crime deserves jungle justice," a Nigerian thief who had swallowed a stolen necklace rather than give it back was reported to have been set ablaze by an angry mob who poured gasoline over him. British journalists covering the royal tour had some bizarre experiences too. Television newscaster Fiona Armstrong had to be dragged from a Chinese restaurant by her crew when the kitchen exploded in midmeal. And Alan Hamilton reported in *The Times* "Diary" that during one trying forty-five-minute drive across Lagos, while trapped in a traffic jam, "this column" was pestered by "itinerant vendors who live on the central reservation" to buy "a television aerial, a doormat, three bunches of bananas, several shirts and T-shirts, a set of car-mirrors, an umbrella, numerous bags of nuts, a telephone, two ironing-boards, a pocket calculator, an inflatable globe, a Japanese microwave oven, and one dead chicken with its feathers on."

NORWAY

In February 1984, making her first solo official overseas visit, Diana arrived in icy Oslo as snowflakes fell and was immediately tagged the Snow Princess by the Press. She emerged from an Andover of the Queen's Flight at Fornebu airport looking particularly chilly in blue tights and a blue outfit, without a hat or gloves. The purpose of the twenty-hour trip was to attend a gala world premiere performance of the new full-length ballet *Carmen* by London City Ballet, of which she is Patron. Wearing a favorite red silk gown with a lacy, sequined top and a dramatic floor-length, deep blue velvet cloak, she was escorted to the ballet at the new Koncerthus by her hosts, Crown Prince Harald and Crown Princess Sonja of Norway, cousins of the Queen. She stayed with them overnight after greeting the cast after the performance and attending a buffet supper at the British Ambassador's residence.

Sonja, a qualified ski instructor, was a commoner, like Diana, before her marriage and reportedly once earned extra cash as a barmaid in a pub in Cambridge, England. The palace where she and Harald live with their children, Maerta Louise and Haakon Magnus (both then pupils at a secondary modern state school in Oslo), is a whitewashed farmhouse in Skaugum. Like Prince Charles, who likes to keep his office windows open in all weather, Sonja is a fresh-air fiend. Her windows are kept open even in temperatures of −25° C, and it is said that sometimes guests are awakened at dawn for a six-mile jog. Security has not been a problem for the Norwegian Royal Family; Sonja and Harald, who then drove a Volvo and an ancient Renault 5, feel free to pedal through Oslo on their bicycles. However, security plans for Diana's visit were reportedly reviewed after a Norwegian government official, who had helped make the arrangements, confessed three weeks before the Princess arrived that he had spied for Russia's KGB for fifteen years.

Before Diana returned home—with various gifts, including a pink teddy bear for Prince William—she planted a spruce tree at the British Embassy, where the ground had to be predug with boiling water because it was frozen solid. Throughout the brief visit, the Princess, then aged twenty-two, seemed rather lost and insecure without her husband at her side. But she needn't have worried because the Norwegians loved her.

Diana was pregnant with Prince Harry at the time. She deliberately kept the news a secret until after her return and even dodged airport Press photographers when she flew in, knowing that the announcement would increase publicity for the ballet company—since the most recent TV film and photographs of her had been taken with its dancers in Oslo. See DANCING.

ORCHESTRAS

The Princess is Patron of two orchestras: the Scottish Chamber Orchestra and the National Children's Orchestra. Her patronage of the Scottish Chamber Orchestra (SCO) began in May 1987, and she opened its new office in Edinburgh. The orchestra, which was formed in 1974, gives regular concerts in Edinburgh, Glasgow, St. Andrews, and Aberdeen; and it has an annual residency in the Highlands. It also holds regular events for youngsters and community groups. In Glasgow in 1990, it gave four world premiere performances of SCO commissions, including the *Strathclyde Concertos No. 3* and *No. 4* by its Associate Composer-Conductor Sir Peter Maxwell Davies; performed his music theater work *The Martyrdom of St. Magnus* in the Tramway; and collaborated in an extended educational project with an Indonesian gamelan orchestra. Principal Conductor of the SCO is Jukka-Pekka Saraste.

The National Children's Orchestra, which actually consists of four different orchestras featuring "the cream" of Britain's young musicians aged seven to thirteen, was founded in 1978 by violinist Vivienne Price, who runs it and also teaches at the Guildhall School of Music. She had been planning the venture since childhood, having taken up the violin "much too late" at fourteen and joined the local youth orchestra, where the other players were aged eighteen to nineteen. Being so much younger, she felt "the odd one out socially." So she decided to start an orchestra for highly talented younger children to provide "an opportunity for them to play with others of the same age and of comparable ability." Since then, some of her young musicians have said how much it has helped because they too felt like "odd ones out" at school—other pupils not understanding why, instead of going out to play, they spent so much time practicing.

Children from all over the country apply to join, most of them put forward by their parents, teachers, or the local authority. Auditions are held in the autumn. In 1990 there were just over a hundred children aged under fourteen in the main symphony orchestra; exactly a hundred under thirteen in the second; and about eighty under twelve in the third. The fourth, which is a string orchestra, trains musicians aged seven to ten and had nearly seventy of them in 1990. The children meet during school vacations and rehearse six to seven hours each day in live-in courses (the student works and sleeps at the same place while the period of study lasts) which culminate in concerts, usually given at the Queen Elizabeth Hall in London. Most years the orchestra also plays in the Edinburgh Festival fringe. (The Edinburgh Festival has its own official program of musical and other events. The Edinburgh Festival fringe consists of unofficial events which take place at the same time as the main festival.) About half the children will probably go on to careers in music when they are older. "There's an enormous amount of musical talent in [Britain]," Miss Price says. "Britain leads the world with youth orchestras in terms of quality."

Diana became Patron in 1982 and has since visited the orchestra several times, in rehearsal and at concerts, showing great interest in what the children are doing. On her first visit, she was presented with a quarter-sized violin which they had had specially made for Prince William; a little boy, aged about ten, played it for her. "The Princess was delighted," Miss Price said.

I believe that Prince Charles is rather keen that his son should learn the cello. The Princess is absolutely super with the children, very natural and easy. She's a terrific woman and more beautiful when you see her face-to-face than in photographs. We all love her. When she came to a gala concert at St. David's Hall in Cardiff in 1986, when the main orchestra played, she took the trouble to wear a dress which exactly matched the orchestra's cherry red color—the girls have red skirts and the boys have red ties. And when somebody commented on it, she said, "Oh I'm so *glad* you noticed. I did it specially." Which I thought was absolutely lovely. [See FASHION.]

ORDERS, DECORATIONS & HONORS

Orders & Decorations

One of the Princess's most treasured possessions is the Royal Family Order, which she was awarded by the Queen. The Order is a form of decoration worn only by senior female members of the Royal Family. It is awarded as a personal gift of and entirely at the discretion of the Sovereign. Such favors date from King George IV in 1820. The Orders are miniature portraits of the Sovereign, worn suspended from ribbon bows pinned on the left shoulder of gowns worn at formal evening events. Diana's Order is an oval portrait of the Queen surrounded with jewels, topped with a jeweled crown, and suspended from a yellow ribbon. She first wore it in November 1982. Others awarded the Royal Family Order by the Queen include the Queen Mother; the Princess Royal; Princess Margaret; Princess Alice, Duchess of Gloucester; the Duchess of Kent; and Princess Alexandra. Significantly, perhaps, at the time of writing neither Fergie nor Princess Michael of Kent had one. In 1982, Diana was also awarded the Grand Cross of the Order of the House of Orange, Netherlands, and the Order of Al Kamal of the Arab Republic of Egypt.

Royal Master of the Bench

Diana is a Royal Bencher of the Honourable Society of the Middle Temple. Established about 1340, the Middle Temple is one of the four Inns of Court which call students to the Bar of England and Wales and thereby confer on them the degree of barrister. The Benchers are its governing body. The other Inns are Lincoln's Inn, the Inner Temple, and Gray's Inn. The Queen Mother has been a Royal Bencher of Middle Temple since 1944, and Diana's induction had her warm approval.

Freedoms

The Princess has been granted the Freedom of the City of Cardiff, the Freedom of the City of London, and the Freedom of the Borough of Northampton. She is also an Honorary Citizen of the State of California.

Livery Companies

Diana is an Honorary Freeman of both the Worshipful Company of Grocers and the Merchant Taylors' Company.

Fellowships

She is an Honorary Fellow of the Royal College of Obstetricians and Gynaecologists; of the Royal College of Physicians and Surgeons of Glasgow, of which she is also Patron; and of the Faculty of Dental Surgery of the Royal College of Surgeons of England.

Memberships

In Britain the Princess is an Honorary Family Member of the Friends of the Imperial War Museum; an Honorary Member of the All England Lawn Tennis and Croquet Club, Wimbledon; the David Lloyd Slazenger Racquet Club; and the Royal Highland Yacht Club, Argyll. Abroad she is an Honorary Member of the Lyford Cay Club, Nassau, Bahamas; and the Royal Guild of St. Sebastian, Bruges, Belgium, which, according to Buckingham Palace, is an ancient Flemish order of archers.

PARKINSON'S DISEASE SOCIETY

In 1989 the Princess became Patron of the Parkinson's Disease Society, a charity formed by patients, their relatives, and friends twenty years before. Through its London headquarters and just over two hundred local branches throughout the U.K., it helps sufferers and their families with problems in the home, collects and distributes helpful information, and uses funds raised to sponsor research into the disease, which affects more than one hundred thousand people in Britain alone. Life expectancy with proper drug therapy is now normal, but unfortunately the disease gets steadily and progressively worse. In February 1990 Diana visited the society's research laboratories at King's College London, Chelsea Campus, to see for herself some of the strenuous efforts being made to discover the elusive cause and cure. "The concern of the Princess has given encouragement to the researchers as well as the sufferers and their carers," an official said. Diana's visit coincided with the beginning of a year of celebration marking the society's twenty-first birthday. In an anniversary letter from Kensington Palace the same month, the Princess wrote:

> In the years since its foundation, the Society has grown enormously and will in the future need to continue to do so, both in the field of research and with its welfare activities.
>
> Thanks to the miracles of modern science, our population is living longer but it is a sad fact that in the over-sixty age group, the occurrence of Parkinson's Disease climbs dramatically from one in five hundred to one in every hundred people. The implication for the future is all too clear and we must all do what we can to help conquer this distressing disease.
>
> The Society brings relief to both patients and their caring relatives, and I know that the local branches of the Society give enormous help to minimize the difficulties and to encourage self-help and mutual support in their community.

Parkinson's disease, named after Dr. James Parkinson (1755–1824) who described the condition in "An Essay on the Shaking Palsy" in 1817, is one of the most common illnesses to affect the human brain. The average age of onset is about fifty-five, although one in seven patients contract it in their thirties and forties. Patients find that movement becomes slower and clumsy and may find increasing difficulty with speech, use of the hands or limbs, and walking. The patient knows what he or she wants to do, but the muscles won't respond; without treatment the patient becomes ever more immobile. However, many can lead full and gratifying lives for years after diagnosis. Despite lurid newspaper headlines, the disease is not a "killer." Although patients can die with Parkinson's disease, they don't die *from* it.

It can affect men and women more or less equally, in all races, and in all parts of the world. Famous Parkinson's patients include Chairman Mao Tse-Tung of China; American President Harry S. Truman; Spain's Generalissimo Franco; millionaire financier Paul Getty; boxing champion Muhammad Ali; surrealist painter Salvador Dali; playwright Eugene O'Neill; U.S. General Douglas MacArthur; the former Poet Laureate Sir John Betjeman; actors Terry-Thomas, Kenneth More, Sir Michael Redgrave, and Dame Anna Neagle; the historian A. J. P. Taylor; and soccer player Ray Kennedy. See HUNGARY.

PETS

Diana does not own a pet though she did keep guinea pigs as a child. See EDUCATION and STAFF. Charles has two Jack Russell terriers called Tigger and Roo. William and Harry have hamsters, a rabbit, and a guinea pig. They also have, or had, four goldfish that Diana won for them at a fair. See SPORT. However, like many mothers, Diana says, "I have to look after them."

The Royal Family is famous for its love of dogs. The Duke and Duchess of Windsor's pets included pug dogs called Disraeli, Trooper, Imp, and Davy Crockett, which they dressed in tiny wing collars and bow ties. The Queen Mother's dogs, Ranger and Dash, have baskets made up with blankets and pillows to look like real beds. And the Queen, using a silver fork and spoon, personally mixes and dishes out cooked meat, gravy, and biscuits brought by a footman on a silver tray for her corgis—Spark,

Myth, Fable, Diamond, Kelpie, Phoenix, and Pharos—and her "dorgis" Piper and Harris—a cross between a corgi and Princess Margaret's frisky stud dachshund, Pipkin.

Diana has at times seemed somewhat bemused at the attention given to the royal dogs. Visiting flood victims in Wales last year, she was told by one family how their dogs had nestled on a bed with them amid the flood waters. "That's dogs," she commented. "They have more priority than mothers-in-law."

PORTUGAL

In February 1987, Charles and Diana made an out-of-season visit to Portugal, being greeted at Lisbon airport by the President, Dr. Mario Soares, amid high winds and heavy rain which bucketed down for virtually the whole of their four days there. See KUWAIT & THE UNITED ARAB EMIRATES. Pulling a cord to unveil a plaque, the tassel came away in the Prince's hand. It was Friday the 13th, and that sort of trip. Noting the fact that the royal couple had separate four-poster beds in adjoining rooms at the magnificent Queluz Palace, reporters asked a Portuguese Government official if that meant they would be sleeping apart. "I suppose that depends on their mood," he replied winking. However, a royal aide declared, "The guidance from Buckingham Palace to host countries is that the royal couple like separate *dressing rooms*. It is not stipulated that they should have separate beds." See BEDS & BEDROOMS.

The purpose of the trip was to commemorate the ancient Anglo-Portuguese alliance and to boost flagging British exports. In Oporto, where students spread their coats at her feet, Walter Raleigh–style (see SPAIN), Diana found her makeup artist, Barbara Daly, promoting her cosmetics at The Body Shop stand at a trade fair. See BEAUTY SECRETS. But the strongest memory which remains from the trip was of the Princess, in a bare-shouldered gown at a banquet at the chilly Ajuda Palace in Lisbon, allegedly asking the sixty-two-year-old President, "If I get cold, will you warm me up?" And then, when he offered her his dinner jacket, Diana, twanging his suspenders (or braces, as the British call them) and saying, "You're a socialist, aren't you? You should be wearing *red* braces." Royal correspondents reckon that Diana, who can be "outrageous" in private, likes to liven up dull tours by causing a few ripples. In wintery, rain-lashed Portugal, according to one report, "She batted her eyelashes at nearly every man she met, and it drove Charles frantic with rage." True or not, her flirting on public occasions has since, it is said, ceased. Sorry, chaps. See MARRIAGE.

PRE-SCHOOL PLAYGROUPS ASSOCIATION

In 1982 Diana became Patron of the Pre-school Playgroups Association (PPA). She is also Patron of its separate sister organizations in Wales, Scotland, and Northern Ireland. The Association was set up thirty years ago following the publication of a letter from Mrs. Belle Tutaev, a London mother with one small daughter, in the *Guardian* newspaper in August 1961. Mrs. Tutaev, organizer of the then little-known Nursery School Campaign, wrote:

> To the rescue of . . . mothers desperate about the lack of facilities for children under 5 comes a newly-formed organization, with a do-it-yourself spirit, the Nursery School Campaign. Beginning as a local effort in St. Marylebone, it has now extended to anyone, mother or teacher, who is concerned about the dismal situation at present and the equally dismal future, and is steadily gaining support not only in London but in many parts of the North and Midlands. The campaign has two aims. One is to gather names for a large-scale national petition to be presented to the Minister of Education asking him for more nursery schools and play facilities for children under 5. The other is to encourage groups of mothers to start their own schools wherever they can find suitable premises, employing trained teachers, especially those who are married with their own small children and who want only part-time jobs. The campaign has received considerable advice and encouragement from the Nursery School Association, the Save The Children Fund, and the Advisory Centre on Education, and many of its members come from the Housebound Housewives Register. Inquiries are welcomed . . . from mothers and teachers who would like to create their own solutions to their problems.

The response was immediate. The petition was presented with 3,588 signatures, and the Pre-school Playgroups Association was born. It is now the single largest provider of preschool care and education in England, with fourteen thousand play groups catering to six hundred thousand children. They cost about £55 million to run, of which around £4 million comes from local authorities and £700,000 from central Government, the remaining £50 million being raised through fees of 40 pence to £1.50 per session and fund-raising efforts by the parents themselves.

Sessions usually last less than four hours, but nearly seven hundred of the groups now offer full-day care or extended hours. Each play group serves about twenty to twenty-four children at a time, and many offer similar facilities. A typical group has a home corner with a children's playhouse with a child's bed, play stove, and dolls; a junk play area where the children use the insides of toilet tissue and kitchen towel rolls to make model animals like dogs and dragons; an area where the children paint watercolor pictures; a sandbox; an area where they roll Play-Doh into shapes and animals; a book corner where an adult will read them a story and get the children to talk about the pictures in the book; a music and rhythm spot where the children sing and play the triangle, tambourines, and drums; and an area where they put shapes and jigsaws together, as Diana was photographed doing with Prince William in the nursery at Kensington Palace in 1985.

In a letter to the PPA in 1983 Diana wrote, ". . . The Association does marvellous work all over the country. . . . Its efforts make a most valuable contribution to family life and to the development of children at a most important stage of their lives." She also gave her "wholehearted support" to the PPA's appeal for a new headquarters, which she opened at a play group in Tavistock by sticking on a self-adhesive brick to the outline of a paper building. Among play groups she has visited was Lewis Lane in Cirencester, which Diana drove over to from Highgrove in her black Ford Escort in 1983. She arrived at the playgroup, which met in an old schoolroom, wearing the PPA's gift of a silver logo on the collar of her rust plaid suit and was instantly amused to spot one group of children making paste sandwiches. Supervisor Shirley Jones reported later in the association's magazine *Contact*:

When [the Press] had gone, the Princess really came into her own, sitting on the floor, reading aloud from *The Tiger Who*

Came to Tea, blowing soap bubbles, attending a tea party in the home corner, giving piggybacks, and helping at the climbing frame. Her Royal Highness fitted into the playgroup so well that we wished we had her on our rota. I especially admired the way she divided her attention between groups of children. She must have enjoyed herself, for she stayed more than twice as long as planned. When at last she had to go, we gave her *The Very Hungry Caterpillar* as a gift for Prince William.

In November 1983, the Princess invited children from PPA's eleven regions to a tea party at Kensington Palace. They arrived bearing balloons (from a trip on a double-decker bus full of balloons) which they had carried as they walked through Kensington Gardens. They were kept amused by an entertainer called Click, who transformed herself into a panda in front of their eyes, before they had tea. Diana knelt at the little tea tables chatting to the children—under-five-year-old tots on one side, older children on the other. Click passed a parcel (a children's party game, popular in the U.K.), and the kiddies sang. One tiny guest named Emmeline recalled later in *Contact* that she'd got a big black spider in her cracker and that the Princess's dress was dotted, adding:

> . . . the sandwiches for tea were round and square; there were cakes and crisps and sausages. The Princess . . . talked to me about my fluffy blue PPA building bug. . . . The balloons went up to the sky at the Palace. I didn't like the cameraman on the bus so I pushed him. But I didn't pick my nose at the Palace. I went into the Princess's dining room, the Princess's reading room, the Princess's loo. There was a long path to the Palace. Tortoises were outside the window in the garden. The panda lady tapped her tambourine and we all stretched our arms up and spread our fingers wide.

Sounds like fun was had by all! A spokeswoman for the PPA said, "The Princess has been absolutely marvelous. She's magic, a complete natural. The adults are slightly in awe of her. But whoever she meets, whatever age they are, she makes people feel special. It's her ability to care and be interested. The warmth she generates is terrific. She's doing a fantastic job." See YOUNG ENGLAND KINDERGARTEN.

PRESIDENCIES & PATRONAGES

Like Prince Charles, Diana is not usually interested in being a mere figurehead, just a name on the top of some charity or organization's stationery. She operates as a *working* President or Patron and tends to take on groups and causes which she feels she can get involved with and help. Although the glitz comes anyway with the royal lifestyle, and she certainly attends plenty of fancy fund-raising film premieres and galas, it is the grit she often seeks in her daylight working hours. It is as if she has taken the Prince of Wales's motto *"Ich dien"* ("I serve") very much to heart—as her father predicted she would—and tries to use the platform and influence her position has given her to do as much genuine good as she can. The charities and other organizations she works with bestow great esteem and affection on her—testimony to the success with which she has carved out a serious role for herself in recent years and the achievements she has made. As President or Patron, she can encourage, promote, campaign, and raise funds. Her involvement confers a virtual seal of approval. And because what she does and says is news, she is able to make the work and objectives of well-known organizations she is linked with become better known. Likewise, she can put those of smaller or newer organizations, which were virtually unknown, on the map.

A particular mark of Diana's work is that she's a pioneer, ready and willing to take risks. She will lend her name to something utterly new, untried, and untested, like the First International Covent Garden Festival held in September 1990. Organizers had problems getting sponsorship because it was the first one, but Diana leapt right in. She risked ridicule from cynics, as Charles does with his championing of alternative, or "complementary," medicine, by giving the seal of approval to chiropractic when she became Patron of the Anglo-European College of Chiropractic, well in advance of the therapy gaining anything like general acceptance in Britain from orthodox medics and the public at large. See HEALTH. With the same gung-ho spirit, she is prepared to work for unpopular causes: fighting world prejudice against AIDS and leprosy; helping people with drug, drink, and mental problems through Turning Point; jumping in at the deep end of the marital mire to help RELATE assist those with marriage and relationship problems—a concern no one before her ever took under a royal wing. Though at school she was no leader, in her work today, as well as in fashion and in the fresh, unstuffy way she brings up her children, she undoubtedly is.

Naturally, she gets more invitations than she could possibly take on; but when she does accept, she generally agrees to become President or Patron for an initial period of five years—unless it involves, for example, a one-time festival, conference, or special anniversary—after which the arrangement is reviewed. The range of organizations under her wing reflects her concern for children and the elderly; the injured and infirm; people affected by drug, alcohol, and relationship problems and the homeless; as well as her personal interests like ballet, opera, music, sport, and bridge. In alphabetical order in each category (with those which have ceased marked with an asterisk), Diana's presidencies and patronages are as follows:

President—Britain:
The Albany Community Centre, southeast London
Barnardo's
The Federation Cup 1991 (Honorary President) [tennis]
General Council and Register of Osteopaths
The Hospital for Sick Children, Great Ormond Street
The National Meningitis Trust
Printers Charitable Corporation 1989*
Royal Academy of Dramatic Art
Royal Academy of Music
The Royal Marsden Hospital
Wales Craft Council

President—Abroad:
Barnardo's, Australia (Royal President)
Barnardo's, New Zealand (International President)

Patron—Britain (Joint Patron means with Prince Charles):
The American Friends of Covent Garden

Anglo-European College of Chiropractic
Arts 2000 Year of Dance 1993
Association for Spinal Injury Research Rehabilitation and
    Reintegration
The Benesh Institute
Birthright
British Bridge League's 1989 World Junior Championships*
British Deaf Association (Royal Patron)
British Lung Foundation
British Red Cross Youth
British Sports Association for the Disabled
British Youth Opera
Chester Music Festival (Joint Patron)
Child Accident Prevention Trust
The Commonwealth Society for the Deaf
Douglas Bader Foudation
Dystrophic Epidermolysis Bullosa Research Association
English National Ballet
English Women's Indoor Bowling Association
EUREKA! (formerly The Children's Museum Ltd.) (Joint Patron)
First International Covent Garden Festival 1990
The Foundation for Conductive Education (Royal Patron) [see
    HUNGARY]
The Freshfield [drug counseling] Service, Truro, Cornwall
Garden Festival Wales 1992 (Joint Patron)
Glasgow Festival 1988 (Joint Patron)*
Gloucestershire County Cricket Club
The Guinness Trust
Headway National Head Injuries Association
Help the Aged
HOME-START Consultancy, Leicester
Institute for the Study of Drug Dependence
International Spinal Research Trust
The Leprosy Mission
Leukaemia Research Appeals for Wales
London City Ballet
London Symphony Chorus
The Malcolm Sargent Cancer Fund for Children
National AIDS Trust

National Children's Orchestra
The National Hospitals for Nervous Diseases (now renamed The
    National Hospital for Neurology and Neurosurgery)
National Rubella Council (now renamed Child 2000—The National
    Council for Child Health)
The Natural History Museum
Newport International Competition for Young Pianists, Gwent
Northern Ireland Pre-school Play Groups Association
Parkinson's Disease Society
Pied Piper Appeal, Gloucestershire
Pre-school Playgroups Association
Pre-school Playgroups Association, Wales
RELATE
Royal Anthropological Institute
Royal College of Physicians and Surgeons of Glasgow
Royal School for the Blind, Leatherhead, Surrey
St Matthew Society (Homes for the Lonely)
Scottish Chamber Orchestra
Scottish Pre-School Play Association
Swansea Festival of Music and the Arts
The Trust for Sick Children in Wales
Turning Point
Welsh Bowling Association
Welsh National Opera
Wishing Well Appeal (Joint Patron)*

Patron—Abroad:
Australian Council on Smoking and Health
Australian Junior Red Cross
Canadian Red Cross Youth Services
Chipangali Wildlife Trust, Zimbabwe
The Malcolm Sargent Cancer Fund for Children, Australia
The Princess of Wales Children's Health Camp, Rotorua, New
    Zealand
Royal Children's Hospital Foundation Appeal, Victoria, Australia
    (Joint Patron)*
Royal New Zealand College of Obstetricians and Gynaecologists
Royal New Zealand Foundation for the Blind
Variety Club of New Zealand

The Princess sometimes agrees to be Patron of a conference or similar event, as she did for a meeting of European respiratory physicians in 1990 (see BRITISH LUNG FOUNDATION) and for the 9th Congress of the European Society for Child and Adolescent Psychiatry in London in September 1991. For positions in the Services, see ARMED FORCES. For Honorary Memberships, etc., see ORDERS, DECORATIONS & HONORS.

PRESS

Diana felt she had been "conned" into posing against the light when she first agreed to be photographed by Press cameramen after her romance with Prince Charles became known in September 1980. See YOUNG ENGLAND KINDERGARTEN. The famous picture which resulted, which revealed the shape of her legs through her skirt because she wasn't wearing a petticoat, made her burst into tears, though Charles appreciatively told her, "I knew your legs were good, but I didn't realize they were that spectacular!" See QUOTES. In fact, that picture was the making of her, because as she stood there, looking innocent, shy, and as nice as pie with two little children from the kindergarten where she worked, she epitomized the kind of girl that the Prince of Wales needed as a wife. Someone young, pure, sweet, and demure who loved babies. That it was her ambition to become the Princess of Wales, and that she had set her cap at Charles, was less evident. Her love for him soon became obvious. So did her guile and steely determination, when she duped Press teams with decoys or left them swearing at stoplights while she sped on in her red Mini Metro to a secret rendezvous with Charles. See MOTORING.

However, the pressure from the Press interest was daunting. Diana got to know the reporters and felt "sorry for them having to wait outside my flat in all weathers." But she also said:

> The whole thing's got out of control. I'm not so much bored as miserable. Everywhere I go, there's someone there. . . . If I go to a restaurant or just out shopping to the supermarket, they're trying to take photographs. . . . It makes everyone's life so bloody, particularly the girls who share my flat. . . . It's a situation I think the Royal Family is not really aware of. I don't

think they really know what's going on down here. . . . You see, they've all grown up with it, so they know what to do because they're used to it.

In December 1980, when Diana had been besieged in her flat at Coleherne Court for months by the Press, her mother, Frances Shand Kydd, wrote a letter to *The Times*, without Diana's knowledge, in which she said:

> May I ask the editors of Fleet Street whether, in the execution of their jobs, they consider it necessary or fair to harass my daughter daily, from dawn until well after dusk? Is it fair to ask any human being, regardless of circumstances, to be treated in this way? The freedom of the press was granted by law, by public demand, for very good reasons. But when these privileges are abused, can the press command any respect, or expect to be shown any respect?

In fact, though her mother was defending her, Diana declared later that she didn't agree with the letter.

Eager for an engagement announcement, photographers turned up en masse at Sandringham for New Year's in 1981. Finding their privacy disturbed, senior royals lost their tempers. The Queen shouted at the photographers, "I wish you would go away!" and Prince Charles wished their Editors "a particularly nasty" New Year. Diana, by contrast, was unfailingly courteous, relaxed, and friendly toward the Press, whom she's said she treats "like children." This swiftly earned her their affection and admiration (and that of the general public), and most of the nation had decided she was the right girl for Charles long before the Prince got around to popping the question. For one so young and inexperienced, the way she handled it all was astonishing. A campaign launched at a cost of millions by the world's top PR men could not have been more successful. Her father, Lord Spencer, commented at the time, "The Press made Diana's life difficult, but she behaved very well. It has proved to be a test, though it wasn't meant to be, and she came through with flying colors. I wouldn't have done it myself at nineteen. I would have collapsed."

But royal courtiers who assumed media interest would drop after the royal wedding were proven wrong. Anxious about the effects of so much Press attention on the Princess, who was now

Throughout her travels, Diana has consistently enchanted the press. (Glenn Harvey/Camera Press London)

pregnant, the Queen called Fleet Street Editors to the Palace to ask them to lay off. Most did for a while, but it was like trying to hold back the tide. Interest never flagged, and the Princess was soon established not only as the leading international cover girl, whose face on a magazine could boost sales 20 percent, but the media personality of the decade. People couldn't get enough of her. In the early years, unable to get away from posses of photographers, Diana started to hate the cameras. She particularly hated being pursued by paparazzi on private vacations, and there were several difficult scenes on ski trips to Europe as a result. See MARRIAGE. But now she loves being famous and exercising the power of her celebrity and beauty. She knows that by batting her eyelashes, she can make strong men weak. The way she won over Republican Prime Minister Bob Hawke in Australia is a legend among diplomats. After her trip to the Arab Gulf States, according to royal reporter Judy Wade, she told journalists, "Oh, you should have seen some of those Arabs going gaga when they saw me on the Gulf tour. I gave them the full treatment, and they were just falling over themselves. I just turned it on and mopped them up." She has even enjoyed teasing and flirting with the Press, including one chap who claims, "She collects scalps."

Prince Charles is the most popular royal with the Press. Diana has long been their number one female, but she won't stand any nonsense. If photographers do something she disapproves of or she's in a bad mood, they say, she'll turn her back on them or make sure some other way that they can't get a good picture of her. She still hates *posing* for Press pictures, which she finds embarrassing, as she explained when she refused during a visit to HMS *Cornwall*. See ARMED FORCES. In Hawaii, posing with Charles against a backdrop of palm trees in the sunset during a private rest break, apparently against her will, she looked so po-faced that hardly anyone published the picture, which may have been what she intended. See HAWAII.

There have of course been problems on both sides. There was a huge row over pictures taken of Diana wearing a bikini on a beach in the Bahamas in February 1982 when she was five months' pregnant with Prince William. A Sunday newspaper published photos of wee Willie having a wee. See X-RATED. And after too many off-the-record royal remarks appeared in print, against strict royal rules, Prince Charles put a stop to the receptions which he and Diana had previously held for the accompanying British and local Press teams on their overseas tours. See SPAIN. In 1990, the *Sun* apologized for printing a front-page photo of Charles hugging his friend Penny Romsey in Majorca after Lord Romsey revealed that he and his wife had just broken the news that one of their children had been diagnosed as having cancer and

that the Prince was offering comfort. See HOLIDAYS and MAR-
RIAGE. But the famous occasion when Diana fled in tears from a
polo field in Tidworth just before her wedding was apparently *not*
the fault of Press cameramen but due to other pressures.

The London-based British royal Press corps who follow
members of the Royal Family around the world are known as the
Rat Pack, the Reptiles, and sometimes, among themselves, as the
Mafia. Their stars include Diana's most faithful chronicler, James
Whitaker of the *Daily Mirror*, who became so friendly with her
during the siege days that he gave her private advice, against his
own interests, to encourage her chances of becoming the Princess
of Wales because he was so certain she was the right person; and
the *Mirror*'s award-winning photographer, Kent Gavin, who
scooped an informal chat with Diana returning on the Concorde
from New York in 1989 when she revealed how sad she was
thinking about the little boy dying of AIDS whom she'd held in
her arms. "It was so moving. I'm still thinking about him now,"
she said. Their major rival, until he moved to the *Mirror* himself
as chief reporter, was Harry Arnold, royal correspondent of the
Sun, who scooped the world by breaking the news of the royal
romance. Referring to the Duke of Edinburgh's remark about the
Press being "scum," Harry once made Prince Charles laugh by
declaring, "We may be the scum, but we're the *crème de la* scum."
Harry's former colleague, the *Sun*'s Cockney photographer, Arthur Edwards (see JAPAN), first spotted Diana watching Prince
Charles play polo in Sussex. Later, more significantly, as James
Whitaker recalled in his book *Settling Down*, he (i.e., Whitaker),
Arthur, and photographer Ken Lennox caught sight of Diana
watching Charles fish on the river Dee at Balmoral where, hiding
behind a tree, she peered back at them with the aid of a hand
mirror. Thinking they could get pictures of this mystery royal
companion by splitting to upstream and downstream positions,
the photographers focused their cameras on either side of the tree
trunk. When she moved to left or right, they figured, one of them
might be able to capture her face on film and then identify her.
Instead, her face and hair concealed beneath a head scarf and cap,
Diana completely outwitted them by disappearing straight up a
steep hill without ever looking around, leaving them none the
wiser. A worthy quarry!

It was Arthur, who often talks in Cockney rhyming slang to the royals, who told the Princess one day, " 'Ere, did you know 'Arry's launched a new trivia game?" "Oh, Sex Trivia, I suppose, is it?" she asked. Harry Arnold explained it was Royal Trivia and tried a couple of questions on her. Who drank the Queen's wine without permission? And what did Henry VIII and Al Capone have in common? Diana was stumped and said, "I think you'd better send me a copy of that game!" So Harry had a special one made for her with the lettering printed in gold. (If you are still puzzling, answers appear at the end of this section.)

The *Sun*'s royal reporter is now Robert Jobson. Alan Hamilton covers royal events for *The Times*, reporter Richard Kay and photographer Mike Forster for the *Daily Mail*, and for many years the royal team on the *Daily Express* has been reporter Ashley Walton and photographer Steve Wood.

Although Diana gets on with the Rat Pack, and Charles has shown great personal kindness to them in times of trouble, the Princess can be moody and difficult. "She can be very truculent, and that's a polite word," Harry Arnold said.

She can be a cow, actually. Other times, she's charming. But I think her relationship with the Press is good because she doesn't seem to bear grudges, doesn't stay in a bad mood for long, and she always keeps that little bit of naturalness. Just when you think she's getting very regal, she'll say, "I'm dying for a pee" or something, and you like her for that. [See NIGE-RIA and X-RATED.] She loves taking the mickey [making fun of someone or something]. She told one journalist from the *Financial Times*, "We used to take that at home." I think she meant her father's home. And when he preened himself, she said, "Yes, we used to line the budgie's cage with it." And during a walkabout, when she saw some guy reading the *Sun*, she said, "I use it as bedding for my children's hamsters"— probably the cook's copy, you understand. I think it's a line she rehearses. Being on the *Sun* at the time, I thought, "Oh, God, how am I going to get round that?" So I rang the office and said, "Look, we can't ignore this. It won't go away. We'll have to tackle it head-on." So we then got vets to talk about how it was wonderful to have your hamsters sleeping on the *Sun* because it would make them romantic and warm and loving, and in twenty tests with twenty hamsters, the *Sun* came out tops. And then the *Daily Mirror* took the mickey the next day and ran a similar piece with two hamsters sitting on the *Sun* and called them Arthur and Harry! It was all good knock-about stuff. She loves a good tease.

It was Harry, having followed Diana's progress from the start, who declared not long ago, "I'm so proud of that girl." Admiration won't stop the Press getting up royal noses on occasion, of course—that sometimes goes with the territory. But they have a difficult job and, with certain exceptions, don't always deserve the criticism they get. Martin Walker, who watched the Rat Pack operate during Diana's solo official visit to New York in 1989, reported in the *Guardian*, "They are one of the hardest-working and most conscientious groups of journalists that I have ever seen in action"—an unusual example of one journalist praising others.

So who *did* drink the Queen's wine without permission? Michael Fagan, the Buckingham Palace intruder. And what did Henry VIII and Al Capone have in common? Don't say it too loud—they both died of syphilis. If, like Diana, you'd like a copy of the Royal Trivia game, write to: Harry Arnold, Royal Trivia, Tanyard House, Hollingbourne, Kent ME17 1TS, U.K.

PUBLIC ENGAGEMENTS

Diana's marriage to Prince Charles launched her straight into the unending royal round of shaking hands, making speeches, planting trees, unveiling plaques, cheering the sick and dying at hospitals and hospices, comforting the grief-stricken after disasters, visiting schools and factories, supporting myriad charities and other organizations (see PRESIDENCIES & PATRONAGES), and making tours at home and abroad. Like the Queen Mother, she gives every appearance of enjoying her duties, though she was terrified at first. She confessed later that after public criticism, she sometimes had to force herself to go out, fearing that the crowds might no longer wish to see her. See TELEVISION and QUOTES. In the early days, Diana would return from her public engagements drained and exhausted, kick her shoes off, and slump in a chair. Now she has learned to pace herself, but enormous energy and stamina are

Princess Diana greets tennis star Boris Becker at one of nearly three hundred public engagements she carries out each year. (Alpha)

still required. "You just grow into the job," the Queen Mother said, and Diana did.

As Prince Charles quickly discovered, somewhat to his irritation when her appeal proved to be more than a mere novelty factor, she immediately became the star attraction, her publicity value putting every other royal in the shade. See MARRIAGE. Her natural, relaxed, unaffected ways; her ability to treat ordinary people on the same level as VIPs; her empathy and sympathy with those in need or in trouble; her sense of fun; the uninhibited way she giggles or slides down a gangplank; her concern and care for children, stopping to pick them up and cuddle them, getting on her knees to chat or play with them or tie up a loose shoelace; and her considerate, tactful, and appropriate emotional responses to the huge variety of individuals and situations she comes across have injected a freshness, humor, warmth, spontaneity, and humanity previously lacking at royal events and brought the image of the Royal Family completely up-to-date. Such is the impact Diana has made that a survey in *Woman* magazine revealed in July 1990 that although an astonishing one in five British children didn't know who the Queen Mother was, they did know Diana (and Mrs. Thatcher, then Prime Minister).

On occasion the excitement of a royal visit can go over the top. In 1985 a twenty-seven-year-old woman who had been visited by Charles and Diana at her home in Sunderland was arrested, but not charged, when police raided a party, held to celebrate the visit, which ended in scuffles. One dedicated royal fan, seventeen-year-old Paul Ratcliffe from Headingley, Leeds, followed the Princess and the Duchess of York around Britain on engagements. By 1988 he claimed he had kissed Diana's hand seven times and Fergie's gloved one on three occasions. ("Oh no, not you again!" Fergie said, spotting him in Warrington in Cheshire in March 1989.) In July 1988, confronting the Princess yet again during a visit to a Barnardo's project in Whitley Bay, Tyne and Wear, Paul boldly asked if he could kiss her cheek instead and was refused somewhat flirtatiously with the remark, "You'd better kiss my hand. You never know where it might lead if you kiss me on the cheek." Meeting her is still such a thrill that he often ends up, he says, standing there "with my mouth wide open." Norman Willis, General Secretary of the Trades Union Congress, was so thrilled when he met the Princess in February 1991 that he went weak at the knees and not only shook her hand but curtsied as well. (Not the first man to do that on meeting royalty.) She giggled.

Diana's first solo public engagement was in November 1981, when she switched on the Christmas lights on London's Regent Street. Encountering singer Cilla Black, who was there with her husband Bobby, she said, "I see you've brought your other half with you. I've left mine at home, watching telly." She now does an average of about 270 public engagements a year at home and abroad, just over five a week. In 1989, after watching proudly as Diana received the Freedom of the Borough of Northampton, where Althorp stands (see ORDERS, DECORATIONS & HONORS), her father, Lord Spencer, told reporters, "I worry about her a lot. Official engagements can be very exacting, and sometimes she does several in one day. In the old days, people usually just did one. Sometimes I think she does too much and works too hard. I know that she enjoys carrying out engagements, but it worries me sometimes that she is putting too much of a strain on her health." See HEALTH.

The Princess had barely traveled abroad before her marriage apart from going on vacation with her mother and stepfather (see

AUSTRALIA) and skiing in Europe. Since then, however, apart from strictly personal trips (see HOLIDAYS and HONEYMOON), the countries she has been to include the following:

1982:	September	Monaco
1983:	March/April	Australia & New Zealand
	June	Canada
1984:	February	Norway
1985:	April/May	Italy
	October	West Germany
	October/ November	Australia
	November	Fiji
	November	Hawaii
	November	America
1986:	April	Austria
	April/May	Canada
	May	Japan
	November	Arab Gulf States
1987:	February	Portugal
	February	France
	April	Spain
	May	France
	September	France
	November	West Germany
1988:	January/February	Australia
	February	Thailand
	November	France
1989:	February	America
	March	Kuwait & the United Arab Emirates
	June	Australia
	November	Indonesia & Hong Kong

1990:	March	Nigeria & Cameroon
	May	Hungary
	October	America
	November	Japan
	December	Belgium
1991:	April	Brazil
	May	Czechoslovakia
	September	Pakistan
	October	Canada
1992:	February	India

Buckingham Palace does not keep tallies of how many public engagements are carried out by members of the Royal Family. However, insurance broker Tim O'Donovan of Datchet, Berkshire, has performed a useful public service over the years by making an annual survey and count of their duties, as listed in the published Court Circular. O'Donovan sends this data annually to the letters columns of *The Times* and the *Daily Telegraph*. Using his figures it is possible to draw Table 3 (on the following page), which charts the number of engagements performed in the U.K.

The duties counted here include official visits, opening ceremonies, charity galas, premieres, receptions, lunches, dinners, banquets, meetings presided over and attended, and audiences given. The table does not reflect the length of a particular engagement, which could last all morning while someone else is doing several short ones. Nor the time taken going through official papers, writing official letters, consulting advisers, or all the preparation needed before engagements in terms of reviewing background details and people to be met, fittings for clothes, travel to and from, and so on. Making the relevant allowances for increasing age, periods of illness or maternity, and other career commitments, Table 3 shows how much harder many members of the Royal Family are working, in particular Princess Anne. Averaging out the number of public engagements carried out per person per year in the U.K. from these figures produces Table 4 (see page 301).

Prince Andrew, serving in the Royal Navy, sometimes carries

TABLE 3: ROYAL ENGAGEMENTS CARRIED OUT
IN THE UNITED KINGDOM

	1979	1980	1981	1982	1983	1984	1985	1986	1987	1988	1989	1990	1991
The Queen	466	351	407	385	337	391	415	430	432	421	488	476	455
Duke of Edinburgh	229	253	302	250	205	298	258	257	322	279	302	294	298
Queen Mother	125	110	97	113	119	115	119	127	105	120	90	118	100
Prince of Wales	196	198	208	216	168	204	286	301	276	359	331	245	301
Princess of Wales			45	66	110	72	206	176	180	191	238	234	258
Duke of York			6	4	14	15	19	61	76	30	65	23	83
Duchess of York								46	132	55	200	85	170
Prince Edward					7	3	6	48	62	98	107	106	195
Princess Royal	119	100	84	168	244	268	330	401	367	429	455	449	504
Princess Margaret	115	105	97	106	116	161	89	98	129	109	121	148	103
Princess Alice, Duchess of Gloucester	50	65	67	64	40	48	57	58	64	57	47	66	51
Duke of Gloucester	89	88	113	130	151	120	154	137	123	151	176	172	144
Duchess of Gloucester	25	61	78	74	86	77	90	104	111	113	99	119	97
Duke of Kent	93	94	120	125	121	109	130	144	130	156	162	172	190
Duchess of Kent	31	71	88	90	33	119	102	109	107	128	139	137	178
Princess Alexandra	75	85	118	115	119	114	125	115	93	94	116	102	148

TABLE 4: AVERAGE NUMBER OF ROYAL ENGAGEMENTS
CARRIED OUT IN THE U.K. PER PERSON PER YEAR
BETWEEN THE YEARS 1979 AND 1991 INCLUSIVE

		Number of engagements	Number of years	Average per year
1	The Queen	5,454	13	419.5
2	Princess Royal	3,918	13	301.3
3	Duke of Edinburgh	3,547	13	272.8
4	Prince of Wales	3,289	13	253
5	Princess of Wales	1,776	11	161.4
6	Duke of Gloucester	1,748	13	134.4
7	Duke of Kent	1,746	13	134.3
8	Princess Margaret	1,497	13	115.1
9	Duchess of York	688	6	114.6
10	Queen Mother	1,458	13	112.1
11	Princess Alexandra	1,419	13	109.1
12	Duchess of Kent	1,327	13	102
13	Duchess of Gloucester	1,134	13	87.2
14	Prince Edward	632	9	70.2
15	Princess Alice, Duchess of Gloucester	734	13	56.4
16	Duke of York	396	11	36

out more public engagements abroad than at home. In fact, the busiest times of all are when members of the Royal Family are on official visits or tours overseas, when schedules are packed tight to make the most of each trip. Diana, for example, instead of doing perhaps three or four public engagements a week as she might at home, may find herself doing an average of five every day when abroad. The greatest globe-trotter in the family is Prince Philip, who, according to Tim O'Donovan's surveys, made sixteen trips abroad in 1979, fourteen in 1980, eleven in 1981, no fewer than thirty-two in 1982, and twenty-one the following year. However, he is rapidly being caught up in terms of time spent abroad by Princess Anne, whose work overseas for the Save the Children

TABLE 5: NUMBER OF DAYS SPENT ABROAD BY MEMBERS OF THE ROYAL FAMILY ON OVERSEAS TOURS, FOLLOWED, WHERE THE INFORMATION IS AVAILABLE, BY THE NUMBER OF ENGAGEMENTS CARRIED OUT THERE

	1984	1985	1986	1987	1988	1989	1990	1991
The Queen	29/121	34/171	39/170	18/87	31/127	18/104	28/94	26/126
Duke of Edinburgh	82/238	99/356	98/341	54/192	81/277	75/267	77/260	71/289
Queen Mother	5/9	10/16		8		5/15	2/4	2/2
Prince of Wales	36/112	36/118	40/169	33/167	30/125	30/140	37/144	34/159
Princess of Wales	2/5	32/93	26/98	17/86	18/58	18/62	22/89	25/139
Duke of York	15/44	10/43	8/8	36/76	28/81	20/74	4/6	9/24
Duchess of York			3/5	36/76	38/98	35/127	16/23	16/43
Prince Edward				20/70	27/78	7/27	35/113	16/56
Princess Royal	64/233	44/130	22/81	67/337	70/236	66/282	82/319	54/241
Princess Margaret	8/25	12/42	12/12	17	16/36	2/7	4/6	
Princess Alice, Duchess of Gloucester	2	1		3	3	2		

	1984	1985	1986	1987	1988	1989	1990	1991
Duke of Gloucester	32	36	11	22	30	16	25	25
Duchess of Gloucester	14	29	4	8	8	4		7
Duke of Kent	31	37	29	33	33	29	27	35
Duchess of Kent	13	37	8	18	22	6	13	20
Princess Alexandra	22	29	36	33	23/72	31/66	29/54	7

Fund has been tireless. From 1984 onward—earlier figures were not available—O'Donovan has calculated how many days members of the Royal Family have spent abroad on official tours and how many engagements they carried out there. From that information, it is possible to draw Table 5 (see pages 302–303).

Combining the figures for public engagements from Tables 3 and 5 provides the following "Top Six" list of the busiest of the senior royals, at home and abroad, 1987–91 inclusive (Table 6). Notice that the workaholic Princess Royal is at the number one position ahead of her parents.

TABLE 6: TOP SIX LIST SHOWING THE BUSIEST SENIOR MEMBERS
OF THE ROYAL FAMILY IN TERMS OF
PUBLIC ENGAGEMENTS CARRIED OUT AT HOME
AND ABROAD 1987–91 INCLUSIVE

	At home	Abroad	Total
1 Princess Royal	2,204	1,415	3,619
2 The Queen	2,272	538	2,810
3 Duke of Edinburgh	1,495	1,285	2,780
4 Prince of Wales	1,512	735	2,247
5 Princess of Wales	1,101	434	1,535
6 Duchess of York	642	367	1,009

Prince William undertook his first public engagement in Cardiff in March 1991, at age eight.

Quotes

Some of Diana's more memorable quotations include these:

Early days:

◆ As a child: "I'll never marry unless I really love someone. If you're not really sure you love someone, then you might get divorced. I never want to be divorced."

◆ On school days: "We used to be very naughty and slide down the back of the bath[tub]."

On herself:

◆ "Brain the size of a pea I've got."

◆ "I'm as thick as a plank."

◆ On the fact that she takes a size 7½ hat, having such a large head: "It may be large, but there's not much in it."

◆ In Italy, when Prince Charles warned her to mind her head as they went under a low arch: "Why? There's nothing in it."

◆ "When I'm nervous I tend to giggle."

◆ Denying stories which claimed that she was domineering: ". . . I don't think I am. I'm a perfectionist with myself, though not necessarily with everyone else."

◆ "I'm a normal person, hopefully, who loves life."

◆ On her keen sense of hearing: "I've got ears like a bat." (Harry says she doesn't like bats.)

◆ "I like playing bridge but I'm no good—I talk too much."

◆ "What's so special about me?"

◆ "Anywhere I see suffering, that is where I want to be—doing what I can."

On and to the Press:

◆ On the famous early Press photograph, posed against the

305

In procession on the way to the state opening of Parliament. (Andy Kyle/
Camera Press London)

light, in which her legs were revealed through her skirt because
she wasn't wearing a petticoat: "I ended up in the papers
looking like I had Steinway piano legs."

◆ Asked whether she was hurt by Press criticism: "Well
obviously you feel very wounded. You think, 'Oh gosh, I don't
want to go out and do my engagement this morning. Nobody
wants to see me. Help! Panic!' But you've got to push yourself
out and remember that some people, hopefully, won't remember
everything they read about you."

◆ "There is far too much about me in the newspapers, far too
much. It horrifies me when there's more important things, like
what goes on in the hospices, or there's been a bomb or
something."

◆ "I simply treat the Press as though they were children."

◆ "You keep writing that I'm on a diet, but I'm not."

◆ "You know everything about me except how many fillings
I've got—and I'm not telling you *that*."

◆ "You won't need me anymore, now you've got Fergie."

On royal life and the Royal Family:

◆ "Life at Buckingham Palace isn't too bad but too many formal dinners—yuk!"

◆ On staff there when she was nineteen: "Everybody is so old around here."

◆ On some of the palace courtiers: "It was as if Charles was married to them, not me, and they are so patronizing it drives me mad."

◆ On what she expected her future royal work to be like: "Thirty percent fantastic, 70 percent sheer slog."

◆ On having to dress up for public engagements: "Imagine having to go to a wedding every day of your life—as the bride. Well, that's a bit what it's like."

◆ On the Queen: "I have the best mother-in-law in the world."

◆ On Princess Anne: "I'm her biggest fan because what she crams into a day I could never achieve. We've always hit it off very well and I just think she's marvelous. . . . She works ten times harder than me and deserves every bit of credit coming her way."

◆ "The trouble with being a princess is that it is so hard to have a pee."

◆ "Being a princess is not all it's cracked up to be."

◆ Laughing about the fact that she could no longer behave the way she once did: "I think that's probably just as well—if you knew how I used to behave!"

◆ To Fergie, on joining the Royal Family: "Be delightful, but be discreet."

On courtship, marriage, and Prince Charles:

◆ Her first impression of him after they met when she was sixteen: "Pretty amazing."

◆ On her instant acceptance of his marriage proposal: "It was what I wanted—it is what I want."

◆ On their engagement: "With Prince Charles beside me, I can't go wrong."

◆ On her sapphire-and-diamond engagement ring: "I can't get used to wearing it yet. The other day I even scratched my nose with it because it's so big—the ring, I mean."

◆ Leaving her new telephone number for her flatmates, as she left Coleherne Court for the last time: "For God's sake, ring me up—I'm going to need you!"

◆ Asked why her fiancé hadn't accompanied her to watch tennis at Wimbledon shortly before their wedding: "It's because he can never sit still. He is like a great big baby. But one day I hope to calm him down enough to enjoy it."

◆ To a blind woman at a Buckingham Palace garden party just before the wedding: "Do you want to feel my engagement ring? I'd better not lose it before Wednesday or they won't know who I am."

◆ On the wedding rehearsal: "Everybody was fighting. I got my heel stuck in some grating and everyone was saying, 'Hurry up, Diana.' I said, 'I can't. I'm stuck.' "

◆ On the enormous breakfast she ate on her wedding day: "I hope that stops my tummy rumbling in St. Paul's."

◆ As she finished the "terrifying" walk down the aisle and reached Prince Charles in her bridal gown, he said, "You look wonderful." "Wonderful for you," she replied.

◆ Making her wedding vows, Diana got the order of Charles's names mixed up and vowed to take "Philip Charles Arthur George" as her husband.

◆ Asked after their honeymoon what she thought of marriage: "I can highly recommend it."

◆ To a bride-to-be, November 1982: "Married life is wonderful, so don't worry."

◆ In 1985: "I feel my role is supporting my husband whenever I can, and always being behind him, encouraging him. And also, most important, being a mother and a wife. And that's what I try to achieve. Whether I do is another thing, but I do try."

◆ "When we first got married, we were everyone's idea of the world's most perfect, ideal couple. Now they say we're leading separate lives. The next thing I know I'll read in some newspaper that I've got a black lover."

◆ "My husband has taught me everything I know."

◆ On Charles and his interests: "He loves his garden, but as soon as he's finished sorting out every inch of it he will get bored with it and take up something else. He's like that."

◆ On Charles being "a bad patient" after breaking his arm playing polo in June 1990: "But then so are all men . . . well, at least 75 percent of them."

◆ In October 1990, saying that Charles was rushing his recovery: "He is going fishing and golfing and other things that men do. He would like to get back on his horse. . . . Like most men, he does what he wants to do. He's doing what he shouldn't do half the time."

On pregnancy and motherhood:
◆ Suffering from morning sickness while expecting Prince William: "Nobody told me I would feel like this."

◆ After William was born: "It's amazing how much happiness a small child brings to people."

◆ On how Charles had taken to fatherhood: "He's a doting Daddy and does everything perfectly."

◆ While pregnant with Prince Harry: "I haven't felt well since Day One. I don't think I'm made for the production line . . . but it's all worth it in the end."

◆ After the birth of Prince Harry: "My husband knows so much about rearing children that I've suggested he has the next one and I'll sit back and give advice."

◆ "If men had to have babies, they would only have one each."

◆ On looking after her two sons: ". . . by Sunday I am a stretcher case."

◆ On rearing children: "It's all hard work and no pay."

◆ "William is just like me—always in trouble."

◆ When William was aged three: "William's a typical three-year-old—because I worked with three-year-olds. Very enthusiastic about things, pushes himself right into it. He's not at all shy, but very polite, extraordinarily enough. Where, perhaps, Harry is quieter and just watches . . . he's certainly a different character altogether.''

◆ When William was to be a pageboy at Fergie's wedding to Prince Andrew: "I'm going to put down a line of Smarties in the aisle at Westminster Abbey so that William will know where to stand, and he's got to stay there. . . . He's terribly excited. I only hope he behaves in the Abbey. He will rise to the occasion. At least, I hope he will.''

◆ "He's [William's] surrounded by a tremendous amount of grown-ups, so his conversation's very forthright.''

◆ On her two sons: "They are little minxes.''

◆ "We're open-minded about William and his education because the bad luck about being number one is trial and error. Number two skates in quite nicely. So we're still learning all the tricks of the trade.''

◆ In 1985, on being asked when she would have her third child: "I'm not a production line, you know.''

◆ In April 1987: "I'm too busy to have any babies for at least a year.''

◆ In March 1990: "I'd like three more babies—but I haven't told my husband yet. I think he may find it a bit of a surprise. You see I grew up in a family of four, but I would like one extra. I think five children make the perfect family.''

On dancing:
◆ "It's my absolute passion.''

◆ On her early ambition to become a ballet dancer: "I overshot the height by a long way. I couldn't imagine some man trying to lift me up above his arms.''

On the British heat wave, summer 1990:
◆ "I just can't stand it when it's this hot.''

On clothes and fashion:
◆ To a freezing housewife in a Glasgow crowd, 1989: "Haven't

you got your thermals on?" And to another in the same crowd: "I'm lovely and warm. I was expecting Scottish weather so I'm wearing thermal underwear."

◆ "Hats give me confidence."

◆ "My clothes are not my priority. I enjoy bright colors and my husband likes me to look smart and presentable, but fashion isn't my big thing at all."

◆ "When I first arrived there were a lot of people to help me. It's now really my choice."

◆ "Clothes are for the job. They've got to be practical. Sometimes I can be a little outrageous, which is quite nice. But only sometimes."

◆ "I just can't win. They either accuse me of spending too much on my clothes or of wearing the same outfit all the time. I wish everyone would stop talking about my clothes."

◆ "I do so like men in uniform."

On tours abroad:
◆ In Australia in 1983 after patting a little boy on the head, she asked him why he wasn't at school and got the reply: "I was sent home because I've got head lice."

◆ After her debut tour: "The first week was a shock. It was like a baptism of fire. But having got into the feeling of it, it got better. By the time I left Australia I felt I'd actually been able to achieve something. I was so amazed that I was capable of that, that New Zealand got easier, and it's sort of built up from there."

◆ To President Mario Soares at a banquet in a chilly palace in Portugal, 1987: "If I get cold, will you warm me up?" After he offered her his dinner jacket, she said, twanging his braces (suspenders): "You're a socialist, aren't you? You should be wearing *red* braces."

On food and drink:
◆ "I don't like champagne."

◆ July 1987: "Contrary to reports in some of our more sensational Sunday newspapers, I have not been drinking and I am not, I can assure you, about to become an alcoholic."

◆ "Oh no! Everywhere I go they give me salad."

◆ "I prefer fish to meat . . . anyway, it's cheaper to eat fish."

◆ "I ate kippers all the time when I was pregnant with William."

◆ "It's so nice to get home and have a bowl of custard."

◆ "I have an enormous appetite, despite what people say, and so has William. He takes after his mother."

◆ "I'm never on what's called a diet. Maybe I'm so scrawny because I take so much exercise."

◆ "I would walk miles for a bacon sandwich."

◆ Asked by *Dangerous Liaisons* star John Malkovich after watching a postsex breakfast scene in the movie: "Is it like that for breakfast at the Palace?," Diana replied, "No. But it beats reading the papers!"

RADIO

Diana is a great fan of Capital Radio, the London independent pop music station. "It's the best," she declared in 1988. Her radio is tuned to Capital from early morning onward. Indeed, the constant rock music, and the baby paraphernalia in evidence during his visits to Kensington Palace on business, were said to tax top royal courtier Edward Adeane, who later quit. See STAFF. Charles himself prefers to tune in to the early-morning farming and "Today" programs on BBC Radio 4 and to classical music on BBC Radio 3, which couldn't be more of a contrast. Sir Richard Attenborough (see SPEECHES) is Chairman of Capital, and another of the royal couple's friends, Lord Romsey, is a Director. See FRIENDS.

In November 1982 the Princess toured Capital Radio, where she was presented with *Tales for a Princess*, a specially produced book to read to baby Prince William containing the fifty-one winning entries in a contest which attracted twenty-five thousand stories from London children. "William says thank you too," she said. While there, she visited studios and saw how a radio station works; talked with John Stoneborough, who went to Gordonstoun school with Prince Charles, about his "PDQ" consumer investigation show; and met top executives and several disc jockeys including Michael Aspel, Graham Dene, Roger Scott (see BATHS & BATHROOMS), and Gary Crowley. During the visit she made it obvious that she was familiar with virtually all the station's programs and even traffic spotter Bryan Wolfe's Flying Eye plane, which cruises over Kensington Palace.

In 1987, Diana made a secret dawn visit to Capital Radio in jeans, taking some of her favorite records with her, and sat beside disc jockey Graham Dene devouring sticky buns and tea while he broadcast his last breakfast show. The final record he played—

Diana's favorite, "Uptown Girl" by Billy Joel—was dedicated to "Charles, back in Kensington." In December that year, Dene played another secret request for her, Paul McCartney's "Once Upon a Long Ago," dedicating it to "Charlie's Angel and her Little Goblins," meaning Prince William and Prince Harry. And after saying, "If the Uptown Girl keeps listening, there'll be something else she likes on soon," he also played Chris de Burgh's Christmas single.

In 1988, when Capital started broadcasting two separate outputs, providing pop music twenty-four hours a day with classic hit records from the last three decades on Capital Gold and the Top 40 format on Capital FM, Diana was asked by her friend Millie Dunne, on behalf of Capital Radio's charity, Help a London Child, to launch its Easter Appeal. She agreed. See FRIENDS. The following year, the Princess donated a carriage clock, which was sold for £17,500, for a celebrity auction at a star-studded lunch at the Café Royal which helped raise funds of £90,000 for the same charity. See COLLECTIONS. Other donations included one of Mrs. Thatcher's handbags, which fetched £1,500, and a tea party at Neil Kinnock's office in the House of Commons, complete with tea brewed by Neil and Welsh cakes baked by his wife Glenys, which went for £2,100.

In 1989, BBC Radio Scotland disc jockey Art Sutter played a special request for Diana's twenty-eighth birthday after receiving a letter from her mother, Mrs. Frances Shand Kydd, which read, "Please will you play a record for my beloved daughter Diana who celebrates her birthday on Saturday. She has the beautiful title Lady of the Isles [see NAMES], so how about the 'Eriskay Love Lilt' sung by Kenneth McKellar? And could you play it towards the end of your programme as I will be on the River Spey hoping to catch a salmon?"

In June 1987, a broadcaster at Beacon Radio in Wolverhampton was suspended for forty-eight hours after calling Diana "a bit of a dog." And in July 1988, a presenter broadcast an apology after branding her "a bimbo" on Radio WM in Birmingham.

About 250 million people listened to the royal wedding on radio around the world. See TELEVISION and WEDDING.

RED CROSS

The Princess is Patron of British Red Cross Youth, Patron of the Australian Junior Red Cross, and Patron of Canadian Red Cross Youth Services. All spring from the International Red Cross, founded by a Swiss, Henry Dunant, which had its 125th anniversary in May 1988. To mark that occasion, Diana was at Paddington railway station in London to name an Inter City 125 power car *The Red Cross*. It was the idea of twelve-year-old Jonathan Frankham, a member of British Red Cross Youth, who was in the cab with the Princess to start *The Red Cross* on its first journey, to Bristol. And watching them were a group of youngsters with disabilities, with their young helpers, who had all taken part in a Red Cross vacation and who met Diana later at a lunch hosted by British Rail.

British Red Cross Youth, which has a membership of around twenty thousand youngsters aged from five to eighteen, began life as the Junior Red Cross in 1924. Its three objectives are the protection of health and life, service to the sick and suffering, and the promotion of international friendship and understanding. In January 1989, visiting British Red Cross headquarters in London, Diana saw how the Red Cross leadership training program prepares workers to identify and be sensitive to problems facing young people in the 1990s, including child abuse and drug and solvent addiction. She also watched the preview of a new HIV/AIDS video education package aimed at thirteen- to sixteen-year-olds. In December 1984, when the Princess joined three hundred members of British Red Cross Youth at a carol service at Bristol Cathedral, it was the first time she had appeared in public in her uniform—a navy blue beret, tunic, and skirt. See UNIFORMS.

RELATE

Diana is a good listener with bags of common sense, a keen interest in other people, plenty of compassion, and a dedication to family life. Coming from a broken home and being caught in the middle of a custody battle as a child, she has had firsthand experience of the painful effects on children of their parents' separation and divorce and, after both her parents remarried, of the sometimes difficult adjustments required when stepparents arrive on the scene. Marriage into the Royal Family has presented special difficulties, and motherhood has also demonstrated the strains, as well as the joys, of parenting. The entire subject of personal relationships, marriage, and the problems which can arise in family life has become of burning interest to the Princess, particularly in more recent years. So it is not surprising that she has made RELATE one of the especially favored organizations to which she commits extra time and energy. Or that its experts have commented time and again that she would make a good marriage counselor herself. With her friends and relatives, she offers a shoulder to cry on and gives advice where necessary. She was quick to show public support for Sir Angus Ogilvy during the painful and much-publicized dispute which he and his wife, Princess Alexandra, had with their pregnant daughter, Marina, over whether she should marry her boyfriend before or after the baby was born. The couple did wed beforehand—as Marina's parents wished, allegedly not relishing the prospect of their branch of the Royal Family producing the first illegitimate baby in living memory. Diana even gave off-the-cuff advice once to a lovelorn girl on a public engagement. See MARRIAGE.

Ironically though, when the Princess was invited to become Patron of RELATE's Golden Jubilee Appeal in 1986, she said no. The organization, set up in 1939 by a small group of clergy, doctors, and lawyers concerned about marriage and family life, was still called the National Marriage Guidance Council. And the fact that it was in the throes of a major upheaval as it brought itself up-to-date may have accounted for the Princess's refusal. However, she did ask to go and see their work, making her first visit in 1988.

In the meantime, a new Director, David French, was appointed in 1987, and the charity changed its name to RELATE (in capital letters) to symbolize its new identity. Old policies went out the window. And the scope of its work and services was widened enormously. Gone were the days when couples had to be married to get help and when the charity's aim was to keep them married, whatever their problems. RELATE, as the name implies, places the emphasis on relationships in general and family life in particular. Nowadays its counselors offer confidential help to anyone, married or single, whatever their age, who has relationship problems with partners or parents. To cope with the ever-increasing demand for help—RELATE has an annual caseload of fifty-five thousand with ten thousand clients on the waiting list at any one time—the charity has about two thousand voluntary trained counselors, based at 160 affiliated centers across Britain. The Home Office provides an annual grant, which in 1989 was just under £1 million, but further funds are constantly needed because the work is expensive. Training for each counselor takes two-and-a-half years and costs an average of £3,850.

Diana's first visit, to RELATE's national headquarters in Rugby in March 1988, proved a revelation. After being greeted by David French and members of staff and seeing an exhibition of the charity's work, she sat in on a counselor training session watching, absolutely riveted, as two counselors played the roles of a husband and wife having a fierce marital row. Such role-play sessions teach trainees how and when to intervene and how to give the battling couple new insight into what their problems are, why they have occurred, and what they can do about them. Diana was hooked. While in Rugby, she visited St. Cross Hospital to see how RELATE counselors there help seriously and terminally ill cancer patients, and their partners, come to terms with their fears. The scene at the hospital that day was very moving. "There were tears in everyone's eyes," one counselor recalled.

Intrigued by her first encounter with RELATE and its work, Diana wanted to see more. So two months later, in May 1988, she visited their community project based at the Doddington council estate (public housing) in Wandsworth, London, which aims to help residents avert family crises quickly. Local mothers who attend a counseling group at the center told her of the support they had received in coping with marital conflicts, financial and housing problems, and their children. There were "no inhibitions" in the discussion, one mother said later, and Diana showed "great sensitivity and understanding" according to project leader Mrs. Alison Crosthwaithe. Renate Olins, Director of RELATE

London Marriage Guidance, which set up the project in September 1986, described her visit to the center as "an inspiration to everyone involved in it." The Princess, of course, has never had to live on a council estate nor is ever likely to have to cope with poverty, but she listened and learned. She recognizes how wearing motherhood can be, however, even though she has nannies to help. "It's tiring work looking after children," she agreed. "I know because I have to look after my two boys and by Sunday I am a stretcher case."

That November, Diana made her third visit, this time to the RELATE center for Barnet, Haringey, and Hertsmere, one of the largest of its kind in Britain, where the clients ranged from teenagers to a couple in their eighties. She joined counselors in one of their regular fortnightly case discussion groups, where difficult and complex cases receive expert attention. To preserve strict confidentiality, even from the Princess, clients were referred to only by their first names. She listened sympathetically as two single mothers talked of the strain and difficulties of bringing up children on their own. One of them was so nervous that it was painful to watch, but Diana quickly made her feel at ease. Then she met an Asian couple plagued with communication problems, the most common cause of relationship breakdown (as the Emanuels, who designed Diana's wedding gown, found; see ASTROLOGY). And she learned that what counselors need most is not a string of GCE O levels (see EDUCATION) or a university degree, but "warmth, openness, and an ability to listen and communicate," qualities which she herself has in abundance. It was an important reassurance for Diana. "She really picked up on that," said Irene Short, the center's Director.

> She has always made a thing about failing O levels. What do O levels matter? To be frank, I didn't expect to be impressed by visiting royalty. But the biggest compliment I can give is that within a few minutes, we had forgotten who she was. She didn't lead the clients at all. She listened and encouraged them to talk about their problems. And they opened up to her in a remarkably short period of time. I would have her on my counseling team any day of the week. She would make a very good counselor.

Thousands of Londoners turned out to see Diana arrive at the center, where she was photographed in a pink coat over a black outfit, standing in front of a poster which read, "IF YOUR OTHER HALF DOESN'T UNDERSTAND YOU, TALK TO SOMEONE WHO DOES." Before she left, the center's Chairman, Jerome Karet, presented her with two fund-raising RELATE bears, wearing bow ties, for Prince William and Prince Harry.

By now Diana's interest was thoroughly aroused. The following month, December 1988, she traveled to RELATE Wolverhampton, where homeless and unemployed men at a hospital told her about the feelings of hopelessness and despair brought on by their plight. Then she sat in on a sex therapy session, hearing all about the intimate problems of a couple in their thirties. Counselor Margaret Brown commented afterward, "She is a very well-informed and sympathetic lady. She was also very relaxed, which helps put the clients at ease."

In January 1989, Diana was off again to a pioneering RELATE family therapy center at Portsmouth, where the subject came very close to home—stepfamilies. According to the charity, just because divorced parents fall in love with and marry someone else does not mean that either set of children "automatically love or even like their new stepparent." This message would not have been lost on Diana or her sisters and brother. Or indeed on their stepmother, Raine, who has at times found the problems of stepfamily relationships "bloody awful." See FAMILY. RELATE says that in stepfamilies generally, children "very often feel resentful, or fear that they won't get as much love and attention from their parents once there is a stepparent around. Meanwhile the couple, instead of having a honeymoon period on their own, have to cope with all the stresses of an instant family in which each individual is adjusting to a lot of new relationships. There can be problems about discipline and divided loyalties, and this can cause conflict between the couple themselves as well."

At the center, the first started in Britain, entire families turn up for counseling. Diana met one of them—a couple with six children aged from six to sixteen from previous marriages. All were nervous, but they soon got engrossed in a thirty-minute heart-to-heart, finding Diana's suggestion that the family have monthly meetings at home where they all air their grievances "marvelous." "She has helped us all," the wife was quoted as saying later. "Although our backgrounds are so different, she understood perfectly some of the problems we are experiencing. She would be an ideal counselor. She actually listens to what you are saying and draws you out." Counselor Sue Woolrych said, "We feared that the meeting might be artificial, but the Princess was really perceptive." At the center, Diana learned that family therapy can also help other families not getting on together, or under other stress, whether this involves constant fights and rows between teenagers and parents, coping with a member of the family who is chronically ill, or a household where three generations strive to live in peace and harmony under the same roof but don't always succeed.

During the five visits she had now made, Diana had impressed counselors with her ability to get clients to talk openly to her about their problems. And she had earned the admiration of David French, who commented, "We are very honored by the interest the Princess of Wales has shown in our work. We see it as a deep caring and belief in the importance of family life in [Britain] today."

Next on Diana's diary for RELATE came the Golden Jubilee Appeal Champagne Luncheon at the Berkeley Hotel in Wilton Place, London, in February 1989, for which she had written a foreword to the brochure, in which she said, "Despite all the change around us, the family remains the bedrock on which modern society is built. RELATE is working to help families: to help couples and thereby to help the children who are so often the victims of marriage breakdown."

When two people see a lot of each other, other people tend to start gossiping about them. And there *was* talk about Diana and RELATE. Yes, she had given the charity an initial brush-off, like the start of one of those romantic novels she devoured as a schoolgirl where the heroine spurns the handsome hero. See BOOKS and EDUCATION. But since then, she had been hooked and unable to stay away. And so, of course, the tongues started wagging. "What it felt like at the time was that RELATE and the Princess of Wales must get married—they're seeing so much of each other!" David French recalled. "It felt a bit like a courtship, particularly because people kept saying to us, 'Isn't she Patron? *Surely* she's Patron? When's she going to *become* Patron?' " In April 1989 it was finally announced that Diana had agreed to become Patron. And not of the Golden Jubilee Appeal, as originally requested, but more importantly of the charity RELATE itself. "In view of the interest she had shown," David French said, "we thought another formal request might be well received, so we asked again and she agreed. And she does an enormous amount for us."

That May she made her first visit as Patron to RELATE Bristol, where she joined a parents' group discussion called "Get to know your child better" which showed parents how constant criticism can damage young children. She also listened as a group of fifteen-year-olds were shown how to communicate better. According to Mrs. Rosie Spurr at the center, Diana was "totally involved" and "seemed to thoroughly enjoy it. She has done her homework and realizes the importance of communication between parents and children."

Afterward the Princess staged an impromptu walkabout among the crowds in Bristol who'd gathered to greet her, anxious that they'd been waiting under a blazing sun in blistering heat. "She was worried for the children," nursery worker Sarah Cartwright said. "But we would have waited all day."

Since then, in addition to other visits, Diana has helped raise funds for RELATE by attending a special performance of the smash-hit musical *Miss Saigon* and the film premiere of *Shirley Valentine*, starring Pauline Collins as yet another wife whose marriage has lost its sparkle. At RELATE Worcestershire in December, she saw the enactment of a scene from a marriage heading for divorce in which counselors played the roles of a wife who is desperate to sort out problems within the marriage and a husband who refuses to recognize there are any and therefore won't talk them through—a situation which would ring bells in homes everywhere. Diana voiced her thoughts on the "rights and wrongs" of the imaginary situation, showing herself to be "both charming and intelligent," said the center's Keith Stanley. And she offered advice to a woman in her forties who was having communication difficulties with her husband. "It was very private," Mr. Stanley said, "but the Princess made some very acute observations on the problem. And she suggested how it might be tackled." In January 1990 she plunged in even more deeply at RELATE's national headquarters and training college in Rugby, where she spent half a day sitting in on a training session herself with sixteen trainee counselors. But Press reports that she has asked to become a counselor herself are untrue, said David French, who added, "I think there's no doubt that she would be very interested in training to be and being a counselor if she weren't who she is. But her royal life proscribes it. However, she is very interested in what makes counseling work, and I think she's recognized that some of the skills that we train people in are things that can actually be very useful to her in the job she does."

On Valentine's Day, 1990, the Princess was guest of honor at the Family of the Year luncheon, held at the Inn on the Park in London. Launched by RELATE with *Woman's Own* magazine, the idea was to find a family who show love, loyalty, care, and support for each other and also contribute to the community by helping people outside the family. Hundreds of families were nominated from all social and cultural backgrounds across Britain: families who had been together for many years or only a few, one-parent families, second marriage and stepfamilies. The response was heartening at a time when 37 percent of marriages end in divorce and when forecasts suggest, following current trends, that in the decade to the year 2000, about three million Britons will experience divorce, involving 1½ million children under the age of sixteen. Heather and Rico Gopaul and their four children from Colchester, Essex, were chosen as the Family of the Year. Diana presented a glass goblet to them after saying:

> The award is really intended as a tribute to the thousands of families whose daily lives are constructive, loving, and unselfish. These are the families who give of their best, to each other and to society, while quietly coping with a daunting array of pressures.
>
> In this room there is no shortage of experts on the subject of marriage breakdown. I'm sure that they all have at their fingertips the statistics which prove the damage of divorce—

felt in education, employment, crime, even in the national economy. I know also, from my own visits to their offices around the country that the experts of RELATE have daily contact with the distress which underlies the statistics.

Marriage offers stability, and maybe that is why nearly seven thousand couples a week begin new family lives of their own. Sadly for many of these marriages, reality fails to live up to expectations. When that happens, most couples discover and draw on new reserves of love and strength. But for many, their own resources are not enough.

More than mere guidance, RELATE offers some marriages the support which will strengthen them to overcome a crisis. To others it offers hope through and after divorce. In short, RELATE helps people keep going. In ways too often unnoticed, its work enriches and supports the fabric of society.

This may all seem a far cry from the Family of the Year. But we should remember that the award celebrates the victory of very simple values over the very complex difficulties confronted by so many modern marriages. I offer my congratulations to all families who remain cheerful, positive and loving in adversity—and I offer my support to everyone who helps them in the task.

It goes without saying that RELATE is delighted to have Diana as Patron. David French said:

The Princess has already begun to influence the way our work is understood by the public at large. The great thing that we see in her all the time is that she has a natural talent for getting on with people. It just naturally flows out of her. She connects with people very, very quickly. That's a pretty essential quality for a counselor, and obviously therefore she finds herself getting on terribly well with people she meets in RELATE. She was enthusiastic from the start. She's developed a very clear understanding of the fact that we are there not to "patch up marriages" or "to dole out advice" but, as one of my colleagues puts it, to hold up a mirror to a couple and enable them to see themselves more clearly. And *they* make the decisions, we don't. The great thing is the warmth that the Princess manages to communicate, coupled with her informality. She's wonderfully unstuffy, which takes a lot of people by surprise.

There is a degree of royal formality, but it's fairly thin. And people take to her very well, partly because of that. She's a very gracious person as well as being very informal, and that's a remarkable combination, I think. She's royal, she's beautiful, and she has this spontaneity and naturalness and openness and warmth. And she combines these things, apparently totally effortlessly, without losing any of her dignity. And I think that's a great gift.

Obviously there's generally a level of apprehension before people meet her, but that evaporates very quickly. We have our share of skeptics around the place, and I can think of one or two people who really weren't enthusiastic, and one felt they were there because they were part of the team and they'd been told they'd got to be on parade, who were saying afterward, "That was really quite something." She's much more intuitive than intellectual. She's on the whole more interested in the practical than the theoretical basis of RELATE's work. She's also deeply interested in finding out from a practical point of view what a man and woman each bring to a relationship from their childhood experiences and what makes the relationship work.

One of the things that I have observed over the last year or two is that she's becoming very much more confident of herself, and I think the work she's doing for RELATE and for the other organizations with which she is linked has played its part in helping her to gain that extra confidence. We are one of the roles that she has found which have helped to give her a distinctive, serious identity of her own. She isn't any longer just the wife of the Prince of Wales. She isn't any longer just a beautiful clotheshorse. She is a serious person with a distinctive role. She'll contribute more valuable insights now during discussions at RELATE and voice her opinions more. I think that is partly because she knows more, she knows more about us, and has learned from other places, and can contribute to a discussion from the basis of what she's learned from the previous one. She makes her own observations on things more and more, in ways which astonish people at how perceptive she is about what's going on around her and about the things that are being discussed, quite often in relation to children but also in relation to things that concern a man's relationship with a woman and vice versa, things to do with family relationships.

Her role is very distinctive. If you look at the things she's taken on, us for example, Turning Point, and so on, very many of them—and I think the great majority of the ones that she is actually most closely involved with—are organizations that ten or fifteen years ago would never have dreamed themselves of getting royal patronage. And the Royal Family would probably never have dreamed of providing it. It's not the kind of cause that people in general, and the Royal Family in particular, were likely to want to support. But the Princess of Wales is happy and willing to take on causes which might once have been considered unpopular—like leprosy or drugs or AIDS—and she is undoubtedly doing a good job. There has also been a stigma, though to a much lesser extent, attached to marriage counseling, which by her involvement with RELATE she is helping to remove. It's noticed that she is our Patron, and it's made an enormous difference to the public perception. Marriage counseling is an essential support to marriage and family life, yet many people still don't accept it. The Princess helps to redress that balance, counteracting the negative, and she has a very positive influence as well. And that's not just in stamping her own fresh, youthful image on RELATE. It's also saying that one of the most popular and best-loved members of the Royal Family is saying it's okay to go there.

And what of Diana's own marriage, dare one ask? Does the expert think she's happily married? Mr. French, put on the spot, paused thoughtfully. "Yes," he said. "This is a field in which it is least appropriate to comment, and of course we don't see her private life. But judging from appearances—yes, I believe she is."

RESIDENCES

Diana was born and spent her childhood at Park House, a spacious Victorian house with ten bedrooms on the Queen's Sandringham estate in Norfolk. Long after she and her family moved out, the house became a Leonard Cheshire Foundation home for disabled people. But during renovation work on the building before the official opening in July 1987, Diana's old nursery window, on which she had scratched friends' names and telephone numbers as a child, was saved and sent to her as a keepsake. She was very attached to her first home, where the whole family had been together before her parents split up.

Prince Harry enjoys a pony ride around the Queen's Sandringham estate.
(Jim Bennett/Alpha)

She is said to have made several visits there in secret to see it
again and to wander nostalgically around the grounds and the
rooms where she had played in happy days of old before the
renovations changed the place forever.

The Spencers left Park House in 1975 when Diana's father
succeeded to the earldom, becoming the 8th Earl Spencer, and
inherited the family stately home, Althorp, in Northampton, to
which they moved. Fifteen generations of Spencers have lived
there since the original medieval manorhouse, then surrounded by
a moat, was bought by the first Sir John Spencer in 1508. In
1573, during the reign of Queen Elizabeth I, the two red-brick
wings enclosing the forecourt were added by his grandson, also Sir
John. In 1666, builders began work on the impressive staircase,
which three centuries later Diana (and later still, William) liked to

toboggan down on a teatray. Around 1790, the house was refaced with silvery white tiles by Henry Holland, called in by the 2nd Earl Spencer. And John Wootton was commissioned to paint the enormous hunting pictures which hang in the splendid entrance hall, where Diana practiced her tap dancing on the marble floor.

Two visions tourists to Althorp are unlikely to catch sight of, however, are Diana herself, who apparently tends to stay with her sister Jane at another house in the grounds, and a ghost. After his stroke (see FAMILY), Diana's father apparently thought that a ghost at Althorp might have brought ill health upon him, so he asked a clergyman friend, the Reverend Victor Malon, to exorcise the place for him. The identity of this ghost is unclear, but it has been suggested that after his death Diana's grandfather, the 7th Earl, haunted Althorp, or at least popped up on occasion. He and Diana's father apparently did not get on.

After she left school and began work (see EDUCATION and JOBS), Diana lived at her mother's house in London at 69 Cadogan Place, which she shared with her schoolfriends Laura Grieg, from West Heath, and Sophie Kimball, from the Swiss finishing school. Then, after coming into an inheritance from her American great-grandmother when she was eighteen (see AMERICA), she bought a flat of her own at 60 Coleherne Court in West London, thought to have cost about £60,000. The flat had three bedrooms, and she initially shared it with Sophie and another friend, Philippa Coaker, and later with the three girls who were there at the time of her engagement to Prince Charles: Carolyn Pride, from West Heath; Ann Bolton, who worked at Savill's, the real estate agents; and Virginia Pitman. Plus a goldfish called Battersea. Once she was engaged, Diana moved out (see QUOTES) to stay briefly with the Queen Mother at Clarence House. Then she moved into a suite of rooms on the same floor as Prince Charles's apartment at Buckingham Palace for a few months before their wedding and until a London base was prepared for them at Kensington Palace.

Meanwhile, with the help of her mother's interior designer, Dudley Poplak, she got to grips with the decorating and furnishing of Highgrove, their country home in Tetbury in Gloucestershire, which the Duchy of Cornwall had bought for Prince Charles for £800,000 in 1980 after he had fallen in love with the walled garden. He was very pleased to be given a complete set of fruit trees as a wedding present from the Fruiterers' Company, a party of whom were later invited to visit Highgrove. The Sussex branch of the Women's Institute provided a herb garden, and Charles's naturalist friend Miriam Rothschild, who is an expert on fleas and watches butterflies as a hobby, helped him develop the wildflower garden he wanted by the front drive.

Highgrove previously belonged to former Tory Prime Minister Harold Macmillan's son Maurice. It is a Georgian mansion with four reception rooms; nine bedrooms; six bathrooms; an impregnable and fully stocked "Iron Room," actually lined with steel, where Charles and Diana and their children could survive for months under any terrorist attack; and a heated swimming pool in the back yard with a hutch nearby for William and Harry's black-and-white rabbit. Together with the original 350 acres of land around the house, Charles also now has Broadfield Farm next door, where he has sheep and a dairy herd. For the interior of the house, Diana chose pastel shades and chintz fabrics. Off the peach entrance hall, where the back French windows lead to the garden terrace, there are four main rooms: Diana's sitting room, Charles's study (which because of his fury if anyone moves anything from his desk has a notice forbidding it), a dining room which can seat twenty, and a main drawing room. The kitchen is an all-electric German one stuffed with gadgets. And the whole house and grounds, of course, bristle with security devices and cameras.

Much the same can be said of Kensington Palace, nicknamed KP and the Aunt Heap. Although the Prince and Princess's address is Apartments Number 8 and 9 Kensington Palace, it is actually a twenty-five-room house with a sun terrace, greenhouse, and barbecue on the roof garden. Apart from the garish green-and-gray carpet, featuring the Prince of Wales's feathers, which greets visitors in the entrance hall, Diana's pastel shades predominate. The ground floor of the three-story, L-shaped building houses offices. The key rooms, as at Highgrove but on the first floor, are the main drawing room, in shades of peach and yellow (where receptions for up to sixty people are held); Diana's sitting room, with the Prince of Wales's feathers on the wallpaper, where the family curl up to watch TV; Charles's study; and a dining room with a huge circular table which seats sixteen and where the twice-yearly planning meetings are held with their aides to fix royal engagements for the months ahead. The main bedroom is also on the first floor, with bathrooms leading off (see BEDS & BEDROOMS and BATHS & BATHROOMS), plus dressing rooms, vast walk-in closets for Diana's clothes, and a room for Charles's uniforms. See UNIFORMS. The children's and nannies' bedrooms are in the nursery suite on the second floor. On a window ledge of Diana's sitting room, she keeps a treasured souvenir from childhood: her old school trunk, made of pine, with her name D. Spencer on the front. Some of the State, but not private, Apartments at Kensington Palace are open to the public.

The couple also have holiday homes. See HOLIDAYS.

In November 1990, Diana officially reopened her family's magnificent old London home, Spencer House, at St. James's Place, which had been restored to glory at a cost of £16 million by the tenant, RIT Capital Partners, whose Chairman is Lord Rothschild. Open to the public from spring 1991, rooms can also be hired for approved functions from £2,500 to £10,000 per night. See FRIENDS.

RESTAURANTS

Restaurants are checked before Diana eats out privately, and her bodyguard sits at the next table. Her favorite restaurants in London include San Lorenzo at Beauchamp Place off Knightsbridge, a popular haunt of London café society and celebrities like Dustin Hoffman and Mick Jagger. Girlfriends she gossips with there over lunch include Caroline Twiston-Davies, who works nearby on Walton Street. The crudités (raw vegetables served as a starter) and hot anchovy sauce are said to be "divine." She has also been spotted lunching with her sister Lady Jane Fellowes at La Fontana, an Italian spot in Pimlico, and Launceston Place, a restaurant close to Kensington Palace, where they both live. With dancer friend Wayne Sleep, Diana has eaten pasta at Luigi's in Covent Garden and monkfish at the Groucho Club in Soho, haunt of literary, television, and other media folk and source of the odd saucy yarn in the British satirical magazine *Private Eye*.

Other friends have taken her to the upstairs restaurant at

L'Escargot on Greek Street, Soho, managed by the legendary Elena Salvoni, formerly of Bianchi's on Frith Street, and frequented by international literati and glitterati, many of whose photographs adorn the walls. Regulars include Melvyn Bragg and John Hurt. It was there, in a party which included portly Member of Parliament Nicholas Soames (see FRIENDS), that Diana was alleged to have wept at the table. The story, apparently leaked to the Press by another customer, was later denied.

The Harvey Nichols store in Knightsbridge used to be a regular lunch spot, handy in the middle of a shopping spree with a girlfriend. She has been seen eating at Mosimann's; Mortons; Harry's Bar; the Caprice; Ménage à Trois; Green's Champagne, Oyster Bar & Restaurant; the Hind's Head at Bray; eating Chinese food at the Tai Pan in Chelsea with Nicholas Soames; enjoying the Mao Tai Special Feast in Parsons Green; and tucking in with Fergie at the Chelsea Harbour restaurant of Ken Lo, who had already given the Duchess a wok and presented them both with Chinese cookery books. Diana's favorite London restaurants before her marriage were Topolino D'Ischia on Draycott Avenue, the Santa Croce on Cheyne Walk, La Poule au Pot on Ebury Street, and the San Quintino on Radnor Walk.

Diana has taken her sons out for hamburgers at McDonald's and, in a party, to the Chicken Rib Shack, where barbecued ribs and chicken were ordered. In November 1990, she drove off the A1 highway at Astwick, Bedfordshire, so that William could have burger and fries with Coca-Cola at a packed Happy Eater restaurant. The boys have also had snacks with Mum at the aptly named Café Diana near Kensington Palace. See COOKING and FOOD & DRINK.

ROYAL PROTECTION SQUAD

Since she became engaged to Prince Charles, Diana has learned what it is never to be alone, even when she's off-duty. For security reasons, she is guarded at all times by armed detectives from the SAS-trained Royal Protection Squad whose proper name is the Royalty Protection Department—the cream of the male crop from the Metropolitan Police force. See MONEY. She can't even go shopping, to church, out to lunch, or on vacation without them. Nor is she supposed to drive anywhere without a detective and a backup car or even to keep her own car keys. It is said that on occasions she goes "absolutely mad" at the lack of privacy, at times whispering, "I wish, I wish . . ." as she yearns for the freedom she has lost. There are, however, compensations. Many women in today's dangerous world would be glad to have some hunky, handsome, armed he-man in tow to protect them, carry the shopping bags, and stop their car from being given the boot when it is parked illegally. When hubby is not around, it is also useful to have another man present to play with the children, help them build sandcastles on the beach, give them swimming lessons in the sea, and take them on a pedalo (children's boat) trip, as William and Harry's bodyguard Detective Sergeant David Sharp did on their vacation in Majorca in 1988. Diana's minder, Inspector Ken Wharf, was reportedly even her tango partner during her moms-and-children vacation on Necker in the Virgin Islands in April 1990. A crackshot former soldier who carries a rapid-fire Smith and Wesson .38 revolver, Wharf is known to colleagues as Mr. Flamboyant.

In September 1989 Sharp replaced Diana's long-term minder, six-foot-four-inch, 230-pound Sergeant Allan Peters, a top marksman, rider, skier, and swimmer nicknamed Big Al and the Hulk, as her personal bodyguard. Peters was the cop who shouted, "Get out of the way!" to clear a path, then grabbed the Princess and declared, "Come on, we're getting out of here," when he sensed potential trouble during her visit in February 1985 to the notorious Broadwater Farm Estate in Tottenham, north London, scene of the later riot in which Police Constable Keith Blakelock was hacked to death. "The one good thing about guarding a woman is that if the worst happens, you can pick her up and run for it," Peters said later. However, the police service still has a macho image, and some cops prefer guarding men.

One of the first minders assigned to Diana, on her engagement, was Chief Inspector Paul Officer, who had long been a bodyguard of Prince Charles. When the Prince was in the Royal Navy in 1974, Officer had saved him from a naval officer with a knife who went berserk and broke into the Prince's quarters at the naval barracks in Portland, Dorset, where Charles was sleeping. But after less than five months at the side of the bride-to-be, Officer asked for a transfer and later took charge of a police station in south London. Another hazard when a man sees a woman as often as Diana's shadows see her—which is more often than many a man sees his spouse—is that the relationship has to be good, but not too good. Diana allegedly found one cop, Detective Inspector David Robinson, overprotective. Since this apparently made her feel nervous and he wasn't overkeen on trailing around shops with her, he went on to guard other members of the Royal Family. Another, Sergeant Barry Mannakee, who was tragically killed later in a motorcycle accident, left amid newspaper claims that he had been "overfamiliar" with the Princess. However, a friend revealed that his transfer had nothing to do with Diana, and Mannakee himself cited "domestic reasons—the job meant long hours away from home," a problem for all those with wives and children who serve the Royal Family, especially those who accompany them on extensive overseas tours. It is seldom a recipe for an easy marriage. See STAFF.

Relationships, of course, also grow with the royal children, whose detectives accompany them to school. David Sharp, one of their bodyguards, apparently became a sort of "deputy Dad" to William and Harry, who both cried when he wasn't at Harry's fourth birthday party in September 1988, from which Charles was alleged to have banned him. When, a year later, he was appointed personal bodyguard to Diana instead, in place of Allan Peters, royalty watchers saw it not so much as a sign of displeasure with Peters but as an attempt by the Princess to nip the children's attachment to Sharp in the bud. After seven years' service with the Princess, and only five months after pouncing on a fifty-six-year-old joiner who had lunged from a crowd and grabbed Diana's arm during a walkabout in Northumberland, Peters, aged forty-two, was switched to the Royal Family's general protection staff.

Diana arranged for her most senior detective, Inspector Graham Smith, nicknamed Smudger, to be awarded the Royal Victorian Order in the 1987 New Year Honor's List as a public thank-you for his service to her since she became engaged. See HOLIDAYS. She has also popped in to have tea with his wife, Eunice. In

December 1989 Diana became the first member of the Royal
Family ever to attend the Royal Protection Squad's annual Christmas party in the Royal Mews.

To ward off any attack, it is said that the Princess, along with
other members of the Royal Family, has learned unarmed combat
from members of the SAS based at Hereford. She has also learned
antiterrorist driving techniques. See MOTORING and BOOKS.
There have been many security scares over the years. In 1985,
two girls broke into Kensington Palace, where sixteen members of
the Royal Family and several royal aides live. On the eve of
Charles and Diana's visit to Portugal in February 1987, while they
and their children slept at Kensington Palace, a man with a knife
and hammer was arrested after a chase and struggle with police in
the grounds. And in September 1989, newsmen alleged, Irish
laborers working on a Palace building project without proper
security passes included a convicted killer and a kidnapper. In
May 1989, two weeks after the incident in Northumberland,
police seized and quizzed a forty-one-year-old man armed with a
gas-powered air pistol in a crowd gathered to welcome Diana in
Cardiff. In May 1990 a former Buckingham Palace swimming
pool attendant complained about lax security checks and claimed
he could have drowned Diana during her morning swims. See
SPORT. In April, there was a bomb scare at Victoria station, where
she and Charles were waiting to greet the President of India. In
June, woods behind Highgrove were combed after a gamekeeper
heard shots. In mid-July 1990, just after Diana opened a conference in Brighton, five demonstrators with placards paraded close
to her on the platform shouting, "Lesbian and gay rights now!" A
week later, a crude incendiary device in a package addressed to the
Princess was intercepted by security staff at Buckingham Palace.
And the same month, she was rushed from Claridge's hotel after
a suspicious case was found. A day later, she had to leave a dinner
in the West End because of a terrorist alert. At the end of July, a
man with a gun was arrested before her walkabout through a
crowded shopping area in Inverness. In November, an Iranian
admirer, twice arrested trying to see her at Kensington Palace, was
ordered to be deported. The previous month, following a series of
IRA outrages, the Princess was protected by police officers in

combat gear openly carrying 9-mm MP5 Heckler and Koch machine guns (also used by the American Secret Service and FBI to protect VIPs) during a visit to Cumbria. (The bullets can pierce bulletproof vests and walls and could even shoot someone dead three rooms away.) And in December, three IRA suspects were arrested in Antwerp prior to Diana's visit to Brussels. See BELGIUM.

No one can forget that Lord Mountbatten was blown to pieces by the IRA, who planted a fifty-pound remote-control bomb on his fishing boat, *Shadow V*, in county Sligo in August 1979. See SPAIN. That an armed man tried to kidnap Princess Anne and shot five people in the process—including *Daily Mirror* journalist Brian McConnell, who went to the rescue—in the Mall in March 1974. Or that Buckingham Palace intruder Michael Fagan managed to slip through security and confront the Queen in her bed in June 1982.

For Diana and the rest of the Royal Family, security is a problem they have to live with daily. At Ludgrove prep school, according to one report, Prince William has to wear an electronic homing device similar to one issued to Prince Charles years ago to keep track of his movements when out hunting and fishing. Scares can also involve security officers themselves. In October 1990, it was reported that Scotland Yard had launched an inquiry into how secret papers listing the addresses and telephone numbers of royal bodyguards had come to be dumped in a truck lot in west London.

But sometimes there are lighter moments. William and Harry laughed with glee when a loud bang made Diana jump at the International Show Jumping Championships at Olympia in London in December 1989. And William's previous school, Wetherby, was evacuated on one occasion when a police sniffer dog "went crazy" during a routine explosives search of lockers at an adjoining school. The "secret cache" in a fourteen-year-old boy's locker which got the labrador excited turned out not to be explosives but two chocolate bars.

There were no smiles, however, on New Year's Eve 1990 when, apparently upset after a quarrel at Sandringham, Diana sparked a major security scare by driving alone to the beach in Snettisham, Norfolk, and walking for almost an hour in solitude through the puddles, head bowed and lost in thought. The peace and sea breezes may have calmed her down; but in the absence of her bodyguards, she had made herself a sitting duck. As it was, fortunately, she became only the target for a cameraman's lens.

S

SHOPPING

Diana hates being tagged a shopaholic, but there is no doubt she loves shopping and shops as no British royal has ever done before. For her, of course, shopping has always been a normal part of life. The difference is that now she's accompanied by a bodyguard and sometimes a Lady-in-Waiting or a friend within the family, like Fergie or Princess Margaret's daughter Lady Sarah Armstrong-Jones. Her favorite stores are Harvey Nichols and Harrods, where she gets special treatment. At Christmas 1984, after Harrods opened early so that she could take Prince William to visit Santa Claus, Diana nipped back a second time to buy a £365 rocking horse he'd spotted, complete with real horsehair and tack, for the royal nursery. She bought most of the children's Christmas presents from Harrods' toy department that year. She has also shopped for toys at the Early Learning Centre in Kensington, where she bought a Think and Match puzzle just before Prince Harry's hernia operation, and at Frog Hollow. See COLLECTIONS.

She has bought sweatshirts, knitwear, and trousers for the children from Benetton's childrenswear shop in Kensington, where manager Sohella Therabaldi said in November 1988, "She always buys two of everything. She's very friendly and informal and always has a chat and a joke." Her favorite childrenswear shop is said to be Anthea Moore Ede in Victoria Grove, where she has bought Viyella shirts, tweed knickerbockers, and Osh Kosh overalls for her sons. She also got Osh Kosh overalls and some sweaters from Meenys on Kensington High Street; and a French dungaree suit for £275 from a rather grand boutique near Edgware Road which also sells mink coats for rich kids. Diana skipped those, no doubt to the relief of Prince Charles, who's been said to turn pale on occasion at his wife's bills. See MONEY. She bought William's hand-smocked silk and satin baby romper suits from the White House on New Bond Street and the blue snowsuit in which he took his first steps at Kensington Palace in December 1983 from Bimbo on Kendal Street.

For her own sweaters, she goes to Inca, a boutique on Elizabeth Street, off Eaton Square, and Warm & Wonderful. Shopping locally in Kensington, she has been to Tomlinson, to Hyper Hyper, and to the adult branch of Benetton, where she has also bought blouses, trousers, and skirts. When she popped in to the Knightsbridge branch to buy T-shirts and a pair of Bermuda shorts in 1983, the manager Guiditta Dellanna told her she was "looking too thin and should eat plenty of lasagne to fatten up." But despite being a regular Benetton customer, Diana has had problems with their strict rules over returning purchases when she has tried to do it without having the receipt. She also selects clothes—size 10—from the Mondi and Laurel catalogs sent to her by Harrods. See BEAUTY SECRETS, FASHION, and JEWELRY.

For household goods, she likes the General Trading Company and has shopped at Casa Pupo. She pops downstairs to the food hall at her local Marks and Spencers to buy muffins and sliced white bread for the bacon sandwiches she adores. "We often see her in here with her bodyguard," said a salesgirl in November 1988. "She always buys convenience food." She also goes to Sainsbury's supermarket in Cromwell Road, a branch so large that some shoppers are said to roller-skate down the aisles, to buy food for the children's tea. She has been spotted with cookies, cakes, cereals, and convenience foods in her wire basket. She once declared that she enjoyed nothing better than pushing a cart around a supermarket. The branch manager, Graham Naylor, said in April 1988, "She comes here about every five weeks. She knows what she wants and is out again in five minutes. Everyone gets caught short of things sometimes, and we are handy for the Palace." "She's usually got jeans on and a sweater," said the parking lot attendant, "and hardly anyone recognizes her. She's brought one of her boys and they get sweets. They also seem to like those little cereal packets. I think the cakes are for Diana. If it wasn't for her detective, nobody would give her a second look. She sort of drags the poor bloke around. He looks proper fed up." See FOOD & DRINK.

When she is at Highgrove, Diana goes shopping—sometimes in baggy shorts, sweatshirt, and a baseball cap—in Cirencester, where she regularly buys greeting cards from the Surprises gift shop, and Bath, where she goes to the Bowes and Bowes book shop and the local branch of The Body Shop. At Tetbury, close to Highgrove, she has nipped into J. and C. News to buy jelly babies for Prince William, visited an antique shop, and shopped at the Safeway supermarket. At Gateway, other customers were surprised to find her queuing at the checkout to buy her purchases, which included a package of hamburgers. While she is at Balmoral, she goes shopping in the town of Ballater, where George Smith sells fishing tackle at one of the very few shops Prince Charles has ever been known to visit to make purchases.

SPAIN

Charles and Diana's four-day visit to Spain in April 1987 began with an embarrassing incident for one of their bodyguards, Allan Peters. See ROYAL PROTECTION SQUAD. He handed his passport to an immigration official at Madrid airport, who found the ink had run and it was barely readable. It seems Allan's wife had put his lightweight jacket into the washing machine the night before without realizing he had already tucked his passport into his inside breast pocket to make sure he didn't leave it behind in the morning! A long line built up behind the royal detective before the matter was sorted out. The tour also began on an irritating note for Charles who, at the controls of the aircraft as he and his wife flew in, was kept stacked up over Madrid. Then he was directed to a cargo bay by Spanish air controllers who apparently thought he was flying a cargo plane, delaying their arrival at the right spot by ten minutes.

At the beginning of the visit, the royal couple toured the famous Prado art gallery, much of whose collection has been built up since the sixteenth century by Spanish monarchs, where Diana displayed an unexpected knowledge of art. "The Princess knew which paintings were by whom," said her guide. "She recognized every Velazquez and Goya before I could say a word." She was particularly interested to see Goya's paintings of the Maja, clothed

Charles, Diana, William, and Harry spend a sunny afternoon in Majorca with King Juan Carlos (at right), Queen Sofia, and Prince Felipe of Spain. (Globe Photos)

and nude. See MARRIAGE. In Salamanca, she was overcome by the heat during a tour of the museum and had to ask for a glass of water before resting in private for ten minutes and going on to the university, the oldest in Europe. There the royal couple were serenaded by students dressed in medieval troubadour costumes, who flung down their cloaks, in the style of Sir Walter Raleigh, for the Princess to walk on. See PORTUGAL. On the final day, King Juan Carlos drove the couple in his gold-painted minibus to the ancient hilltop city of Toledo, where they walked around the narrow cobbled streets like tourists, shopping for souvenirs. If Prince Charles was growing increasingly irritated by the limelight thrown on his wife and she was aware of it, it may explain why in Spain, and later at Cannes, she seemed to be placing herself more in the background and walking three steps behind him.

However, there was no such reticence in some of her clothes, though these had probably been ordered months before. Indeed, 1987 was a vintage year for Diana's fashion-gimmick disasters—

an orangy red satin jacket with a black bow tie for the ballet in Lisbon that February; a white, gold-braided majorette suit, also known as her "chocolate soldier outfit," for a visit to Sandhurst Military Academy in April; a ridiculous puffball dress in Cannes that May; and for a fashion show in Madrid, she donned a hideous theatrical turquoise blue outfit with gold braiding by Rifat Ozbek, which the Press declared would have been better suited to a pantomime principal boy.

The tour was also notable for the row which erupted when an off-the-record remark made by Prince Charles at a reception for British and Spanish Press covering the tour appeared in print. In view of the security laid on to guard the royal couple in Spain, where Basque separatists have been active for years (see BOOKS), a local journalist had raised the question of terrorism with the Prince. "I wouldn't have thought I was a target," Charles said. "If I am, it would be more likely with the IRA [see ROYAL PROTEC- TION SQUAD]. But if your name is on the bullet, there's nothing you can do about it." The remark was published in newspapers in Spain and Britain. It was by no means the first time that this sort of leak had occurred from such receptions, which have been a feature of royal tours for decades. But later it became clear that the royal couple had had enough when Press receptions usually held at the start of the Prince and Princess's overseas visits were stopped. British journalist Harry Arnold (see PRESS) says now:

> There were a number of stories which appeared in print which came out of the Press receptions. Sometimes it was foreign journalists, in some cases it was us Brits. And because of that the Prince of Wales said he didn't want to hold any more meetings with the Press. My theory is that it was a bit of an excuse. He knows, and so does the Queen and Diana, when they're tempting you too strongly. After his famous remark in Spain, I thought, "How could he really think that would *not* get into print?" He's much too aware of what makes newspa- pers tick not to realize otherwise.

At the end of the tour, the Prince and Princess went to stay with their friends, the Marquess of Douro, heir to the 8th Duke of Wellington, and his wife Antonia (see FRIENDS) on the family's

2,200-acre estate near Granada, given to the 1st Duke by Madrid as a thank-you for helping to drive Napoleon from Spain. There Charles got back to his sketching while Diana sunbathed.

Diana then returned home to the children, while Charles flew to Italy to receive an award, sketch, and see friends. However, the reason for his Italian trip, and even the fact that he was going there, was not announced by the Palace in advance. This led (before the facts were discovered) to a lot of unnecessary Press digging and speculation about the Prince and a lovely Italian Contessa, Fiammetta Frescobaldi (who later wed), which no doubt added to Charles's aggravation.

SPEECHES

Diana has always been terrified of making speeches. In this respect she is in the shadow of Fergie, who can confidently give passionate orations in English *and* French, one of Diana's worst subjects at school. However, they're both put in the shade by Prince Charles, who on visits overseas has made responses, however brief, in numerous languages, some of which most of us have never heard of. Nevertheless, Diana has always been a trier. When she made her first-ever speech as the Princess of Wales in October 1981, receiving the Freedom of the City of Cardiff, she also hazarded her first public words in Welsh. Very nervously but with moral support from Prince Charles on the sidelines, she said:

> I am extremely grateful to you, Lord Mayor, and to the City Council and to the City of Cardiff for granting me the Freedom of the City. I realize that this is a very great honor and I am most grateful. I would like to try to express my thanks to you in Welsh also.
>
> Y mae'n bleser cael dod i Cymru. Hoffwn ddod eto yn faun. Diolch yn fawr.
>
> I do hope that bore some relationship to what I meant to say, which is basically that it is a very great pleasure for me to come to Wales and to its capital, Cardiff. I look forward to returning many times in the future. Also I'd just like to add how proud I am to be Princess of such a beautiful place and of the Welsh people, who are very special to me.

In her first three years as a princess, Diana spoke barely five hundred words in public and having recognized herself that speeches were not her forte (see EDUCATION) has made remarkably few since. At first, through sheer nerves, she would gabble out the words in a rush. Then, after learning to talk more slowly, she would break up sentences in a stilted way, making the sense difficult to follow. She still tends to speak in a monotone, and she would benefit from lowering her voice and being more relaxed. Imagining she's speaking to *one* person, like her mother—the trick that's supposed to help if you appear on TV or radio—might help. But she has improved, apparently with guidance from the royals' friend Sir Richard Attenborough (see RADIO), the actor, film producer and director, and Chairman of the Royal Academy of Dramatic Art, of which Diana is President.

As she has become more and more involved with the aims and concerns of the charities and organizations she represents, she has also learned to replace blandness in her speeches with more commitment and passion, proving to be an effective campaigner. She still on occasion needs to identify more clearly the central message she is trying to get across, and then to express it as simply as possible. But once she is relaxed enough to *enjoy* making speeches, she will no doubt get much better. See BARNARDO'S, CHILD ACCIDENT PREVENTION TRUST, DEAF, DRUGS, EDUCATION, HIV, NATIONAL RUBELLA COUNCIL, RELATE, and TURNING POINT.

Sport

Diana was very sporty at school and still is. See EDUCATION. She particularly loves swimming, and a diving cup which she won as a schoolgirl now stands in her dressing room at Highgrove. At Park House, where she spent her childhood, there was a heated swimming pool, which Prince Andrew and Prince Edward used to pop across from Sandringham House to use. The Princess swims to relax rather than to keep trim, and she likes to do twenty lengths every morning. Usually she nips to the pool at Buckingham Palace, though she is also reported to have taken William and Harry to a local swimming pool closer to Kensington Palace. All

On holiday in Lichtenstein, Diana enjoys a downhill run. (Glenn Harvey/ Camera Press London)

three go swimming at a nearby club when they are at Balmoral. See HEALTH. And Diana likes to make sure she gets her daily morning dip on tour abroad when possible, though this can produce problems. See HONG KONG. The pink-and-black swim-suit she wore on vacation at Necker in the Virgin Islands in January 1989 was made from neoprene, a material developed from a synthetic rubber worn by British frogmen during the war, and it gave rubber swimwear the royal stamp of approval. Rubber swimsuits became hot fashion—yet another of the trends Diana has set. See FASHION.

Since childhood Diana has been a big tennis fan. She always

watched Wimbledon on television at school and used to be taken there on the first Saturday each year by her mother. The Royal Family on the whole are not tennis fans. The Queen has attended Wimbledon fortnight on only three occasions, in 1957, 1962, and 1977. The lack of interest is sad in view of the fact that King George VI, then the Duke of York (who often played tennis with Diana's grandfather, Lord Fermoy), won the 1926 RAF doubles at Wimbledon with Louis Greig. He was also the first royal to compete in the actual Wimbledon tournament, though he and Greig conceded after three sets. King Henry VIII popularized the forerunner of the modern game, known as real or royal tennis in Britain, court tennis in the United States, royal tennis in Australia, and *jeu de paume* in France, where it originated. (Five hundred years ago, before they had rackets, players used the palm of their hands to hit the ball.) There is still one of the extraordinary indoor, real tennis courts—with window nets and a bell which rings if you hit the ball into the right spot—in use at Hampton Court Palace today. Built in 1625, it is possible to see it, play there, and take lessons, provided you book well in advance. But be warned: the rules and scoring are complicated. Prince Edward is a very keen player and a member of the club there, which is called the Royal Tennis Court.

Diana was able to watch the semifinals and finals at Wimbledon from the Royal Box for the first time in 1981. Charles, who has shown little enthusiasm for the game though she hopes to kindle his interest, wasn't with her. When tennis star Chrissie Evert (then married to English tennis player John Lloyd) asked why not, Diana replied, "It's because he can never sit still. He is like a great big baby. But one day I hope to calm him down enough to enjoy it." Charles has said in the past that he's a doer, not a watcher, and anyway he prefers dangerous sports like polo, hunting, and skiing in which life and limb are often at risk. One of the Princess's tennis heroes is John "You're the Pits" McEnroe. At Wimbledon in 1989, Diana sat on the center court with Fergie and their friend Kate Menzies watching as McEnroe beat Mats Wilander and giggling at some private joke. The source of their amusement seemed to be the size of the enormous floppy straw hat worn by McEnroe's wife, Tatum O'Neal, or the contrast between that and the black cloche obscuring the forehead of her female companion.

Diana laughed even more the following year during the ladies' semifinal between Steffi Graf and Zena Garrison when a pied-wagtail raising five chicks in a nest beneath the Royal Box, named Waddle after the way it walked, disturbed play by hopping round the court and setting off the "magic eye" electronic bleeper signaling service faults. Steffi lost the match and was wiped out of the tournament. The previous year, when Steffi was Wimbledon champion, Diana had hoped to watch her play in the women's final, but the match was rained out until the following day. Steffi recalled then that it was "a very sad Princess" who called at her dressing room and said, "I have waited the whole day in the hope of seeing your final . . . and tomorrow I've no time, worst luck." The twenty-year-old German star also revealed that Diana had asked her to coach seven-year-old Prince William. "She has asked me several times if I can give her son an hour's lesson," Steffi said. "She told me he is absolutely mad about tennis. Of course I shall treat him more gently than I did Martina Navratilova!" In 1988, Steffi had played a mixed doubles match at the swish Vanderbilt Racquet Club in Shepherd's Bush, London, with Diana, who had remarked before they began, "I'm very nervous. I'm not very good, you know. But I love the game." Of her playing, Steffi said, "She was very good—she surprised me. She has a good serve and forehand, but perhaps her backhand needs a little work." They beat two of the club's male players 6–5.

The Vanderbilt has held doubles tournaments to raise funds for Birthright, of which Diana is Patron (see BIRTHRIGHT), and she presented the trophies. In the first two in which Diana competed, she was twice knocked out in the second round. She has lessons from the club's senior coach, Rex Seymour-Lyn. The co-owner, Charles Swallow, is a former history master at Harrow, comprehensive school headmaster, and rackets champion. See FRIENDS. William and Harry have tennis tuition there too. Diana is also an Honorary Member of the All England Lawn Tennis and Croquet Club, Britain's first and foremost tennis club, founded in 1877, which holds Wimbledon fortnight, and of the David Lloyd Slazenger Club at Hounslow in Middlesex. She apparently doesn't use the court at Highgrove because of whiffs from the nearby compost heap, but she has played locally at the Hare and Hounds Hotel in Westonbirt. She was Honorary President of the Federation Cup 1991, the fifty-six-nation women's team tennis championship played in Nottingham that July, sponsored by the Japanese communications company NEC.

Diana's family had their own cricket pitch at Park House and have one at Althorp, and both her father and brother love playing. Viscount Althorp plays home matches at Althorp with his own side and also skippered a team from NBC television, his former employer. After Prince Harry was born, Lord Spencer remarked that he hoped Harry would grow up "to play cricket for Gloucestershire." Perhaps with that in mind, Diana accepted an invitation in 1985 to become Patron of Gloucestershire County Cricket Club. She and her two sons, who were made Honorary Members, were given club sweaters (miniature ones for William and Harry), and the boys were also given tiny cricket bats autographed by the players. Diana has visited several club functions and matches and has helped raise funds. "The Princess does a splendid job as our Patron," a club official said. "She may not be too well versed in the technicalities of cricket, but in no way is she just a figurehead. I doubt if any other club Patron takes a keener personal interest. Every time she visits us, she makes a special point of spending most time with the players and their wives and children, many of whom she obviously remembers well."

Unlike most of her in-laws, including Fergie, Diana is not horsey. It is said that she lost her nerve for riding at the age of eight when she fell from her pony, Romany, and broke her arm, which took more than two months to mend. (Prince Charles once had to overcome a fear of horses.) However, horsey pursuits are a way of life with the Royal Family. On rare occasions since her marriage, Diana has been seen back in the saddle riding with the Queen, which one suspects were duty rides to please her mother-in-law. She cheered Charles on when he tried steeplechasing before their marriage, and she watches racing with the Queen and other members of the Royal Family at Royal Ascot each year. Prince Philip, another doer rather than watcher who prefers carriage racing anyway, is said to sometimes pop a transistor radio under his top hat at the races so that he can listen to cricket.

Diana has also been to the greyhound races in London, where she won £130 personally and helped raise more than £50,000 for London City Ballet. See DANCING. In one race she backed Hardy King, a greyhound owned by Princess Anne, which came in second to last. Prince Edward has a winning greyhound called Druids Johno, and in the sixties Prince Philip's dog, Camira Flash, won the premier prize, the Greyhound Derby.

Charles is a very keen huntsman who has hunted with forty-six of Britain's two hundred packs including the Beaufort, Berkeley, and Bicester Hunts near Highgrove, and the Belvoir and Quorn in Leicestershire. He has a hunter called Old Minto, who likes mints, and apparently hopes his sons will also hunt when they are old enough. According to royal correspondent Judy Wade, Diana has followed him by car and has also tried hunting herself. "She had a hunter but it was so spirited that Charles got rid of it," Judy said. "But she actually said she loved it. She doesn't like riding, but she said the galloping gave her a fantastic sense of freedom. She saw what he sees in it."

William was apparently first lifted on to the saddle of a fell pony called Martin when he was less than eighteen months old. He and Harry were both taught to ride by Marion Cox, the groom at Highgrove. They started on a Shetland pony called Smokey, lent by Princess Anne, and William progressed to Llanerch Topaz, a white Welsh mountain pony. In May 1989, under fake names, William, then aged six, and Harry, then aged four, competed at the Minchinhampton Pony Club show in Avening, Gloucestershire, and won rosettes for being well turned-out. It was Harry's first gymkhana. In July 1990, William competed on Topaz at the Purton Gymkhana near Swindon, riding fearlessly despite almost falling twice. Diana, however, still prefers to stay out of the saddle. That April, when the boys cantered around Windsor Great Park with their father, Mum opted out.

Diana and the children have often watched Charles playing polo, his great passion. See DANCING. He has been known to play six days a week, including weekends, during the season, which lasts from spring to autumn. He has encouraged the boys to take an interest in the game, which their grandfather, Prince Philip, played and which Lord Mountbatten proclaimed himself "completely dippy" about, even writing a book called *An Introduction to Polo* under the pen name Marco. In June 1990 at Cirencester Park, home of the Earls of Bathurst in Gloucestershire where their father was playing (and later broke his arm), William and Harry, watched by their new nanny Jessie Webb, played on their own, on foot, with miniature polo sticks, getting a kiss on the forehead from Dad between chukkas. At home William plays from his BMX bicycle. After Charles's accident, which was followed by two operations on his arm (see HEALTH and MARRIAGE), doubt was expressed about when, if ever, he would be able to play again. The accident was a great blow for the Prince since the game has always helped him let off steam, and he has remarked that playing helps preserve his sanity. "If I didn't get the exercise, or have something to take my mind off things, I would go potty," he once declared. One of Diana's American relatives did go potty as a result of a polo accident. See AMERICA. However, Charles played polo again in 1991, despite medical warnings, this time over his bad back—apparently an old problem—which had given him intense pain.

Diana is an angler, like Charles. She was first spotted at Balmoral watching him fish for salmon in the river Dee, and fishing was cited on their engagement as one of the interests they had in common. However, Diana does not appear to have become a great fan of the sport, unlike her mother (see RADIO) and the Queen Mother, who taught Charles. But Charles's interest is such that he even fished at the start of their honeymoon at Broadlands. See HONEYMOON.

Diana was first introduced to the Prince at a shoot at Althorp, and he first started asking her out as a friend after the Queen invited Diana and her sister Sarah to join a shooting party at Sandringham. Shooting is a sport Diana grew up with, and she is making sure that her children do the same. In December 1986, when Charles was out pheasant shooting at Sandringham with ex-King Constantine of Greece and King Juan Carlos of Spain, she took William, then aged four, to have lunch with them. And Harry was at a shoot organized by Prince Philip, ironically a key figure in wildlife conservation worldwide, two years later. Traditionally the British Royal Family have always had a passion for blood sports—and even shot big game until a quarter of a century ago—and Charles, who is a renowned shot, apparently wants William and Harry to learn to shoot as soon as is feasible. Diana is said to be a good shot. According to Sir John Junor's memoirs, in 1984 Charles denied claims that she had tried to stop him hunting and shooting. She did "nothing of the kind," he said. "My wife actually likes hunting and shooting. It is I who have turned against it."

Both he and Diana are good skiers, and Charles usually spends a week skiing early each year in Klosters. But since the avalanche which nearly killed him, and which did kill their friend Major Hugh Lindsay (see FRIENDS), Diana has not returned there. However, she accompanied William and Harry to dry ski slopes in Hillingdon and Gloucester before taking them on their very first snow skiing vacation to Lech in Austria at Easter this year. Prince Charles was apparently too busy working on his own projects to join them.

When Diana became Patron of the English Women's Indoor Bowling Association and of the Welsh Bowling Association, the first woman to be associated with the Welsh organization in nearly ninety years, she knew nothing about the game. Curiously, though, on the first two or three occasions she was seen playing in public, including once during her tour of Indonesia, exactly the same thing happened. Her first wood shot too far across the green into the ditch, but her second was a corker! When it happened at the opening of a £600,000 indoor rink in Luton in October 1988—where she was presented with a set of bowls for her sons—Diana, in stockinged feet, jumped with joy as her second 3-pound-4-ounce wood hit the jack and then stopped within four inches. Only a few seconds before, she had been shown elementary basics like how to hold the bowl. "It was an absolutely perfect shot," said Pamela Allison of the English Women's Indoor Bowling Association. "She was quite excited, and of course everybody clapped. Nobody could believe it. I said, 'We could do with you in our international team!' and she laughed." Chris Mills, Editor of *Bowls International*, called it "an incredible 1,000-to-1 shot," adding, "I have never known anything like it from a beginner." "It was just a bit of luck," said Diana, who has since practiced bowls at Windsor.

At a youth club in Newcastle in March 1982, the Princess threw her first three darts in public and scored 10, 2, and double 3. In October 1990, visiting Tetbury Fair with Harry, she won three goldfish—plus an extra one so that her sons could have two each—when she hit nine playing cards with her darts at a stall and was declared "a very good shot." On some public engagements, she has been invited to try snooker. The Queen Mother, a skilled player, once demonstrated a near-perfect break at a community center in east London, and also impressed players at the Press Club in London, including Peter Grosvenor, Literary Editor of the *Daily Express*, who declared that she played "a mean Southpaw." But when Diana was offered her chance at a youth club, she had to be shown how to hold the cue.

Diana jogs in a tracksuit or shorts and running shoes in Kensington Gardens, and she allegedly got reprimanded in October 1990 for jogging there alone without a bodyguard. In June 1988, running barefoot, she won the mothers' seventy-three-meter (eighty-yard) sprint at Prince William's school sports day, though she was beaten in a photo finish in the race the following year and finished well down the field of thirteen moms in 1990. William grew to love soccer at Wetherby prep school and is a supporter of the Arsenal soccer team. Although his father is not a fan of soccer, William reportedly pestered both of his parents to take him to see the (British) Cup Final at Wembley Stadium in May 1991—Charles and Diana's first Cup Final visit together. However, on the day, William was not there with them. The Princess had presented the Cup to the winning team in 1988.

In June 1986 the Princess became Patron of the British Sports Association for the Disabled, inaugurated in 1961, which has ninety-eight-thousand members, provides sports and recreational facilities for the disabled, organizes sports championships, and trains and coordinates teams for international competitions including the Paralympics.

In terms of games rather than sport, Diana likes playing bridge and poker, which she prefers to dominoes. But she says

she's not very good at bridge because she talks too much. See
FRIENDS and PRESS.

STAFF

The first boy Diana ever kissed in an innocent game of catch-the-
ball when they were both fourteen was Paul Betts, the son of
Bertie and Elsie Betts, her father's valet-butler and cook at Park
House, her childhood home. Later she sent him a holiday post-
card from Scotland signed "Tons of love, Diana xxxx," asking,
"How are my pigs?," a reference to her pet guinea pigs, Pinky and
Peanuts, which he looked after while she was away. See EDUCA-
TION. She invited several of the staff from Althorp, where her
family moved shortly after, to the royal wedding, including Betty
Andrew, the housekeeper; Mr. Pendry, their former butler; Mr.
Smith, the gamekeeper; and Mr. Watters, the clerk of works. And
a gilt-edged invitation was also sent to Ally, Diana's former gov-
erness at Park House, which the old lady was allegedly found
holding in her hand when she died shortly before the wedding.

Diana's friendliness and kindness to her own staff and others
who serve her is well known. She has dropped in for tea with her
butler, Harold Brown, a former Palace footman and a member of
the strict Plymouth Brethren religious sect, and to see his collection of Victorian postcards. She has visited the Knightsbridge flat
of Anne Beckwith-Smith, her first Lady-in-Waiting and for a time
her Assistant Private Secretary, to have scrambled eggs and a chat
and watch TV. She calls Anne "darling" and after her debut
overseas tour of Australasia in 1983 gave her a diamond brooch,
saying, "I couldn't have done it without you." When hairdresser
Kevin Shanley went abroad with her on tour, she wrote thanking
his wife for "lending" him to her. See AUSTRALIA and BEAUTY
SECRETS. Her dresser Evelyn Dagley, a former housemaid at
Buckingham Palace whom she calls Ev, uses Diana's car to go
shopping. When another dresser, Fay Marshalsea, was discovered
to have cancer two weeks before her wedding to her RAF sweetheart Steven Appleby in October 1987, which the Princess attended, Diana provided practical help and support and even
accompanied her on one occasion to the hospital for treatment.
"She gave me encouragement to carry on," said Fay, who has since

With an ever-present detective in tow, Diana takes a stroll. (Srdja Djukanovic/Camera Press London)

left the Palace. "She is a lovely person to work for, and very special to me." In June 1990, the Princess gave up a day off to visit Fay and her twin boys, Nicholas and Benjamin, in the hospital where they were born in Devon.

Charles and Diana celebrated the seventieth birthday of Paddy Whiteland, a lovable Liverpudlian inherited with Highgrove who acts as a general factotum there, with a special lunch party for him at a local hotel. When his wife Nesta, their house-keeper, died two years later in 1986, Diana flew down from Scotland to attend the funeral, then took Paddy back to Balmoral with her to keep him company in his grief. (In 1987 she also made a trip from Balmoral to Ballater to comfort the grieving parents of royal baker Kenny Murdoch, who died in a horrific road accident in which three others were also killed.) To celebrate the birthday of Charles's twice-wed valet, Ken Stronach, an ex-Marine and former valet and chauffeur to Lord Mountbatten, champagne and a special birthday cake were presented to him in flight while the royal party flew to Australia in October 1985. She has also shown kindness to her bodyguards. See ROYAL PROTECTION SQUAD. Diana sends birthday cards to the staff, who also include a second valet, Michael Fawcett (nicknamed Winge after he made a com-plaint to a shop during the 1983 Australian tour and was called "a wingeing Pom"—that is, a complaining Englishman); a Gurkha oddjob man named Ek Gurung; and Diana's Ladies-in-Waiting, who are unpaid apart from a clothing allowance and minor ex-penses: Lavinia Baring; former amateur jockey Hazel West; Vis-countess Campden; Jean Pike, who works part-time at Christie's and is the daughter of Major General Lord Michael Fitzalan-Howard, the former Marshal of the Diplomatic Corps; Alexandra Loyd; and Laura Greig, who is Mrs. James Lonsdale. See FRIENDS.

Despite that, dozens of employees have left since her mar-riage, and several royal bodyguards have also moved on. The huge turnover of staff led to many suggestions that Charles and Diana were not the easiest couple to work for. Charles, known as the Boss, is a perfectionist who gets cross quickly, particularly at delays and inefficiency. Diana has denied being bossy, saying, "I am a perfectionist with myself, though not necessarily with every-one else." In June 1985, she told James Whitaker, royal corre-spondent of the *Daily Mirror*, "I want you to understand that I am not responsible for any sackings. I just don't sack people." How-ever, her brother, Viscount Althorp, revealed in *Woman* magazine in January 1987, "She is an exceptionally kind and thoughtful person but nobody's saying she is a fool. She's weeded out quite a few hangers-on that she found around her husband and his family in a subtle way." Whitaker wrote the same month, "Without question, the Princess of Wales is the single most charming person I have met. . . . But you cross her at your peril." One royal method is simply to freeze out those who have fallen from favor until they get the message and resign. Another is to get an aide to do the sacking for them. Other staff leave of their own volition for better-paid work elsewhere, for jobs which allow them more time at home with their families, or for other reasons.

Stephen Barry began work at Buckingham Palace as a £7-a-week junior footman and rose to become Prince Charles's valet, serving him loyally for twelve years. He left saying that he felt there was no place for him after the royal wedding. Barry had been more like an aide than a servant. Apart from taking care of the Prince's wardrobe and waking him in the morning to prepare for the day, he did his shopping, sorted his books, papers, and photo albums, and even—astoundingly—went with him on some of his public engagements. He also advised the traditional and rather square Charles on the purchase of clothes, in terms of color, style, and taste, and sounded somewhat piqued when he later commented, "I could never get him to wear yellow. Then along came the Princess and the next moment I see him in a yellow sweater!" Barry's position of trust with Charles, who relied on him heavily, gave him a certain standing, and off-duty he would mix with the famous at premieres and book promotions as if he were a celebrity himself.

However, he frequented gay clubs and was once photographed in a scuffle on the floor of a nightclub with another man. He further blotted his copybook, it is claimed, by trying to stop Diana from entering Charles's study before they were engaged, claiming the Prince was "too busy" to see her, and after their marriage by walking into their bedroom without knocking, catching Diana in her nightdress. Other allegations were that Barry, who even used to dress like the Prince in clothes from the same top-flight tailors, was "totally infatuated" with him and that Diana issued the ultimatum to Charles: "Either he goes, or I do." She was said to be "horrified" that a homosexual should have played such a close role as a servant in Charles's life, but she was very naive in those days. Her former hairdresser Kevin Shanley revealed in the *Sunday Mirror* that she had once asked him to explain newspaper references she kept spotting to the "gay Mafia" at the Palace. "I don't even know what the gay scene is all about," she said.

Many dedicated royal servants are gay. Despite off-duty scandals which have sometimes rocked the Palace, they are often valued for the quality of their work and the extra hours they put in. In years since, the Princess has campaigned for public acceptance of AIDS patients, many of them gay. See HIV. But one early claim was that she did not want gay staff around her and her husband; and after Barry's departure, it was said that a Palace purge began. A friend of Stephen Barry's was quoted as saying later, "He used to say he resigned, but he was pushed. And she did the pushing. He called her a spoilt brat." Barry went to the United States, where he made a fortune from his memoirs, which were never published in Britain. Gaunt and gray at thirty-seven, he died at St. Stephen's hospital in west London in October 1986 from AIDS-related pneumonia, though an ex-royal steward claimed he had really died "of a broken heart." Prince Charles, who has since shown interest in the work done on behalf of AIDS patients by the Terrence Higgins Trust, was very upset and wrote a letter of sympathy to Barry's sister. Barry's replacement, Corporal Paul Chant, only stayed eight months.

In 1982, Alan Fisher, aged fifty-two, whose wife, Norma, worked as a nurserymaid at Buckingham Palace when Charles was a tot, joined the staff as the Prince and Princess's butler but left for America two years later, revealing, "I was bored there. They never did any entertaining." Or at least not on the scale of his previous employers, who included the Duke and Duchess of Windsor and Bing Crosby. (Some staff are said to refer to Highgrove, the royal couple's country retreat, as "Highgrave.") But of Charles and Diana, he said, "They are the most wonderful people in the world. Truly."

The same year saw the resignation of Oliver Everett, formerly Assistant Private Secretary to Charles and a keen polo player like his boss—Everett once played polo from the back of an elephant in Nepal—who rushed to the Prince's rescue when Charles collapsed with heatstroke after playing polo in Palm Beach, Florida, in 1980, saying, "Please help me, Oliver. I think I'm dying." After Charles and Diana became engaged, he was recalled from diplomatic service at the British Embassy in Madrid to take charge of the ensuing correspondence and to help Diana in her new role. He became her Private Secretary in July 1981, at a salary of about £16,000 a year, and also Comptroller. However, there were rumors of clashes with Diana, particularly about her last-minute changes to schedules which he had arranged months before, and he quit to become Deputy Librarian at Windsor Castle.

The new Comptroller was Lieutenant-Colonel Philip Creasy, a former Gurkha officer who was reportedly nicknamed Colonel Bossy Boots by the staff for trying to run the Household like a military operation. He left in 1986. Assistant Private Secretary Francis Cornish returned to his career as a diplomat in 1984, becoming High Commissioner in Brunei. The same year, the Household Secretary and Accountant, Michael Colborne, who was said to hate the snobbery at the Palace, left too. In 1986, Diana's Equerry, Lieutenant-Commander Peter Eberle—who had served briefly with Prince Charles on HMS *Jupiter* and had a lucky escape as warfare officer on the frigate *Argonaut* when it was twice hit by Argentine bombs during the Falklands conflict—returned to his duties with the Royal Navy, having been on secondment (loan) to Diana since October 1983. His replacement, Lieutenant-Commander Richard Aylard, was in turn replaced by a further naval officer, Lieutenant-Commander Patrick Jephson, who in January 1990 took over as Diana's Assistant Private Secretary from Anne Beckwith-Smith. In 1991, Aylard, who was by then promoted to Commander, was made Private Secretary to Prince Charles, and Jephson became Private Secretary to the Princess. Her Equerry then was Wing Commander David Barton, RAF. Diana's big, bluff, no-nonsense Canadian Press Secretary, Victor Chapman was a former professional soccer player who once worked for Canadian Prime Minister Pierre Trudeau. He was with her from September 1982 until 1987, when he returned to Ottawa and died within two months at the age of fifty-three. Michael Shea, the Queen's Press Secretary and a thriller writer in his spare time, played a key Press role for Charles and Diana, but in 1987 he also left the Palace and joined the Hanson Trust.

One of the biggest shocks came with the sudden departure in 1985 of the Honorable Edward Adeane, whose family had served British monarchs since Queen Victoria. A godson of King George VI, he was made a Page of Honor by the Queen while he was a fourteen-year-old student at Eton. In 1979, he gave up his career as a successful libel lawyer to become Private Secretary to Prince Charles, a friend with whom he went shooting and fishing, and in 1984 he became Private Secretary to Diana as well. He had also been Treasurer to Charles from the start, and to them both since their marriage, and had been expected to remain at their side at least until the Prince succeeds to the throne. A courtier's courtier, when he left journalists suggested that he had found it taxing discussing business with Diana at Kensington Palace against the blare of pop music and surrounded with baby paraphernalia, alleging he had told a friend, "If I ever see another knitted bootie, I will go mad." However, it is inconceivable that an adviser of Adeane's background and caliber would quit such an important post over something so frivolous. The real reason he left, others alleged at the time, was because of differences with Prince Charles, who would often "disregard advice" and go his own way.

One cannot help wondering whether any "differences" could have concerned the royal couple's forthcoming Italian tour, which took place shortly after Adeane left—in particular the Prince's alleged wish to attend a private Mass with the Pope at the Vatican. In April 1985, while the royal couple were in Italy, Buckingham Palace denied Press reports that the Queen, who is head of the Church of England, had vetoed such a plan. Yet the Vatican apparently adamantly maintained that the Mass *was* on until the Palace stepped in. According to John Pearson in *The Ultimate Family*, "it was only Her Majesty's direct, last-minute intervention that prevented it. Intense embarrassment ensued, particularly for the Prince himself." A Mass attended by the future head of the Church of England and the head of the Church of Rome would be the most historic rapprochement in 450 years of English royal, constitutional, and ecclesiastical history, with what could be far-reaching and, to some, alarming consequences.

It was Henry VIII in the sixteenth century who initiated the

English Reformation, which destroyed papal authority in England, and who, under the 1534 Act of Supremacy, was proclaimed supreme head of the English Church. Protestantism finally became the established religion of the Church of England under Elizabeth I. The Act of Settlement of 1701, which established the Hanoverian succession to the English throne, states that the monarch must be a Protestant. The fact that Catholics are still kept distanced from the throne was evidenced in recent times when Prince Michael of Kent, who was only sixteenth in line and therefore unlikely ever to be King, nevertheless had to give up his right of succession to the throne in order to wed the Catholic Marie-Christine von Reibnitz. Pearson claimed that the Queen, aware that serious controversy could damage the monarchy, had prevented the Mass to play "very safe in one area where, as traditional Defender of the Faith, [she] herself could easily become the center of bitter and impassioned religious controversy—particularly in Northern Ireland, where there is quite enough religious bigotry already."

If Charles, as the next King and Defender of the Faith, had said before going to Italy that he wished to attend Mass with the Pope, it seems likely he would have been advised against such a plan. And if he chose to reject that advice, on such an important and controversial issue, an adviser might well have concluded that the time had come to throw in the towel. Which, of course, is all conjecture. Whatever his reasons—and we may never know—Adeane quit. However, since 1985 he has been an Extra Equerry to Charles and remains on good terms with the Princess. (In 1989, after a later Private Secretary, Sir John Riddell, decided to quit, Chris Hutchins in *Today* suggested that there was a move to bring Adeane back. Hutchins claimed that Charles had become ever more outspoken since he left and quoted a senior courtier as saying, "The greatest challenge now facing the Royal Family is to control the future King and keep him out of controversy.")

Following Adeane's departure, David Roycroft took over, but later left to become a senior television executive. At that point Sir John Riddell, Executive Director of the Credit Suisse First Boston Bank in London and Deputy Chairman of the Independent Broadcasting Authority, became Private Secretary. But having decided in 1989 to leave the £60,000-a-year job, he rejoined his bank in 1990, apparently after differences about Diana's last-minute changes to schedules, the same complaint allegedly made by Oliver Everett years before. It is a tricky problem because many of the royal couple's engagements are scheduled months ahead at twice-yearly planning meetings and have to be because of the number of people and amount of advance organization involved. Nevertheless, Charles has talked of trying not to let his life get set in concrete, and Diana clearly likes to maintain some spontaneity. After all, they're people, not robots. But suddenly deciding to go to someone's wedding or christening or add a walkabout can obviously cause problems if it means last-minute changes to a program that has already been fixed. Riddell was replaced by Major-General Sir Christopher Airy, who recruited Britain's first black Guardsman after Charles complained that all seven thousand troops who guard the Royal Family were white. Airy left in 1991. Charles and Diana's Press Secretary is Dickie Arbiter, a former independent radio journalist, assisted by Kiloran McGrigor.

Their first chef, Roseanna Lloyd, whose culinary talents they discovered when she worked at a hotel in Wales, was with them for only a short while before she left to marry a farmer. Another chef, Graham Newbold, quit to work at a hotel in Scotland. Chef Mervyn Wycherley, an ex-boxer known as Seth, was also reported to be thinking of leaving when the royal couple employed a special Italian chef, named Enrico Derflinger, to cook pasta. See FOOD & DRINK. But it was Derflinger who went. He felt too homesick to take up a job offer in America with President George Bush. Instead, he moved to a restaurant in Siena, Italy, where Charles continued to call him for recipes. Butcher's daughter Valerie Gibbs, who worked as Diana's personal maid but reportedly complained of job stress, left in August 1984 to wed former Kensington Palace chauffeur Richard Lord. That November, two live-in maids, Sally Palmer and Julie Spinelli, who liked to drink off-duty in the nearby Prince of Wales pub on Kensington Church Street, were reportedly ordered by royal minder Chief Inspector Colin Trimming, nicknamed Haircut 100 "because of his hair-spray," to be in by 10:30 P.M. and not to bring boyfriends back to

Kensington Palace for a good-night cuddle. A second report the following month claimed that when Julie's six-month contract came up for renewal, she decided to leave and go home to Cornwall. Other staff who have left include Palace cleaner Sheila Tilly, royal chauffeurs John Clarke and Joe Last, both former soldiers, and Joan Bodman, who retired after three years as head housekeeper at Highgrove in July 1987.

Diana has always been a real mother to her children, rather than leaving their care to a nanny, but since work often takes her away from home or abroad, good nursery staff have always been essential. She believes in never raising her voice or a hand in anger to her offspring (she is said to follow the child care ideas given in the book *Parent Effectiveness Training* by Dr. Thomas Gordon) and doesn't expect the Palace nannies to either. William's first nanny was Barbara Barnes, who accompanied him on the tour of Australia and New Zealand in 1983. Though she was not formally trained for the job, she came highly recommended, having worked for fifteen years as a "wonderful, marvelous nanny" to the children of Lady Anne Tennant, an Extra Lady-in-Waiting to Princess Margaret and the wife of Princess Margaret's former escort, the Honorable Colin Tennant, now the 3rd Baron Glenconner. Lady Anne is the daughter of the 5th Earl of Leicester, who had known Barbara from childhood since she grew up on the twenty-nine-thousand-acre estate surrounding his magnificent Palladian mansion at Holkham, Norfolk—close to Sandringham—where her father William Barnes was a forestry worker until he retired. William and Harry grew very fond of her.

But on the day in January 1987 that William, then four, started at Wetherby prep school in west London, Buckingham Palace made the surprise announcement: "As Prince William is now to attend school full-time, it has been mutually agreed by Miss Barnes and the Prince and Princess that it is an appropriate time for her to move," adding that the matter had been under discussion for ten days. This plus the fact that Barbara, then aged forty-two, had no job to go to and a replacement for her had not been selected, clearly indicated a rift. Amid much Press speculation, it was claimed that Prince Charles wanted William, who had proved a real handful, to have much stricter discipline, like the kind *he* had had from his stern Scottish nanny, Mabel Anderson, who spent more than thirty years rearing royal children; that Miss Barnes had got fed up with what she regarded as Charles's "fussiness"; and that having twice planned to quit but been persuaded by Diana to stay, this time her resignation had been accepted. The *Today* newspaper quoted a member of the royal staff as saying, "Barbara did the right job up to now, but the Prince is determined that William should not be allowed to be so boisterous and naughty. The children get away with a lot when they are with their mother or nanny, but when the Prince is there the atmosphere is much colder. He is a stickler for everything being correct." Shades of Prince Philip perhaps. But since he was bringing up the heir to the throne, a task now assigned to Charles, hardly surprising. Ruth Wallace joined deputy nanny Olga Powell as Barbara's replacement, but she left amicably in March 1990 to be replaced two months later by new nanny Jessie Webb.

Like the glamorous Marlene Dietrich, who loved getting down on her knees and scrubbing floors, the Princess is still a charlady at heart. See JOBS. Despite her exalted position and the domestic staff she has to do the chores, she absolutely loves washing up and also enjoys cleaning, tidying, vacuuming, dusting, and ironing. See TELEVISION.

$\mathcal{T}$

TELEVISION

Diana is a great soap opera addict, and has followed "Cross-roads," "Dynasty," "Dallas," "EastEnders," "Brookside," "Neighbours," and "Home and Away." Charles isn't but confessed in 1985 that she'd got him watching "Dallas" and "Dynasty," whose star Joan Collins, with whom he danced in Palm Beach, once allegedly told the Princess, "We will get you a part in 'Dynasty' when you come to Los Angeles." See AMERICA. Like millions of "Dallas" fans, Diana was very intrigued to discover who shot JR. And according to one report, she didn't break the news of her engagement to her flatmates until after she had watched "Crossroads." The Queen is a fan of "Coronation Street," judging by the congratulatory telegram she sent on its thirtieth anniversary in 1990. Charles has also seen "Emmerdale." However, when he and Diana watched the filming of a Japanese soap opera at a Tokyo TV studio in 1986 and Charles was asked if it reminded him of "EastEnders," he replied, "You'd better ask my wife." Princess Anne had clearly never seen "East-Enders" when she met two of its stars, including Leslie Grantham who played Dirty Den, and had to ask, "Who are you?" Diana, who classed Den as "a lovable rogue," tired of that soap eventually, commenting, "I've gone off 'EastEnders' and now I prefer 'Brookside.'" A staff member videotapes episodes for her when she's out. See VIDEOS.

As a child at Park House, Diana would curl up in front of the nursery fire and watch TV after tea. At school at West Heath, she never missed the tennis from Wimbledon and liked "Charlie's Angels," starring Farrah Fawcett-Majors, who once caught Prince Charles's eye. Other programs she has enjoyed include "The Generation Game" and "Not the Nine O'Clock News," starring Pamela Stephenson with whom Diana and Fergie later staged their

policewomen stunt on Prince Andrew's stag night. See UNI-
FORMS. "The Muppet Show" (see COLLECTIONS) was a big
favorite too. Later so was "Bread." She adores romantic films and
watched the TV miniseries of bestselling books by two of her
favorite authors (see BOOKS)—Barbara Taylor Bradford's *A
Woman of Substance*, starring Jenny Seagrove, and Colleen McCullough's *The Thorn Birds*, starring Richard Chamberlain as the
priest, whose long-awaited fall from grace kept practically the
entire nation glued to their seats and caused a massive drain on
water and electricity at the end when millions of viewers got up to
go to the bathroom and put the kettle on for a cup of tea. She is
also a fan of Cilla Black's "Blind Date" show. Her fashion interest
prompts her to tune in to "The Clothes Show," starring look-
alike Selina Scott, a former fancy of Prince Andrew, and she once
went to watch Selina at work in a breakfast TV studio.

Both Selina and David Frost (see BIRTHRIGHT) have been
suggested in the past as the interviewers most likely to land the
plum job of conducting the Princess's first solo interview on
television. Another contender might be Michael Aspel, whom
Diana has met. She listened to his show on Capital Radio. And he
and Charles once struggled manfully through a TV interview at
Highgrove although both of them were ill. Diana has also met, and
danced with, TV star Robert Kilroy-Silk. See DANCING. But the
best bet is on youthful, trendy Jonathan Ross. In October 1990
the *Daily Star* claimed that Diana wanted to scotch upsetting
rumors about her marriage by appearing as the "real me" on
Ross's TV talk show. Three weeks later, the Princess reportedly
said of Ross, "I prefer him to Terry Wogan. I've sat next to him
twice at functions and I think he's wonderful."

Like everyone else, Diana and Charles have TV suppers on
their laps while they watch the box (see FAVORITE THINGS). The
Prince frequently spends evenings going through all the paper-
work he has to deal with in his cluttered study, sometimes falling
asleep at his desk, while his wife stays in her superneat sitting
room, glued to the television, sometimes doing the ironing at the
same time.

Charles's favorite TV programs have included comedy shows
like "The Goodies" and "Monty Python's Flying Circus," and

serious documentary series like "Horizon," "The World About Us," and "Life on Earth." He watched too much television as a child, the Queen said, but as an often-lonely bachelor, it kept him company. He twice watched "Edward and Mrs. Simpson," the TV version of the Duke of Windsor's romance and abdication saga, starring Edward Fox. His sons watch cartoons on television and saw the BBC program "Going Live." But other shows have caused their mother some anxiety. In 1985, visiting a London drug unit, Diana said she was concerned about some of the things William, then aged three, said after watching TV. Mentioning "Starsky and Hutch" and "Bergerac," she said she was worried that some shows demonstrated "how clever" drug smugglers are, hiding drugs, for example, inside a teddy bear. The comment prompted remarks that William must be going to bed rather late if he was watching those shows. One expert declared, "Princess Diana should control his viewing. A three-year-old should watch things such as 'Postman Pat' and 'Mr. Ben.' Programs such as 'Bergerac' show ordinary people, who look like Mummy and Daddy, involved in violence. This is certainly harmful to children." Diana was also concerned that showing people drinking in soap operas could have harmful effects. See TURNING POINT.

The Queen Mother is a great fan of " 'Allo 'Allo!," a hilarious comedy based in Nazi-occupied France, which is on in the early evening. She has apparently been known to delay joining the Queen for predinner cocktails in order to watch it. Another royal TV favorite is "Only Fools and Horses," a sitcom based around working-class south London street market characters.

Although the Princess loves watching television, appearing on it is another matter. Unlike some members of the Royal Family, including Prince Charles, Princess Anne, Prince Andrew, Fergie, and Princess Michael of Kent, she has not, at the time of this writing, appeared on a TV talk show. Nor, because Charles apparently forbade it, did she appear with other royals in that undignified and much-criticized display on the "It's a Knockout" show which Prince Edward helped to organize. She dreaded giving her first brief TV interview with Charles at the time of their engagement, seen by five hundred million viewers, though Charles, a TV veteran since 1969, did much of the talking. The questions were harmless and had been screened, but Diana hated seeing herself on television later and covered her face with her hands, declaring, "Oh God, I look awful. Why did I say that?" Four years went by before she agreed to subject herself to a TV quizzing again.

At Christmas 1983, BBC TV broadcast a fifty-minute documentary called "The Princess and the People," which covered the royal year, including Diana's first overseas tours of Australia, New Zealand, and Canada. This was the first time an entire program had been devoted to Diana. A request for the Princess to give an interview to go with the documentary was apparently made but refused on the grounds that she "didn't give interviews." One newspaper journalist made the presumptuous suggestion that she didn't want to risk "upstaging" the Queen's Christmas Day message two days later. A more likely reason is that she still hadn't conquered her nerves and didn't yet feel ready to go on camera. However, in July 1985, without a request from the BBC but at the prompting of TV's ubiquitous "Jim'll Fix It" celebrity, Jimmy (now Sir James) Savile, Diana made a brief surprise appearance on "Drugwatch," the BBC's two-hour television special on the drug problem, where she became the first person to sign her name to the "Just Say No" antidrug campaign. See DRUGS.

In the years following the royal wedding, which was watched on television by seven hundred million people in seventy-four countries (and by the bride and groom on video afterward, see VIDEOS), a bizarre contrast developed between the public Diana and what, according to some reports, she was like in private. Rumor had it that, behind closed Palace doors, the royal couple had a rocky marriage and that while "potty" Charles tried to summon up the late Lord Mountbatten via a ouija board, the "shy Di" we had all loved as a fairy-tale bride had turned into a restless, demanding, money-squandering, tantrum-throwing, staff-sacking shrew who domineered her "wimpish" husband and made his life miserable. Charles's frustration at the "rubbish" written about him and, in particular, about his wife, was no doubt increased by the fact that she felt so wounded and upset reading that sort of stuff that she found it harder to face carrying out her public engagements. As she herself said later on British TV, "You think, 'Oh gosh, I don't want to go out and do my engagement this morning. Nobody wants to see me, help, panic.' But you have got to push yourself out and remember that some people hopefully won't remember everything they read about you." In an effort to set the record straight and let the public see and hear them for themselves, Charles and Diana agreed to be interviewed together in their drawing room at Kensington Palace by Sir Alastair Burnet for a forty-five-minute ITN TV program called "In Person: The Prince and Princess of Wales." Diana was coached in advance by Sir Richard Attenborough, who showed her how to look relaxed, hold her head, and speak clearly (see SPEECHES). At her request, ITN gave her a trial run first. The company was allowed to film Charles and Diana at home with their children, but the royal couple insisted on having final editorial approval and on proceeds going to the Prince of Wales' Charities Trust. In the end, twenty million viewers saw Diana emerge poised and confident on their screens to answer the critics and talk of her life as a wife and mother, her work, and her interests. And though she clearly *had* changed, indeed transformed herself from the nervous teenager who had been seen in the Buckingham Palace summerhouse only four years before, the changes came across as wholly positive. Even the momentary bickering between her and Charles as to whether they had rows (see MARRIAGE) underlined the normality of their relationship rather than anything else.

The Prince, for his part, scotched all the ouija board nonsense, stating that he didn't even know what a ouija board was. He came across, as usual, as a highly intelligent, sensitive, and thoughtful man.

The interview was broadcast in Britain on Sunday, October 20, 1985, and got rave reviews. The book of the program, published by ITN and Michael O'Mara Books with color photographs by one of Diana's favorite photographers, Tim Graham, spent three months at the top of the bestseller lists. In the United States, edited down for the American audience to about twenty-five minutes, the interview was shown during prime time by ABC News' "20/20" on November 7, 1985. Enchanted, the public wanted more. So, of course, did the TV people. A second program and book, *In Public—In Private: The Prince and Princess of Wales*, followed in 1986. This time ITN, Sir Alastair, and Tim

Graham were allowed to follow the royal couple at home and abroad, on- and off-duty, for about nine months. Proceeds again went to the Prince of Wales' Charities Trust.

The highest viewing audience ever recorded for any television broadcast in Britain was for Charles and Diana's wedding on July 29, 1981, when thirty-nine million people tuned in, Kleenex at the ready. See AMERICA, JAPAN, and WEDDING. By comparison, 30 million in Britain watched "Live Aid," and 27.3 million U.K. "Dallas" fans, no doubt including Diana, switched on in 1980 to find out who shot JR.

Diana's brother, Viscount Althorp, a TV man himself (see FAMILY), was caught in a Candid Camera–type stunt trying to help a woman get a large desk into her car outside a London auctioneers, by TV star Esther Rantzen, disguised as a traffic warden, for the BBC "Hearts of Gold" show broadcast on October 14, 1990. He suspected something was up, and when Esther produced her hidden microphone, he declared, "Oh dear, I've been had!" Diana once told Cyril Fletcher, who used to deliver Odd Odes on Esther's consumer program, "I really miss you on 'That's Life.' "

And guess who revealed on "The Oprah Winfrey Show" that his mother thought Di was the only woman for him? *Rocky/Rambo* star Sylvester Stallone!

In March 1991 it was announced that Twiggy had signed with an American TV network to play an aristocratic English girl sharing a New York penthouse with two Americans, to be played by Fran Drescher and Julie Haggerty, in a comedy, "Princesses." (Diana shared her London apartment with three friends before her marriage. See RESIDENCES and FRIENDS.) A TV spokesman was quoted as telling a British newspaper, "Americans can't get enough of your Royal Family, so we decided to base Twiggy's character on Lady Di." But Twiggy, born in the humble London suburb of Neasden with far from an upper-crust accent, denied this. "I'm hardly Diana material, am I?" she asked. "Anyway, I'm a great fan of the Royal Family, especially Diana, who is so lovely. I wouldn't want to offend any of them." Sadly for Twiggy's fans, before the year's end, "Princesses" had been axed.

THAILAND

"Thai Di!" ran one headline after Charles and Diana's visit to Thailand in February 1988 as part of the sixtieth birthday celebrations of the jazz-loving King Bhumibol Adulyadej, who plays the saxophone. Thailand was called Siam until 1939, and the King is the great-great-grandson of King Mongkut (Rama IV), who was popularized in the novel *Anna and the King of Siam*. He became even more famous, as played by Yul Brynner, in the classic Rodgers and Hammerstein musical, *The King and I* (which is banned in Thailand, apparently because it is thought to bring the monarchy into disrepute.)

However, Diana loves musicals and knows all the lyrics of her favorite songs. So it is tempting to wonder, as the plane touched down at Bangkok airport, whether she revealed, " 'I Have Dreamed' of being greeted by 'The March of the Siamese Children' " or even of crowds singing 'Hello, Young Lovers.' " But she might have thought it would be nice to "Whistle a Happy Tune" as she walked along the red welcome carpet. Especially as she was shaded from the sun by a young man carrying a huge mauve ceremonial parasol which, had she and Charles been in private, would have allowed the Prince to say "We Kiss in a Shadow." "Something Wonderful" awaited her at the Bosang umbrella factory in Chiang Mai province: an enormous red sun umbrella decorated with flowers and the message: A WARM WELCOME TO HER ROYAL HIGHNESS THE PRINCESS OF WALES. She played "Getting to Know You" at a local senior citizens project supported by Help the Aged, of which she is Patron. And with Charles, she visited the Grand Palace and the Emerald Buddha Temple. For the Crown Prince's banquet in Bangkok, the Princess wore an exotic Catherine Walker fuchsia-and-purple silk chiffon gown, with matching silk flowers in her hair. She looked gorgeous enough to make any monarch sing the "Song of the King" or suggest "Shall We Dance?"

TURNING POINT

Diana is Patron of Turning Point, founded in 1964, which has over forty projects in Britain providing residential, day care, and street-level advice and counseling services to help people deal with drug, alcohol, and mental health problems. The charity's PR manager, Deborah Newbury, says, "The Princess has helped draw public attention to our work, and to break down stereotypes about 'junkies and drunks.' Our fund-raising capacity has also gone up significantly since she became Patron because, apart from having the 'royal seal of approval,' we are also able to put on fund-raising events like the film premiere of *When Harry Met Sally*" (at which, incidentally, Diana laughed not only at the famous restaurant scene but all the way through. See X-RATED.). The Princess has made at least twenty-seven visits since becoming Patron in 1987, and in February 1990 she hosted a reception at Kensington Palace for the charity and its statutory supporters— health and local authorities. William and Harry turned up too, shook hands with over 150 people, and insisted on having name badges like everyone else, so special ones were made for them on the spot. In a speech Diana made at the charity's conference in London in May 1989 on drug and alcohol problems at work, sponsored by the Whitbread Brewery, she said:

> 1989 marks the Silver Jubilee of Turning Point, a charity which, during its twenty-five years, has gained enormous experience in dealing with problems related to drug and alcohol misuse. Today, Turning Point is the largest national voluntary organization catering for those with drink, drug and mental health problems.
>
> Before going any further, I should make it clear that what I have to say is not the result of any special expertise; but in my time as Patron, I have seen at firsthand some of the work undertaken by Turning Point around the country, and the conclusions I have drawn are perhaps those any layman might reach given a similar opportunity.
>
> I was quickly made aware of the fact that drug and alcohol problems are on the increase, especially among the young. I will not trouble you now with the statistics (no doubt better-qualified speakers will do so later), but anybody who reads the newspapers, listens to the radio, and watches television will recognize the underlying contributions made by drugs and alcohol to many of the problems which afflict society.

The next discovery came as more of a surprise. Those who imagine that drug and alcohol problems mainly affect the less fortunate members of our community would be quite wrong. On the contrary, addiction can strike any who suffer stress in their personal or professional lives. For alcohol and drugs do not respect age, sex, class or occupation and the line between recreational use and creeping addiction is perilously thin.

We must remember, then, that the majority of Turning Point's clients come from ordinary communities. Very few of them resemble the stereotype junkie or drunk. Most have, or certainly had, a normal family and working life. For many, the tragic consequence of their addiction is that they have lost their jobs, and hurt and confused their families.

As I have learned more about the problems which Turning Point seeks to help, I have been increasingly concerned by the effects on families of drug and alcohol abuse. Very often, it is in the home that the climate for addiction is created and, equally often, it is in the home that its worst consequences are felt. A stable domestic background where the simple duties of family life are shared and understood can do much to strengthen those tempted to find refuge in drink or drugs.

It is sometimes argued that addicts bring their problems on themselves. But I have noticed that those such as Turning Point, who have first-hand knowledge of what these problems are, seem less inclined to pass judgment. Instead, I suggest that we each consider what part we can play in the fight against addiction, whether as parent, friend, colleague or employer.

I know that today's conference will concentrate on drug and alcohol problems, but I should also mention Turning Point's work in the field of mental health. As more mental patients leave [the] hospital to join the community, there will be increasing demand on Turning Point's services.

The charity's three mental health projects help ex-patients make the transition from the institutionalized life of a mental hospital to a more normal existence in the outside world. For people who have been in [the] hospital for as long as they can remember, learning to fend for themselves can be a frightening experience. Even the simplest tasks, such as understanding money or using household appliances, may have to be learned from scratch. This is an area of growing demand and Turning

Point has received many requests from local authorities to extend its services for the long-term mentally ill.

Mental health, like the problem of drug and alcohol misuse, does not easily attract public sympathy. There are many charities which campaign for more appealing causes. In overcoming this disadvantage, Turning Point has developed an innovative approach to its work, typified by this joint venture with a major brewery. I believe that Whitbread and Turning Point are to be congratulated for their initiative, which is just one example of the charity's strategy of building a strong partnership with industry and business to help fight drug and alcohol problems at work.

Now in its twenty-fifth year, Turning Point faces greater challenges than ever before. Its partnerships with Government and industry offer much hope for the future. Conferences such as today's will, I am sure, make valuable progress toward the elimination of drug and alcohol problems at work. But just as Turning Point believes these problems must be tackled on a painstaking, individual level, so we in turn must recognize the part that individuals can play in caring for all the casualties of our society.

In October 1987, Diana said she was worried about the increasing number of women with drinking problems and wondered aloud whether women viewers might be influenced by watching stars drinking in soap operas on television. She is a soap opera fan herself. See TELEVISION. But after hearing claims about her own drinking, she once declared that she was "not about to become an alcoholic." See FOOD & DRINK.

At Turning Point's annual general meeting in December 1990, the Princess, who has visited mental hospitals like Rampton, spoke on the controversial topic of care in the community: the charity's policy for twenty-six years and now Government policy too. The words, she said, conjured up "a rosy picture of a warm-hearted society, generously protecting and comforting its less fortunate members, just as in the best type of family." But, she added, "Everyone here knows that the reality is far from rosy." To reach the ideal demanded "imagination, sympathy and very unglamorous hard work," plus precise planning, cooperation between many specialist groups, resources to do the job properly, and awareness in the community of "who it is supposed to be caring for."

Turning Point did not have an easy task "explaining that the causes of drink, drug and mental health problems are usually deep-seated and formidably complex." Yet the charity's projects, Diana said, "are living proof that the journey from institutional to normal life can be made with dignity and a high degree of success . . . and, moreover, without frightening the neighbours. . . . It . . . takes professionalism to convince a doubting public that it should accept back into its midst many of those diagnosed as psychotics, neurotics and other sufferers whom Victorian communities decided should be kept out of sight in the safety of mental hospitals."

The Princess said she was "shocked" to "learn the number of our fellow citizens who fall victim to normally bearable pressures which—like a sudden landslide—carry them down to the confusion of mental illness and drug misuse. Fear of the unknown runs deep—even in our modern, enlightened society. Only when there is wider understanding of the frailty of our mental health will care in the community really mean what it should. . . ."

In March, as Patron of Turning Point, Diana became the first member of the Royal Family to visit Broadmoor, the top-security hospital in Crowthorne in Berkshire, which has been tagged the most dangerous place in Britain. The hospital, originally known as Broadmoor Asylum, houses five hundred patients with mental illness and violent criminals and sex offenders with psychiatric disorders, among them some of Britain's most feared killers— including the infamous Yorkshire Ripper, Peter Sutcliffe, who was convicted in 1981 of the murder of thirteen women.

U

UNIFORMS

Among the first uniforms Diana wore after her marriage was a
fake policewoman's uniform from a theatrical costumer in which
she and Fergie, also dressed like someone from *Police Woman*,
tried to gate-crash Prince Andrew's stag night. They ended up, in
their disguise, at Annabel's nightclub in Berkeley Square. But the
first official uniform she wore as the Princess of Wales was her
smart Red Cross navy blue beret, tunic, and skirt which she
donned, as Patron of British Red Cross Youth, for a carol service
in Bristol in December 1984. She looked super.

Diana has an eye for a chap in uniform, which is fortunate
because Prince Charles is said to have about a hundred of them.
See RESIDENCES. "I do so like men in uniform," she said, meeting
dozens of blue-and-gold uniformed cops at London's ancient
Guildhall in April 1989 to mark the 150th anniversary of the
founding of the City of London police force. William and Harry
have been given miniature military camouflage uniforms, which
they wore for a wonderful Boys' Own hour clambering around
over army equipment and hiding in a reconnaissance vehicle when
Diana took them on a visit to the Queen's Life Guards. They have
also been seen on television wearing them while playing in the
backyard at Highgrove. Diana has worn combat dress while visiting the Royal Hampshire Regiment, of which she is Colonel-in-
Chief. See ARMED FORCES. And for a regimental dinner with
them in February 1990, Gieves and Hawkes of Savile Row made
her a special scarlet mess jacket and white waistcoat, based on a
regimental style which had been replaced in 1966, which she wore
with a black bow tie, black trousers, and white blouse. The jacket
had yellow cuffs and yellow facings which had two of the regiment's "Hampshire rose" badges embroidered in gold and silk
thread on them. Another version of a "uniform" which stunned

Diana's tailored white dress and matching sailor's hat complement Charles's uniform. (Peter Abbey/Camera Press London)

her hosts was the white-and-gold military-style "majorette" outfit made for her by Catherine Walker which Diana wore in April 1987 for a visit to Sandhurst Military Academy. See SPAIN. She also has her own versions of the tuxedo. See FASHION.

$\mathcal{V}$

VIDEOS

Although the royals can see new-release films of their choice at their private cinema facilities, Charles and Diana also have a large selection of videos for home viewing. And when they have to be out on official engagements, they get staff to tape their favorite TV programs for them as well. One of Charles's favorite videos is the Merchant Ivory movie of E. M. Forster's *A Room with a View*, which he's seen over and over again and urged his friends to buy. One reason for its royal appeal, no doubt, is that the romance featured in the story is set partly against the backdrop of classical Florence, one of the Prince's favorite cities. In the summer of 1990 after Charles broke his arm playing polo, Diana stood in for various of his engagements, but he used a video link-up to address some meetings he'd been due to attend, including a doctors' conference that July. See HEALTH.

In 1988, Diana had a secret video made of herself dancing on stage to Andrew Lloyd Webber's song "All I Ask of You" on the set of *Phantom of the Opera*, her favorite musical, at Her Majesty's Theatre, as a surprise seventh wedding anniversary gift for her husband. The same year, ballet star Wayne Sleep, with whom she had danced in public on stage at the Royal Opera House in 1985 (see DANCING) announced that he would be making a couple of videos on "ballobics," aerobics for six- to ninety-year-olds based on ballet exercises, which were meant to rival Jane Fonda's aerobics videos. Early in 1988, it was reported that pop star Michael Jackson, a huge fan of the Princess, wanted to make a video to show at his July concerts at Wembley Stadium in which he planned to superimpose himself onto TV film of Diana playing the piano on her recent Australian tour (see MUSIC) to give the impression they were playing a duet together. However, it seems Whacko Jacko, who met Diana at one of the Wembley concerts,

375

was persuaded that this wouldn't get the go-ahead.

On New Year's Day 1989 it was reported that the Queen had banned naughty videos (those that might offend viewers with delicate sensibilities) from future Royal Family gatherings after the Queen Mother—of whom several videos were produced to commemorate her ninetieth birthday in 1990—objected to swearing in the violent thriller *Pelham 123*, shown at Sandringham that Christmas. She had left the room after half an hour, saying, "I don't really think this is for us." Charles, Andrew, and others watched to the end. See X-RATED.

In March 1990, Buckingham Palace revealed that the Queen had given her backing to a new project for filming at the Palace, due to begin with that autumn's investitures, which would allow the two thousand people who receive honors from her each year to buy videos of their big moment for £130 each. A Palace spokesman was quoted as saying, "These videos would be available to all recipients of honors. At the moment no pictures of any kind are allowed. But we have now asked a video company to make inquiries to see if it is possible."

Prince Charles did a comedy double act with John Cleese in a twenty-five-minute video film called *Grime Goes Green*, which was first screened at a London hotel in November 1990 to promote an environment-awareness guide for business published by Business in the Community, of which Charles is President. "If there was ever a revolution," Cleese said later, "Prince Charles would have a great career as a comic actor. His timing was excellent, he has a great sense of humor, and he certainly makes me laugh."

Charles and Diana did of course videotape their wedding, which they watched later. Before the big day, Diana declared mischievously, "I'm going to videotape it. Then I'll be able to run back over the best bits—and when it comes to the part that says 'I will,' I'm going to take that out and put something else!"

In March 1991 it was reported that a one-hour BBC video made up of clips from royal documentaries, to mark the couple's tenth wedding anniversary and Diana's thirtieth birthday that year, had proved a bestseller with overseas buyers.

W

WALES

Diana is the 9th Princess of Wales, the last being May of Teck, later Queen Mary, wife of George V, who with her stiff, starched reserve and cold demeanor couldn't be more of a contrast to the modern-day Princess. Diana's first major engagement after the royal wedding, in October 1981, was a three-day tour of the Principality with her husband, who presented her to the people of Wales from a balcony at Caernarfon Castle, where his investiture as Prince of Wales had been held in 1969. The cheers might have been even louder had everyone known that the Princess was already pregnant with their son and heir, Prince William.

A novice as a royal, Diana was scared stiff behind her smiles but got off to a good start by dressing in the Welsh colors, an outfit in red and green. From the beginning, it was clear that she was different—a flesh-and-blood royal who wanted to make real contact with people in the most warm, human, and sympathetic way. She reached out and touched people in the crowds, shook hands without the usual royal gloves, which she seldom wears (see FASHION), and, acknowledging the bitter wind, told one woman who had been waiting for hours to see her, "Poor you! I feel cold myself. My hands are freezing—and you must be much worse. Thank you for waiting for us." Her sensitivity touched many hearts, though not all. Threats had been made, two fire bombs were found, paint was sprayed on the royal car, placards demanded "Go Home, Diana" and "Go Home, English Prince," Welsh Nationalists chanted slogans, and in Bangor students staged a noisy demonstration, complete with stink bombs, which led to scuffles and arrests.

But thousands of others across the Land of Song from the seaside resorts of North Wales to the Rhondda Valley gave the royal couple a rousing welcome which the Princess never forgot. "The people who stood outside for hours and hours, five or six

Charles and Diana spend an afternoon with little William, the future Prince of Wales. (Lionel Cherruault/Camera Press London)

hours in torrential rain, that's what I remember," she said long after. "They were so welcoming. Because I was terrified. [It was] the most frightening thing I've ever done, because I was just married. But they made it much easier for me." In her first-ever speech, made at the end of the four-hundred-mile tour when she was granted the Freedom of the City of Cardiff, the only woman apart from the Queen to be given that honor, she delighted everyone by speaking a few words in Welsh. See SPEECHES.

Since then Diana has made numerous visits to Wales. In October 1987, all eyes were upon her and Charles when they were briefly reunited, after weeks apart, on a visit to victims of the flood in Carmarthen which followed Britain's famous freak hurricane which had taken weathermen by surprise. See MARRIAGE. Wearing leek badges on their lapels, they made another special visit on St. David's Day in March 1990 to comfort and cheer some of the two thousand people made homeless by violent storms and a giant tide which had smashed away six hundred feet of the sea wall and flooded the village of Towyn. Hundreds of villagers were camping out with their children in sleeping bags at an emergency center set up at Bodelwyddan Castle. When a seventy-seven-year-old woman told Charles that it was pension day but she couldn't claim her money because her pension book was still in her flooded house, he told his aides to ensure that pensions would be paid. The royal couple turned tears to laughter at the refugee center when they joked with the families. See BEDS & BEDROOMS and BATHS & BATHROOMS. Mrs. Fran O'Rourke, a sixty-two-year-old widow who had been rescued from her flooded bungalow, raised a laugh when she told Prince Charles that the only thing the villagers were short of was "clean knickers" (underwear).

But he and Diana, who saw the devastated area from a helicopter during a thirty-minute flight made despite gales, were shocked by the flood damage and said it was "very worrying." The Prince, who had flown back from a ski trip in Klosters after learning of the disaster, was later reported to have made a sizeable private donation to help. Months later, however, after a disappointing response to a public appeal, the people of Towyn were still suffering from the disaster and in "a terrible mess." In October 1990, when Diana revisited Towyn eight months after the floods, more than two hundred people were still unable to return to their damaged homes. If you would like to help, please send a check or postal order made out to North Wales Mayors' Flood Disaster Appeal to the Appeal at: Civic Centre, Colwyn Bay, Clwyd, North Wales, U.K.

Diana is Patron of several organizations in Wales, including the Newport International Competition for Young Pianists in Gwent; the Pre-school Playgroups Association, Wales; Swansea Festival of Music and the Arts; the Welsh Bowling Association; the Welsh National Opera; the Trust for Sick Children in Wales; and the Leukaemia Research Appeal for Wales. She is also President of Wales Craft Coucil.

WEDDING

At 11:00 A.M. Greenwich Mean Time on March 3, 1981, it was announced from Buckingham Palace that Prince Charles and Lady Diana Spencer would marry at St. Paul's Cathedral in London on Wednesday, July 29, 1981. They had chosen the cathedral in preference to Westminster Abbey, where royal weddings usually take place, because they both love St. Paul's and because Charles thought it would be a magnificent setting visually and a spectacular one acoustically for the musical wedding he had always wanted. "I think I shall spend half the time in tears," he said in advance. The choice of St. Paul's meant the carriage procession had further to go, but when it was pointed out to the Prince that extra soldiers would be required to line the longer route, he simply declared, "Well, stand them further apart."

Diana had chosen designers David and Elizabeth Emanuel to make her wedding dress, after liking a chiffon blouse they designed which she wore for a formal photo session with Lord Snowdon. The wedding dress, prepared in great secrecy (see NAMES) was a fairy-tale crinoline of ivory silk taffeta, embroidered with mother-of-pearl sequins and pearls, with lace flounces at the V-shaped neckline and on the puff sleeves, a tiny gold horseshoe and a little blue bow sewn at the waist for good luck, and a magnificent twenty-five-foot train. (A white bridal gown, though more traditional, would have caused "flare" on TV.) In order to practice maneuvering the train, Diana is said to have walked up and down the ballroom at St. James's Palace trailing yards of tissue paper pinned to her head. And because of the width of the crinoline skirt, she also rehearsed getting into, and out of, the Glass Coach which was to take her and her father, Lord Spencer, from the Queen Mother's home, Clarence House, where Diana spent the night before her wedding, to St. Paul's Cathedral. Diana's tulle veil was designed to be worn with a Spencer family diamond tiara and like her delicate wedding slippers, which were made by Clive Shilton with a heart design on the front, was of ivory silk with mother-of-pearl sequins. The "something old" was the Carrickmacross lace, also on the bodice, which had belonged to Queen Mary; the "something borrowed" were diamond earrings from Diana's mother.

Similar dresses were made for the five bridesmaids: maid of honor Lady Sarah Armstrong-Jones, the seventeen-year-old daughter of Princess Margaret and Lord Snowdon; India Hicks, aged thirteen, Lord Mountbatten's granddaughter and the daughter of interior designer David Hicks; Sarah-Jane Gaselee, the eleven-year-old daughter of Prince Charles's racehorse trainer, Nick Gaselee; Catherine Cameron, aged six, the daughter of another friend, Donald Cameron of Locheil; and five-year-old

Clementine Hambro, the great-granddaughter of Sir Winston Churchill, who is named after his wife. See YOUNG ENGLAND KINDERGARTEN and FRIENDS. The two pageboys, Lord Nicholas Windsor, aged eleven, the son of the Duke and Duchess of Kent, and eight-year-old Edward van Cutsem, the son of the Prince's friend Hugh van Cutsem, wore Royal Navy cadet's summer uniforms dating from 1863, the date of the last State wedding of a Prince of Wales (later Edward VII).

The florists Longmans prepared Diana's sweet-scented bridal bouquet of gardenias, freesias, stephanotis, white odontoglossom orchids, lilies of the valley, a sprig of myrtle from a bush planted from Queen Victoria's wedding bouquet, and, in his memory, golden roses named after Lord Mountbatten.

Because of the noise from the wedding-eve royal fireworks display in Hyde Park—where Prince Charles lit the first of a chain of celebration royal beacons throughout the United Kingdom—and from the thousands who gathered to watch it and the crowds already assembling in the Mall (some of whom had been reserving their positions for days), Diana did not get much sleep that night. Neither did her makeup artist, Barbara Daly, who turned up with her kit at 4:00 A.M. on the wedding day to make certain she was on time. See BEAUTY SECRETS. Diana in turn ensured that her stomach wouldn't rumble during the wedding ceremony by eating an enormous breakfast. By the time her hairdresser, Kevin Shanley, and his wife, Clare, arrived at 7:00 A.M. to help prepare her for the biggest day in her life, there was already a carnival atmosphere on the streets. Before leaving for the cathedral herself, in an eau-de-Nil (greenish color) outfit, the Queen Mother popped in to see the bride, declaring, "My dear, you look simply enchanting." Diana was so happy, and so relaxed, that when she climbed into the Glass Coach and the Emanuels carefully tucked her train into the carriage behind her, she serenaded them, Shanley, and the others with a burst of "Just One Cornetto." At 10:37 A.M. the Glass Coach drove off, taking Diana and her father past the cheering throngs of an estimated one to two million people who lined the route up the Mall and on to St. Paul's. In order to see, many in the crowds watched through tall red, white, and blue periscopes.

At the cathedral, guests who had accepted the 2,650 invitations sent out by the Lord Chamberlain were already seated. They included most of the crowned heads of Europe (apart from King Juan Carlos and Queen Sofia of Spain, who stayed away because of the bride and groom's plan to set off on their honeymoon cruise from the disputed territory of Gibraltar); kings from the Middle East, Africa, Asia, and the South Pacific, including the King of Tonga, for whom a special chair was built to accommodate his 350-pound frame; Nancy Reagan, First Lady of the United States; more than 160 foreign Presidents and Prime Ministers; heads of industry and the diplomatic and civil services; stars of sport and show biz, including several of Charles's favorite "Goon Show" stars; more than two hundred members of the Queen's staff from Buckingham Palace, Sandringham, Windsor Castle, and Balmoral; and family and friends of the bride and groom, including Diana's former flatmates and headmistresses, staff from Althorp and the kindergarten where she worked (see STAFF and YOUNG ENGLAND KINDERGARTEN), and staff from the stables of Nick Gaselee at Lambourn. Two people who weren't invited, but should have been, were Betty Vacani, of the dance school where Diana briefly worked (see JOBS), who was apparently missed by an oversight, and Barbara Cartland, the mother of Diana's stepmother, Raine. See FAMILY.

The Queen and other members of the Royal Family arrived at the cathedral, as did Prince Charles and his "supporters," Prince Andrew and Prince Edward, and took their places. The bride, arriving several minutes late in keeping with tradition, was greeted at St. Paul's with cheers so loud they rang across London. As Diana stepped down from the Glass Coach, seven hundred million viewers watching TV coverage relayed by more than eighty companies broadcasting to seventy-four countries around the world were able to get their first proper look at her wedding gown. The crinoline skirt at that stage, it has to be said, looked crumpled and creased and in need of a good pressing. But Diana, as expected, made a breathtaking bride. Lord Spencer, still frail as a result of his serious illness three years before, had to be helped up the red-carpeted steps to the cathedral. As they entered to a trumpet fanfare, Diana whispered to her father about her bridegroom, "Is he here?" Lord Spencer managed the long proud walk down the aisle with Diana on his arm without faltering. He has since said he would like to go through the whole wedding all over again. Diana found that long walk to her royal future "terrifying," but when she reached Prince Charles, who was wearing the full-dress uniform of a Royal Navy commander, he smiled and said, "You look wonderful." "Wonderful for you," she replied.

During the seventy-five-minute wedding ceremony, conducted by the Archbishop of Canterbury, Dr. Robert Runcie, both bride and groom made gaffes. Diana got Charles's names in the wrong order, calling him Philip Charles Arthur George by mistake. "She's married my father!" Prince Andrew exclaimed. And Charles enhanced his reputation for being stingy by vowing to share all *her* worldly goods, instead of his own. He should have said, "And all my worldly goods with thee I share" but actually declared, "And all thy goods with thee I share." "*That* was no mistake!" Princess Anne declared. Diana did not promise to "obey" him. The wedding ring was the last to be made from a nugget of Welsh gold found sixty years before in a mine at Bontddu, Gwynedd, which had been used to make wedding rings for the Queen Mother, the Queen, Princess Margaret, and Princess Anne. Charles's friend George Thomas, then Speaker of the House of Commons, now Lord Tonypandy, read the lesson. Dr. Runcie gave an address, beginning, "Here is the stuff of which fairy tales are made. . . ." The anthem "I Was Glad" was sung as the couple moved further up the aisle toward the high altar. Lady guests, their wide-brimmed hats contrasting with the Arab headdresses of sheikhs in the congregation, fanned themselves with their wedding programs to keep cool in the heat. Diana's favorite hymn, "I Vow to Thee My Country," was sung before the Blessing and a drum roll and trumpets which led into the national anthem. The Queen, in pale blue, looked very solemn. Then the Archbishop led the bride and groom off to sign the register while their favorite female opera singer, Dame Kiri Te Kanawa, and the Bach Choir (see MUSIC) sang the aria "Let the Bright Seraphim" by Handel. A trumpet fanfare heralded the return of the bride and groom, who emerged smiling, the veil now thrown back from Diana's face. She gave a deep curtsy to the Queen, her first as the Princess of Wales, as they walked back down the aisle to the strains of Elgar's *Pomp and Circumstance March No. 4 in G* and Walton's *Crown Imperial*.

Out in the sunshine beyond the West Door, where Diana grinned and waved, acknowledging the huge roar from the crowds, peals of bells from the cathedral's northwest tower were echoed by church bells throughout the City of London. Then, waved off from the top of the cathedral steps by the Queen and the Royal Family and Diana's parents, the Prince and Princess moved off in the open 1902 State Postillion Landau for the twenty-minute drive down Fleet Street and the Strand, through Admiralty Arch and back down the Mall to Buckingham Palace, cheered by spectators waving Union Jacks and showering them with rice. Diana's first tradition-breaking act as the Princess of Wales was to encourage Charles to unbend and give her that famous bridal kiss on the Palace balcony, as the crowds wanted. Another huge roar of approval went up. This was followed by curses from 150 of the world's best Press photographers, perched opposite on a special stand on the Queen Victoria Memorial, nicknamed the Wedding Cake, only three of whom—according to Rosalyn Grose in her book *The Sun-sation*—managed to catch the unrepeatable shot.

The royal party posed for some charming and unusually relaxed official wedding photographs taken inside the Palace by Patrick Lichfield, the Queen's cousin, who had precisely eighteen minutes to do them, and blew a whistle to attract everyone's attention when it was time to smile for the birdie. Then 118 guests sat down to a three-course wedding breakfast, actually lunch, based around Diana's favorite foods (fish, chicken, and fruit) of brill in lobster sauce, *suprême de volaille Princesse de Galles*, and strawberries and cream. The royal couple cut the giant five-foot-tall, five-tiered, six-sided, 255-pound official wedding cake (large enough it was said, to be cut into a thousand slices) with Charles's ceremonial sword, and he replied to toasts proposed by his two brothers. The cake was made under the direction of master baker Chief Petty Officer David Avery at the Royal Navy cookery school in Chatham. At the special request of the Prince, navy rum had been added to the ingredients, which included cherries, raisins, sultanas, and currants which took four men two days to pit and remove the stems. The icing included colored pictures of the bride's and groom's family crests, coats of arms, and their homes.

Fifteen other wedding cakes, displayed at the wedding breakfast, had arrived among the ten thousand wedding presents sent to the couple, which later went on public display at St. James's Palace, the proceeds going to a charity nominated by Prince Charles. Prince Andrew and Prince Edward decorated the going-away carriage with a large "Just Married" card and numerous silver and blue helium balloons bearing the Prince of Wales's feathers. And, amid further cheers and showers of confetti, Charles and Diana, who wore a going-away outfit of coral pink by Bellville Sassoon with an ostrich-feathered hat by John Boyd, were taken to Waterloo railway station for their journey to Romsey, near Southampton. There, on Platform 12, Diana kissed and thanked those who had organized the wedding—the Lord Chamberlain, Lord Maclean, and Sir Johnnie Johnston, the Queen's Comptroller. Then she and Charles boarded the Royal Train which took them to Broadlands for the start of their honeymoon.

Millions reached for their Kleenex as tears welled up at the emotion of the wedding day, heightened by the splendor of all the pageantry, pomp, and ceremony at which Britain excels and the obvious happiness of the royal couple. Even Prince Charles revealed that on the wedding eve he had watched from the Palace as "all night people were sitting out on the steps there singing 'Rule Britannia' and every kind of thing. . . . I found myself standing in the window with tears pouring down my face." Three months later, he declared, "We still cannot get over what happened that day. Neither of us can get over the atmosphere. It was electric, I felt, and so did my wife. I remember several occasions that were similar—the Coronation, and the Jubilee, and various major national occasions. All of them were special in their own way, but our wedding was quite extraordinary as far as we were concerned. It made us both extraordinarily proud to be British."

The wedding fervor affected even the most unexpected people. In October 1990, solicitor Benedict Birnberg, defending the two men who were eventually tried, but acquitted, in June 1991, of helping spy George Blake escape from jail, revealed on "Midweek" on BBC Radio 4 that in the course of his inquiries, he had visited Blake at his flat in Moscow and spotted a Charles and Diana wedding plate (and a picture of Windsor Castle) on the wall. See HONEYMOON, MARRIAGE, RADIO, TELEVISON, and VIDEOS.

X-RATED

X-rated in Britain does not mean pornographic but was the old term (pre-1982) for movies containing steamy sex scenes, violence, or swearing that could only be seen by moviegoers aged eighteen and over. The term has now passed into general use in the U.K. to refer to anything sexy, saucy, or wicked.

The vital statistics of members of the Royal Family are never revealed, but Diana's were estimated to be 35-29-35 in 1988 and 34-26-36 in 1990. In May 1989, the Princess referred to the *Sun* newspaper's famous topless pin-ups pictured on Page 3 when she playfully asked some building site workers in Cornwall, "Do you read Page Three in the *Sun?*" "We love the *Sun* girls," one of them commented later, "but we all agree Di takes some beating." She almost made the Page Three pin-up spot herself in March 1981, when she created a sensation on her first public engagement as Prince Charles's fiancée by arriving at Goldsmiths' Hall in the City of London in a breathtaking strapless black dress from the Emanuels. A dress so low-cut that as she emerged from the royal car toward a battery of Press and TV cameras—with Charles, proud of how glamorous and grown-up she looked, saying, "Wait till you see this!"—more than the onlookers' eyes popped out. At least, that's what some claim; others disagree. Independent Television News (ITN), with the usual somber commentary by Sir Alastair Burnet, even ran film of the big moment frame by frame so that viewers could decide for themselves. Diana has not worn the dress in public since. See FASHION.

She is said to enjoy sunbathing nude on the roof garden at Kensington Palace, swimming in the nude at Highgrove (having first allegedly switched off the remote-control police surveillance camera), and skinny-dipping in the pool at Windsor Castle with Princess Margaret. A butler at Althorp once revealed that in the middle of a party, she'd gone skinny-dipping in the pool there. Former royal reporter Harry Arnold (see PRESS) has a photograph, alleged to be of Diana, aged about thirteen, sitting nude by a swimming pool. "I think it's her," he says. "If you heard there was a picture of the Princess of Wales in the nude, you'd think, 'My God!' and conjure up all sorts of visions. But it's very, very unsexy. I used to keep it pinned up in the bathroom, and if she ever came the old madam on a job in the morning, I used to look at it in the evening and think, 'I knew you when you were a nobody.' " Other photos of Diana at seventeen on a French skiing holiday, which showed her standing towel-wrapped in the snow waving a bra, were obtained by the French magazine *Paris Match*. When the *Sun*'s Cockney photographer Arthur Edwards (see PRESS) asked why she had worn an old gown to the opera in Italy, she teased, "Oh, I suppose you'd like it better if I came naked?" "Well, at least then I'd get a picture of ya in the paper," he replied. See ITALY.

Before her marriage, the *Sunday Mirror* alleged that Diana had had a late-night tryst with Prince Charles in the Royal Train, parked in a siding. Since much had been made of her youthful innocence and lack of previous serious boyfriends (her uncle, Lord Fermoy, declared publicly, "Diana, I can assure you, has never had a lover"), this allegation caused a storm, reduced Diana to tears, and brought furious denials and a demand from the Palace for a retraction. In March 1990, Iraq made a bizarre verbal attack on the British Royal Family, claiming that Prince Charles married Diana "knowing that she had many lovers before him, including Prince Andrew," and accusing the Queen of "not feeling any shame despite members of her family hanging out their dirty linen in public." The attack was seen as retaliation following worldwide condemnation after Iraq hanged *Observer* journalist Farzad Bazoft.

Diana once remarked, "The trouble with being a princess is that it is so hard to have a pee." See NIGERIA and PRESS. Prince Charles has said that when he's out fishing, he always fears that some Press photographer will catch him out taking a leak, though King Henry IV of France once avoided an assassin by peeing in a pig sty. When George V met pioneer aviator Charles Lindbergh after his first solo flight across the Atlantic, the first thing he wanted to know was, "What did you do about peeing?" And when the Shah of Persia visited Queen Victoria in 1873, it's claimed he "failed to use the lavatories," which lets the imagination run wild. Toastmaster Ivor Spencer got crowned when he popped into a bathroom reserved for Prince Charles at a dinner in 1982 and the towel dispenser collapsed on his head.

The *People* newspaper actually published a photograph of schoolboy Prince William having a pee. The Editor, Wendy Henry, got fired shortly afterward but apparently not, as many thought, for that reason. Other famous royal photographs include the one showing Diana's legs through her skirt. See PRESS. Another, circulated but never published, was taken after Princess Anne became engaged to Mark Phillips when the Captain, somewhat naively, was apparently persuaded by photographers to pose astride the barrel of a tank at his barracks, with his hands holding onto the barrel.

Swearing is nothing new to the Royal Family. Prince Philip, being a Royal Navy man, doesn't mince his words. It was Princess Anne, of course, who made the phrase "Naff off!" famous. Diana has been heard to cuss. So has Charles, who once cried, "Oh, God, my bloody bit of paper!" when his notes were blown awry in Australia, just as he was reportedly about to make a speech which included the line "Swearing is contemptible and foolish." Even the Queen swore during the police delay after intruder Michael Fagan broke into her bedroom at Buckingham Palace, when she told them, "Oh, come on. Get a bloody move on!"

No longer a naive kindergarten assistant but a woman of the world, Diana can be outrageous in private and enjoys saucy comments and blue jokes, though she has yet to be reported watching blue movies on video. Prince Andrew and his fellow officers were banned from viewing such films at the Royal Navy Air Station in Culdrose in 1981. See VIDEOS. When he sat next to the Princess at the premiere of the movie *Dangerous Liaisons*, its star, John Malkovich, said he hoped she wouldn't be embarrassed by the eighteenth-century tale of lust and revenge among the French aristocracy. "I'm not easily shocked," she replied. Malkovich recalled, "After Valmont has deflowered the virgin, they're having breakfast and he is pulling faces. I said, 'Is it like that for breakfast at the Palace?' She smiled, 'No. But it beats reading the papers!' "

Unlike the Duke of Windsor, who is reported to have had a remarkably small pecker, Charles is said to be well endowed. The Duke, incidentally, is said to have had a foot fetish (see BEAUTY SECRETS). Of all things, before leaving for France after his abdication as Edward VIII, he spent time having the corns on his feet attended.

During his bachelor years, Prince Charles was endlessly pursued by females worldwide throwing themselves at him and kissing him. Like his brother Prince Andrew—nicknamed "Randy Andy" in *his* bachelor days, whose girlfriends included former soft-porn star Koo Stark and saucy model Vicki Hodge—Charles's dates included a girl who had posed naked for *Penthouse* magazine. Girlfriends with whom Charles had affairs had to remember to call him "Sir" even when passing his underpants. But he was very discreet. His former valet, Stephen Barry, recalled later, "The relationships he did have were arranged with the most enormous discretion. In all those twelve years that I worked for him, if he was meant to be in his bed in the morning when I went in to wake him up, he was in bed—alone." He added, "Buckingham Palace was totally unsuitable for anything indiscreet to take place. It would have been impossible for a girl to have spent any time there without a footman or his policeman or me not being aware that she was there. . . . I sometimes thought the limitations on his privacy were part of the reason for his participation in so many energetic activities." During his Koo Stark era, Prince Andrew reportedly put a "Do Not Disturb" sign on his bedroom door and ordered staff not to barge in with breakfast for two.

In Hawaii in 1985, when Charles's oversize shorts took a dive while he was surfing at Sandy Beach, a girl watching the royal display remarked, "Now I know what Diana sees in him." And when another girl trying to present him with a traditional Hawaiian garland of flowers asked the Prince, "Can I give you a lei?," he laughed and replied, "Oh, why not?" The Prince's nice line in saucy comments was also shown when he asked a Welsh Guardsman whether he and his wife had any children and was told, "Not yet, Sir—we're keeping our fingers crossed." "You certainly won't get one that way!" he declared. In Nigeria in 1990, Diana blushed deeply when she was greeted in Port Harcourt by tribal dancers, including one wearing a three-foot-tall dance mask bearing two carved figures—meant to be her and Charles making love. See NIGERIA.

In the cellar at Highgrove, where a vast assortment of curious gifts to the royal couple is kept, there is a green woolen willy-warmer which someone once bought Charles for Christmas. (Given as a gag gift, a willy-warmer is usually a brightly colored knitted garment, often with a bow, meant to cover a particular part of the male anatomy.) During one royal Christmas, attempts were made to take down Charles's trousers by Prince Andrew and Diana, who was wearing a set of false boobs over her clothes. Charles was once photographed dancing in South America with an exotic scantily clad beauty whose boob popped out of her costume as she swayed to the rhythm. The Prince likes an ample well-rounded bosom. Margaret Trudeau, former wife of the Canadian Prime Minister, revealed that when she sat next to him in a low-cut dress at dinner, "He looked long and hard down my cleavage." During a trip to Fiji, Charles was treated to the spectacle of some buxom Fijian maidens doing a bare-breasted fertility dance. "Well," he remarked when he'd recovered his breath, "it beats the Changing of the Guard, doesn't it?"

Diana was claimed to have gone disco-dancing during one royal ski trip in Switzerland in a sexy blouse and braless. The Princess, who lost inches from her most vital curves when her early babyfat disappeared, once bemoaned her smaller bosom to astounded journalists as she recalled the old days, saying, "Do you remember how I was then? I used to have lots up top, remember? Well it's all gone now, isn't it?"

Prince Philip once refused to disclose the color of his underwear to a reporter in Chicago. Prince Charles, who has never allowed his inside leg measurement to be revealed (or to give up his battered old dressing gown), wears boxer shorts rather than briefs because Diana prefers them. And she wears thermal underwear when it's cold. See FASHION.

Despite the advice of Queen Victoria's consort, Prince Albert, that practical jokes "should never be permitted," members of the Royal Family enjoy them. Prince Philip once pursued the Queen around the Royal Train wearing a pair of Dracula fangs. And in 1957, when he returned, bearded, from a visit to the South Pacific, she and her Ladies-in-Waiting all wore false beards to greet him. (Beards are not liked by most of the ladies of the Royal Family with the exception of Princess Michael of Kent. Philip, Charles, and Andrew have all in the past had to shave off beards they'd grown.) Diana has short-sheeted beds for guests. And Prince Charles, who was once responsible for the Moderator of the Church of Scotland ending up in a fountain at Balmoral, also passed around exploding cigars at a dinner in Dartmouth and once put a whoopee cushion on the Bishop of Norwich's chair at Sandringham.

There are at least a couple of windy stories concerning the Royal Family. When one of the Queen's corgies broke wind during lunch at Buckingham Palace, entertainer Max Bygraves made Her Majesty laugh by exclaiming, "I hope you don't think that was me." And according to another tale, which is probably apocryphal, when the Queen apologized to an African potentate after one of the horses drawing their carriage farted, he replied airily, "Oh, don't worry. If you hadn't apologized, I would have thought it was the horse."

𝒴

YOUNG ENGLAND KINDERGARTEN

Diana's last job before her marriage was at the Young England kindergarten, in a church hall in St. George's Square, Pimlico, where she worked as an assistant and was known to the children as Miss Diana. See JOBS. The school, which then had ten teachers catering for about fifty children under the age of five, the off-spring of well-heeled local residents, was run by Victoria Wilson and Kay Seth-Smith. Kay had also been educated at West Heath. See EDUCATION. So had her sister Janie, who had been there at the same time as Diana's sister Jane, and it was through them that Diana was taken on to help, initially for three afternoons each week and later, when her natural affinity with children became obvious, in the mornings too. Diana, who has been described by her mother as "a positive Pied Piper with children," helped them with their artwork, tidied up, washed mugs, and, when necessary, quelled squabbles, dried tears, and dispensed cuddles.

Once news of the royal romance broke in September 1980, Diana was besieged by journalists at her flat and at the kinder-garten. She agreed to pose for Press cameramen, provided they then kept away from the school. She was photographed with two of the children in the gardens outside, but she burst into tears at the published result. See PRESS.

After her engagement, Diana returned to the kindergarten, where the children climbed all over her and gave her a collage they had made as a memento. She invited all ten of her colleagues there to the royal wedding. Her youngest bridesmaid, five-year-old Clementine Hambro, Sir Winston Churchill's great-granddaughter, had been one of her charges at Young England.

Z

Zoo

Though Diana's academic progress at school was enough to give her the blues, she was such a trier that for her seventh birthday, when twenty children had been invited to have a party with Jell-O and birthday cake on the lawn at Park House, her father hired a camel called Bert from Dudley Zoo as a special treat. Diana and her friends were allowed to climb on the camel's back in twos to be led around the garden by its keeper. For Prince William's eighth birthday in June 1990, the Princess treated him and Harry and about twenty of their young friends to an outing to London Zoo in Regent's Park, where they all wore 95-pence zoo plastic raincoats to keep off the rain while they went to see the elephants and giraffes. Watched carefully by a keeper, William even got to hold a giant royal python. They had a smashing birthday tea, complete with a birthday cake shaped like an elephant and cookies shaped like other animals, plus sandwiches, Jell-O, potato chips, and orange juice, in the insect house at the zoo. The kids were surrounded by all manner of creepy-crawlies including stick insects and spiders—a little boys' paradise! Diana missed Ladies' Day at Royal Ascot in order to prepare for the treat and to go shopping for all sorts of party goodies little boys love from a shop called Party. Charles, who left Ascot early to be with them, is an associate member of the Zoological Society of London. The zoo has more recently been fighting the threat of closure.

The first elephant in England was sent as a gift from the King of France to King Henry III, top zookeeper in Western Europe, who kept it with three leopards, a lion, a camel, a bear, and buffalo in his menagerie at the Tower of London.

Bibliography

(All books published in London, U.K., unless otherwise stated.)

Arch, Nigel, and Marschner, Joanna. *The Royal Wedding Dresses.* Sidgwick & Jackson, 1990.

Arnold, Harry. *Charles and Diana.* New English Library, 1981.

Ash, Russell. *The Top 10 of Everything.* Macdonald, Queen Anne Press, 1989.

Barr, Ann, and York, Peter. *The Official Sloane Ranger Directory.* Ebury Press, 1984.

Brown, Alan (Tim Brown and Alan Rustage). *Princess.* Penguin, 1989.

Brown, Craig, and Cunliffe, Lesley. *The Book of Royal Lists.* Routledge & Kegan Paul, 1982.

Brown, Michèle. *Ritual of Royalty: The Ceremony and Pageantry of Britain's Monarchy.* Sidgwick & Jackson, 1983.

Burnet, Alastair. *In Person: The Prince and Princess of Wales.* ITN/Michael O'Mara Books, 1985.

Burnet, Alastair. *In Private—In Public: The Prince and Princess of Wales.* ITN/Michael O'Mara Books, 1986.

Burnet, Alastair. *The Queen Mother.* ITN/Michael O'Mara Books, 1990.

Campbell, Judith. Introduction by Brough Scott. *Royal Horses.* New English Library, 1983.

Cathcart, Helen. *Charles: Man of Destiny.* W. H. Allen, 1988.

Cayzer, Beatrice. *The Royal World of Animals.* Sidgwick & Jackson, 1989.

Courtney, Nicholas. *Diana, Princess of Wales.* Park Lane Press, 1982.

Courtney, Nicholas. *Sisters-in-Law: A Palace Revolution.* Weidenfeld & Nicolson, 1988.

Dempster, Nigel. *HRH The Princess Margaret*. Quartet Books, 1981.

Dunlop, Janice. *Charles and Diana: A Royal Romance*. Coronet Books, 1981.

Edgar, Donald. *Palace*. W. H. Allen, 1983.

Everingham, Barry. *MC: The Adventures of a Maverick Princess*. Bantam Press, 1985.

Fincher, Jayne and Terry. *Debrett's Illustrated Fashion Guide: The Princess of Wales*. Webb & Bower, 1989.

Fincher, Jayne. *Travels with a Princess: A Decade of Photographing Royalty*. Weidenfeld & Nicolson, 1990.

Frischauer, Willi. *Margaret: Princess Without a Cause*. Michael Joseph, 1977.

Garner, Valerie. *Debrett's Queen Elizabeth, the Queen Mother*. Webb & Bower, 1990.

Garrett, Richard. *Royal Travel*. Blandford Press, Poole, Dorset, 1982.

Golby, J. M., and Purdue, A. W. *The Monarchy and the British People*. Batsford, 1988.

Graham, Tim. *Diana: HRH The Princess of Wales*, introduced by Clive James. Michael O'Mara Books, 1988.

Graham, Tim. *The Royal Year 1989*. Michael O'Mara Books/ITN, 1989.

Grose, Rosalyn. *The Sun-sation*. Angus & Robertson, 1989.

Hall, Trevor. *Born to Be King: Prince William of Wales*. Colour Library Books, 1982.

Hall, Trevor. *The Royal Family: At Home and Abroad*. W. H. Smith Exclusive Books, 1990.

Hamilton, Alan. *The Real Charles*. William Collins, 1988.

Hamilton, Alan. *The Royal Handbook*. Mitchell Beazley, 1985.

Hibbert, Christopher. *A Guide to Royal London*. Macmillan, 1987.

Hibbin, Sally. *The Official James Bond Movie Book*. Hamlyn, 1987.

Hichens, Phoebe, and Oxley, Rosie. *Dear Princess*. Macmillan Children's Books, 1984.

Hoey, Brian. *Anne: The Princess Royal*. Grafton Books, 1989.

Hoey, Brian. *Monarchy: Behind the Scenes with the Royal Family*. BBC Books, 1988.

Hoey, Brian. *The New Royal Court.* Sidgwick & Jackson, 1990.

Holden, Anthony. *Charles.* Weidenfeld & Nicolson, 1988.

Holden, Anthony. *Charles, Prince of Wales.* Weidenfeld & Nicolson, 1979.

Holden, Anthony. *The Queen Mother: A 90th Birthday Tribute.* Sphere, 1990 edition.

Household, Joanna (ed.). *Debrett's Guide to Britain: Where to Go and What to See.* Webb & Bower, 1983.

James, Paul. *Anne: The Working Princess.* Judy Piatkus, 1987.

Junor, Sir John. *Listening for a Midnight Train: The Memoirs of Sir John Junor.* Chapmans, 1990.

Junor, Penny. *Charles.* Sidgwick & Jackson, 1987.

Junor, Penny. *Charles and Diana: Portrait of a Marriage.* Headline, 1991.

Junor, Penny. *Diana, Princess of Wales.* Sidgwick & Jackson, 1982.

Keay, Douglas. *Royal Pursuit: The Palace, the Press and the People.* Severn House, 1983.

Lacey, Robert. *Majesty.* Hutchinson, 1977.

Lane, Peter. *Prince Charles: A Study in Development.* Robert Hale, 1988.

Levenson, David, and Hall, Trevor. *Charles and Diana's First Royal Tour.* Colour Library Books, 1983.

Lichfield, Patrick. *Not the Whole Truth.* Headline, 1987.

Liversidge, Douglas. *Prince Charles: Monarch in the Making.* Arthur Barker, 1975.

Longford, Elizabeth. *Elizabeth R.* Weidenfeld & Nicolson, 1983.

Longford, Elizabeth. *The Oxford Book of Royal Anecdotes.* Oxford University Press, 1989.

Longford, Elizabeth. *The Royal House of Windsor.* Weidenfeld & Nicolson, 1974.

Menkes, Suzy. *The Royal Jewels.* Grafton Books, 1985.

Montague-Smith, Patrick. *The Royal Family Pop-Up Book.* Deans International Publishing, 1984.

Moore, Sally. *Lucan—Not Guilty.* Sidgwick & Jackson, 1987.

Morrow, Ann. *Princess.* Chapmans, 1991.

Morrow, Ann. *The Queen.* Granada, 1983.

Morrow, Ann. *The Queen Mother.* Granada, 1984.

Morton, Andrew. *Diana's Diary*. Michael O'Mara Books, 1990.

Morton, Andrew. *Duchess*. Michael O'Mara Books, 1988.

Morton, Andrew. *Inside Kensington Palace*. Michael O'Mara Books, 1987.

Owen, Jane. *Diana, Princess of Wales: The Book of Fashion*. Colour Library Books, 1983.

Packard, Jerrold M. *The Queen & Her Court*. Robson Books, 1981.

Palmer, Alan and Veronica. *Royal England: A Historical Gazetteer*. Methuen, 1983.

Parker, John. *The Princess Royal*. Coronet Books, 1989.

Pearson, John. *The Ultimate Family: The Making of the Royal House of Windsor*. Michael Joseph, 1986.

Pepper, Frank S. *20th Century Anecdotes*. Sphere, 1990.

Quine, Judith Balaban. *The Bridesmaids—Grace Kelly and Six Intimate Friends*. Weidenfeld & Nicolson, 1989.

Roberts, Gary Boyd, and Reitwiesner, W. A. *American Ancestors and Cousins of The Princess of Wales*. The Genealogical Publishing Company of Baltimore, 1984 (U.S.A.).

Russell, Peter, and James, Paul. *At Her Majesty's Service*. William Collins, 1986.

Sakol, Jeannie, and Latham, Caroline. *The Royals*. W. H. Allen Planet, 1988.

Satchell, Tim. *Astaire: The Biography*. Hutchinson, 1987.

Sayers, N., and Viney, C. *The Bad News Zodiac*. Grafton Books, 1985.

Seward, Ingrid. *Diana*. Weidenfeld & Nicolson, 1988.

Sinclair, Marianne, and Litvinoff, Sarah. *The Wit & Wisdom of the Royal Family*. Plexus, 1990.

Sunday Express Magazine, The. *A Week in the Life of the Royal Family*, introduced by Anthony Holden. Weidenfeld & Nicolson, 1983.

Talbot, Godfrey. *The Book of the Royal Family*. Country Life Books, 1983.

Talbot, Godfrey. *The Country Life Book of Queen Elizabeth, the Queen Mother*. Country Life Books, 1983.

Talbot, Godfrey. *Queen Elizabeth, the Queen Mother*. Foreword by HRH The Prince of Wales. Mandarin, 1990.

Thornton, Michael. *Royal Feud*. Michael Joseph, 1985.

Vickers, Hugo. *Debrett's Book of the Royal Wedding*. Debrett's Peerage, 1981.

Wade, Judy. *Charles & Diana, Inside a Royal Marriage*. Angus & Robertson, 1987.

Warwick, Christopher. *Princess Margaret*. Weidenfeld & Nicolson, 1983.

Watson, Lyall. *The Channel Four Book of Sumo*. Sidgwick & Jackson, 1989.

Whitaker, James. *Settling Down*. Quartet Books, 1981.

Whitaker, Yvonne. *Royal Cooking*. Time-Scan, 1982.

Zec, Donald. *The Queen Mother*. Sidgwick & Jackson, 1990.

Ziegler, Philip. *Mountbatten*. William Collins, 1985.